Blackstone's Statutes on

PUBLIC LAW

Blackstone's Statutes on
PUBLIC LAW

Edited by
Peter Wallington MA, LLM, Barrister
Professor of Law, Brunel University

and

Robert G. Lee LLB
Director of Education, Wilde Sapte, Solicitors, London

With assistance from Clive Lewis MA(Cantab), LLM,
Selwyn College, Cambridge

BLACKSTONE
PRESS LIMITED

First published in Great Britain 1988 by Blackstone Press Limited, Aldine Place, London W12 8AA

ISBN: 1 85431 020 8

Typeset by LKM Typesetting Ltd, London EC1
Printed by Redwood Burn Ltd, Trowbridge

CONTENTS

EDITORS' PREFACE

The adage that Britain has no written constitution, while still technically true, is an increasingly unhelpful and unreal starting point for the study of Constitutional and Administrative Law. As in many other areas of the law, statute has assumed an increasingly pervasive role. And while there is no domestic constitutional document to use as a starting point for studying 'the British Constitution', international sources play an increasing part in the regulation of power in the UK, and the continuing controversy over Bills of Rights makes it important to look for comparison at the constitutional approach of some other jurisdictions. The volume of statutory and analogous material to which students in the field of Public Law now need to refer has become such that a separate set of materials is a necessary guide. Hence this book.

We have assembled here a collection of statutes on all aspects of Constitutional and Administrative Law and Civil Liberties. It is not intended to replace textbooks or cases and materials books, but to complement them and to provide necessary and quick reference to essential texts. Since it contains no commentary it is suitable — and we hope will be adopted — for reference in examinations in these subjects (but do check with your faculty or department whether this is so). We hope it will also encourage students to become more accustomed to reading and unravelling the language of Parliament — one of the most basic skills of a lawyer.

The selection of materials for a new collection of statutes is a matter of sometimes arbitrary editorial judgment. Our selection is based on the knowledge that courses vary in content and an attempt to meet the major needs of a fairly broad range of undergraduate courses. This means the book will contain some material irrelevant to your particular course — but much that is central, or a valuable supplement, to any course in the Public Law area (including important parts of English Legal System courses). The book is designed to be used by English, Welsh and Scottish students; the territorial extent of each Act is indicated and where there is parallel English and Scottish legislation we have included both (with exceptions, especially in the field of Local Government). For reasons of space this approach was not possible for Northern Ireland, but we have included those parts of Northern Irish legislation of most interest to students elsewhere in the UK.

As well as statutes, we include the Bill of Rights amendments to the United States Constitution, the European Convention on Human Rights, parts of the Treaty of Rome (and an example of a Regulation and a Directive made under it) and major extracts from the key Codes of Practice issued under the Police and Criminal Evidence Act 1984.

Because this is a text for students rather than practitioners we have been able to be more selective in cutting material down to a manageable length. Omissions are indicated by a row of asterisks. Provisions as to commencement, etc. have also been omitted. The text is printed, where appropriate, as subsequently amended; new materials are shown by square brackets and repeats by dots. Statutes are printed in chronological order; other material is gathered together in Part II. The texts are as in force on 1 January 1988.

We gratefully acknowledge the help we have received from Clive Lewis of Selwyn College, Cambridge, who has advised on content and carefully checked the manuscript. We are also indebeted to Jeremy McBride of the University of Birmingham both for suggestions as to inclusions and for the benefits of collaboration over the years in the internal production of statutory materials for students at Cambridge, Birmigham and Lancaster. Finally our thanks are due to our publishers for their willingness to take this book on at the earliest stages of their new existence, and for their speed and efficiency in production. The responsibility for errors is the editors' alone.

Peter Wallington
Robert G. Lee

PART I

STATUTES OF THE UK PARLIAMENT AND ITS PREDECESSORS

MAGNA CARTA
(Statute 25 Edw. 1, 1297)

Territorial extent England and Wales, Northern Ireland

The Great Charter of the Liberties of England, and of the Liberties of the Forest; confirmed by King Edward, in the Twenty-fifth Year of his Reign.
Edward by the grace of God King of England, Lord of Ireland, and Duke of Guyan, to all archbishops, bishops, &c. We have seen the Great Charter of the Lord Henry sometimes King of England, our father, of the liberties of England in these words:

Henry by the grace of God King of England, Lord of Ireland, Duke of Normandy and Guyan, and Earl of Anjou, to all archbishops, bishops, abbots, priors, earls, barons, sheriffs, provosts, officers, and to all bailiffs, and other our faithful subjects, which shall see this present charter, greeting: Know ye, that we, unto the honour of Almighty God, and for the salvation of the souls of our progenitors and successors Kings of England, to the advancement of holy church and amendment of our realm, of our meer and free will, have given and granted to all archbishops, bishops, abbots, priors, earls, barons, and to all freemen of this our realm, these liberties following, to be kept in our kingdom of England for ever.

Chapter 1 Confirmation of liberties
First, we have granted to God, and by this our present charter have confirmed, for us and our heirs for ever, that the church of England shall be free, and shall have all her whole rights and liberties inviolable. We have granted also, and given to all the freemen of our realm, for us and our heirs for ever, these liberties underwritten, to have and to hold to them and their heirs, of us and our heirs for ever.

Chapters 2-28 . . .

Chapter 29 Imprisonment, etc. contrary to law
No freeman shall be taken or imprisoned, or be disseised of his freehold, or liberties, or free customs, or be outlawed, or exiled, or any other wise destroyed; nor will we not pass upon him, nor condemn him, but by lawful judgment of his peers, or by the law of the land. We will sell to no man, we will not deny or defer to any man either justice or right.

Chapters 30-36 . . .
[Chapter 37 (Escuage) omitted]

TREASON ACT 1351
(25 Edw. 3 Stat 5, c. 2)

Territorial extent United Kingdom

Declaration what offences shall be adjudged treason

Item, whereas divers opinions have been before this time in what case treason shall be said, and in what not; the King, at the request of the lords and of the commons, hath made a declaration in the manner as hereafter followeth, that is to say; when a man doth compass or imagine the death of our lord the King, or of our lady his Queen or of their eldest son and heir; or if a man do violate the King's companion, or the King's eldest daughter unmarried, or the wife the King's eldest son and heir; or if a man do levy war against our lord the King in his realm, or be adherent to the King's enemies in his realm, giving to them aid and comfort in the realm, or elsewhere, and thereof be probably attainted of open deed by the people of their condition: . . . and if a man slea the chancellor, treasurer, or the King's justices of the one bench or the other, justices in eyre, or justices of assise, and all other justices assigned to hear and determine, being in their places, doing their offices: and it is to be understood, that in the cases above rehearsed, that ought to be judged treason which extends to our lord the King, and his royal majesty: . . .

JUSTICES OF THE PEACE ACT 1361
(34 Edw. 3, c. 1)

Who shall be justices of the peace — Their jurisdiction over offenders; rioters; barrators; and vagabonds — Commissions of general inquiries to end — Fines to be reasonable

Territorial extent England and Wales, Northern Ireland (in part — see Magistrates' Courts Act (Northern Ireland) 1964. Sch. 2).

First, that in every county of England shall be assigned for the keeping of the peace, one lord, and with him three or four of the most worthy in the county, with some learned in the law, and they shall have power to restrain the offenders, rioters, and all other barrators and to pursue, arrest, take, and chastise them according their trespass or offence; and to cause them to be imprisoned and duly punished according to the law and customs of the realm, and according to that which to them shall seem best to do by their discretions and good advisement; . . . and to take and arrest all those that they may find by indictment, or by suspicion, and to put them in prison; and to take of all them that be not of good fame, where they shall be found, sufficient surety and mainprise of their good behaviour towards the King and his people, and the other duly to punish; to the intent that the people be not by such rioters or rebels troubled nor endamaged, nor the peace blemished, nor merchants nor other passing by the highways of the realm disturbed, nor put in the peril which may happen of such offenders . . .

THE BILL OF RIGHTS (1688)
(1 Will. & Mar. sess 2, c. 2)

An Act declaring the Rights and Liberties of the Subject and Setleing the Succession of the Crowne

Territorial extent England and Wales, Northern Ireland (for Scotland see the equivalent Act of the Scottish Parliament, the Claim of Right 1689).

Whereas the lords spirituall and temporall and comons assembled at Westminster lawfully fully and freely representing all estates of the people of this realme did upon the thirteenth day of February in the yeare of our Lord one thousand six hundred eighty eight present unto their Majesties then called and known by the names and stile of William and Mary Prince and Princesse of Orange being present in their proper persons a certaine declaration in writeing made by the said lords and comons in the words following viz

The heads of declaration of lords and commons, recited — Whereas the late King James the Second by the assistance of diverse evill councillors judges and ministers imployed by him did endeavour to subvert and extirpate the Protestant religion and the lawes and liberties of this kingdome

Dispensing and suspending power — By assumeing and exerciseing a power of dispensing with and suspending of lawes and the execution of lawes without consent of Parlyament.

Committing prelates — By committing and prosecuting diverse worthy prelates for humbly petitioning to be excused from concurring to the said assumed power.

Ecclasiastical commission — By issueing and causeing to be executed a commission under the great seale for erecting a court called the court of commissioners for ecclesiasticall causes.

Levying money — By levying money for and to the use of the Crowne by pretence of prerogative for other time and in other manner then the same was granted by Parlyament.

Standing army — By raising and keeping a standing army within this kingdome in time of peace without consent of Parlyament and quartering soldiers contrary to law.

Disarming Protestants, etc. — By causing severall good subjects being protestants to be disarmed at the same time when papists were both armed and imployed contrary to law.

Violating elections — By violating the freedome of election of members to serve in Parlyament.

Illegal prosecutions — By prosecutions in the Court of King's Bench for matters and causes cognizable onely in Parlyament and by diverse other arbitrary and illegall courses.

Juries — And whereas of late yeares partiall corrupt and unqualifyed persons have beene returned and served on juryes in tryalls and particularly diverse jurors in tryalls for high treason which were not freeholders.

Excessive bail — And excessive baile hath beene required of persons committed in criminall cases to elude the benefitt of the lawes made for the liberty of the subjects.

Fines — And excessive fines have beene imposed.

Punishments — And illegall and cruell punishments inflicted.

Grants of fines, etc., before conviction, etc. — And severall grants and promises made of fines and forfeitures before any conviction or judgement against the persons upon whome the same were to be levyed.

All which are uterly and directly contrary to the knowne lawes and statutes and freedome of the realme.

And whereas the said late King James the Second haveing abdicated the government and the throne being thereby vacant his Highnesse the Prince of Orange (whome it hath pleased Almighty God to make the glorious instrument of delivering this kingdome from popery and arbitrary power) did (by the advice of the lords spirituall and temporall and diverse principall persons of the commons) cause letters to be written to the lords spirituall and temporall being protestants and other letters to the severall countyes cityes universities boroughss and cinque ports for the choosing of such persons to represent them as were of right to be sent to Parlyament to meete and sitt at Westminster upon the two and twentyeth day of January in this yeare one thousand six hundred eighty and eight in order to such an establishment as that their religion lawes and liberties might not againe be in danger of being subverted, upon which letters elections haveing beene accordingly made.

The subject's Rights — And thereupon the said lords spirituall and temporall and commons pursuant to their respective letters and elections being now assembled in a full and free representative of this nation takeing into their most serious consideration the best meanes for attaining the ends aforesaid doe in the first place (as their auncestors in like case have usually done) for the vindicating and asserting their auntient rights and liberties, declare

[1] **Suspending power** — That the pretended power of suspending of laws or the execution of laws by regall authority without consent of Parlyament is illegall.

Late dispensing power — That the pretended power of dispensing with laws or the execution of laws by regall authoritie as it hath beene assumed and exercised of late is illegall.

Ecclesiastical courts illegal — That the commission for erecting the late court of commissioners for ecclesiasticall causes and all other commissions and courts of like nature are illegal and pernicious.

Levying money — That levying money for or to the use of the Crowne by pretence of prerogative without grant of Parlyament for longer time or in other manner than the same is or shall be granted is illegal.

Right to petition — That it is the right of the subjects to petition the King and all commitments and prosecutions for such petitioning are illegal.

Standing army — That the raising or keeping a standing army within the kingdome in time of peace unlesse it be with consent of Parlyament is against law.

Subject's arms — That the subjects which are protestants may have arms for their defence suitable to their conditions and as allowed by law.

Freedom of election — That election of members of Parlyament ought to be free.

Freedom of speech — That the freedome of speech and debates or proceedings in Parlyament ought not to be impeached or questioned in any court or place out of Parlyament.

Excessive bail — That excessive baile ought not to be required nor excessive fines imposed nor cruell and unusuall punishments inflicted.

Juries — That jurors ought to be duly impannelled and returned . . .

Grants of forfeitures — That all grants and promises of fines and forfeitures of particular persons before conviction are illegal and void.

Frequent Parliaments — And that for redresse of all grievances and for the amending strengthening and preserving of the lawes Parlyaments ought to be held frequently.

The said right claimed, tender of the crown, regal power exercised, limitation of the crown, new oaths of allegiance, etc. — And they doe claime demand and insist upon all and singular the premises as their undoubted rights and liberties and that noe declarations judgements doeings or proceedings to the prejudice of the people in any of the said premisses ought in any wise to be drawne hereafter into consequence or example. To which demand of their rights they are particularly encouraged by the declaration of his Highnesse the Prince of Orange as being the only meanes for obtaining a full redresse and remedy therein. Haveing therefore an intire confidence that his said Highnesse the Prince of Orange will perfect the deliverance soe farr advanced by him and will still preserve them from the violation of their rights which they have here asserted and from all other attempts upon their religion rights and liberties. The said lords spirituall and temporall and commons assembled at Westminster doe resolve that William and Mary Prince and Princesse of Orange be and be declared King and Queene of England France and Ireland and the dominions thereunto belonging to hold the crowne and royall dignity of the said kingdomes and dominions to them the said prince and princesse dureing their lives and the life of the survivour of them. And that the sole and full exercise of the regall power be onely in and executed by the said Prince of Orange in the names of the said prince and princesse dureing their joynt lives and after their deceases the said crowne and royall dignitie of the said kingdoms and dominions to be to the heires of the body of the said princesse and for default of such issue to the Princesse Anne of Denmarke and the heires of her body and for default of such issue to the heires of the body of the said Prince of Orange. And the lords spirituall and temporall and commons doe pray the said prince and princesse to accept the same accordingly. And that the oathes hereafter mentioned be taken by all persons of whome the oathes of allegiance and supremacy might be required by law instead of them and that the said oathes of allegiance and supremacy be abrogated.

I A B doe sincerely promise and sweare that I will be faithfull and beare true allegiance to their Majestyes King William and Queen Mary

Soe helpe me God

I A B doe sweare that I doe from my heart abhorr, detest and abjure as impious and hereticall this damnable doctrine and position that princes excommunicated or deprived by the Pope or any authority of the see of Rome may be deposed or murdered by their subjects or any other whatsoever. And I doe declare that noe forreigne prince person prelate, state or potentate hath or ought to have any jurisdiction power superiority preeminence or authoritie ecclesiasticall or spirituall within this realme.

Soe help me God

[**Note** for the modern version of this effectively obsolete oath see the Accession Declaration Act 1910, Sch.]

Acceptance of the crown, the two Houses to sit, subjects' liberties to be allowed, and ministers hereafter to serve according to the same, William and Mary declared King and Queen, limitation of the crown, papists debarred the crown, every King, etc, shall make the declaration of 30 Car 2, if under 12 years old, to be done after attainment thereof, King's and Queen's assent. Upon which their said Majestyes did accept the crowne and royall dignitie of the kingdoms of England France and Ireland and the dominions thereunto belonging according to the resolution and desire of the said lords and commons contained in the said declaration. And thereupon their Majestyes were pleased that the said lords spirituall and temporall and commons being the two Houses of Parlyament should continue to sitt and with their Majesties royall concurrence make effectuall provision for the settlement of the religion lawes and liberties of this kingdome soe that the same for the future might not be in danger againe of being subverted, to which the said lords spirituall and temporall and commons did agree and proceede to act accordingly. Now in pursuance of the premises the said lords spirituall and temporall and commons in Parlyament assembled for the ratifying confirming and establishing the said declaration and the articles clauses matters and things therein contained by the force of a law made in due forme by authority of Parlyament doe pray that it may be declared and enacted that all and singular the rights and liberties asserted and claimed in the said declaration are the true auntient and indubitable rights and liberties of the people of this kingdome and soe shall be esteemed allowed adjudged deemed and taken to be and that all and every the paritculars aforesaid shall be firmly and strictly holden and observed as they are expressed in the said declaration. And all officers and ministers whatsoever shall serve their Majestyes and their successors according to the same in all times to come. And the said lords spirituall and temporall and commons seriously considering how it hath pleased Almighty God in his marvellous providence and mercifull goodness to this nation to provide and preserve their said Majestyes royall persons most happily to raigne over us upon the throne of their auncestors for which they render unto him from the bottome of their hearts their humblest thanks and praises doe truely firmely assuredly and in the sincerity of their hearts thinke and doe hereby recognize acknowledge and declare that King James the Second haveing abdicated the government and their Majestyes having accepted the crowne and royall dignity as aforesaid their said Majestyes did become were are and of right ought to be by the lawes of the realme our soveraigne liege lord and lady King and Queene of England France and Ireland and the dominions thereunto belonging in and to whose princely persons the royall state crowne and dignity of the said realmes with all honours stiles titles regalities prerogatives powers jurisdictions and authorities to the same belonging and appertaining are most fully and rightfully and intirely invested and incorporated united and annexed. And for preventing all questions and divisions in this realme by reason of any pretended titles to the crowne and for preserveing a certainty in the succession thereof in and upon which the unity peace tranquillity and safety of this nation doth under God wholly consist and depend the said lords spirituall and temporall and commons doe beseech their Majestyes that it may be enacted established and declared that the crowne and regall government of the said kingdoms and dominions with all and singular the premisses thereunto belonging and appertaining shall bee and continue to their said Majestyes and the survivour of them dureing their lives and the life of the survivour of them and that the entire perfect and full exercise of the regall power and government be onely in and executed by his Majestie in the names of both their Majestyes dureing their joynt lives and after their deceases the said crowne and premisses shall be and remaine to the heires of the body of her Majestie and for default of such issue to her royall Highnesse the Princess Anne of Denmarke and the heires of her body and for default of such issue to the heires of the body of his said Majestie And thereunto the said lords spirituall and temporall and commons doe in the name of all the people aforesaid most humbly and faithfully submitt themselves their heires and posterities for ever and doe faithfully promise that they will stand to maintaine and defend their said Majesties and alsoe the limitation and succession of the crowne herein specified and contained to the utmost of their powers with their lives and estates against all persons whatsoever that shall attempt any thing to the contrary. And whereas it hath beene found by experience that it is inconsistent with the safety and welfaire of this protestant kingdome to be governed by a popish prince or by any King or Queene marrying a papist the said lords spirtuall and temporall and commons doe further pray that it may be enacted that all and every person and persons that is are or shall be reconciled to or shall hold communion with the see or church of Rome or shall professe the popish religion or shall marry a papist shall be excluded and be for ever uncapeable to inherit possesse or enjoy the crowne and government of this realme and Ireland and the dominions thereunto belonging or any part of the same or to have use or exercise any regall power authoritie or jurisdiction within the same And in all and every such case or cases the people of these realmes shall be and are hereby absolved of their allegiance and the said crowne and government shall from time to time descend to and be enjoyed by such person or persons being protestants as should have inherited and enjoyed the same in case the said person or persons soe reconciled holding communion or professing or marrying as aforesaid were naturally dead And that every King and Queene of this realme who at any time hereafter shall come to and succeede in the imperiall crowne of this kingdome shall on the first day of the meeting of the first Parlyament next after his or her comeing to the crowne sitting in his or her throne in the House of Peeres in the presence of the lords and commons therein assembled or at his or her coronation before such person or persons who shall administer the coronation oath to him or her at the time of his or her takeing the said oath (which shall first happen) make subscribe and audibly repeate the declaration mentioned in the Statute made in the thirtyeth yeare of the raigne of King Charles the Second entituled An Act for the more effectuall preserveing the Kings person and government by disableing papists from sitting in either House of Parlyament But if it shall happen that such King or Queene upon his or her succession to the crowne of this realme shall be under the age of twelve yeares then every such King or Queene shall make subscribe and audibly repeate the said declaration at his or her coronation or the first day of the meeting of the first Parlyament as aforesaid which shall first happen after such King or Queene shall have attained the said age of twelve years. All which their Majestyes are contented and pleased shall be declared enacted and established by authoritie of this present Parliament and shall stand remaine and be the law of this realme for ever And the same are by their said Majesties by and with the advice and consent of the lords spirituall and temporall and commons in Parlyament assembled and by the authoritie of the same declared enacted and established accordingly

2 Non obstantes made void

. . . noe dispensation by non obstante of or to any statute or any part thereof shall be allowed but . . . the same shall be held void and of noe effect except a dispensation be allowed of in such statute . .

3 . . .

CROWN AND PARLIAMENT RECOGNITION ACT 1689
(2 Will. & Mar., c. 1)

An Act for Recognizing King William and Queene Mary and for avoiding all Questions touching the Acts made in the Parliament assembled at Westminster the thirteenth day of February one thousand six hundred eighty eight

Territorial extent England and Wales, Northern Ireland (effectively extended to Scotland by the Union with Scotland Act 1706, below).

Wee your Majestyes most humble and loyall subjects the lords spirituall and temporall and commons in this present Parlyament assembled doe beseech your most excellent Majestyes that it may be publisehd and declared in this High Court of Parlyament and enacted by authoritie of the same that we doe recognize and acknowledge your Majestyes were are and of right ought to be by the laws of this realme our soveraigne liege lord and lady King and Queene of England France and Ireland and the dominions thereunto belonging in and to whose princely persons the royall state crowne and dignity of the said realms with all honours stiles tiles regalities prerogatives powers jurisdictions and authorities to the same belonging and appertaining are most fully rightfully and intirely invested and incorporated united and annexed. And for the avoiding of all disputes and questions concerning the being and authority of the late Parliament assembled at Westminster the thirteenth day of February one thousand six hundred eighty eight wee doe most humbly beseech your Majestyes that it may be enacted and bee it enacted by the King and Queenes most excellent Majestyes by and with the advice and consent of the lords spirituall and temporall and commons in this present Parlyament assembled and by authoritie of the same that all and singular the Acts made and enacted in the said Parlyament were and are laws and statutes of this kingdome and as such ought to be reputed taken and obeyed by all the people of this kingdome.

THE ACT OF SETTLEMENT (1700)
(12 & 13 Will. 3, c. 2)

An Act for the further Limitation of the Crown and better securing the Rights and Liberties of the Subject

Territorial extent England and Wales, Northern Ireland; effectively extended to Scotland by the Union With Scotland Act 1706.

Whereas in the first year of the reign of your Majesty and of our late most gracious soverign lady Queen Mary (of blessed memory) an Act of Parliament was made intituled (An Act for declaring the rights and liberties of the subject and for setling the succession of the crown) wherein it was (amongst other things) enacted established and declared that the crown and regall government of the kingdoms of England France and Ireland and the dominions thereunto belonging should be and continue to your Majestie and the said late Queen during the joynt lives of your Majesty and the said Queen and to the survivor and that after the decease of your Majesty and of the said Queen the said crown and regall government should be and remain to the heirs of the body of the said late Queen and for default of such issue to her royall Highness the Princess Ann of Denmark and the heirs of her body and for default of such issue to the heirs of the body of your Majesty And it was thereby further enacted that all and every person and persons that then were or afterwards should be reconciled to or shall hold communion with the see or church of Rome or should professe the popish religion or marry a papist should be excluded and are by that Act made for ever incapable to inherit possess or enjoy the crown and government of this realm and Ireland and the dominions thereunto belonging or any part of the same or to have use or exercise any regall power authority or jurisdiction within the same and in all and every such case and cases the people of these realms shall be and are thereby absolved of their allegiance and that the said crown and government shall from time to time descend to and be enjoyed by such person or persons being protestants as should have inherited and enjoyed the same in case the said person or persons so reconciled holding communion professing or marrying as aforesaid were naturally dead After the making of which Statute and the settlement therein contained your Majesties good subjects who were restored to the full and free possession and enjoyment of their religion rights and liberties by the providence of God giving success to your Majesties just undertakings and unwearied endeavours for that purpose had no greater temporall felicity to hope or wish for than to see a royall progeny descending from your Majesty to whom (under God) they owe their tranquility and whose ancestors have for many years been principall assertors of the reformed religion and the liberties of Europe and from our said most gracious sovereign lady whose memory will always be precious to the subjects of these realms And it having since pleased Almighty God to take away our said sovereign lady and also the most hopefull Prince William Duke of Gloucester (the only surviving issue of her royall Highness the Princess Ann of Denmark) to the unspeakable grief and sorrow of your Majesty and your said good subjects who under such losses being sensibly put in mind that it standeth wholly in the pleasure of Almighty God to prolong the lives of your Majesty and of her royall Highness and to grant to your Majesty or to her royall Highness such issue as may be inheritable to the crown and regall government aforesaid by the respective limitations in the said recited Act contained doe constantly implore the divine mercy for those blessings And your Majesties said subjects having daily experience of your royall care and concern for the present and future welfare of these kingdoms and particularly recommending from your throne a further provision to be made for the succession of the crown in the protestant line for the happiness of the nation and the security of our religion and it being absolutely necessary for the safety peace and quiet of this realm to obviate all doubts and contentions in the same by reason of any pretended titles to the crown and to maintain a certainty in the succession thereof to which your subjects may safely have recourse for their protection in case the limitations in the said recited Act should determine Therefore for a further provision of the succession of the crown in the protestant line we your Majesties most dutifull and loyal subjects the lords spirituall and temporall and commons in this present Parliament assembled do beseech your Majesty that it may be enacted and declared and be it enacted and declared by the Kings most excellent Majesty by and with the advice and consent of the lords spirituall and temporall and commons in this present Parliament assembled and by the authority of the same that

1 The Princess Sophia, Electress and Duchess dowager of Hanover, daughter of the late Queen of Bohemia, daughter of King James the First, to inherit after the King and the Princess Anne, in default of issue of the said princess and his Majesty, respectively; and the heirs of her body, being protestants

the most excellent Princess Sophia Electress and Dutchess dowager of Hanover daughter of the most excellent Princess Elizabeth late Queen of Bohemia daughter of our late sovereign lord King James the First of happy memory be and is hereby declared to be the next in succession in the protestant line to the imperiall crown and dignity of the [said] realms of England France and Ireland with the dominions and territories thereunto belonging after his Majesty and the Princess Ann of Denmark and in default of issue of the said Princess Ann and of his Majesty respectively and that from and after the deceases of his said Majesty our own soveriegn lord and of her royall Highness the Princess Ann of Denmark and for default of issue of the said Princess Ann and of his Majesty respectively the crown and regall government of the said kingdoms of England France and Ireland and of the dominions thereunto belonging with the royall state and dignity of the said realms and all honours stiles titles regalities prerogatives powers jurisdictions and authorities to the same belonging and appertaining shall be remain and continue to the said most excellent Princess Sophia and the heirs of her body being protestants And thereunto the said lords spirituall and temporall and commons shall and will in the name of all the people of this realm most humbly and faithfully submitt themselves their heirs and posterities and do faithfully promise that after the deceases of his Majesty and her royall Highness and the failure of the heirs of their respective bodies to stand to maintain and defend the said Princess Sophia and the heirs of her body being protestants according to the limitation and succession of the crown in this Act specified and contained to the utmost of their powers with their lives and estates against all persons whatsoever that shall attempt any thing to the contrary.

2 The persons inheritable by this Act, holding communion with the church of Rome, incapacitated as by the former Act; to take the oath at their coronation, according to Stat 1 W & M c. 6
Provided always and it is hereby enacted that all and every person and persons who shall or may take or inherit the said crown by vertue of the limitation of this present Act and is are or shall be reconciled to or shall hold communion with the see or church of Rome or shall profess the popish religion or shall marry a papist shall be subject to such incapacities as in such case or cases are by the said recited Act provided enacted and established. And that every King and Queen of this realm who shall come to and succeed in the imperiall crown of this kingdom by vertue of this Act shall have the coronation oath administered to him her or them at their respective coronations according to the Act of Parliament made in the first year of the reign of his Majesty and the said late Queen Mary intituled An Act for establishing the coronation oath and shall make subscribe and repeat the declaration in the Act first above recited mentioned or referred to in the manner and form thereby prescribed.

3 Further provisions for securing the religions, laws, and liberties of these realms
And whereas it is requisite and necessary that some further provision be made for securing our religion laws and liberties from and after the death of his Majesty and the Princess Ann of Denmark and in default of issue of the body of the said princess and of his Majesty respectively Be it enacted by the Kings most excellent Majesty by and with the advice and consent of the lords spirituall and temporall and commons in Parliament and by the authority of the same

That whosoever shall hereafter come to the possession of this crown shall joyn in communion with the Church of England as by law established

That in case the crown and imperiall dignity of this realm shall hereafter come to any person not being a native of this kingdom of England this nation be not obliged to ingage in any warr for the defence of any dominions or territories which do not belong to the crown of England without the consent of Parliament

. . . . .

That after the said limitation shall take effect as aforesaid no person born out of the kingdoms of England Scotland or Ireland or the dominions thereunto belonging (although he be . . . made a denizen (except such as are born of English parents)) shall be capable to be of the privy councill or a member of either House of Parliament or to enjoy any office or place of trust either civill or military or to have any grant of lands tenements or hereditaments from the Crown to himself or to any other or others in trust for him.

. . . . .

That no pardon under the great seal of England be pleadable to an impeachment by the commons in Parliament.

4 The laws and statutes of the realm confirmed
And whereas the laws of England are the birthright of the people thereof and all the Kings and Queens who shall ascend the throne of this realm ought to administer the government of the same according to the said laws and all their officers and ministers ought to serve them respectively according to the same The said lords spirituall and temporall and commons do therefore further humbly pray that all the laws and statutes of this realm for securing the established religion and the rights and liberties of the people thereof and all other laws and statutes of the same now in force may be ratified and confirmed And the same are by his Majesty by and with the advice and consent of the said lords spirituall and temporall and commons and by authority of the same ratified and confirmed accordingly.

UNION WITH SCOTLAND ACT 1706
(6 Anne, c. 11)

An Act for an Union of the Two Kingdoms of England and Scotland

Territorial extent England, Wales and Scotland (by the combined effect of this Act and the equivalent Act of the Parliament of Scotland (APS, XI, 406)); subsequently applied to Northern Ireland.

Most Gracious Sovereign
Whereas articles of union were agreed on the twenty second day of July in the fifth year of your Majesties reign by the commissioners nominated on behalf of the kingdom of England under your Majesties great seal of England bearing date at Westminster the tenth day of April then last past in pursuance of an Act of Parliament made in England in the third year of your Majesties reign and the commissioners nominated on the behalf of the kingdom of Scotland under your Majesties great seal of Scotland bearing date the twenty-seventh day of February in the fourth year of your Majesties reign in pursuance of the fourth Act of the third session of the present Parliament of Scotland to treat of and concerning an union of the said kingdoms And whereas an Act hath passed in the Parliament of Scotland at Edinburgh the sixteenth day of January in the fifth year of your Majesties reign wherein 'tis mentioned that the estates of Parliament considering the said articles of union of the two kingdoms had agreed to and approved of the said articles of union with some additions and explanations and that your Majesty with advice and consent of the estates of Parliament for establishing the Protestant religion and Presbyterian Church government within the kingdom of Scotland had passed in the same session of Parliament an Act intituled Act for securing of the Protestant religion and Presbyterian Church government which by the tenor thereof was appointed to be inserted in any Act ratifying the treaty and expresly declared to be a fundamental and essential condition of the said treaty or union in all times coming the tenor of which articles as ratified and approved of with additions and explanations by the said Act of Parliament of Scotland follows.

Article I

The kingdoms united; ensigns armorial — That the two kingdoms of England and Scotland shall upon the first day of May which shall be in the year one thousand seven hundred and seven and for ever after be united into one kingdom by the name of Great Britain and that the ensigns armorial of the said United Kingdom be such as her Majesty shall appoint and the crosses of St. George and St. Andrew be conjoyned in such manner as Her Majesty shall think fit and used in all flags banners standards and ensigns both at sea and land.

Article II

Succession to the monarchy — That the succession to the monarchy of the United Kingdom of Great Britain and of the dominions thereto belonging after her most sacred Majesty and in default of issue of her Majesty be remain and continue to the most excellent Princess Sophia Electoress and Dutchess dowager of Hanover and the heirs of her body being protestants upon whom the crown of England is settled by an Act of Parliament made in England in the twelfth year of the reign of his late Majesty King William the Third intituled An Act for the further limitation of the crown and better securing the right and liberties of the subject And that all papists and persons marrying papists shall be excluded from and for ever incapable to inherit possess or enjoy the imperial crown of Great Britain and the dominions thereunto belonging or any part thereof and in every such case the crown and government shall from time to time descend to and be enjoyed by such person being a protestant as should have inherited and enjoyed the same in case such papist or person marrying a papist was naturally dead according to the provision for the descent of the crown of England made by another Act of Parliament in England in the first year of the reign of their late Majesties King William and Queen Mary intituled An Act declaring the rights and liberties of the subject and settling the succession of the crown.

Article III

Parliament — That the United Kingdom of Great Britain be represented by one and the same Parliament to be stiled the Parliament of Great Britain.

Article IIII

Trade and navigation and other rights — That all the subjects of the United Kingdom of Great Britain shall from and after the union have full freedom and intercourse of trade and navigation to and from any port or place within the said United Kingdom and the dominions and plantations thereunto belonging and that there be a communication of all other rights privileges and advantages which do or may belong to the subjects of either kingdom except where it is otherwise expressly agreed in these articles.

Article V . . .

Article VI

Regulations of trade, duties, etc — That all parts of the United Kingdom for ever from and after the union shall have the same allowances encouragements and drawbacks and be under the same prohibitions restrictions and regulations of trade and liable to the same customs and duties on import and export and that the allowances encouragements and drawbacks prohibitions restrictions and regulations of trade and the customs and duties on import and export settled in England when the union commences shall from and after the union take place throughout the whole United Kingdom . . .

* * * * *

Article XVIII

Laws concerning public rights; private rights — That the laws concerning regulation of trade customs and such excises to which Scotland is by virtue of this treaty to be liable be the same in Scotland from and after the union as in England and that all other laws in use within the kingdom of Scotland do after the union and notwithstanding thereof remain in the same force as before (except such as are contrary to or inconsistent with this treaty) but alterable by the Parliament of Great Britain with this difference betwixt the laws concerning publick right policy and civil government and those which concern private right that the laws which concern publick right policy and civil government may be made the same throughout the whole United Kingdom. But that no alteration be made in laws which concern private right except for evident utility of the subjects within Scotland

* * * * *

Article XXV

Laws inconsistent with the articles, void — That all laws and statutes in either kingdom so far as they are contrary to or inconsistent with the terms of these articles or any of them shall from and after the union cease and become void and shall be so declared to be by the respective Parliaments of the said kingdoms.

As by the said articles of union ratified and approved by the said Act of Parliament of Scotland relation being thereunto had may appear.

* * * * *

5 Cap 8 ante, and the said Act of Parliament of Scotland to be observed as fundamental conditions of the said union; and the said articles and Acts of Parliament to continue the union

And it is hereby further enacted by the authority aforesaid that the said Act passed in this present session of Parliament intituled An Act for securing the Church of England as by law established and all and every the matters and things therein contained and also the said Act of Parliament of Scotland intituled Act for securing the Protestant religion and Presbyterian Church government with the establishment in the said Act contained be and shall for ever be held and adjudged to be and observed as fundamental and essential conditions of the said union and shall in all times coming be taken to be and are hereby declared to be essential and fundamental parts of the said articles and union and the said articles of union so as aforesaid ratified approved and confirmed by Act of Parliament of Scotland and by this present Act and the said Act passed in this present session of Parliament intituled an Act for securing the Church of England as by law established and also the said Act passed in the Parliament of Scotland intituled Act for securing the Protestant religion and Presbyterian Church government are hereby enacted and ordained to be and continue in all times coming the complete and intire union of the two kingdoms of England and Scotland.

* * * * *

METROPOLITAN POLICE ACT 1839
(2 & 3 Vict., c. 47)

An Act for further improving the Police in and near the Metropolis.

Territorial extent Metropolitan Police Area and City of London

* * * * *

52 Commissioners may make regulations for the route of carriages, and persons, and for preventing obstruction of the streets during public processions, etc., or in the neighbourhood of public buildings, etc.

. . . It shall be lawful for the commissioners of police from time to time, and as occasion shall require, to make regulations for the route to be observed by all carts, carriages, horses, and persons, and for preventing obstruction of the streets and thoroughfares within the metropolitan police district, in all times of public processions, public rejoicings, or illuminations, and also to give directions to the constables for keeping order and for preventing any obstruction of the thoroughfares in the immediate neighbourhood of her Majesty's palaces and the public offices, the High Court of Parliament, the courts of law and equity, the police courts, the theatres, and other places of public resort, and in any case when the streets or thoroughfares may be thronged or may be liable to be obstructed.

* * * * *

PARLIAMENTARY PAPERS ACT 1840
(3 & 4 Vict., c. 9)

An Act to give summary Protection to Persons employed in the Publication of Parliamentary Papers

Territorial extent United Kingdom

[1] Proceedings, criminal or civil, against persons for publication of papers printed by order of Parliament to be stayed upon delivery of a certificte and affidavit to the effect that such publication is by order of either House of Parliament

. . . It shall and may be lawful for any person or persons who now is or are, or hereafter shall be, a defendant or defendants in any civil or criminal proceedings commenced or prosecuted in any manner soever, for or on account or in respect of the publication of any such report, paper, votes, or proceedings by such person or persons, or by his, her, or their servant or servants, by or under the authority of either House of Parliament, to bring before the court in which such proceeding shall have been or shall be so commenced or prosecuted, or before any judge of the same (if one of the superior courts at Westminster), first giving twenty-four hours notice of his intention so to do to the prosecutor or plaintiff in such proceeding, a certificate under the hand of the lord high chancellor of Great Britain, or the lord keeper of the great seal, or of the speaker of the House of Lords, for the time being, or of the clerk of the Parliaments, or of the speaker of the House of Commons, or of the clerk of the same house, stating that the report, paper, votes, or proceedings, as the case may be, in respect whereof such civil or criminal proceeding shall have been commenced or prosecuted, was published by such person or persons, or by his, her, or their servant or servants, by order or under the authority of the House of Lords or of the House of Commons, as the case may be, together with an affidavit verifying such certificate; and such court or judge shall thereupon immediately stay such civil or criminal proceeding, and the same, and every writ or process issued therein, shall be and shall be deemed and taken to be finally put an end to, determined, and superseded by virtue of this Act.

2, 3 *****

4 Act not to affect the privileges of Parliament
Provided always . . . that nothing herein contained shall be deemed or taken, or held or construed, directly or indirectly, by implication or otherwise, to affect the privileges of Parliament in any manner whatsoever.

TREASON FELONY ACT 1848
(11 & 12 Vict., c. 12)

An Act for the better Security of the Crown and Government of the United Kingdom

Territorial extent See section 3.

*****

3 Offences herein mentioned declared to be felonies
. . . If any person whatsoever shall, within the United Kingdom or without, compass, imagine, invent, devise, or intend to deprive or depose our Most Gracious Lady the Queen, . . . from the style, honour, or royal name of the imperial crown of the United Kingdom, or of any other of her Majesty's dominions and countries, or to levy war against her Majesty, . . . within any part of the United Kingdom, in order by force or constraint to compel her . . . to change her . . . measures or counsels, or in order to put any force or constraint upon or in order to intimidate or overawe both Houses or either House of Parliament, or to move or stir any foreigner or stranger with force to invade the United Kingdom or any other of her Majesty's dominions or countries under the obeisance of her Majesty, . . . and such compassings, imaginations, inventions, devices, or intentions, or any of them, shall express, utter, or declare, by publishing any printing or writing, . . . or by any overt act or deed, every person so offending shall be guilty of felony, and being convicted thereof shall be liable, . . . to be transported beyond the seas for the term of his or her natural life . . .
. . .

6 Saving as to 25 Edw 3 stat 5 c 2
Provided always, . . . that nothing herein contained shall lessen the force of or in any manner affect any thing enacted by the Treason Act 1351.

*****

EXTRADITION ACT 1870
(33 & 34 Vict., c. 52)

An Act for amending the Law relating to the Extradition of Criminals

Territorial extent United Kingdom

Note For extradition between the United Kingdom and the Republic of Ireland see the Backing of Warrants (Republic of Ireland) Act 1965, not included in this book for reasons of space.

Preliminary

1 Short title
This Act may be cited as "The Extradition Act 1870."

2 Where arrangement for surrender of criminals made, Order in Council to apply Act
Where an arrangement has been made with any foreign state with respect to the surrender to such state of any fugitive criminals, Her Majesty may, by Order in Council, direct that this Act shall apply in the case of such foreign state.

Her Majesty may, by the same or any subsequent order, limit the operation of the order, and restrict the same to fugitive criminals who are in or suspected of being in the part of Her Majesty's dominions specified in the order, and render the operation thereof subject to such conditions, exceptions, and qualifications as may be deemed expedient.

Every such order shall recite or embody the terms of the arrangement, and shall not remain in force for any longer period than the arrangement.

Every such order shall be laid before both Houses of Parliament within six weeks after it is made, or, if Parliament be not then sitting, within six weeks after the then next meeting of Parliament, and shall also be published in the London Gazette.

3 Restrictions on surrender of criminals
The following restrictions shall be observed with respect to the surrender of fugitive criminals:

(1) A fugitive criminal shall not be surrendered if the offence in respect of which his surrender is demanded is one of a political character, or if he prove to the satisfaction of the police magistrate or the court before whom he is brought on habeas corpus, or to the Secretary of State, that the requisition for his surrender has in fact been made with a view to try or punish him for an offence of a political character:

(2) A fugitive criminal shall not be surrendered to a foreign state unless provision is made by the law of that state, or by arrangement that the fugitive criminal shall not, until he has been restored or had an opportunity of returning to Her Majesty's dominions, be detained or tried in that foreign state for any offence committed prior to his surrender other than the extradition crime proved by the facts on which the surrender is grounded:

(3) A fugitive criminal who has been accused of some offence within English jurisdiction not being the offence for which his surrender is asked, or is undergoing sentence under any conviction in the United Kingdom, shall not be surrendered until after he has been discharged, whether by acquittal or on expiration of his sentence or otherwise:

(4) A fugitive criminal shall not be surrendered until the expiration of fifteen days from the date of his being committed to prison to await his surrender.

* * * * *

6 Liability of criminal to surrender
Where this Act applies in the case of any foreign state, every fugitive criminal of that state who is in or suspected of being in any part of Her Majesty's dominions, or that part which is specified in the Order applying this Act (as the case may be), shall be liable to be apprehended and surrendered in manner provided by this Act, whether the crime in

respect of which the surrender is sought was committed before or after the date of the Order, and whether there is or is not any concurrent jurisdiction in any court of Her Majesty's dominions over that crime.

7 Order of Secretary of State for issue of warrant in United Kingdom if crime is not of a political character

A requisition for the surrender of a fugitive criminal of any foreign state, who is in or suspected of being in the United Kingdom, shall be made to a Secretary of State by some person recognised by the Secretary of State as a diplomatic representative of that foreign state. A Secretary of State may, by order under his hand and seal, signify to a police magistrate that such a requisition has been made, and require him to issue his warrant for the apprehension of the fugitive criminal.

If the Secretary of State is of opinion that the offence is one of a political character, he may, if he think fit, refuse to send any such order, and may also at any time order a fugitive criminal accused or convicted of such offence to be discharged from custody.

8 Issue of warrant by police magistrate, justice, etc.

A warrant for the apprehension of a fugitive criminal, whether accused or convicted of crime, who is in or suspected of being in the United Kingdom, may be issued—

1. By a police magistrate on the receipt of the said order of the Secretary of State, and on such evidence as would in his opinion justify the issue of the warrant if the crime had been committed or the criminal convicted in England; and

2. By a police magistrate or any justice of the peace in any part of the United Kingdom, on such information or complaint and such evidence or after such proceedings as would in the opinion of the person issuing the warrant justify the issue of a warrant if the crime had been committed or the criminal convicted in that part of the United Kingdom in which he exercises jurisdiction.

Any person issuing a warrant under this section without an order from a Secretary of State shall forthwith send a report of the fact of such issue, together with the evidence and information or complaint, or certified copies thereof, to a Secretary of State, who may if he think fit order the warrant to be cancelled, and the person who has been apprehended on the warrant to be discharged.

A fugitive criminal, when apprehended on a warrant issued without the order of a Secretary of State, shall be brought before some person having power to issue a warrant under this section, who shall by warrant order him to be brought and the prisoner shall accordingly be brought before a police magistrate.

A fugitive criminal apprehended on a warrant issued without the order of a Secretary of State shall be discharged by the police magistrate, unless the police magistrate, within such reasonable time as, with reference to the circumstances of the case, he may fix, receives from a Secretary of State an order signifying that a requisition has been made for the surrender of such criminal.

9 Hearing of case and evidence of political character of crime

When a fugitive criminal is brought before the police magistrate, the police magistrate shall hear the case in the same manner, and have the same jurisdiction and powers, as near as may be, as if the prisoner were brought before him charged with an indictable offence committed in England.

The police magistrate shall receive any evidence which may be tendered to show that the crime of which the prisoner is accused or alleged to have been convicted is an offence of a political character or is not an extradition crime.

10 Committal or discharge of prisoner

In the case of a fugitive criminal accused of an extradition crime, if the foreign warrant authorising the arrest of such criminal is duly authenticated, and such evidence is produced as (subject to the provisions of this Act) would, according to the law of England, justify the committal for trial of the prisoner if the crime of which he is accused had been committed in England, the police magistrate shall commit him to prison, but otherwise shall order him to be discharged.

In the case of a fugitive criminal alleged to have been convicted of an extradition crime, if such evidence is produced as (subject to the provisions of this Act) would, according to the law of England, prove that the prisoner was convicted of such crime, the police magistrate shall commit him to prison, but otherwise shall order him to be discharged.

If he commits such criminal to prison, he shall commit him . . ., there to await the warrant of a Secretary of State for his surrender, and shall forthwith send to a Secretary of State a certificate of the committal, and such report upon the case as he may think fit.

11 Surrender of fugitive to foreign state by warrant of Secretary of State

If the police magistrate commits a fugitive criminal to prison, he shall inform such criminal that he will not be surrendered until after the expiration of fifteen days, and that he has a right to apply for a writ of Habeas corpus.

Upon the expiration of the said fifteen days, or, if a writ of Habeas corpus is issued, after the decision of the court upon the return to the writ, as the case may be, or after such further period as may be allowed in either case by a Secretary of State, it shall be lawful for a Secretary of State, by warrant under his hand and seal, to order the fugitive criminal (if not delivered on the decision of the court) to be surrendered to such person as may in his opinion be duly authorized to receive the fugitive criminal by the foreign state from which the requisition for the surrender proceeded, and such fugitive criminal shall be surrendered accordingly.

It shall be lawful for any person to whom such warrant is directed and for the person so authorized as aforesaid to receive, hold in custody, and convey within the jurisdiction of such foreign state the criminal mentioned in the warrant; and if the criminal escapes out of any custody to which he may be delivered on or in pursuance of such warrant, it shall be lawful to retake him in the same manner as any person accused of any crime against the laws of that part of Her Majesty's dominions to which he escapes may be retaken upon an escape.

12 Discharge of persons apprehended if not conveyed out of United Kingdom within two months

If the fugitive criminal who has been committed to prison is not surrendered and conveyed out of the United Kingdom within two months after such committal, or, if a writ of Habeas corpus is issued, after the decision of the court upon the return to the writ, it shall be lawful for any judge of one of Her Majesty's Superior Courts at Westminster, upon application made to him by or on behalf of the criminal, and upon proof that reasonable notice of the intention to make such application has been given to a Secretary of State, to order the criminal to be discharged out of custody, unless sufficient cause is shown to the contrary.

* * * * *

General provisions

19 Criminal surrendered by foreign state not triable for previous crime

Where, in pursuance of any arrangement with a foreign state, any person accused or convicted of any crime which, if committed in England, would be one of the crimes described in the first schedule to this Act is surrendered by that foreign state, such person shall not, until he has been restored or had an opportunity of returning to such foreign state, be triable or tried for any offence committed prior to the surrender in any part of Her Majesty's dominions other than such of the said crimes as may be proved by the facts on which the surrender is grounded.

* * * * *

CONSPIRACY AND PROTECTION OF PROPERTY ACT 1875
(38 & 39 Vict., C. 86)

An Act for amending the Law relating to Conspiracy, and to the Protection of Property, and for other purposes

Territorial extent United Kingdom

* * * * *

7 Penalty for intimidation or annoyance by violence or otherwise

Every person who, with a view to compel any other person to abstain from doing or to do any act which such other person has a legal right to do or abstain from doing, wrongfully and without legal authority,—

1. Uses violence to or intimidates such other person or his wife or children, or injures his property; or,
2. Persistently follows such other person about from place to place; or,
3. Hides any tools, clothes, or other property owned or used by such other person, or deprives him of or hinders him in the use thereof; or,
4. Watches or besets the house or other place where such other person resides, or works, or carries on business, or happens to be, or the approach to such house or place; or,
5. Follows such other person with two or more other persons in a disorderly manner in or through any street or road,

shall [be liable on conviction to imprisonment for a term not exceeding 6 months or a fine not exceeding level 5 on the standard scale, or both.]

[A constable may arrest without warrant anyone he resonably suspects is committing an offence under this section.]

Note Increased penalties and power of arrest added by the Public Order Act 1986, Sch. 2.

* * * * *

15 Definition of "maliciously"

The word "maliciously" used in reference to any offence under this Act shall be construed in the same manner as it is required by the fifty-eighth section of the Malicious Damage Act 1861 to be construed in reference to any offence committed under such last-mentioned Act.

* * * * *

CUSTOMS CONSOLIDATION ACT 1876
(39 & 40 Vict., c. 36)

An Act to consolidate the Customs Laws

Territorial extent United Kingdom

AS TO THE IMPORTATION, PROHIBITION, ENTRY, EXAMINATION, LANDING, AND WAREHOUSING OF GOODS

. . .

42 Prohibitions and restrictions

The goods enumerated and described in the following table of prohibitions and restrictions inwards are hereby prohibited to be imported or brought into the United Kingdom, save as thereby excepted . . .

A TABLE OF PROHIBITIONS AND RESTRICTIONS INWARDS

Goods prohibited to be imported

Indecent or obscene prints, paintings, photographs, books, cards, lithographic or other engravings, or any other indecent or obscene articles.

* * * * *

RIOT (DAMAGES) ACT 1886
(49 & 50 Vict., c. 38)

An Act to provide compensation for Losses by Riots

Territorial extent England and Wales. (For Scotland see the Riotous Assembly (Scotland) Act 1822.)

1 Short title
This act may be cited for all purposes as the Riot (Damages) Act 1886.

2 Compensation to persons for damage by riot
(1) Where a house, shop, or building in any police district has been injured or destroyed, or the property therein has been injured, stolen, or destroyed, by any persons riotously and tumultuously assembled together, such compensation as herein-after mentioned shall be paid out of [the police fund] of such district to any person who has sustained loss by such injury, stealing, or destruction; but in fixing the amount of such compensation regard shall be had to the conduct of the said person, whether as respects the precautions taken by him or as respects his being a party or accessory to such riotous or tumultuous assembly, or as regards any provocation offered to the persons assembled or otherwise.

(2) Where any person having sustained such loss as aforesaid has received, by way of insurance or otherwise, any sum to recoup him, in whole or in part, for such loss, the compensation otherwise payable to him under this Act shall, if exceeding such sum, be reduced by the amount thereof, and in any other case shall not be paid to him, and the payer of such sum shall be entitled to compensation under this Act in respect of the sum so paid in like manner as if he had sustained the said loss, and any policy of insurance given by such payer shall continue in force as if he had made no such payment, and where such person was recouped as aforesaid otherwise than by payment of a sum, this enactment shall apply as if the value of such recoupment were a sum paid.

Note Section 10 of the Public Order Act 1986 provides that 'riotous' and 'riotously' are to be construed in accordance with the definition of 'riot' in that Act.

PUBLIC MEETING ACT 1908
(8 Edw. 7, c. 66)

An Act to prevent disturbance of Public Meetings

Territorial extent England and Wales, Scotland

1 Penalty on endeavour to break up public meeting
(1) Any person who at a lawful public meeting acts in a disorderly manner for the purpose of preventing the transaction of the business for which the meeting was called together shall be guilty of an offence [and shall on summary conviction be liable to imprisonment for a term not exceeding six months or to a fine not exceeding [level 5 on the standard scale] or to both] . . .

(2) Any person who incites others to commit an offence under this section shall be guilty of a like offence.

[(3) If any constable reasonably suspects any person of committing an offence under the foregoing provisions of this section, he may if requested so to do by the chairman of the meeting require that person to declare to him immediately his name and address and, if that person refuses or fails so to declare his name and address or gives a false name and address he shall be guilty of an offence under this subsection and liable on summary conviction thereof to a fine not exceeding [level 1 on the standard scale], . . .

[(4) This section does not apply as respects meetings to which section 97 of the Representation of the People Act 1983 applies.]

OFFICIAL SECRETS ACT 1911
(1 & 2 Geo. 5, c. 28)

An Act to re-enact the Official Secrets Act 1889, with Amendments

Territorial extent United Kingdom. See also s. 10(1).

Note Printed as amended by the Official Secrets Act 1920.

1 Penalties for spying

(1) If any person for any purpose prejudicial to the safety or interests of the State—

(a) approaches [inspects, passes over] or is in the neighbourhood of, or enters any prohibited place within the meaning of this Act; or

(b) makes any sketch, plan, model, or note which is calculated to be or might be or is intended to be directly or indirectly useful to an enemy; or

(c) obtains, [collects, records, or publishes,] or communicates to any other person [any secret official code word or pass word, or] any sketch, plan, model, article, or note, or other document or information which is calculated to be or might be or is intended to be directly or indirectly useful to an enemy;

he shall be guilty of felony . . .

(2) On a prosecution under this section, it shall not be necessary to show that the accused person was guilty of any particular act tending to show a purpose prejudicial to the safety or interests of the State, and, notwithstanding that no such act is proved against him, he may be convicted if, from the circumstances of the case, or his conduct, or his known character as proved, it appears that his purpose was a purpose prejudicial to the safety or interests of the State; and if any sketch, plan, model, article, note, document, or information relating to or used in any prohibited place within the meaning of this Act, or anything in such a place [or any secret official code word or pass word], is made, obtained, [collected, recorded, published], or communicated by any person other than a person acting under lawful authority, it shall be deemed to have been made, obtained, [collected, recorded, published] or communicated for a purpose prejudicial to the safety or interests of the State unless the contrary is proved.

2 Wrongful communication, etc, of information

(1) If any person having his possession or control [any secret official code word, or pass word, or] any sketch, plan, model, article, note, document, or information which relates to or is used in a prohibited place or anything in such a place, or which has been made or obtained in contravention of this Act, or which has been entrusted in confidence to him by any person holding office under His Majesty or which he has obtained [or to which he has had access] owing to his position as a person who holds or has held office under His Majesty, or as a person who holds or has held a contract made on behalf of His Majesty, or as a person who is or has been employed under a person who holds or has held such an office or contract,—

(a) communicates the [code word, pass word,] sketch, plan, model, article, note, document, or information to any person, other than a person to whom he is authorised to communicate it, or a person to whom it is in the interest of the State his duty to communicate it, or, [(aa) uses the information in his possession for the benefit of any foreign power or in any other manner prejudicial to the safety or interests of the State;]

(b) retains the sketch, plan, model, article, note, or document in his possession or control when he has no right to retain it or when it is contrary to his duty to retain it [or fails to comply with all directions issued by lawful authority with regard to the return or disposal thereof] [or

(c) fails to take reasonable care of, or so conducts himself as to endanger the safety of the sketch, plan, model, article, note, document, secret official code or pass word or information:]

that person shall be guilty of a misdemeanour.

[1A] If any person having in his possession or control any sketch, plan, model, article, note, document, or information which relates to munitions of war, communicates it directly or indirectly to any foreign power, or in any other manner prejudicial to the safety or interests of the State, that person shall be guilty of a misdemeanour.]

(2) If any person receives any [secret official code word, or pass word, or] sketch, plan, model, article, note, document, or information, knowing, or having reasonable ground to believe, at the time when he receives it, that the [code word, pass word,] sketch, plan, model, article, note, document, or information is communicated to him in contravention of this Act, he shall be guilty of a misdemeanour, unless he proves that the communication to him of the [code word, pass word,] sketch, plan, model, article, note, document, or information was contrary to his desire.

(3) . . .

3 Definition of prohibited place

For the purposes of this Act, the expression "prohibited place" means—

(a) any work of defence, arsenal, naval or air force establishment or station, factory, dockyard, mine, minefield, camp, ship, or aircraft belonging to or occupied by or on behalf of His Majesty, or any telegraph, telephone, wireless or signal station, or office so belonging or occupied, and any place belonging to or occupied by or on behalf of His Majesty and used for the purpose of building, repairing, making, or storing any munitions of war, or any sketches, plans, models, or documents relating thereto, or for the purpose of getting any metals, oil, or minerals of use in time of war];

(b) any place not belonging to His Majesty where any [munitions of war], or any [sketches, models, plans] or documents relating thereto, are being made, repaired, [gotten] or stored under contract with, or with any person on behalf of, His Majesty, or otherwise on behalf of His Majesty; and

(c) any place belonging to [or used for the purposes of] His Majesty which is for the time being declared [by order of a Secretary of State] to be a prohibited place for the purposes of this section on the ground that information with respect thereto, or damage thereto, would be useful to an enemy; and

(d) any railway, road, way, or channel, or other means of communication by land or water (including any works or structures being part thereof or connected therewith), or any place used for gas, water, or electricity works or other works for purposes of a public character, or any place where any [munitions of war], or any [sketches, models, plans] or documents relating thereto, are being made, repaired, or stored otherwise than on behalf of His Majesty, which is for the time being declared [by order or a Secretary of State] to be a prohibited place for the purposes of this section, on the ground that information with respect thereto, or the destruction or obstruction thereof, or interference therewith, would be useful to an enemy.

4, 5 . . .

6 Power of arrest
Any person who is found committing an offence under this Act . . . or who is reasonably suspected of having committed, or having attempted to commit, or being about to commit, such an offence, may be apprehended and detained . . .

7 *****

8 Restriction on prosecution
A prosecution for an offence under this Act shall not be instituted except by or with the consent of the Attorney-General:

. . . . .

9 Search warrants
(1) If a justice of the peace is satisfied by information on oath that there is reasonable ground for suspecting that an offence under this Act has been or is about to be committed, he may grant a search warrant authorising any constable . . . to enter at any time any premises or place named in the warrant, if necessary, by force, and to search the premises or place and every person found therein, and to seize any sketch, plan, model, article, note, or document, or anything of a like nature or anything which is evidence of an offence under this Act having been or being about to be committed, which he may find on the premises or place or on any such person, and with regard to or in connexion with which he has reasonable ground for suspecting that an offence under this Act has been or is about to be committed.

(2) Where it appears to a superintendent of police that the case is one of great emergency and that in the interests of the State immediate action is necessary, he may by a written order under his hand give to any constable the like authority as may be given by the warrant of a justice under the section.

10 Extent of Act and place of trial of offence
(1) This Act shall apply to all acts which are offences under this Act when committed in any part of His Majesty's dominions, or when committed by British officers or subjects elsewhere.

*****

PARLIAMENT ACT 1911
(1 & 2 Geo. 5, c. 13)

An Act to make provision with respect to the powers of the House of Lords in relation of the House of Commons, and to limit the duration of Parliament

Territorial extent United Kingdom

Note The words in square brackets in s. 2 were substituted by the Parliament Act 1949, and are included without prejudice to the suggestions of some writers that the 1949 Act (itself passed under the procedure of the 1911 Act) is not a valid Act of Parliament.

Preamble
Whereas it is expedient that provision should be made for regulating the relations between the two Houses of Parliament:

And whereas it is intended to substitute for the House of Lords as it at present exists a Second Chamber constituted on a popular instead of hereditary basis, but such substitution cannot be immediately brought into operation:

And whereas provision will require hereafter to be made by Parliament in a measure effecting such substitution for limiting and defining the powers of the new Second Chamber, but it is expedient to make such provision as in this Act appears for restricting the existing powers of the House of Lords:

1 Powers of House of Lords as to Money Bills

(1) If a Money Bill, having been passed by the House of Commons, and sent up to the House of Lords at least one month before the end of the session, is not passed by the House of Lords without amendment within one month after it is so sent up to that House, the Bill shall, unless the House of Commons direct to the contrary, be presented to His Majesty and become an Act of Parliament on the Royal Assent being signified, notwithstanding that the House of Lords have not consented to the Bill.

(2) A Money Bill means a Public Bill which in the opinion of the Speaker of the House of Commons contains only provisions dealing with all or any of the following subjects, namely, the imposition, repeal, remission, alteration, or regulation of taxation; the imposition for the payment of debt or other financial purposes of charges on the Consolidated Fund, [the National Loans Fund] or on money provided by Parliament, or the variation or repeal of any such charges; supply; the appropriation, receipt, custody, issue or audit of accounts of public money; the raising or guarantee of any loan or the repayment thereof; or subordinate matters incidental to those subjects or any of them. In this subsection the expressions "taxation", "public money", and "loan" respectively do not include any taxation, money, or loan raised by local authorities or bodies for local purposes.

(3) There shall be endorsed on every Money Bill when it is sent up to the House of Lords and when it is presented to His Majesty for assent the certificate of the Speaker of the House of Commons signed by him that it is a Money Bill. Before giving his certificate, the Speaker shall consult, if practicable, two members to be appointed from the Chairmen's Panel at the beginning of each Session by the Committee of Selection.

2 Restriction of the powers of the House of Lords as to Bills other than Money Bills

(1) If any Public Bill (other than a Money Bill or a Bill containing any provision to extend the maximum duration of Parliament beyond five years) is passed by the House of Commons [in two successive sessions] (whether of the same Parliament or not), and, having been sent up to the House of Lords at least one month before the end of the session, is rejected by the House of Lords in each of those sessions, that Bill shall, on its rejection [for the second time] by the House of Lords, unless the House of Commons direct to the contrary, be presented to His Majesty and become an Act of Parliament on the Royal Assent being signified thereto, notwithstanding that the House of Lords have not consented to the Bill: Provided that this provision shall not take effect unless [one year has elapsed] between the date of the second reading in the first of those sessions of the Bill in the House of Commons and the date on which it passes the House of Commons [in the second of those sessions].

(2) When a Bill is presented to His Majesty for assent in pursuance of the provisions of this section, there shall be endorsed on the Bill the certificate of the Speaker of the House of Commons signed by him that the provisions of this section have been duly complied with.

(3) A Bill shall be deemed to be rejected by the House of Lords if it is not passed by the House of Lords either without amendment or with such amendments only as may be agreed to by both Houses.

(4) A Bill shall be deemed to be the same Bill as a former Bill sent up to the House of Lords in the preceding session if, when it is sent up to the House of Lords, it is identical with the former Bill or contains only such alterations as are certified by the Speaker of the House of Commons to be necessary owing to the time which has elapsed since the date of the former Bill, or to represent any amendments which have been made by the House of Lords in the former Bill in the preceding sesion, and any amendments which are certified by the Speaker to have been made by the House of Lords [in the second session] and agreed to by the House of Commons shall be inserted in the Bill as presented for Royal Assent in pursuance of this section:

Provided that the House of Commons may, if they think fit, on the passage of such a Bill through the House [in the second session], suggest any further amendments without inserting the amendments in the Bill, and any such suggested amendments shall be considered by the House of Lords, and, if agreed to by that House, shall be treated as amendments made by the House of Lords and agreed to by the House of Commons; but the exercise of this power by the House of Commons shall not affect the operation of this section in the event of the Bill being rejected by the House of Lords.

3 Certificate of Speaker
Any certificate of the Speaker of the House of Commons given under this Act shall be conclusive for all purposes, and shall not be questioned in any court of law.

4 Enacting words
(1) In every Bill presented to His Majesty under the preceding provisions of this Act, the words of enactment shall be as follows, that is to say:—

> "Be it enacted by the King's most Excellent Majesty, by and with the advice and consent of the Commons in this present Parliament assembled, in accordance with the provisions of [the Parliament Acts 1911 and 1949], and by authority of the same, as follows."

(2) Any alteration of a Bill necessary to give effect to this section shall not be deemed to be an amendment of the Bill.

5 Provisional Order Bills excluded
In this Act the expression "Public Bill" does not include any Bill for confirming a Provisional Order.

6 Saving for existing rights and privileges of the House of Commons
Nothing in this Act shall diminish or qualify the existing rights and privileges of the House of Commons.

7 Duration of Parliament
Five years shall be substituted for seven years as the time fixed for the maximum duration of Parliament under the Septennial Act, 1715.

EMERGENCY POWERS ACT 1920
(10 & 11 Geo. 5, c. 55)

An Act to make exceptional provision for the Protection of the Community in cases of Emergency

Territorial extent England and Wales, Scotland

Note Section 1 is printed as amended by the Emergency Powers Act 1964.

1 Issue of proclamations of emergency
(1) If at any time it appears to His Majesty that [there have occurred, or are about to occur, events of such a nature] as to be calculated, by interfering with the supply and distribution of food, water, fuel, or light, or with the means of locomotion, to deprive the community, or any substantial portion of the community, of the essentials of life, His Majesty may, by proclamation (hereinafter referred to as a proclamation of emergency), declare that a state of emergency exists.

No such proclamation shall be in force for more than one month, without prejudice to the issue of another proclamation at or before the end of that period.

(2) Where a proclamation of emergency has been made the occasion thereof shall forthwith be communicated to Parliament, and, if Parliament is then separated by such adjournment or prorogation as will not expire within five days, a proclamation shall be issued for the meeting of Parliament within five days, and Parliament shall accordingly meet and sit upon the day appointed by that proclamation, and shall continue to sit and act in like manner as if it had stood adjourned or prorogued to the same day.

2 Emergency regulations

(1) Where a proclamation of emergency has been made, and so long as the proclamation is in force, it shall be lawful for His Majesty in Council, by Order, to make regulations for securing the essentials of life to the community, and those regulations may confer or impose on a Secretary of State or other Government department, or any other persons in His Majesty's service or acting on His Majesty's behalf, such powers and duties as His Majesty may deem necessary for the preservation of the peace, for securing and regulating the supply and distribution of food, water, fuel, light, and other necessities, for maintaining the means of transit or locomotion, and for any other purposes essential to the public safety and the life of the community, and may make such provisions incidental to the powers aforesaid as may appear to His Majesty to be required for making the exercise of those powers effective:

Provided that nothing in this Act shall be construed to authorise the making of any regulations imposing any form of compulsory military service or industrial conscription:

Provided also that no such regulation shall make it an offence for any person or persons to take part in a strike, or peacefully to persuade any other person or persons to take part in a strike.

(2) Any regulations so made shall be laid before Parliament as soon as may be after they are made, and shall not continue in force after the expiration of seven days from the time when they are so laid unless a resolution is passed by both Houses providing for the continuance thereof.

(3) The regulations may provide for the trial, by courts of summary jurisdiction, of persons guilty of offences against the regulations; so, however, that the maximum penalty which may be inflicted for any offence against any such regulations shall be imprisonment with or without hard labour for a term of three months, or a fine [not exceeding level 3 on the standard scale] or both such imprisonment and fine, together with the forfeiture of any goods or money in respect of which the offence has been committed: Provided that no such regulations shall alter any existing procedure in criminal cases, or confer any right to punish by fine or imprisonment without trial.

(4), (5) * * * * *

GOVERNMENT OF IRELAND ACT 1920
(10 & 11 Geo. 5, c. 67)

An Act to provide for the better Government of Ireland

Territorial extent Northern Ireland

* * * * *

75 Saving for supreme authority of the Parliament of the United Kingdom
Notwithstanding . . . anything contained in this Act, the supreme authority of the parliament of the United Kingdom shall remain unaffected and undiminished over all persons, matters, and things in Ireland and every part thereof.

OFFICIAL SECRETS ACT 1920
(10 & 11 Geo. 5, c. 75)

An Act to amend the Official Secrets Act 1911

Territorial extent United Kingdom

1 Unauthorised use of uniforms; falsification of reports, forgery, personation, and false documents

(1) If any person for the purpose of gaining admission, or of assisting any other person to gain admission, to a prohibited place, within the meaning of the Official Secrets

Act 1911 (hereinafter referred to as "the principal Act"), or for any other purpose prejudicial to the safety or interests of the State within the meaning of the said Act—

(a) uses or wears, without lawful authority, any naval, military, air-force, police, or other official uniform, or any uniform so nearly resembling the same as to be calculated to deceive, or falsely represents himself to be a person who is or has been entitled to use or wear any such uniform; or

(b) orally, or in writing in any declaration or application, or in any document signed by him or on his behalf, knowingly makes or connives at the making of any false statement or any omission; or

(c) . . . tampers with any passport or any naval, military, air-force, police, or official pass, permit, certificate, licence, or other document of a similar character (hereinafter in this section referred to as an official document), . . . or has in his possession any . . . forged, altered, or irregular official document; or

(d) personates, or falsely represents himself to be a person holding, or in the employment of a person holding office under His Majesty, or to be or not to be a person to whom an official document or secret official code word or pass word has been duly issued or communicated, or with intent to obtain an official document, secret official code word or pass word, whether for himself or any other person, knowingly makes any false statement; or

(e) uses, or has in his possession or under his control, without the authority of the Government Department or the authority concerned, any die, seal, or stamp of or belonging to, or used, made or provided by any Government Department, or by any diplomatic, naval, military, or air force authority appointed by or acting under the authority of His Majesty, or any die, seal or stamp so nearly resembling any such die, seal or stamp as to be calculated to deceive, or counterfeits any such die, seal or stamp, or uses, or has in his possession, or under his control, any such counterfeited die, seal or stamp;

he shall be guilty of a misdemeanour.

(2) If any person—

(a) retains for any purpose prejudicial to the safety or interests of the State any official document, whether or not completed or issued for use, when he has no right to retain it, or when it is contrary to his duty to retain it, or fails to comply with any directions issued by any Government Department or any person authorised by such department with regard to the return or disposal thereof; or

(b) allows any other person to have possession of any official document issued for his use alone, or communicates any secret official code word or pass word so issued, or, without lawful authority or excuse, has in his possession any official document or secret official code word or pass word issued for the use of some person other than himself, or on obtaining possession of any official document by finding or otherwise, neglects or fails to restore it to the person or authority by whom or for whose use it was issued, or to a police constable; or

(c) without lawful authority or excuse, manufactures or sells, or has in his possession for sale any such die, seal or stamp as aforesaid;

he shall be guilty of a misdemeanour.

(3) In the case of any prosecution under this section involving the proof of a purpose prejudicial to the safety or interests of the State, subsection (2) of section one of the principal Act shall apply in like manner as it applies to prosecutions under that section.

2-5 * * * * *

6 Duty of giving information as to commission of offences

[(1) Where a chief officer of police is satisfied that there is reasonable ground for suspecting that an offence under section one of the principal Act has been committed and for believing that any person is able to furnish information as to the offence or suspected offence, he may apply to a Secretary of State for permission to exercise the powers conferred by this subsection and, if such permission is granted, he may authorise a superintendent of police, or any police officer not below the rank of inspector, to require the person believed to be able to furnish information to give any information in his power relating to the offence or suspected offence, and, if so required and on tender of his reasonable expenses, to attend at such reasonable time and place as may be specified by the superintendent or other officer; and if a person required in pursuance of such an authorisation to give information, or to attend as aforesaid, fails to comply with any such requirement or knowingly gives false information, he shall be guilty of a misdemeanour.

(2) Where a chief officer of police has reasonable grounds to believe that the case is one of great emergency and that in the interest of the State immediate action is necessary, he may exercise the powers conferred by the last foregoing subsection without applying for or being granted the permission of a Secretary of State, but if he does so shall forthwith report the circumstances to the Secretary of State.

7 *****

8 Provisions as to trial and punishment of offences

(1) Any person who is guilty of a felony under the principal Act or this Act shall be liable to penal servitude for a term of not less than three years and not exceeding fourteen years.

(2) Any person who is guilty of a misdemeanour under the principal Act or this Act shall be liable on conviction on indictment to imprisonment with or without hard labour, for a term not exceeding two years, or, on conviction under the Summary Jurisdiction Acts, to imprisonment, with or without hard labour, for a term not exceeding three months or to a fine not exceeding [the prescribed sum], or both such imprisonment and fine:

Provided that no misdemeanour under the principal Act or this Act shall be dealt with summarily except with the consent of the Attorney General.

(3) For the purposes of the trial of a person for an offence under the principal Act or this Act, the offence shall be deemed to have been committed either at the place in which the same actually was committed, or at any place in the United Kingdom in which the offender may be found.

(4) In addition and without prejudice to any powers which a court may possess to order the exclusion of the public from any proceedings if, in the course of proceedings before a court against any person for an offence under the principal Act or this Act or the proceedings on appeal, or in the course of the trial of a person for felony or misdemeanour under the principal Act or this Act, application is made by the prosecution, on the ground that the publication of any evidence to be given or of any statement to be made in the course of the proceedings would be prejudicial to the national safety, that all or any portion of the public shall be excluded during any part of the hearing, the court may make an order to that effect, but the passing of sentence shall in any case take place in public.

(5) Where the person guilty of an offence under the principal Act or this Act is a company or corporation, every director and officer of the company or corporation shall be guilty of the like offence unless he proves that the act or omission constituting the offence took place without his knowledge or consent.

*****

JUDICIAL PROCEEDINGS (REGULATION OF REPORTS) ACT 1926
(16 & 17 Geo. 5, c. 61)

An Act to regulate the publication of reports of judicial proceedings in such manner as to prevent injury to public morals

Territorial extent England and Wales, Scotland

1 Restriction on publication of reports of judicial proceedings

(1) It shall not be lawful to print or publish, or cause or procure to be printed or published—

(a) in relation to any judicial proceedings any indecent matter or indecent medical, surgical or physiological details being matter or details the publication of which would be calculated to injure public morals;

(b) in relation to any judicial proceedings for dissolution of marriage, for nullity of marriage, or for judicial separation, or for restitution of conjugal rights, any particulars other than the following, that is to say:—

(i) the names, addresses and occupations of the parties and witnesses;

(ii) a concise statement of the charges, defences and countercharges in support of which evidence has been given;

(iii) submissions on any point of law arising in the course of the proceedings, and the decision of the court thereon;

(iv) the summing-up of the judge and the finding of the jury (if any) and the judgment of the court and observations made by the judge in giving judgment:

Provided that nothing in this part of this subsection shall be held to permit the publication of anything contrary to the provisions of paragraph (a) of this subsection.

(2) If any person acts in contravention of the provisions of this Act, he shall in respect of each offence be liable, on summary conviction, to imprisonment for a term not exceeding four months, or to a fine not exceeding [level 5 on the standard scale], or to both such imprisonment and fine:

Provided that no person, other than a proprietor, editor, master printer or publisher, shall be liable to be convicted under this Act.

(3) No prosecution for an offence under this Act shall be commenced in England and Wales by any person without the sanction of the Attorney-General.

(4), (5) * * * * *

THE STATUTE OF WESTMINSTER 1931
(22 & 23 Geo. 5, c. 4)

An Act to give effect to certain resolutions passed by Imperial Conferences held in the years 1926 and 1930

Territorial extent As indicated in the Act (and see note to section 4).

Whereas the delegates of His Majesty's Governments in the United Kingdom, the Dominion of Canada, the Commonwealth of Australia, the Dominion of New Zealand, the Union of South Africa, the Irish Free State and Newfoundland, at Imperial Conferences holden at Westminster in the years of our Lord nineteen hundred and twenty-six and nineteen hundred and thirty did concur in making the declarations and resolutions set forth in the Reports of the said Conferences:

And whereas it is meet and proper to set out by way of preamble to this Act that, inasmuch as the Crown is the symbol of the free association of the members of the British Commonwealth of Nations, and as they are united by a common allegiance to the Crown, it would be in accord with the established constitutional position of all the members of the Commonwealth in relation to one another that any alteration in the law touching the Succession to the Throne or the Royal Style and Titles shall hereafter require the assent as well of the Parliaments of all the Dominions as of the Parliament of the United Kingdom:

And whereas it is in accord with the established constitutional position that no law hereafter made by the Parliament of the United Kingdom shall extend to any of the said Dominions as part of the law of that Dominion otherwise than at the request and with the consent of that Dominion:

And whereas it is necessary for the ratifying, confirming and establishing of certain of the said declarations and resolutions of the said Conferences that a law be made and enacted in due form by authority of the Parliament of the United Kingdom:

And whereas the Dominion of Canada, the Commonwealth of Australia, the Dominion of New Zealand, the Union of South Africa, the Irish Free State and Newfoundland have severally requested and consented to the submission of a measure to the Parliament of the United Kingdom for making such provision with regard to the matters aforesaid as is hereafter in this Act contained:

1 Meaning of "Dominion" in this Act
In this Act the expression "Dominion" means any of the following Dominions, that is to say, the Dominion of Canada, the Commonwealth of Australia, the Dominion of New Zealand, . . . the Irish Free State and Newfoundland.

2 Validity of laws made by Parliament of a Dominion
(1) The Colonial Laws Validity Act 1865 shall not apply to any law made after the commencement of this Act by the Parliament of a Dominion.

(2) No law and no provision of any law made after the commencement of this Act by the Parliament of a Dominion shall be void or inoperative on the ground that it is repugnant to the law of England, or to the provisions of any existing or future Act of Parliament of the United Kingdom, or to any order, rule or regulation made under any such Act, and the powers of the Parliament of a Dominion shall include the power to repeal or amend any such Act, order, rule or regulation in so far as the same is part of the law of the Dominion.

3 Power of Parliament of Dominion to legislate extra-territorally
It is hereby declared and enacted that the Parliament of a Dominion has full power to make laws having extra-territorial operation.

4 Parliament of United Kingdom not to legislate for Dominion except by consent
No Act of Parliament of the United Kingdom passed after the commencement of this Act shall extend, or be deemed to extend, to a Dominion as part of the law of that Dominion unless it is expressly declared in that Act that that Dominion has requested, and consented to, the enactment thereof.

Note This section has been repealed in relation to Canada by the Canada Act 1982 s. 1, Sch B and in relation to Australia by the Australia Act 1986 s. 12.

INCITEMENT TO DISAFFECTION ACT 1934
(24 & 25 Geo. 5, c. 56)

An Act to make better provision for the prevention and punishment of endeavours to seduce members of His Majesty's forces from their duty or allegiance

Territorial extent United Kingdom

1 Penalty on persons endeavouring to seduce members of His Majesty's forces from their duty or allegiance
If any person maliciously and advisedly endeavours to seduce any member of His Majesty's forces from his duty or allegiance to His Majesty, he shall be guilty of an offence under this Act.

2 Provisions for the prevention and detection of offences under this Act
(1) If any person, with intent to commit or to aid, abet, counsel, or procure the commission of an offence under section one of this Act, has in his possession or under his control any document of such a nature that the dissemination of copies thereof among members of His Majesty's forces would constitute such an offence, he shall be guilty of an offence under this Act.

(2) If a judge of the High Court is satisfied by information on oath that there is reasonable ground for suspecting that an offence under this Act has been committed, and that evidence of the commission thereof is to be found at any premises or place specified in the information, he may, on an application made by an officer of police of a rank not lower than that of inspector, grant a search warrant authorising any such officer as aforesaid named in the warrant together with any other persons named in the warrant and any other officers of police to enter the premises or place at any time within one month from the date of the warrant, if necessary by force, and to search the premises or place and every person found therein, and to seize anything found on the premises or place or on any such person which the officer has reasonable ground for suspecting to be evidence of the commission of such an offence as aforesaid:

Provided that—

(a) a search warrant shall only be issued in respect of an offence suspected to have been committed within the three months prior to the laying of the information thereof; and

(b) if a search warrant under this Act has been executed on any premises, it shall be the duty of the officer of police who has conducted or directed the search to notify the occupier that the search has taken place, and to supply him with a list of any documents or other objects which have been removed from the premises, and where any documents have been removed from any other person to supply that person with a list of such documents.

(3) No woman shall, in pursuance of a warrant issued under the last foregoing subsection, be searched except by a woman.

(4) * * * * *

3 Provisions as to punishment of offences

(1) A person guilty of an offence under this Act shall be liable, on conviction on indictment to imprisonment for a term not exceeding two years or to a fine . . . or on summary conviction to imprisonment for a term not exceeding four months or to a fine not exceeding [the prescribed sum], or (whether on conviction on indictment or on summary conviction) to both such imprisonment and fine.

(2) No prosecution in England under this Act shall take place without the consent of the Director of Public Prosecutions.

(3) Where a prosecution under this Act is being carried on by the Director of Public Prosecutions, a court of summary jurisdiction shall not deal with the case summarily without the consent of the Director.

(4) Where any person is convicted of an offence under this Act, the court dealing with the case may order any documents connected with the offence to be destroyed or dealt with in such other manner as may be specified in the order, but no documents shall be destroyed before the expiration of the period within which an appeal may be lodged, and if an appeal is lodged no document shall be destroyed until after the appeal has been heard and decided.

4 * * * * *

HIS MAJESTY'S DECLARATION OF ABDICATION ACT 1936
(1 Edw. 8 & 1 Geo. 6, c. 3)

An Act to give effect to His Majesty's declaration of abdication; and for purposes connected therewith

Territorial extent United Kingdom (and the Empire as in 1936; See Preamble as to application to named Dominions under the Statute of Westminster 1931).

Whereas His Majesty by His Royal Message of the tenth day of December in this present year has been pleased to declare that He is irrevocably determined to renounce the Throne for Himself and His descendants, and has for that purpose executed the Instrument of Abdication set out in the Schedule to this Act, and has signified His desire that effect thereto should be given immediately:

And whereas, following upon the communication to His Dominions of His Majesty's said declaration and desire, the Dominion of Canada pursuant to the provisions of section four of the Statute of Westminster 1931 has requested and consented to the enactment of this Act, and the Commonwealth of Australia, the Dominion of New Zealand, and the Union of South Africa have assented thereto:

1 Effect of His Majesty's declaration of abdication

(1) Immediately upon the Royal Assent being signified to this Act the Instrument of Abdication executed by His present Majesty on the tenth day of December, nineteen hundred and thirty-six, set out in the Schedule to this Act, shall have effect, and thereupon His Majesty shall cease to be King and there shall be a demise of the Crown, and accordingly the member of the Royal Family then next in succession to the Throne shall succeed thereto and to all the rights, privileges, and dignities thereunto belonging.

(2) His Majesty, His issue, if any, and the descendants of that issue, shall not after His Majesty's abdication have any right, title or interest in or to the succession to the Throne, and section one of the Act of Settlement shall be construed accordingly.

(3) The Royal Marriages Act 1772 shall not apply to His Majesty after His abdication nor to the issue, if any, of His Majesty or the descendants of that issue.

SCHEDULE

I, Edward the Eighth, of Great Britain, Ireland, and the British Dominions beyond the Seas, King, Emperor of India, do hereby declare My irrevocable determination to renounce the Throne for Myself and for My descendants, and My desire that effect should be given to this Instrument of Abdication immediately.

In token whereof I have hereunto set My hand this tenth day of December, nineteen hundred and thirty-six, in the presence of the witnesses whose signatures are subscribed.

EDWARD R.I.

Signed at Fort Belvedere
in the presence of
ALBERT.
HENRY.
GEORGE.

PUBLIC ORDER ACT 1936
(1 Edw. 8 & 1 Geo. 6, c. 6)

An Act to prohibit the wearing of uniforms in connection with political objects and the maintenance by private persons of associations of military or similar character; and to make further provision for the preservation of public order on the occasion of public processions and meetings and in public places

Territorial extent England and Wales, Scotland

1 Prohibition of uniforms in connection with political objects

(1) Subject as hereinafter provided, any person who in any public place or at any public meeting wears uniform signifying his association with any political organisation or with the promotion of any political object shall be guilty of an offence:

Provided that, if the chief officer of police is satisfied that the wearing of any such uniform as aforesaid on any ceremonial, anniversary, or other special occasion will not be likely to involve risk of public disorder, he may, with the consent of a Secretary of State, by order permit the wearing of such uniform on that occasion either absolutely or subject to such conditions as may be specified in the order.

(2) Where any person is charged before any court with an offence under this section, no further proceedings in respect thereof shall be taken against him without the consent of the Attorney-General [except such as are authorised by [section 6 of the Prosecution of

Offences Act 1979]] so, however, that if that person is remanded in custody he shall, after the expiration of a period of eight days from the date on which he was so remanded, be entitled to be [released on bail] without sureties unless within that period the Attorney-General has consented to such further proceedings as aforesaid.

2 Prohibition of quasi-military organisations

(1) If the members or adherents of any association of persons, whether incorporated or not, are—

(a) organised or trained or equipped for the purpose of enabling them to be employed in usurping the functions of the police or of the armed forces of the Crown; or

(b) organised and trained or organised and equipped either for the purpose of enabling them to be employed for the use or display of physical force in promoting any political object, or in such manner as to arouse reasonable apprehension that they are organised and either trained or equipped for that purpose;

then any person who takes part in the control or management of the association, or in so organising or training as aforesaid any members or adherents thereof, shall be guilty of an offence under this section:

Provided that in any proceedings against a person charged with the offence of taking part in the control or management of such an association as aforesaid it shall be a defence to that charge to prove that he neither consented to nor connived at the organisation, training, or equipment of members or adherents of the association in contravention of the provisions of this section.

(2) No prosecution shall be instituted under this section without the consent of the Attorney-General.

(3), (4) * * * * *

(5) If a judge of the High Court is satisfied by information on oath that there is reasonable ground for suspecting that an offence under this section has been committed, and that evidence of the commission thereof is to be found at any premises or place specified in the information, he may, on an application made by an officer of police of a rank not lower than that of inspector, grant a search warrant authorising any such officer as aforesaid named in the warrant together with any other persons named in the warrant and any other officers of police to enter the premises or place at any time within one month from the date of the warrant, if necessary by force, and to search the premises or place and every person found therein, and to seize anything found on the premises or place or on any such person which the officer has reasonable ground for suspecting to be evidence of the commission of such an offence as aforesaid:

Provided that no woman shall, in pursuance of a warrant issued under this subsection, be searched except by a woman.

(6) Nothing in this section shall be construed as prohibiting the employment of a reasonable number of persons as stewards to assist in the preservation of order at any public meeting held upon private premises, or the making of arrangements for that purpose or the instruction of the persons to be so employed in their lawful duties as such stewards, or their being furnished with badges or other distinguishing signs.

3, 4, 5, 5A . . . (Repealed by the Public Order Act 1986, Sch. 3).

6 (Amends the Public Meeting Act 1908, printed above as amended).

7 Enforcement

(1) Any person who commits an offence under section two of this Act shall be liable on summary conviction to imprisonment for a term not exceeding six months or to a fine not exceeding [the prescribed sum], or to both such imprisonment and fine, or, on conviction on indictment, to imprisonment for a term not exceeding two years or to a fine . . . or to both such imprisonment and fine.

(2) Any person guilty of [any offence under this Act other than an offence under section 2 . . .] shall be liable on summary conviction to imprisonment for a term not exceeding three months or to a fine not exceeding [level 4 on the standard scale], or to both such imprisonment and fine.

(3) A constable may without warrant arrest any person reasonably suspected by him to be committing an offence under section one . . . of this Act.

8 Application to Scotland

This Act shall apply to Scotland subject to the following modifications:—

(1) Subsection (2) of section one and subsection (2) of section two of this Act shall not apply.

(2) In subsection (3) of section two the Lord Advocate shall be substituted for the Attorney-General and the Court of Session shall be substituted for the High Court.

(3) Subsection (5) of section two shall have effect as if for any reference to a judge of the High Court there were substituted a reference to the Sheriff and any application for a search warrant under the said subsection shall be made by the procurator fiscal instead of such officer as is therein mentioned.

(4) The power conferred on the sheriff by subsection (5) of section two, as modified by the last foregoing paragraph, shall not be exercisable by an honorary sheriff-substitute.

* * * * *

9 Interpretation, etc

(1) In this Act the following expressions have the meanings hereby respectively assigned to them, that is to say:—

. . .

"Meeting" means a meeting held for the purpose of the discussion of matters of public interest or for the purpose of the expression of views on such matters;

"Private premises" means premises to which the public have access (whether on payment or otherwise) only by permission of the owner, occupier, or lessee of the premises;

"Public meeting" includes any meeting in a public place and any meeting which the public or any section thereof are permitted to attend, whether on payment or otherwise;

["Public place" includes any highway and any other premises or place to which at the material time the public have or are permitted to have access, whether on payment or otherwise;]

. . .

"Recognised corps" means a rifle club, miniature rifle club or cadet corps approved by a Secretary of State under the Firearms Acts 1920 to 1936, for the purposes of those Acts.

* * * * *

REGENCY ACT 1937
(1 Edw. 8 & 1 Geo. 6, c. 16)

An Act to make provision for a Regency in the event of the Sovereign being on His Accession under the age of eighteen years, and in the event of the incapacity of the Sovereign through illness, and for the performance of certain of the royal functions in the name and on behalf of the Sovereign in certain other events; to repeal the Lords Justice Act 1837; and for purposes connected with the matters aforesaid

Territorial extent United Kingdom

1 Regency while the Sovereign is under eighteen

(1) If the Sovereign is, at His Accession, under the age of eighteen years, then, until He attains that age, the royal functions shall be performed in the name and on behalf of the Sovereign by a Regent.

(2) * * * * *

2 Regency during total incapacity of the Sovereign

(1) If the following persons or any three or more of them, that is to say, the wife or husband of the Sovereign, the Lord Chancellor, the Speaker of the House of Commons, the Lord Chief Justice of England, and the Master of the Rolls, declare in writing that they are satisfied by evidence which shall include the evidence of physicians that the Sovereign is by reason of infirmity of mind or body incapable for the time being of performing the royal functions or that they are satisfied by evidence that the Sovereign is for some definite cause not available for the performance of those functions, then, until it is declared in like manner that His Majesty has so far recovered His health as to warrant His resumption of the royal functions or has become available for the performance thereof, as the case may be, those functions shall be performed in the name and on behalf of the Sovereign by a Regent.

(2) A declaration under this section shall be made to the Privy Council and communicated to the Governments of His Majesty's Dominions and to the Government of India.

3 The Regent

(1) If a Regency becomes necessary under this Act, the Regent shall be that person who, excluding any persons disqualified under this section, is next in the line of succession to the Crown.

(2) A person shall be disqualified from becoming or being Regent, if he is not a British subject of full age and domiciled in some part of the United Kingdom, or is a person who would, under section two of the Act of Settlement, be incapable of inheriting, possessing, and enjoying the Crown; and section three of the Act of Settlement shall apply in the case of a Regent as it applies in the case of a Sovereign.

(3) If any person who would at the commencement of a Regency have become Regent but for the fact that he was not then of full age becomes of full age during the Regency, he shall, if he is not otherwise disqualified under this section, thereupon become Regent instead of the person who has theretofore been Regent.

(4), (5) * * * * *

4 Oaths to be taken by, and limitations of power of, Regent

(1) The Regent shall, before he acts in or enters upon his office, take and subscribe before the Privy Council the oaths set out in the Schedule to this Act, and the Privy Council are empowered and required to administer those oaths and to enter them in the Council Books.

(2) The Regent shall not have power to assent to any Bill for changing the order of succession to the Crown or for repealing or altering an Act of the fifth year of the reign of Queen Anne made in Scotland entitled "An Act for Securing the Protestant Religion and Presbyterian Church Government".

5-8 * * * * *

Section 4

SCHEDULE

OATHS TO BE TAKEN BY THE REGENT

1. I swear that I will be faithful and bear true allegiance to [*here insert the name of the Sovereign*] his heirs and successors according to law. So help me God.

2. I swear that I will truly and faithfully execute the office of Regent, and that I will govern according to law, and will, in all things, to the utmost of my power and ability,

consult and maintain the safety, honour, and dignity of [*here insert the name of the Sovereign*] and the welfare of his people. So help me God.

3. I swear that I will inviolably maintain and preserve in England and in Scotland the Settlement of the true Protestant religion as established by law in England and as established in Scotland by the laws made in Scotland in prosecution of the Claim of Right, and particularly by an Act intituled "An Act for Securing the Protestant Religion and Presbyterian Church Government" and by the Acts passed in the Parliament of both Kingdoms for Union of the two Kingdoms, together with the Government, Worship, Discipline, Rights, and Privileges of the Church of Scotland. So help me God.

BANK OF ENGLAND ACT 1946
(9 & 10 Geo. 6,c. 27)

An Act to bring the capital stock of the Bank of England into public ownership and bring the Bank under public control, to make provision with respect to the relations between the Treasury, the Bank of England and other banks and for purposes connected with the matters aforesaid

[14 February 1946]

Territorial extent United Kingdom

1-3 *****

4 Treasury directions to the Bank and relations of the Bank with other banks

(1) The Treasury may from time to time give such directions to the Bank as, after consultation with the Governor of the Bank, they think necessary in the public interest.

(2) Subject to any such directions, the affairs of the Bank shall be managed by the court of directors in accordance with such provisions (if any) in that behalf as may be contained in any charter of the Bank for the time being in force and any byelaws made thereunder.

(3) The Bank, if they think it necessary in the public interest, may request information from and make recommendations to bankers, and may, if so authorised by the Treasury, issue directions to any banker for the purpose of securing that effect is given to any such request or recommendation:

Provided that:—

(a) no such request or recommendations shall be made with respect to the affairs of any particular customer of a banker; and

(b) before authorising the issue of any such directions the Treasury shall give the banker concerned, or such person as appears to them to represent him, an opportunity of making representations with respect thereto.

(4) If, at any time before any recommendations or directions are made or given in writing to a banker under the last foregoing subsection, the treasury certify that it is necessary in the public interest that the recommendations or directions should be kept secret, and the certificate is transmitted to the banker together with the recommendations or directions, the recommendations or directions shall be deemed, for the purpose of section two of the Official Secrets Act 1911, as amended by any subsequent enactment, to be a document entrusted in confidence to the banker by a person holding office under His Majesty; and the provisions of the Official Secrets Act 1911 to 1939 shall apply accordingly.

(5) Save as provided in the last foregoing subsection, nothing in the Official Secrets Acts 1911 to 1939 shall apply to any request, recommendations or directions made or given to a banker under subsection (3) of this section.

(6)-(7) *****

5, 6 *****

STATUTORY INSTRUMENTS ACT 1946
(9 & 10 Geo. 6, c. 36)

An Act to repeal the Rules Publication Act, 1893, and to make further provision as to the instruments by which statutory powers to make orders, rules, regulations and other subordinate legislation are exercised [26 March 1946]

Territorial extent United Kingdom

1 Definition of "Statutory Instrument"

(1) Where by this Act or any Act passed after the commencement of this Act power to make, confirm or approve orders, rules, regulations or other subordinate legislation is conferred on His Majesty in Council or on any Minister of the Crown then, if the power is expressed—

(a) in the case of a power conferred on His Majesty, to be exercisable by Order in Council;

(b) in the case of a power conferred on a Minister of the Crown, to be exercisable by statutory instrument,

any document by which that power is exercised shall be known as a "statutory instrument" and the provisions of this Act shall apply thereto accordingly.

(2) Whereby any Act passed before the commencement of this Act power to make statutory rules within the meaning of the Rules Publication Act, 1893, was conferred on any rule-making authority within the meaning of that Act, any document by which that power is exercised after the commencement of this Act shall, save as is otherwise provided by regulations made under this Act, be known as a "statutory instrument" and the provisions of this Act shall apply thereto accordingly.

2 Numbering, printing, publication and citation

(1) Immediately after the making of any statutory instrument, it shall be sent to the King's printer of Acts of Parliament and numbered in accordance with regulations made under this Act, and except in such cases as may be provided by any Act passed after the commencement of this Act or prescribed by regulations made under this Act, copies thereof shall as soon as possible be printed and sold by the King's printer of Acts of Parliament.

(2) Any statutory instrument may, without prejudice to any other mode of citation, be cited by the number given to it in accordance with the provisions of this section, and the calendar year.

3 Supplementary provisions as to publication

(1) Regulations made for the purposes of this Act shall make provision for the publication by His Majesty's Stationery Office of lists showing the date upon which every statutory instrument printed and sold by the King's printer of Acts of Parliament was first issued by that office; and in any legal proceedings a copy of any list so published purporting to bear the imprint of the King's printer shall be received in evidence as a true copy, and an entry therein shall be conclusive evidence of the date on which any statutory instrument was first issued by His Majesty's Stationery Office.

(2) In any proceedings against any person for an offence consisting of a contravention of any such statutory instrument, it shall be a defence to prove that the instrument had not been issued by His Majesty's Stationery Office at the date of the alleged contravention unless it is proved that at that date reasonable steps had been taken for the purpose of bringing the purport of the instrument to the notice of the public, or of persons likely to be affected by it, or of the person charged.

(3) Save as therein otherwise expressly provided, nothing in this section shall affect any enactment or rule of law relating to the time at which any statutory instrument comes into operation.

4 Statutory instruments which are required to be laid before Parliament

(1) Where by this Act or any Act passed after the commencement of this Act any statutory instrument is required to be laid before Parliament after being made, a copy of the instrument shall be laid before each House of Parliament and, subject as hereinafter provided, shall be so laid before the instrument comes into operation:

Provided that if it is essential that any such instrument should come into operation before copies thereof can be so laid as aforesaid, the instrument may be made so as to come into operation before it has been so laid; and where any statutory instrument comes into operation before it is laid before Parliament, notification shall forthwith be sent to the Lord Chancellor and to the Speaker of the House of Commons drawing attention to the fact that copies of the instrument have yet to be laid before Parliament and explaining why such copies were not so laid before the instrument came into operation.

(2) Every copy of any such statutory instrument sold by the King's printer of Acts of Parliament shall bear on the face thereof—

(a) a statement showing the date on which the statutory instrument came or will come into operation; and

(b) either a statement showing the date on which copies thereof were laid before Parliament or a statement that such copies are to be laid before Parliament.

(3) * * * * *

5 Statutory instruments which are subject to annulment by resolution of either House of Parliament

(1) Where by this Act or any Act passed after the commencement of this Act, it is provided that any statutory instrument shall be subject to annulment in pursuance of resolution of either House of Parliament, the instrument shall be laid before Parliament after being made and the provisions of the last foregoing section shall apply thereto accordingly, and if either House, within the period of forty days beginning with the day on which a copy thereof is laid before it, resolves that an Address be presented to His Majesty praying that the instrument be annulled, no further proceedings shall be taken thereunder after the date of the resolution, and His Majesty may by Order in Council revoke the instrument, so, however, that any such resolution and revocation shall be without prejudice to the validity of anything previously done under the instrument or to the making of a new statutory instrument.

(2) * * * * *

6 Statutory instruments of which drafts are to be laid before Parliament

(1) Where by this Act or any Act passed after the commencement of this Act it is provided that a draft of any statutory instrument shall be laid before Parliament, but the Act does not prohibit the making of the instrument without the approval of Parliament, then, in the case of an Order in Council the draft shall not be submitted to His Majesty in Council, and in any other case the statutory instrument shall not be made, until after the expiration of a period of forty days beginning with the day on which a copy of the draft is laid before each House of Parliament, or, if such copies are laid on different days, with the later of the two days, and if within that period either House resolves that the draft be not submitted to His Majesty or that the statutory instrument be not made, as the case may be, no further proceedings shall be taken thereon, but without prejudice to the laying before Parliament of a new draft.

(2) * * * * *

* * * * *

CROWN PROCEEDINGS ACT 1947
(10 & 11 Geo. 6, c. 44)

An Act to amend the law relating to the civil liabilities and rights of the Crown and to civil proceedings by and against the Crown, to amend the law relating to the civil liabilities of persons other than the Crown in certain cases involving the affairs or property of the Crown, and for purposes connected with the matters aforesaid [31 July 1947]

Territorial extent United Kingdom (ss. 2, 4, 11, 21, 40), England and Wales and Northern Ireland (ss. 1, 17, 25, 28), Scotland (ss. 41, 42, 43, 47).

PART I
SUBSTANTIVE LAW

1 Right to sue the Crown

Where any person has a claim against the Crown after the commencement of this Act, and, if this Act had not been passed, the claim might have been enforced, subject to the grant of His Majesty's fiat, by petition of right, or might have been enforced by a proceeding provided by any stautory provision repealed by this Act, then, subject to the provisions of this Act, the claim may be enforced as of right, and without the fiat of His Majesty, by proceedings taken against the Crown for that purpose in accordance with the provisions of this Act.

2 Liability of the Crown in tort

(1) Subject to the provisions of this Act, the Crown shall be subject to all those liabilities in tort to which, if it were a private person of full age and capacity, it would be subject—

(a) in respect of torts committed by its servants or agents;

(b) in respect of any breach of those duties which a person owes to his servants or agents at common law by reason of being their employer; and

(c) in respect of any breach of the duties attaching at common law to the ownership, occupation, possession or control of property:

Provided that no proceedings shall lie against the Crown by virtue of paragraph (a) of this subsection in respect of any act or omission of a servant or agent of the Crown unless the act or omission would apart from the provisions of this Act have given rise to a cause of action in tort against that servant or agent or his estate.

(2) Where the Crown is bound by a statutory duty which is binding also upon persons other than the Crown and its officers, then, subject to the provisions of this Act, the Crown shall, in respect of a failure to comply with that duty, be subject to all those liabilities in tort (if any) to which it would be so subject if it were a private person of full age and capacity.

(3) Where any functions are conferred or imposed upon an officer of the Crown as such either by any rule of the common law or by statute, and that officer commits a tort while performing or purporting to perform those functions, the liabilities of the Crown in respect of the tort shall be such as they would have been if those functions had been conferred or imposed solely by virtue of instructions lawfully given by the Crown.

(4) Any enactment which negatives or limits the amount of the liability of any Government department or officer of the Crown in respect of any tort committed by that department or officer shall, in the case of proceedings against the Crown under this section in respect of a tort committed by that department or officer, apply in relation to the Crown as it would have applied in relation to that department or officer if the proceedings against the Crown had been proceedings against that department or officer.

(5) No proceedings shall lie against the Crown by virtue of this section in respect of anything done or omitted to be done by any person while discharging or purporting to discharge any responsibilities of a judicial nature vested in him, or any responsibilities which he has in connection with the execution of judicial process.

(6) No proceedings shall lie against the Crown by virtue of this section in respect of any act, neglect or default of any officer of the Crown, unless that officer has been directly or indirectly appointed by the Crown and was at the material time paid in respect of his duties as an officer of the Crown wholly out of the Consolidated Fund of the United Kingdom, moneys provided by Parliament, . . ., or any other Fund certified by the

Treasury for the purposes of this subsection or was at the material time holding an office in respect of which the Treasury certify that the holder thereof would normally be so paid.

3 * * * * *

4 Application of law as to indemnity, contribution, joint and several tortfeasors, and contributory negligence

(1) Where the Crown is subject to any liability by virtue of this Part of this Act, the law relating to indemnity and contribution shall be enforceable by or against the Crown in respect of the liability to which it is so subject as if the Crown were a private person of full age and capacity.

(2) . . .

(3) Without prejudice to the general effect of section one of this Act, the Law Reform (Contributory Negligence) Act 1945 (which amends the law relating to contributory negligence) shall bind the Crown.

5-9 * * * * *

10 (Repealed by the Crown Proceedings (Armed Forces) Act 1987) . . .

11 Saving in respect of acts done under prerogative and statutory powers

(1) Nothing in Part I of this Act shall extinguish or abridge any powers or authorities which, if this Act had not been passed, would have been exercisable by virtue of the prerogative of the Crown, or any powers or authorities conferred on the Crown by any statute, and, in particular, nothing in the said Part I shall extinguish or abridge any powers or authorities exercisable by the Crown, whether in time of peace or of war, for the purpose of the defence of the realm or of training, or maintaining the efficiency of, any of the armed forces of the Crown.

(2) Where in any proceedings under this Act it is material to determine whether anything was properly done or omitted to be done in the exercise of the prerogative of the Crown, . . . a Secretary of State may, if satisfied that the act or omission was necessary for any such purpose as is mentioned in the last preceding subsection, issue a certificate to the effect that the act or omission was necessary for that purpose; and the certificate shall, in those precedings, be conclusive as to the matter so certified.

12-16 * * * * *

PART II
JURISDICTION AND PROCEDURE

17 Parties to proceedings

(1) [The Minister for the Civil Service] shall publish a list specifying the several Government departments which are authorised departments for the purposes of this Act, and the name and address for service of the person who is, or is acting for the purposes of this Act as, the solicitor for each such department, and may from time to time amend or vary the said list.

Any document purporting to be a copy of a list published under this section and purporting to be printed under the superintendence or the authority of His Majesty's Stationery Office shall in any legal proceedings be received as evidence for the purpose of establishing what departments are authorised departments for the purposes of this Act, and what person is, or is acting for the purposes of this Act as, the solicitor for any such department.

(2) Civil proceedings by the Crown may be instituted either by an authorised Government department in its own name, whether that department was or was not at the commencement of this Act authorised to sue, or by the Attorney General.

(3) Civil proceedings against the Crown shall be instituted against the appropriate authorised Government department, or, if none of the authorised Government

departments is appropriate or the person instituting the proceedings has any reasonable doubt whether any and if so which of those departments is appropriate, against the Attorney General.

(4), (5) * * * * *

18-20 * * * * *

21 Nature of relief

(1) In any civil proceedings by or against the Crown the court shall, subject to the provisions of this Act, have power to make all such orders as it has power to make in proceedings between subjects, and otherwise to give such appropriate relief as the case may require:

Provided that:—

(a) where in any proceedings against the Crown any such relief is sought as might in proceedings between subjects be granted by way of injunction or specific performance, the court shall not grant an injunction or make an order for specific performance, but may in lieu thereof make an order declaratory of the rights of the parties; and

(b) in any proceedings against the Crown for the recovery of land or other property the court shall not make an order for the recovery of the land or the delivery of the property, but may in lieu thereof make an order declaring that the plaintiff is entitled as against the Crown to the land or property or to the possession thereof.

(2) The court shall not in any civil proceedings grant any injunction or make any order against an officer of the Crown if the effect of granting the injunction or making the order would be to give any relief against the Crown which could not have been obtained in proceedings against the Crown.

22-24 * * * * *

PART III
JUDGMENTS AND EXECUTION

25 Satisfaction of orders against the Crown

(1) Where in any civil proceedings by or against the Crown, or in any proceedings on the Crown side of the King's Bench Division, or in connection with any arbitration to which the Crown is a party, any order (including an order for costs) is made by any court in favour of any person against the Crown or against a Government department or against an officer of the Crown as such, the proper officer of the court shall, on an application in that behalf made by or on behalf of that person at any time after the expiration of twenty-one days from the date of the order or, in case the order provides for the payment of costs and the costs require to be taxed, at any time after the costs have been taxed, whichever is the later, issue to that person a certificate in the prescribed form containing particulars of the order:

Provided that, if the court so directs, a separate certificate shall be issued with respect to the costs (if any) ordered to be paid to the applicant.

(2) A copy of any certificate issued under this section may be served by the person in whose favour the order is made upon the person for the time being named in the record as the solicitor, or as the person acting as solicitor, for the Crown or for the Governmet department or officer concerned.

(3) If the order provides for the payment of any money by way of damages or otherwise, or of any costs, the certificate shall state the amount so payable, and the appropriate Government department shall, subject as hereinafter provided, pay to the person entitled or to his solicitor the amount appearing by the certificate to be due to him together with the interest, if any, lawfully due thereon:

Provided that the court by which any such order as aforesaid is made or any court to which an appeal against the order lies may direct that, pending an appeal or otherwise, payment of the whole of any amount so payable, or any part thereof, shall be suspended, and if the certificate has not been issued may order any such directions to be inserted therein.

(4) Save as aforesaid no execution or attachment or process in the nature thereof shall be issued out of any court for enforcing payment by the Crown of any such money or costs as aforesaid, and no person shall be individually liable under any order for the payment by the Crown, or any Government department, or any officer of the Crown as such, of any such money or costs.

26-27 *****

PART IV
MISCELLANEOUS AND SUPPLEMENTAL

Miscellaneous

28 Discovery

(1) Subject to and in accordance with rules of court and county court rules:—

(a) in any civil proceedings in the High Court or a county court to which the Crown is a party, the Crown may be required by the court to make discovery of documents and produce documents for inspection; and

(b) in any such proceedings as aforesaid, the Crown may be required by the court to answer interrogatories:

Provided that this section shall be without prejudice to any rule of law which authorises or requires the withholding of any document or the refusal to answer any question on the ground that the disclosure of the document or the answering of the question would be injurious to the public interest.

Any order of the court made under the powers conferred by paragraph (b) of this subsection shall direct by what officer of the Crown the interrogatories are to be answered.

(2) Without prejudice to the proviso to the preceding subsection, any rules made for the purposes of this section shall be such as to secure that the existence of a document will not be disclosed if, in the opinion of a Minister of the Crown, it would be injurious to the public interest to disclose the existence thereof.

29-33, 35-38 *****

34, 39 . . .

40 Savings

(1) Nothing in this Act shall apply to proceedings by or against, or authorise proceedings in tort to be brought against, His Majesty in His private capacity.

(2)-(5) *****

PART V
APPLICATION TO SCOTLAND

41 Application of Act to Scotland

The provisions of this Part of this Act shall have effect for the purpose of the application of this Act to Scotland.

42 Exclusion of certain provisions

Section one, Part II (except section thirteen so far as relating to proceedings mentioned in the First Schedule and section twenty-one), Part III (except section twenty-six) and section twenty-eight of this Act shall not apply to Scotland.

43 Interpretation for purposes of application to Scotland

In the application of this Act to Scotland:—

(a) for any reference to the High Court (except a reference to that Court as a prize court) there shall be substituted a reference to the Court of Session; for any reference to the county court there shall be substituted a reference to the sheriff court; the expression "plaintiff" means pursuer; the expresion "defendant" means defender; the expression "county court rules" means Act of Sederunt applying to the sheriff court; and the expression "injunction" means interdict;

(b) the expression "tort" means any wrongful or negligent act or omission giving rise to liability in reparation, and any reference to liability or right or action or proceedings in tort shall be construed accordingly; and for any reference to Part II of the Law Reform (Married Women and Tortfeasors) Act, 1935, there shall be substituted a reference to section three of the Law Reform (Miscellaneous Provisions) (Scotland) Act, 1940.

44-46 * * * * *

47 Recovery of documents in possession of Crown

Subject to and in accordance with Acts of Sederunt applying to the Court of Session and the sheriff court, commission and diligence for the recovery of documents in the possession of the Crown may be granted in any action whether or not the Crown is a party thereto, in like manner in all respects as if the documents were in the possession of a subject:

Provided that—

(i) this subsection shall be without prejudice to any rule of law which authorises or requires the withholding of any document on the ground that its disclosure would be injurious to the public interest; and

(ii) the existence of a document shall not be disclosed if, in the opinion of a Minister of the Crown, it would be injurious to the public interest to disclose the existence thereof.

48-53 * * * * *

WIRELESS TELEGRAPHGY ACT 1949
(12, 13 & 14 Geo. 6, c. 54)

An Act to amend the law relating to wireless telegraphy [30 July 1949]

Territorial extent United Kingdom

PART I

Regulation of Wireless Telegraphy

1 Licensing of wireless telegraphy

(1) No person shall establish or use any station for wireless telegraphy or instal or use any apparatus for wireless telegraphy except under the authority of a licence in that behalf granted by the [Secretary of State] and any person who establishes or uses any station for wireless telegraphy or instals or uses any apparatus for wireless telegraphy except under and in accordance with such a licence shall be guilty of an offence under this Act:

Provided that the [Secretary of State] may by regulations exempt from the provisions of this subsection the establishment, installation or use of stations for wireless telegraphy or wireless telegraphy apparatus of such classes or descriptions as may be specified in the regulations, either absolutely or subject to such terms, provisions and limitations as may be so specified.

(2) A licence granted under this section (hereafter in this Act referred to as a wireless telegraphy licence) may be issued subject to such terms, provisions and limitations as the [Secretary of State] may think fit, including in particular in the case of a licence to establish a station, limitations as to the position and nature of the station, the purposes for which, the circumstances in which, and the persons by whom the station may be used, and the apparatus which may be installed or used therein, and, in the case of any other licence, limitaions as to the apparatus which may be installed or used, and the places where the purposes for which, the circumstances in which and the persons by whom the apparatus may be used.

(3) A wireless telegraphy licence shall, unless previously revoked by the [Secretary of State], continue in force for such period as may be specified in the licence.

(4) A wireless telegraphy licence may be revoked, or the terms, provisions or limitations thereof varied, by a notice in writing of the [Secretary of State] served on the holder of the licence or by a general notice applicable to licences of the class to which the licence in question belongs published in such manner as may be specified in the licence.

(5) * * * * *

(6) Nothing in this section shall authorise the inclusion, in any wireless telegraphy licence relating solely to apparatus not designed or adapted for emission (as opposed to reception), of any term or provision requiring any person to concede any form of right of entry into any private dwelling-house.

* * * * *

POST OFFICE ACT 1953
(1 & 2 Eliz. 2, c. 36)

An Act to consolidate certain enactments relating to the Post Office with corrections and improvements made under the Consolidation of Enactments (Procedure) Act 1949

[31 July 1953]

Territorial extent United Kingdom

1-7 . . .

General provisions as to transmission of postal packets

8 Conditions of transit of postal packets

(1), (2) . . .

(3) If any postal packet is posted or sent by post in contravention of this Act or of any . . . regulation made thereunder, the transmission thereof may be refused and the packet may, if necessary, be detained and opened in the post office and may be returned to the sender thereof or forwarded to its destination, subject in either case to any . . . regulations as to additional postage or other charges, or may be destroyed or otherwise disposed of as [the Post Office] may direct.

(4) . . .

9 . . .

10 * * * * *

11 Prohibition on sending by post of certain articles

(1) A person shall not send or attempt to send or procure to be sent a postal packet which—

(a) save as [the Post Office] may either generally or in any particular case allow, encloses any explosive, dangerous, noxious or deleterious substance, any filth, any sharp instrument not properly protected, any noxious living creature, or any creature, article or thing whatsoever which is likely to injure either other postal packets in course of conveyance or [a person engaged in the business of the Post Office]; or

(b) encloses any indecent or obscene print, painting, photograph, lithograph, engraving, cinematograph film, book, card or written communication, or any indecent or obscene article whether similar to the above or not; or

(c) has on the packet, or on the cover thereof, any words, marks or designs which are grossly offensive or of an indecent or obscene character.

(2) If any person acts in contravention of the foregoing subsection, he shall be liable on summary conviction to a fine not exceeding [the prescribed sum] or on conviction on indictment to imprisonment for a term not exceeding twelve months.

* * * * *

58 Opening or delaying of postal packets by officers of the Post Office

(1) If any [person engaged in the business of the Post Office], contrary to his duty, opens, or procures or suffers to be opened, any postal packet in course of transmission by post, or wilfully detains or delays, or procures or suffers to be detained or delayed, any such postal packet, he shall be guilty of a misdemeanour and be liable to imprisonment [for a term not exceeding two years] or to a fine, or to both:

Provided that nothing in this section shall extend to the opening, detaining or delaying of a postal packet returned for want of a true direction, or returned by reason that the person to whom it is directed has refused it, or has refused or neglected to pay the postage thereof, or that the packet cannot for any other reason be delivered, or to the opening, detaining or delaying of a postal packet under the authority of this Act or in obedience to [a warrant issued by the Secretary of State under section 2 of the Interception of Communications Act 1985].

* * * * *

CHILDREN AND YOUNG PERSONS (HARMFUL PUBLICATIONS) ACT 1955 (3 & 4 Eliz. 2, c. 28)

An Act to prevent the dissemination of certain pictorial publications harmful to children and young persons [6 May 1955]

Territorial extent United Kingdom

1 Works to which this Act applies

This Act applies to any book, magazine or other like work which is of a kind likely to fall into the hands of children or young persons and consists wholly or mainly of stories told in pictures (with or without the addition of written matter), being stories portraying—

(a) the commission of crimes; or

(b) acts of violence or cruelty; or

(c) incidents of a repulsive or horrible nature;

in such a way that the work as a whole would tend to corrupt a child or young person into whose hands it might fall.

2 Penalty for printing, publishing, selling, &c, works to which this Act applies

(1) A person who prints, publishes, sells or lets on hire a work to which this Act applies, or has any such work in his possession for the purpose of selling it or letting it on hire, shall be guilty of an offence and liable, on summary conviction, to imprisonment for a term not exceeding four months or to a fine not exceeding [level 3 on the standard scale] or to both:

Provided that, in any proceedings taken under this subsection against a person in respect of selling or letting on hire a work or of having it in his possession for the purpose of selling it or letting it on hire, it shall be a defence for him to prove that he had not examined the contents of the work and had no reasonable cause to suspect that it was one to which this Act applies.

(2) A prosecution for an offence under this section shall not, in England or Wales, be instituted except by, or with the consent of, the Attorney General.

* * * * *

Note Section 3 (not reproduced) provides for the granting of search warrants and forfeiture of offending material on conviction; s. 4 prohibits importation of material subject to the Act.

LIFE PEERAGES ACT 1958
(6 & 7 Eliz. 2, c. 21)

An Act to make provision for the creation of life peerages carrying the right to sit and vote in the House of Lords [30 April 1958]

Territorial extent United Kingdom

1 Power to create life peerages carrying right to sit in the House of Lords

(1) Without prejudice to Her Majesty's powers as to the appointment of Lords of Appeal in Ordinary, Her Majesty shall have power by letters patent to confer on any person a peerage for life having the incidents specified in subsection (2) of this section.

(2) A peerage conferred under this section shall, during the life of the person on whom it is conferred, entitle him—

(a) to rank as a baron under such style as may be appointed by the letters patent; and

(b) subject to subsection (4) of this section, to receive writs of summons to attend the House of Lords and sit and vote therein accordingly,

and shall expire on his death.

(3) A life peerage may be conferred under this section on a woman.

(4) Nothing in this section shall enable any person to receive a writ of summons to attend the House of Lords, or to sit and vote in that House, at any time when disqualified therefor by law.

PUBLIC RECORDS ACT 1958
(6 & 7 Eliz. 2, c. 51)

An Act to make new provision with respect to public records and the Public Record Office, and for connected purposes [23 July 1958]

Territorial extent England and Wales, Scotland

1 General responsibility of the Lord Chancellor for public records

(1) The direction of the Public Record Office shall be transferred from the Master of the Rolls to the Lord Chancellor, and the Lord Chancellor shall be generally responsible for the execution of this Act and shall supervise the care and preservation of public records.

(2) There shall be an Advisory Council on Public Records to advise the Lord Chancellor on matters concerning public records in general and, in particular, on those aspects of the work of the Public Record Office which affect members of the public who make use of the facilities provided by the Public Record Office.

The Master of the Rolls shall be chairman of the said Council and the remaining members of the Council shall be appointed by the Lord Chancellor on such terms as he may specify.

(3) The Lord Chancellor shall in every year lay before both Houses of Parliament a report on the work of the Public Record Office, which shall include any report made to him by the Advisory Council on Public Records.

2 * * * * *

3 Selection and preservation of public records

(1) It shall be the duty of every person responsible for public records of any description which are not in the Public Record Office or a place of deposit appointed by the Lord Chancellor under this Act to make arrangements for the selection of those records which ought to be permanently preserved and for their safe-keeping.

(2) Every person shall perform his duties under this section under the guidance of the Keeper of Public Records and the said Keeper shall be responsible for co-ordinating and supervising all action taken under this section.

(3) All public records created before the year sixteen hundred and sixty shall be included among those selected for permanent preservation.

(4)-(8) *****

4 *****

5 Access to public records

(1) Public records in the Public Record Office, other than those to which members of the public had access before their transfer to the Public Record Office, shall not be available for public inspection [until the expiration of the period of thirty years beginning with the first day of January in the year next after that in which they were created, or such other period], either longer or shorter, as the Lord Chancellor may, with the approval, or at the request, of the Minister or other person, if any, who appears to him to be primarily concerned, for the time being prescribe as respects any particular class of public records.

(2) Without prejudice to the generality of the foregoing subsection, if it appears to the person responsible for any public records which have been selected by him under section three of this Act for permanent preservation that they contain information which was obtained from members of the public under such conditions that the opening of those records to the public after the period determined under the foregoing subsection would or might constitute a breach of good faith on the part of the Government or on the part of the persons who obtained the information, he shall inform the Lord Chancellor accordingly and those records shall not be available in the Public Record Office for public inspection even after the expiration of the said period except in such circumstances and subject to such conditions, if any, as the Lord Chancellor and that person may approve, or, if the Lord Chancellor and that person think fit, after the expiration of such further period as they may approve.

(3)-(5) *****

6-13 *****

Section 10

FIRST SCHEDULE
DEFINITION OF PUBLIC RECORDS

1. The provisions of this Schedule shall have effect for determining what are public records for the purposes of this Act.

Departmental records

2.—(1) Subject to the provisions of this paragraph, administrative and departmental records belonging to Her Majesty, whether in the United Kingdom or elsewhere, in right of Her Majesty's Government in the United Kingdom and, in particular,—

(a) records, of, or held in, any department of her Majesty's Government in the United Kingdom, or

(b) records of any office, commission or other body or establishment whatsoever under Her Majesty's Government in the United Kingdom,

shall be public records.

(2) Sub-paragraph (1) of this paragaph shall not apply—

(a) to records of any government department or body which is wholly or mainly concerned with Scottish affairs, or which carries on its activities wholly or mainly in Scotland, or

(b) to registers, or certified copies of entries in registers, being registers or certified copies kept or deposited in the General Register Office under or in pursuance of any enactment, whether past or future, which provides for the registration of births, deaths, marriages or adoptions, or

(c) except so far as provided by paragraph 4 of this Schedule, to records of the Duchy of Lancaster, or

(d) to records of the office of the Public Trustee relating to individual trusts.

OBSCENE PUBLICATIONS ACT 1959
(7 & 8 Eliz. 2, c. 66)

An Act to amend the law relating to the publication of obscene matter; to provide for the protection of literature; and to strengthen the law concerning pornography [29 July 1959]

Territorial extent England and Wales

1 Test of obscenity

(1) For the purposes of this Act an article shall be deemed to be obscene if its effect or (where the article comprises two or more distinct items) the effect of any one of its items is, if taken as a whole, such as to tend to deprave and corrupt persons who are likely, having regard to all relevant circumstances, to read, see or hear the matter contained or embodied in it.

(2) In this Act "article" means any description of article containing or embodying matter to be read or looked at or both, any sound record, and any film or other record of a picture or pictures.

(3) For the purposes of this Act a person publishes an article who—

(a) distributes, circulates, sells, lets on hire, gives, or lends it, or who offers it for sale or for letting on hire; or

(b) in the case of an article containing or embodying matter to be looked at or a record, shows, plays or projects it:

Provided that paragraph (b) or this subsection shall not apply to anything done in the course of . . . television or sound broadcasting.

2 Prohibition of publication of obscene matter

(1) Subject as hereinafter provided, any person who, whether for gain or not, publishes an obscene article [or who has an obscene article for publication for gain (whether gain to himself or gain to another)] shall be liable—

(a) on summary conviction to a fine not exceeding [the prescribed sum] or to imprisonment for a term not exceeding six months;

(b) on conviction on indictment to a fine or to imprisonment for a term not exceeding three years or both.

(2) . . .

(3) A prosecution . . . for an offence against this section shall not be commenced more than two years after the commission of the offence.

[(3A) Proceedings for an offence under this section shall not be instituted except by or with the consent of the Director of Public Prosecutions in any case where the article in question is a moving picture film of a width of not less than sixteen millimetres and the relevant publication or the only other publication which followed or could reasonably have been expected to follow from the relevant publication took place or (as the case may be) was to take place in the course of a [film exhibition]; and in this subsection "the relevant publication" means—

(a) in the case any proceedings under this section for publishing an obscene article, the publication in respect of which the defendant would be charged if the proceedings were brought; and

(b) in the case of any proceedings under this section for having an obscene article for publication for gain, the publication which, if the proceedings were brought, the defendant would be alleged to have had in contemplation.]

(4) A person publishing an article shall not be proceeded against for an offence at common law consisting of the publication of any matter contained or embodied in the article where it is of the essence of the offence that the matter is obscene.

[(4A) Without prejudice to subsection (4) above, a person shall not be proceeded against for an offence at common law—

(a) in respect of a [film exhibition] or anything said or done in the course of a [film exhibition], where it is of the essence of the common law offence that the exhibition or, as the case may be, what was said or done was obscene, indecent, offensive, disgusting or injurious to morality; or

(b) in respect of an agreement to give a [film exhibition] or to cause anything to be said or done in the course of such an exhibition where the common law offence consists of conspiring to corrupt public morals or to do any act contrary to public morals or decency.]

(5) A person shall not be convicted of an offence against this section if he proves that he had not examined the article in respect of which he is charged and had no reasonable cause to suspect that it was such that his publication of it would make him liable to be convicted of an offence against this section.

(6) In any proceedings against a person under this section the question whether an article is obscene shall be determined without regard to any publication by another person unless it could reasonably have been expected that the publication by the other person would follow from publication by the person charged.

[(7) In this section "film exhibition" has the same meaning as in the Cinemas Act 1985.]

3 Powers of search and seizure

(1) If a justice of the peace is satisfied by information on oath that there is reasonable ground for suspecting that, in any premises in the petty sessions area for which he acts, or on any stall or vehicle in that area, being premises or a stall or vehicle specified in the information, obscene articles are, or are from time to time, kept for publication for gain, the justice may issue a warrant under his hand empowering any constable to enter (if need be by force) and search the premises, or to search the stall or vehicle . . . and to seize and remove any articles found therein or thereon which the constable has reason to believe to be obscene articles and to be kept for publication for gain.

(2) A warrant under the foregoing subsection shall, if any obscene articles are seized under the warrant, also empower the seizure and removal of any documents found in the premises or, as the case may be, on the stall or vehicle which relate to a trade or business carried on at the premises or from the stall or vehicle.

(3) [Subject to subsection (3A) of this section] any articles seized under subsection (1) of this section shall be brought before a justice of the peace acting for the same petty sessions area as the justice who issued the warrant, and the justice before whom the articles are brought may thereupon issue a summons to the occupier of the premises or, as the case may be, the user of the stall or vehicle to appear on a day specified in the summons before a magistrates' court for that petty sessions area to show cause why the articles or any of them should not be forfeited; and if the court is satisfied, as respects any of the articles, that at the time when they were seized they were obscene articles kept for publication for gain, the court shall order those articles to be forfeited:

Provided that if the person summoned does not appear, the court shall not make an order unless service of the summons is proved.

[Provided also that this subsection does not apply in relation to any article seized under subsection (1) of this section which is returned to the occupier of the premises or, as the case may be, to the user of the stall or vehicle in or on which it was found.]

[(3A) Without prejudice to the duty of a court to make an order for the forfeiture of an article where section 1(4) of the Obscene Publications Act 1964 applies (orders made on conviction), in a case where by virtue of subsection (3A) of section 2 of this Act proceedings under the said section 2 for having an article for publication for gain could not be instituted except by or with the consent of the Director of Public Prosecutions, no order for the forfeiture of the article shall be made under this section unless the warrant under which the article was seized was issued on an information laid by or on behalf of the Director of Public Prosecutions.]

(4) In addition to the person summoned, any other person being the owner, author or maker of any of the articles brought before the court, or any other person through whose hands they had passed before being seized, shall be entitled to appear before the court on the day specified in the summons to show cause why they should not be forfeited.

(5)-(8) * * * * *

4 Defence of public good

(1) [Subject to subsection (1A) of this section] a person shall not be convicted of an offence against section two of this Act, and an order for forfeiture shall not be made under the foregoing section, if it is proved that publication of the article in question is justified as being for the public good on the ground that it is in the interests of science, literature, art or learning, or of other objects of general concern.

[(1A) Subsection (1) of this section shall not apply where the article in question is a moving picture film or soundtrack, but—

(a) a person shall not be convicted of an offence against section 2 of this Act in relation to any such film or soundtrack, and

(b) an order for forfeiture of any such film or soundtrack shall not be made under section 3 of this Act,

if it is proved that publication of the film or soundtrack is justified as being for the public good on the ground that it is in the interests of drama, opera, ballet or any other art, or of literature or learning.]

(2) It is hereby declared that the opinion of experts as to the literary, artistic, scientific or other merits of an article may be admitted in any proceedings under this Act either to establish or to negative the said ground.

[(3) In this section "moving picture soundtrack" means any sound record designed for playing with a moving picture film, whether incorporated with the film or not.]

ADMINISTRATION OF JUSTICE ACT 1960
(8 & 9 Eliz. 2, c. 65)

An Act to make further provision for appeals to the House of Lords in criminal cases; to amend the law relating to contempt of court, habeas corpus and certiorari; and for purposes connected with the matters aforesaid [27 October 1960]

Territorial extent England and Wales

* * * * *

Contempt of Court, habeas corpus and certiorari

11 . . . [Repealed by the Contempt of Court Act 1981, s. 3(4)]

12 Publication of information relating to proceedings in private

(1) The publication of information relating to proceedings before any court sitting in private shall not of itself be contempt of court except in the following cases, that is to say—

(a) where the proceedings relate to the wardship or adoption of an infant or wholly or mainly to the guardianship, custody, maintenance or upbringing of an infant, or rights of access to an infant;

(b) where the proceedings are brought under Part VIII of the Mental Health Act 1959, or under any provision of that Act authorising an application or reference to be made to a Mental Health Review Tribunal or to a county court;

(c) where the court sits in private for reasons of national security during that part of the proceedings about which the information in question is published;

(d) where the information relates to a secret process, discovery or invention which is in issue in the proceedings;

(e) where the court (having power to do so) expressly prohibits the publication of all information relating to the proceedings or of information of the description which is published.

(2) Without prejudice to the foregoing subsection, the publication of the text or a summary of the whole or part of an order made by a court sitting in private shall not of itself be contempt of court except where the court (having power to do so) expressly prohibits the publication.

(3) In this section references to a court include references to a judge and to a tribunal and to any person exercising the functions of a court, a judge or a tribunal; and references to a court sitting in private include references to a court sitting in camera or in chambers.

(4) Nothing in this section shall be construed as implying that any publication is punishable as contempt of court which would not be so punishable apart from this section.

13 Appeal in cases of contempt of court

(1) Subject to the provisions of this section, an appeal shall lie under this section from any order or decision of a court in the exercise of jurisdiction to punish for contempt of court (including criminal contempt); and in relation to any such order or decision the provisions of this section shall have effect in substitution for any other enactment relating to appeals in civil or criminal proceedings.

(2) An appeal under this section shall lie in any case at the instance of the defendant and, in the case of an application for committal or attachment, at the instance of the applicant; and the appeal shall lie—

(a) from an order or decision of any inferior court not referred to in the next following paragraph, to a Divisional court of the High Court;

(b) from an order or decision of a county court or any other inferior court from which appeals generally lie to the Court of Appeal, and from an order or decision . . ., of a single judge of the High Court or of a judge of that court, to the Court of Appeal;

[(bb) from an order or decision of the Crown Court to the Court of Appeal];

(c) from an order or decision of a Divisional Court or the Court of Appeal (including a decision of either of those courts on an appeal under this section), and from an order or decision of the Court of Criminal Appeal or the Courts-Martial Appeal Court, to the House of Lords.

(3) The court to which an appeal is brought under this section may reverse or vary the order or decision of the court below, and make such other order as may be just; and without prejudice to the inherent powers of any court referred to in subsection (2) of this section, provision may be made by rules of court for authorising the release on bail of an appellant under this section.

(4)-(6) * * * * *

PUBLIC BODIES (ADMISSION TO MEETINGS) ACT 1960
(8 & 9 Eliz. 2, c. 67)

An Act to provide for the admission of representatives of the press and other members of the public to the meetings of certain bodies exercising public functions [27 October 1960]

Territorial extent England and Wales, Scotland

1 Admission of public to meetings of local authorities and other bodies

(1) Subject to subsection (2) below, any meeting of a . . . body exercising public functions, being [a body] to which this Act applies, shall be open to the public.

(2) A body may, by resolution, exclude the public from a meeting (whether during the whole or part of the proceedings) whenever publicity would be prejudicial to the public interest by reason of the confidential nature of the business to be transacted or for other special reasons stated in the resolution and arising from the nature of that business or of the

proceedings; and where such a resolution is passed, this Act shall not require the meeting to be open to the public during proceedings to which the resolution applies.

(3) A body may under subsection (2) above treat the need to receive or consider recommendations or advice from sources other than members, committees or sub-committees of the body as a special reason why publicity would be prejudicial to the public interest, without regard to the subject or purport of the recommendations or advice; but the making by this subsection of express provision for that case shall not be taken to restrict the generality of subsection (2) above in relation to other cases (including in particular cases where the report of a committee or sub-committee of the body is of a confidential nature).

(4) Where a meeting of a body is required by this Act to be open to the public during the proceedings or any part of them, the following provisions shall apply, that is to say,—

(a) public notice of the time and place of the meeting shall be given by posting it at the offices of the body (or, if the body has no offices, then in some central and conspicuous place in the area with which it is concerned) three clear days at least before the meeting or, if the meeting is convened at shorter notice, then at the time it is convened;

(b) there shall, on request and on payment of postage or other necessary charge for transmission, be supplied for the benefit of any newspaper a copy of the agenda for the meeting as supplied to members of the body (but excluding, if thought fit, any item during which the meeting is likely not to be open to the public), together with such further statements or particulars, if any, as are necessary to indicate the nature of the items included or, if thought fit in the case of any item, with copies of any reports or other documents supplied to members of the body in connection with the item;

(c) while the meeting is open to the public, the body shall not have power to exclude members of the public from the meeting and duly accredited representatives of newspapers attending for the purpose of reporting the proceedings for those newspapers shall, so far as practicable, be afforded reasonable facilities for taking their report and, unless the meeting is held in premises not belonging to the body or not on the telephone, for telephoning the report at their own expense.

(5) Where a meeting of a body is required by this Act to be open to the public during the proceedings or any part of them, and there is supplied to a member of the public attending the meeting, or in pursuance of paragraph (b) of subsection (4) above there is supplied for the benefit of a newspaper, any such copy of the agenda as is mentioned in that paragraph, with or without further statements or particulars for the purpose of indicating the nature of any item included in the agenda, the publication thereby of any defamatory matter contained in the agenda or in the further statements or particulars shall be privileged, unless the publication is proved to be made with malice.

(6) When a body to which this Act applies resolves itself into committee, the proceedings in committee shall for the purposes of this Act be treated as forming part of the proceedings of the body at the meeting.

(7) Any reference in this section to a newspaper shall apply also to a news agency which systematically carries on the business of selling and supplying reports or information to newspapers, and to any organisation which is systematically engaged in collecting news for sound or television broadcasts [or for programmes to be included in a cable programme service which is or does not require to be licensed]; but nothing in this section shall require a body to permit the taking of photographs of any proceedings, or the use of any means to enable persons not present to see or hear any proceedings (whether at the time or later), or the making of any oral report on any proceedings as they take place.

(8) The provisions of this section shall be without prejudice to any power of exclusion to suppress or prevent disorderly conduct or other misbehaviour at a meeting.

2, 3 * * * * *

OBSCENE PUBLICATIONS ACT 1964
(1964, c. 74)

An Act to strengthen the law for preventing the publication for gain of obscene matter and the publication of things intended for the production of obscene matter [31 July 1964]

Territorial extent England and Wales

1 Obscene articles intended for publication for gain

(1) . . .

(2) For the purpose of any proceedings for an offence against the said section 2 a person shall be deemed to have an article for publication for gain if with a view to such publication he has the article in his ownership, possession or control.

(3) In proceedings brought against a person under the said section 2 for having an obscene article for publication for gain the following provisions shall apply in place of subsections (5) and (6) of that section, that is to say,—

(a) he shall not be convicted of that offence if he proves that he had not examined the article and had no reasonable cause to suspect that it was such that his having it would make him liable to be convicted of an offence against that section; and

(b) the question whether the article is obscene shall be determined by reference to such publication for gain of the article as in the circumstances it may reasonably be inferred he had in contemplation and to any further publication that could reasonably be expected to follow from it, but not to any other publication.

(4) Where articles are seized under section 3 of the Obscene Publications Act 1959 (which provides for the seizure and forfeiture of obscene articles kept for publication for gain), and a person is convicted under section 2 of the Act of having them for publication for gain, the court on his conviction shall order the forfeiture of those articles:

★★★★★

Note 'The said section 2' in subsections (2) and (3) is section 2 of the Obscene Publications Act 1959.

POLICE ACT 1964
(1964, c. 48)

An Act to re-enact with modifications certain enactments relating to police forces in England and Wales, to amend the Police (Scotland) Act 1956, and to make further provision with respect to the police [10 June 1964]

Territorial extent England and Wales (provisions relating to Scotland not reproduced).

PART I
ORGANISATION OF POLICE FORCES

County, county borough and combined forces

1 Police areas

[(1) Subject to the provisions of this Act, a police force shall be maintained—

(a) for every county in England and Wales which is not comprised in a combined area constituted by an amalgamation scheme or in the Northumbria police area;

(b) for every combined area constituted by an amalgamation scheme; and

(c) for the Northumbria police area.

(1A) For the purposes of this Act the Northumbria police area shall consist of the county of Tyne and Wear and the county of Northumberland.]

(2), (3) . . .

(4) For the purposes of this section, any part of a county which is for the time being comprised in the metropolitan police district shall be treated as not forming part of that county.

2 Police authorities for counties and county boroughs

(1) The police authority for [a police area consisting of a non-metropolitan county] . . . shall be a committee of the council of the county . . . constituted in accordance with the provisions of this section, to be known, . . ., as the police committee and, . . .

(2) The police committee for [a police area consisting of a non-metropolitan county] shall consist of such number of persons as may be determined by the council of the county, and of that number—

(a) two thirds shall be members of the council of the county appointed by that council;

(b) [. . .] one third shall be appointed from among their own number by the magistrates for the county in accordance with a scheme made by the magistrates' courts committee for, or for an area including, the county and approved by the Secretary of State].

[(c) . . .]

(3) . . .

(4) The magistrates to be appointed members of a police committee . . . shall be appointed at such times, in such manner and for such terms as may be prescribed by rules made by the Secretary of State; and the other members of a police committee . . . shall be appointed at such times, in such manner and for such term as may from time to time be determined by the council responsible for appointing them.

(5)-(7) *****

2A, 3 *****

4 General functions of police authorities

(1) It shall be the duty of the police authority for every police area for which a police force is required to be maintained by section 1 of this Act to secure the maintenance of an adequate and efficient police force for the area, and to exercise for that purpose the powers conferred on a police authority by this Act.

(2) The police authority for every such police area shall, subject to the approval of the Secretary of State and to regulations under Part II of this Act, appoint the chief constable of the police force maintained by that authority and determine the number of persons of each rank in that force which is to constitute the establishment of the force.

(3) The police authority for any such area may, subject to the consent of the Secretary of State, provide and maintain such buildings, structures and premises, and make such alterations in any buildings, structures or premises already provided, as may be required for police purposes of the area.

(4) The police authority for any such police area may, subject to any regulations under Part II of this Act, provide and maintain such vehicles, apparatus, clothing and other equipment as may be required for police purposes of the area.

(5) *****

5 Chief constables

(1) The police force maintained for a police area under section 1 of this Act shall be under the direction and control of the chief constable appointed under section 4(2) of this Act.

(2) The same person may, with the consent of the police authorities concerned, be appointed chief constable of more than one police force.

(3) The Secretary of State shall not approve the appointment as first chief constable of a combined force of any person other than the chief constable of a police force which ceases to exist in consequence of the formation of the combined force unless the Secretary

of State is satisfied, having regard to the size and character of the combined force and any exceptional circumstances, that some other person should be appointed.

(4) Without prejudice to any regulations under Part II of this Act or under the Police Pensions Act 1948, the police authority, acting with the approval of the Secretary of State, may call upon the chief constable to retire in the interests of efficiency.

(5) Before seeking the approval of the Secretary of State under subsection (4) of this section the police authority shall give the chief constable an opportunity to make representations and shall consider any representations so made.

(6) A chief constable who is called upon to retire as aforesaid shall retire on such date as the police authority may specify or on such earlier date as may be agreed upon between him and the police authority.

6 Deputy and assistant chief constables

(1) In every police force maintained under section 1 of this Act there shall be a [person holding the rank of] deputy chief constable, who shall have all the powers and duties of the chief constable—

(a) during any absence, incapacity or suspension from duty of the chief constable;

(b) during any vacancy in the office of chief constable;

but shall not have power to act by virtue of this subsection for any continuous period exceeding three months except with the consent of the Secretary of State.

(2) The provisions of subsection (1) above shall be in addition to, and not in substitution for, any other enactment which makes provision for the exercise by any other person of the powers conferred by that enactment on a chief constable.

(3) The establishment of any such police force as aforesaid may include one or more persons holding the rank of assistant chief constable.

(4) [Appointments or promotions to the rank of deputy chief constable or] assistant chief constable, shall be made, in accordance with regulations under Part II of this Act, by the police authority after consultation with the chief constable and subject to the approval of the Secretary of State.

(5) Subsections (2), (4), (5) and (6) of section 5 of this Act shall apply to a deputy chief constable, and subsections (4), (5) and (6) of that section shall apply to an assistant chief constable, as they apply to a chief constable.

6A, 7-10 * * * * *

11 Questions on police matters by members of county councils

Arrangements shall be made (whether by standing orders or otherwise) for enabling questions on the discharge of the functions of the police authority for [any non-metropolitan county], . . . or combined area to be put, in the course of the proceedings of the council for that county or . . ., as the case may be, of a constituent council, by members of that council for answer by a member thereof who is also a member of the police authority and is nominated by that authority for that purpose.

General provisions

12 Reports by chief constables to police authorities

(1) Every chief constable shall, as soon as possible after the end of each calendar year, submit to the police authority, submit to that authority a general report in writing on the policing during that year of the year for which his force is maintained.

(2) The chief constable of a police force shall, whenever so required by the police authority, submit to that authority a report in writing on such matters as may be specified in the requirement, being matters connected with the policing of the area for which the force is maintained.

(3) If it appears to the chief constable that a report in compliance with any such requirement of the police authority would contain information which in the public interest ought not to be disclosed, or is not needed for the discharge of the functions of the police

authority, he may request that authority to refer the requirement to the Secretary of State; and in any such case the requirement shall be of no effect unless it is confirmed by the Secretary of State.

(4) This section applies to the City of London police force as if for references to the chief constable there were substituted references to the Commissioner.

13 *****

14 Aid of one police force by another

(1) The chief officer of police of any police force may, on the application of the chief officer of police of any other police force, provide constables or other assistance for the purpose of enabling the other force to meet any special demand on its resources.

(2) If it appears to the Secretary of State to be expedient in the interests of public safety or order that any police force should be reinforced or should receive other assistance for the purpose of enabling it to meet any special demand on its resources, and that satisfactory arrangements under subsection (1) above cannot be made, or cannot be made in time, he may direct the chief officer of police of any police force to provide such constables or other assistance for that purpose as may be specified in the direction.

(3) While a constable is provided under this section for the assistance of another police force he shall, notwithstanding section 5(1) of this Act, be under the direction and control of the chief officer of police of that other force.

(4) The police authority maintaining a police force for which assistance is provided under this section shall pay to the police authority maintaining the force from which that assistance is provided such contribution as may be agreed upon between those authorities, or, in default of any such agreement, as may be provided by any agreement subsisting at the time between all police authorities generally, or, in default of such general agreement, as may be determined by the Secretary of State.

15 Provision of special services

(1) The chief officer of police of any police force may provide, at the request of any person, special police services at any premises or in any locality in the police area for which the force is maintained, subject to the payment to the police authority of charges on such scales as may be determined by that authority.

(2) In the application of this section to the metropolitan police, for the reference in subsection (1) to the police authority there shall be substituted a reference to the Receiver for the Metropolitan Police District.

16, 17 *****

18 Attestation of constables

Every member of a police force maintained for a police area and every special constable appointed for a police area shall, on appointment, be attested as a constable by making a declaration in the form set out in Schedule 2 to this Act—

(a) in the case of the metropolitan police district, before the Commissioner or an Assistant Commissioner of Police of the Metropolis;

(b) in any other case, before a justice of the peace having jurisdiction within the police area.

19 Jurisdiction of constables

(1) A member of a police force shall have all the powers and privileges of a constable throughout England and Wales.

(2) A special constable shall have all the powers and privileges of a constable in the police area for which he is appointed.

(3)-(6) *****

20-27 *****

PART II
CENTRAL SUPERVISION, DIRECTION AND FACILITIES

Functions of Secretary of State

28 General duty of Secretary of State

The Secretary of State shall exercise his power under this Act in such manner and to such extent as appears to him to be best calculated to promote the efficiency of the police.

29 Removal of chief constables &c.

(1) The Secretary of State may require a police authority to exercise their power under Part I of this Act to call upon the chief constable to retire in the interests of efficiency.

(2) Before requiring the exercise of that power or approving the exercise of that or the similar power exercisable with respect to [a deputy or assistant chief constable], the Secretary of State shall give the chief constable or deputy or assistant chief constable an opportunity to make representations to him and shall consider any representations so made.

(3) Where representations are made under this section the Secretary of State may, and in a case where he proposes to require the exercise of the power mentioned in subsection (1) of this section shall, appoint one or more persons (one at least of whom shall be a person who is not an officer of police or of a Government department) to hold an inquiry and report to him and shall consider any report made under this subsection.

(4) The costs incurred by a chief constable or deputy or assistant chief constable in respect of an inquiry under this section, taxed in such manner as the Secretary of State may direct, shall be defrayed out of the police fund.

30 Reports from chief constables

(1) The Secretary of State may require any chief constable to submit to him a report on such matters as may be specified in the requirement, being matters connected with the policing of his area.

(2) Every chief constable shall, as soon as possible after the end of each calendar year, submit to the Secretary of State the like report as is required by subsection (1) of section 12 of this Act to be submitted to the police authority.

31 Police grant

(1) The Secretary of State may make grants in respect of expenses incurred for police purposes—

(a) by any police authority maintaining a county police force, . . . or combined police force;

(b) by the Receiver for the Metropolitan Police District or by the Common Council of the City of London;

[(c) by the Northumbria police authority].

(2) Grants under this section shall be of such amounts, be payable at such times, in such manner, and subject to such conditions, and be carried to such funds, as the Secretary of State may with the approval of the Treasury by order determine; and any such order may provide for the deduction from grants under this section of such sums as may be determined by or under the order on account of expenditure of the Secretary of State under section 41, 44 or 45 of this Act.

(3) Any statutory instrument made under this section shall be subject to annulment in pursuance of a resolution of either House of Parliament.

(4) * * * * *

32 Local inquiries

(1) The Secretary of State may cause a local inquiry to be held by a person appointed by him into any matter connected with the policing of any area.

(2) Any inquiry under this section shall be held in public or in private as the Secretary of State may direct.

(3) Subsections (2) and (3) of section 290 of the Local Government Act 1933 (power to summon and examine witnesses) shall apply to any inquiry held under this section as they apply to an inquiry held under that section.

(4) Where the report of the person holding an inquiry under this section is not published, a summary of his findings and conclusions shall be made known by the Secretary of State so far as appears to him consistent with the public interest.

(5) The Secretary of State may direct that the whole or part of the costs incurred by any person for the purposes of any inquiry held under this section shall be defrayed out of the police fund or, if the inquiry relates to more than one police area, out of the police funds concerned in such proportions as may be specified in the direction; and any costs payable under this section shall be subject to taxation in such manner as the Secretary of State may direct.

33 Regulations for police forces

(1) Subject to the provisions of this section, the Secretary of State may make regulations as to the government, administration and conditions of service of police forces.

(2) Without prejudice to the generality of subsection (1) above, regulations under this section may make provision with respect to the following matters, that is to say:—

(a) the ranks to be held by members of police forces;

(b) the qualifications for appointment and promotion of members of police forces;

(c) periods of service on probation;

(d) voluntary retirement of members of police forces;

(e) the maintenance of discipline in police forces;

(f) the suspension of members of a police force from membership of that force and from their office as constable;

(g) the maintenance of personal records of members of police forces;

(h) the duties which are or are not to be performed by members of police forces;

(i) the treatment as occasions of police duty of attendance at meetings of the Police Federations and of any body recognised by the Secretary of State for the purposes of section 47 of this Act;

(j) the hours of duty, leave, pay and allowances of members of police forces; and

(k) the issue, use and return of police clothing, personal equipment and accoutrements.

(3) . . .

(4) Regulations under this section for regulating pay and allowances may be made with retrospective effect to any date specified therein, but nothing in this subsection shall be construed as authorising pay or allowances payable to any person to be reduced retrospectively.

(5) Regulations under this section may make different provision for different cases and circumstances, and may authorise the Secretary of State to make provision for any purposes specified in the regulations.

(6) Any statutory instrument made under this section shall be subject to annulment in pursuance of a resolution of either House of Parliament.

Note The current disciplinary regulations made under this section are The Police Regulations 1987 SI 851.

34-36 * * * * *

[37 Disciplinary appeals to Secretary of State

(1) A member of a police force who is dealt with for an offence against discipline may appeal to the Secretary of State—

(a) against the decision on the disciplinary charge which was preferred against him;

(b) against any punishment awarded,

except where he has a right of appeal to some other person; and in that case he may appeal to the Secretary of State from any decision of that other person.

(2) On an appeal the Secretary of State may make an order allowing or dismissing the appeal.

(3) Subject to subsection (4) below, in any case where it appears to him that it is appropriate to do so, he may substitute some other punishment.

(4) The Secretary of State may not substitute another punishment unless it appears to him—

(a) that the person or tribunal who heard the disciplinary charge could have awarded it; and

(b) that it is less severe than the punishment awarded by that person or tribunal.

(5) The Secretary of State may direct an appellant to pay the whole or any part of his own costs; but, subject to any such direction, all the costs and expenses of an appeal under this section, including the costs of the parties, shall be defrayed out of the police fund.

Inspectors of constabulary

38 Appointment and functions of inspectors of constabulary

(1) Her Majesty may appoint such number of inspectors (to be known as "Her Majesty's Inspectors of Constabulary") as the Secretary of State may with the consent of the Treasury determine, and of the persons so appointed one may be appointed as chief inspector of constabulary.

(2) It shall be the duty of the inspectors of constabulary to inspect, and report to the Secretary of State on the efficiency of, all police forces maintained under section 1 of this Act and the City of London police force.

(3) The inspectors of constabulary shall carry out such other duties for the purpose of furthering police efficiency as the Secretary of State may from time to time direct.

(4) The chief inspector of constabulary shall in each year submit to the Secretary of State a report in such form as the Secretary of State may direct, and the Secretary of State shall lay a copy of that report before Parliament.

(5) The inspectors of constabulary shall be paid such salary and allowances as the Secretary of State may with the consent of the Treasury determine.

39-44 * * * * *

PART III
POLICE REPRESENTATIVE INSTITUTIONS

45 . . .

46 * * * * *

47 Membership of trade unions

(1) Subject to the provisions of this section, a member of a police force shall not be a member of any trade union, or of any association having for its objects, or one of its objects, to control or influence the pay, pensions or conditions of service of any police force:

Provided that where a person was a member of a trade union before becoming a member of a police force, he may, with the consent of the chief officer of police, continue to be a member of that union during the time of his service in the police force.

(2) If any question arises whether any body is a trade union or an association to which this section applies, the question shall be determined by the chief registrar of friendly societies.

(3) This section applies to police cadets as it applies to members of a police force, and references to a police force or to service in a police force shall be construed accordingly.

(4) Nothing in this section applies to membership of the Police Federations, or of any body recognised by the Secretary of State for the purposes of this section as representing members of police forces who are not members of those Federations.

PART IV
MISCELLANEOUS AND GENERAL

Remedies and complaints against police

48 Liability for wrongful acts of constables

(1) The chief officer of police for any police area shall be liable in respect of torts committed by constables under his direction and control in the performance or purported performance of their functions in like manner as a master is liable in respect of torts committed by his servants in the course of their employment, and accordingly shall in respect of any such tort be treated for all purposes as a joint tortfeasor.

(2) There shall be paid out of the police fund—

(a) any damages or costs awarded against the chief officer of police in any proceedings brought against him by virtue of this section and any costs incurred by him in any such proceedings so far as not recovered by him in the proceedings; and

(b) any sum required in connection with the settlement of any claim made against the chief officer of police by virtue of this section, if the settlement is approved by the police authority.

(3) Any proceedings in respect of a claim made by virtue of this section shall be brought against the chief officer of police for the time being or, in the case of a vacancy in that office, against the person for the time being performing the functions of the chief officer of police; and references in the foregoing provisions of this section to the chief officer of police shall be construed accordingly.

(4) A police authority may, in such cases and to such extent as they think fit, pay any damages or costs awarded against a member of the police force maintained by them, or any constable for the time being required to serve with that force by virtue of section 14 of this Act, or any special constable appointed for their area, in proceedings for a tort committed by him, any costs incurred and not recovered by him in any such proceedings, and any sum required in connection with the settlement of any claim that has or might have given rise to such proceedings; and any sum required for making a payment under this subsection shall be paid out of the police fund.

49, 50 . . .

Offences

51 Assaults on constables

(1) Any person who assaults a constable in the execution of his duty, or a person assisting a constable in the execution of his duty, shall be guilty of an offence and liable [on summary conviction to imprisonment for a term not exceeding six months or to a fine not exceeding [level 5 on the standard scale] or to both].

(2) Subsection (2) of section 23 of the Firearms Act 1937 (additional penalty for possession of firearms when committing certain offences) shall apply to offences under subsection (1) of this section.

(3) Any person who resists or wilfully obstructs a constable in the execution of his duty, or a person assisting a constable in the execution of his duty, shall be guilty of an offence and liable on summary conviction to imprisonment for a term not exceeding one month or to a fine not exceeding [level 3 on the standard scale], or to both.

52 * * * * *

53 Causing disaffection

(1) Any person who causes, or attempts to cause, or does any act calculated to cause, disaffection amongst the members of any police force, or induces or attempts to induce, or does any act calculated to induce, any member of a police force to withhold his services or to commit breaches of discipline, shall be guilty of an offence and liable—

(a) on summary conviction, to imprisonment for a term not exceeding six months or to a fine not exceeding [the prescribed sum], or to both;

(b) on conviction on indictment, to imprisonment for a term not exceeding two years or to a fine or to both.

(2) This section applies to special constables appointed for a police area as it applies to members of a police force.

* * * * *

Section 18

SCHEDULE 2
FORM OF DECLARATION

I, ... of .. .. do solemnly and sincerely declare and affirm that I will well and truly serve Our Sovereign Lady the Queen in the office of constable, without favour or affection, malice or ill will; and that I will to the best of my power cause the peace to be kept and preserved, and prevent all offences against the persons and properties of Her Majesty's subjects; and that while I continue to hold the said office I will to the best of my skill and knowledge discharge all the duties thereof faithfully according to law.

* * * * *

WAR DAMAGE ACT 1965
(1965, c. 18)

An Act to abolish rights at common law to compensation in respect of damage to, or destruction of, property effected by, or on the authority of, the Crown during, or in contemplation of the outbreak of, war [2 June 1965]

Territorial extent United Kingdom

1 Abolition of rights at common law to compensation for certain damage to, or destruction of, property

(1) No person shall be entitled at common law to receive from the Crown compensation in respect of damage to, or destruction of, property caused (whether before or after the passing of this Act, within or outside the United Kingdom) by acts lawfully done by, or on the authority of, the Crown during, or in contemplation of the outbreak of, a war in which the Sovereign was, or is, engaged.

(2) Where any proceedings to recover at common law compensation in respect of such damage or destruction have been instituted before the passing of this Act, the court shall, on the application of any party, forthwith set aside or dismiss the proceedings, subject only to the determination of any question arising as to costs or expenses.

CRIMINAL LAW ACT 1967
(1967, c. 58)

An Act to amend the law of England and Wales by abolishing the division of crimes into felonies and misdemeanours and to amend and simplify the law in respect of matters arising from or related to that division or the abolition of it; to do away (within or without England and Wales) with certain obsolete crimes together with the torts of maintenance and champerty; and for purposes connected therewith [21 July 1967]

Territorial extent England and Wales

PART I
FELONY AND MISDEMEANOUR

1 * * * * *

2 . . . (Repealed by the Police and Criminal Evidence Act 1984)

3 Use of force in making arrest, etc.

(1) A person may use such force as is reasonable in the circumstances in the prevention of crime, or in effecting or assisting in the lawful arrest of offenders or suspected offenders or of persons unlawfully at large.

(2) Subsection (1) above shall replace the rules of the common law on the question when force used for a purpose mentioned in the subsection is justified by that purpose.

* * * * *

FUGITIVE OFFENDERS ACT 1967
(1967, c. 68)

An Act to make fresh provision for the return from the United Kingdom to other Commonwealth countries and United Kingdom dependencies of persons accused or convicted of offences in those countries and dependencies; to regulate the treatment of persons accused or convicted of offences in the United Kingdom who are returned from such countries and dependencies; to authorise the making of corresponding provisions for United Kingdom dependencies, including provisions for the return from such dependencies of persons accused or convicted in the Republic of Ireland; and for purposes connected with the matters aforesaid [27 July 1967]

Territorial extent United Kingdom

Return of offenders to Commonwealth countries and United Kingdom dependencies

1 Persons liable to be returned

Subject to the provisions of this Act, a person found in the United Kingdom who is accused of a relevant offence in any other country being—

(a) a Commonwealth country designated for the purposes of this section under subsection (1) of section 2 of this Act; or

(b) a United Kingdom dependency as defined by subsection (2) of that section, or who is alleged to be unlawfully at large after conviction of such an offence in any such country, may be arrested and returned to that country as provided by this Act.

2 Designated Commonwealth countries and United Kingdom dependencies

(1) Her Majesty may by Order in Council designate for the purposes of section 1 of this Act any country for the time being mentioned in [Schedule 3 to the British Nationality Act 1981] (countries having separate citizenship), or any other country within the Commonwealth; and any country so designated is in this Act referred to as a designated Commonwealth country.

(2)-(6) * * * * *

3 Relevant offences

(1) For the purposes of this Act an offence of which a person is accused or has been convicted in a designated Commonwealth country or United Kingdom dependency is a relevant offence if—

(a) in the case of an offence against the law of a designated Commonwealth country, it is an offence which, however described in that law, falls within any of the descriptions set out in Schedule 1 to this Act, and is punishable under that law with imprisonment for a term of twelve months or any greater punishment;

(b) in the case of an offence against the law of a United Kingdom dependency, it is punishable under that law, on conviction by or before a superior court, with imprisonment for a term of twelve months or any greater punishment; and

(c) in any case, the act or omission constituting the offence, or the equivalent act or omission, would constitute an offence against the law of the United Kingdom if it took place within the United Kingdom or, in the case of an extra-territorial offence, in corresponding circumstances outside the United Kingdom.

(2)-(4) * * * * *

4 General restrictions on return

(1) A person shall not be returned under this Act to a designated Commonwealth country, or committed to or kept in custody for the purposes of such return, if it appears to the Secretary of State, to the court of committal or to the High Court or High Court of Justiciary on an application for habeas corpus or for review of the order of committal—

(a) that the offence of which that person is accused or was convicted is an offence of a political character;

(b) that the request for his return (though purporting to be made on account of a relevant offence) is in fact made for the purpose of prosecuting or punishing him on account of his race, religion, nationality or political opinions; or

(c) that he might, if returned, be prejudiced at his trial or punished, detained or restricted in his personal liberty by reason of his race, religion, nationality or political opinions.

(2) A person accused of an offence shall not be returned under this Act to any country, or committed to or kept in custody for the purposes of such return, if it appears as aforesaid that if charged with that offence in the United Kingdom he would be entitled to be discharged under any rule of law relating to previous acquittal or conviction.

(3) A person shall not be returned under this Act to any country, or committed to or kept in custody for the purposes of such return, unless provision is made by the law of that country, or by an arrangement made with that country, for securing that he will not, unless he has first been restored or had an opportunity of returning to the United Kingdom, be dealt with in that country for or in respect of any offence committed before his return under this Act other than—

(a) the offence in respect of which his return under this Act is requested;

(b) any lesser offence proved by the facts proved before the court of committal; or

(c) any other offence being a relevant offence in respect of which the Secretary of State may consent to his being so dealt with.

(4) Any such arrangement as is mentioned in subsection (3) of this section may be an arrangement made for the particular case or an arrangement of a more general nature; and for the purposes of that subsection a certificate issued by or under the authority of the Secretary of State confirming that existence of an arrangement with any country and stating its terms shall be conclusive evidence of the matters contained in the certificate.

(5) The reference in this section to an offence of a political character does not include an offence against the life or person of the Head of the Commonwealth or any related offence described in subsection (3) of section 3 of this Act.

4A, 5-7 * * * * *

Proceedings for return

8 Application for habeas corpus etc.

(1) Where a person is committed to custody under section 7 of this Act, the court shall inform him in ordinary language of his right to make an application for habeas corpus or to apply to the High Court of Justiciary for review of the order of committal, and shall forthwith give notice of the committal to the Secretary of State.

(2) A person committed to custody under the said section 7 shall not be returned under this Act—

(a) in any case, until the expiration of the period of fifteen days beginning with the day on which the order for his committal is made;

(b) if an application for habeas corpus, or an application to the High Court of Justiciary for review of the order of committal, is made in his case, so long as proceedings on that application are pending.

(3) On any such application the High Court or High Court of Justiciary may, without prejudice to any other jurisdiction of the court, order the person committed to be discharged from custody if it appears to the court that—

(a) by reason of the trivial nature of the offence of which he is accused or was convicted; or

(b) by reason of the passage of time since he is alleged to have committed it or to have become unlawfully at large, as the case may be; or

(c) because the accusation against him is not made in good faith in the interests of justice,

it would, having regard to all the circumstances, be unjust or oppressive to return him.

(4) On any such application the High Court or the High Court of Justiciary may receive additional evidence relevant to the exercise of their jurisdiction under section 4 of this Act or under subsection (3) of this section.

(5) * * * * *

9 Order for return to requesting country

(1) Where a person is committed to await his return and is not discharged by order of the High Court or the High Court of Justiciary, the Secretary of State may by warrant order him to be returned to the country by which the request for his return was made unless the return of that person is prohibited, or prohibited for the time being, by section 4 of this Act or this section, or the Secretary of State decides under this section to make no such order in his case.

(2) An order shall not be made under this section in the case of a person who is serving a sentence of imprisonment or detention, or is charged with an offence, in the United Kingdom—

(a) in the case of a person serving such a sentence, until the sentence has been served;

(b) in the case of a person charged with an offence, until the charge is disposed of or withdrawn and, if it results in a sentence of imprisonment (not being a suspended sentence), until the sentence has been served.

(3) The Secretary of State shall not make an order under this section in the case of any person if it appears to the Secretary of State, on the grounds mentioned in subsection (3) of section 8 of this Act; that it would be unjust or oppressive to return that person, and may decide to make no order under this section in the case of a person accused or convicted of an offence in a United Kingdom dependency if he considers, on any such grounds as are mentioned in paragraphs (a) to (c) of subsection (1) of section 4 of this Act, that the order ought not to be made.

(4) The Secretary of State may decide to make no order under this section in the case of a person accused or convicted of a relevant offence not punishable with death in Great Britain if that person could be or has been sentenced to death for that offence in the country by which the request for his return is made.

(5), (6) * * * * *

* * * * *

Treatment of persons returned from Commonwealth countries and United Kingdom dependencies

14 Restriction upon proceedings for other offences

(1) This section applies to any person accused or convicted of an offence under the law of any part of the United Kingdom who is returned to the United Kingdom—

(a) from any designated Commonwealth country, under any law of that country corresponding with this Act;

(b) from any United Kingdom dependency, under this Act as extended to that dependency or under any corresponding law of that dependency.

(2) A person to whom this section applies shall not, during the period described in subsection (3) of this section, be dealt with in the United Kingdom for or in respect of any offence committed before he has returned to the United Kingdom other than—

(a) the offence in respect of which he was returned;

(b) any lesser offence proved by the facts proved for the purposes of securing his return; or

(c) any other offence in respect of which the Government of the country or Governor of the Dependency from which he was returned may consent to his being dealt with.

(3) The period referred to in subsection (2) of this section in relation to a person to whom this section applies is the period beginning with the day of his arrival in the United Kingdom on his return as mentioned in subsection (1) of this section and ending forty-five days after the first subsequent day on which he has the opportunity to leave the United Kingdom.

*****

Section 3

SCHEDULE 1
DESCRIPTION OF RELEVANT OFFENCES IN DESIGNATED COMMONWEALTH COUNTRIES

1. Murder of any degree.
2. Manslaughter or culpable homicide.
3. An offence against the law relating to abortion.
4. Maliciously or wilfully wounding or inflicting grievous bodily harm.
5. Assault occasioning actual bodily harm.
6. Rape.
7. Unlawful sexual intercourse with a female.
8. Indecent assault.
9. Procuring, or trafficking in, women or young persons for immoral purposes.
10. Bigamy.
11. Kidnapping, abduction or false imprisonment, or dealing in slaves.
12. Stealing, abandoning, exposing or unlawfully detaining a child.
13. Bribery.
14. Perjury or subornation of perjury or conspiring to defeat the course of justice.
15. Arson or fire-raising.
16. An offence concerning counterfeit currency.
17. An offence against the law relating to forgery.
18. Stealing, embezzlement, fraudulent conversion, fraudulent false accounting, obtaining property or credit by false pretences, receiving stolen property or any other offence in respect of property involving fraud.
19. Burglary, housebreaking or any similar offence.
20. Robbery.
21. Blackmail or extortion by means of threats or by abuse of authority.
22. An offence against bankruptcy law or company law.
23. Malicious or wilful damage to property.
24. Acts done with the intention of endangering vehicles, vessels or aircraft.
25. An offence against the law relating to dangerous drugs or narcotics.
26. Piracy.

27. Revolt against the authority of the master of a ship or the commander of an aircraft.

28. Contravention of import or export prohibitions relating to precious stones, gold and other precious metals.

Note Other offences have been brought within the ambit of this schedule by later Acts; for a full list see 17 *Halsbury's Statutes* (4th ed.) 536.

*****

PARLIAMENTARY COMMISSIONER ACT 1967
(1967, c. 13)

An Act to make provision for the appointment and functions of a Parliamentary Commissioner for the investigation of administrative action taken on behalf of the Crown, and for purposes connected therewith [22 March 1967]

Territorial extent United Kingdom

Note This Act is printed as extensively amended by the Parliamentary and Health Service Commissioners Act 1987.

The Parliamentary Commissioner for Administration

1 Appointment and tenure of office

(1) For the purpose of conducting investigations in accordance with the following provisions of this Act there shall be appointed a Commissioner, to be known as the Parliamentary Commissioner for Administration.

(2) Her Majesty may by Letters Patent from time to time appoint a person to be the Commissioner, and any person so appointed shall (subject to [subsections (3) and (3A)] of this section) hold office during good behaviour.

(3) A person appointed to be the Commissioner may be relieved of office by Her Majesty at his own request, or may be removed from office by Her Majesty in consequence of Addresses from both Houses of Parliament, and shall in any case vacate office on completing the year of service in which he attains the age of sixty-five years.

[(3A) Her Majesty may declare the office of Commissioner to have been vacated if satisfied that the person appointed to be the Commissioner is incapable for medical reasons—

(a) of performing the duties of his office; and

(b) of requesting to be relieved of it.]

(4), (5) . . .

2 *****

3 Administrative provisions

(1) The Commissioner may appoint such officers as he may determine with the approval of the Treasury as to numbers and conditions of service.

(2), (3) . . .

3A *****

[4 Departments etc. subject to investigation

(1) Subject to the provisions of this section and to the notes contained in Schedule 2 to this Act, this Act applies to the government departments, corporations and unincorporated bodies listed in that Schedule; and references in this Act to an authority to which this Act applies are references to any such corporation or body.

(2) Her Majesty may by Order in Council amend Schedule 2 to this Act by the alteration of any entry or note, the removal of any entry or note or the insertion of any additional entry or note.

(3) An Order in Council may only insert an entry if—

(a) it relates—

(i) to a government department; or

(ii) to a corporation or body whose functions are exercised on behalf of the Crown; or

(b) it relates to a corporation or body—

(i) which is established by virtue of Her Majesty's prerogative or by an Act of Parliament or an Order in Council or order made under an Act of Parliament or which is established in any other way by a Minister of the Crown in his capacity as a Minister or by a government department;

(ii) at least half of whose revenues derive directly from money provided by Parliament, a levy authorised by an enactment, a fee or charge of any other description so authorised or more than one of those sources; and

(iii) which is wholly or partly constituted by appointment made by Her Majesty or a Minister of the Crown or government department.

(4) No entry shall be made in respect of a corporation or body whose sole activity is, or whose main activities are, included among the activities specified in subsection (5) below.

(5) The activities mentioned in subsection (4) above are—

(a) the provision of education, or the provision of training otherwise than under the Industrial Training Act 1982;

(b) the development of curricula, the conduct of examinations or the validation of educational courses;

(c) the control of entry to any profession or the regulation of the conduct of members of any profession;

(d) the investigation of complaints by members of the public regarding the actions of any person or body, or the supervision or review of such investigations or of steps taken following them.

(6) No entry shall be made in respect of a corporation or body operating in an exclusively or predominantly commercial manner or a corporation carrying on under national ownership an industry or undertaking or part of an industry or undertaking.

(7) Any statutory instrument made by virtue of this section shall be subject to annulment in pursuance of a resolution of either House of Parliament.

(8) * * * * *

5 Matters subject to investigation

(1) Subject to the provisions of this section, the Commissioner may investigate any action taken by or on behalf of a government department or other authority to which this Act applies, being action taken in the exercise of administrative functions of that department or authority, in any case where—

(a) a written complaint is duly made to a member of the House of Commons by a member of the public who claims to have sustained injustice in consequence of maladministration in connection with the action so taken; and

(b) the complaint is referred to the Commissioner, with the consent of the person who made it, by a member of that House with a request to conduct an investigation thereon.

(2) Except as hereinafter provided, the Commissioner shall not conduct an investigation under this Act in respect of any of the following matters, that is to say—

(a) any action in respect of which the person aggrieved has or had a right of appeal, reference or review to or before a tribunal constituted by or under any enactment or by virtue of Her Majesty's prerogative;

(b) any action in respect of which the person aggrieved has or had a remedy by way of proceedings in any court of law:

Provided that the Commissioner may conduct an investigation notwithstanding that the person aggrieved has or had such a right or remedy if satisfied that in the particular circumstances it is not reasonable to expect him to resort or have resorted to it.

(3) Without prejudice to subsection (2) of this section, the Commisioner shall not conduct an investigation under this Act in respect of any such action or matter as is described in Schedule 3 to this Act.

(4) Her Majesty may by Order in Council amend the said Schedule 3 so as to exclude from the provisions of that Schedule such actions or matters as may be described in the Order; and any statutory instrument made by virtue of this subsection shall be subject to annulment in pursuance of a resolution of either House of Parliament.

(5) In determining whether to initiate, continue or discontinue an investigation under this Act, the Commissioner shall, subject to the foregoing provisions of this section, act in accordance with his own discretion; and any question whether a complaint is duly made under this Act shall be determined by the Commissioner.

6 Provisions relating to complaints

(1) A complaint under this Act may be made by any individual, or by any body of persons whether incorporated or not, not being—

(a) a local authority or other authority or body constituted for purposes of the public service or of local government or for the purposes of carrying on under national ownership any industry or undertaking or part of an industry or undertaking;

(b) any other authority or body whose members are appointed by Her Majesty or any Minister of the Crown or government department, or whose revenues consist wholly or mainly of moneys provided by Parliament.

(2) Where the person by whom a complaint might have been made under the foregoing provisions of this Act has died or is for any reason unable to act for himself, the complaint may be made by his personal representative or by a member of his family or other individual suitable to represent him; but except as aforesaid a complaint shall not be entertained under this Act unless made by the person aggrieved himself.

(3) A complaint shall not be entertained under this Act unless it is made to a member of the House of Commons not later than twelve months from the day on which the person aggrieved first had notice of the matters alleged in the complaint; but the Commissioner may conduct an investigation pursuant to a complaint not made within that period if he considers that there are special circumstances which make it proper to do so.

(4) [Except as provided in subsection (5) below] a complaint shall not be entertained under this Act unless the person aggrieved is resident in the United Kingdom (or, if he is dead, was so resident at the time of his death) or the complaint relates to action taken in relation to him while he was present in the United Kingdom or on an installation in a designated area within the meaning of the Continental Shelf Act 1964 or on a ship registered in the United Kingdom or an aircraft so registered, or in relation to rights or obligations which accrued or arose in the United Kingdom or on such an installation, ship or aircraft.

[(5) A complaint may be entertained under this Act in circumstances not falling within subsection (4) above where—

(a) the complaint relates to action taken in any country or territory outside the United Kingdom by an officer (not being an honorary consular officer) in the exercise of a consular function on behalf of the Government of the United Kingdom; and

(b) the person aggrieved is a citizen of the United Kingdom and Colonies who, under section 2 of the Immigration Act 1971, has the right of abode in the United Kingdom.]

7 Procedure in respect of investigations

(1) Where the Commissioner proposes to conduct an investigation pursuant to a complaint under this Act, he shall afford to the principal officer of the department or

authority concerned, and to any person who is alleged in the complaint to have taken or authorised the action complained of, an opportunity to comment on any allegations contained in the complaint.

(2) Every such investigation shall be conducted in private, but except as aforesaid the procedure for conducting an investigation shall be such as the Commissioner considers appropriate in the circumstances of the case; and without prejudice to the generality of the foregoing provision the Commissioner may obtain information from such persons and in such manner, and make such inquiries, as he thinks fit, and may determine whether any person may be represented, by counsel or solicitor or otherwise, in the investigation.

(3), (4) * * * * *

8 Evidence

(1) For the purposes of an investigation under this Act the Commissioner may require any Minister, officer or member of the department or authority concerned or any other person who in his opinion is able to furnish information or produce documents relevant to the investigation to furnish any such information or produce any such document.

(2) For the purposes of any such investigation the Commissioner shall have the same powers as the Court in respect of the attendance and examination of witnesses (including the administration of oaths or affirmations and the examination of witnesses abroad) and in respect of the production of documents.

(3) No obligation to maintain secrecy or other restriction upon the disclosure of information obtained by or furnished to persons in Her Majesty's service, whether imposed by any enactment or by any rule of law, shall apply to the disclosure of information for the purposes of an investigation under this Act; and the Crown shall not be entitled in relation to any such investigation to any such privilege in respect of the production of documents or the giving of evidence as is allowed by law in legal proceedings.

(4) No person shall be required or authorised by virtue of this Act to furnish any information or answer any question relating to proceedings of the Cabinet or of any committee of the Cabinet or to produce so much of any document as relates to such proceedings; and for the purposes of this subsection a certificate issued by the Secretary of the Cabinet with the approval of the Prime Minister and certifying that any information, question, document or part of a document so relates shall be conclusive.

(5) * * * * *

9 Obstruction and contempt

(1) If any person without lawful excuse obstructs the Commissioner or any officer of the Commissioner in the performance of his functions under this Act, or is guilty of any act or omission in relation to any investigation under this Act which, if that investigation were a proceeding in the Court, would constitute contempt of court, the Commissioner may certify the offence to the Court.

(2) Where an offence is certified under this section, the Court may inquire into the matter and, after hearing any witnesses who may be produced against or on behalf of the person charged with the offence, and after hearing any statement that may be offered in defence, deal with him in any manner in which the court could deal with him if he had committed the like offence in relation to the Court.

(3) * * * * *

10 Reports by Commissioner

(1) In any case where the Commissioner conducts an investigation under this Act or decides not to conduct such an investigation, he shall send to the member of the House of Commons by whom the request for investigation was made (or if he is no longer a member of that House, to such member of that House as the Commissioner thinks appropriate) a report of the results of the investigation or, as the case may be, a statement of his reasons for not conducting an investigation.

(2) In any case where the Commissioner conducts an investigation under this Act, he shall also send a report of the results of the investigation to the principal officer of the department or authority concerned and to any other person who is alleged in the relevant complaint to have taken or authorised the action complained of.

(3) If, after conducting an investigation under this Act, it appears to the Commissioner that injustice has been caused to the person aggrieved in consequence of maladministration and that the injustice has not been, or will not be, remedied, he may, if he thinks fit, lay before each House of Parliament a special report upon the case.

(4) The Commissioner shall annually lay before each House of Parliament a general report on the performance of his functions under this Act and may from time to time lay before each House of Parliament such other reports with respect to those functions as he thinks fit.

(5) * * * * *

11 Provision for secrecy of information

(1) It is hereby declared that the Commissioner and his officers hold office under Her Majesty within the meaning of the Official Secrets Act 1911.

(2)-(4) * * * * *

11A * * * * *

Supplemental

12 Interpretation

(1), (2) * * * * *

(3) It is hereby declared that nothing in this Act authorises or requires the Commissioner to question the merits of a decision taken without maladministration by a government department or other authority in the exercise of a discretion vested in that department or authority.

13, 14 * * * * *

Section 3

SCHEDULE 2

DEPARTMENTS ETC. SUBJECT TO INVESTIGATION

Advisory, Conciliation and Arbitration Service.
Agricultural wages committee.
Ministry of Agriculture, Fisheries and Food.
Arts Council of Great Britain.
British Council.
British Library Board.
Building Societies Commission.
Certification Officer.
Charity Commission.
Civil Service Commission.
Co-operative Development Agency.
Countryside Commission.
Countryside Commission for Scotland.
Craft Council.
Crofters Commission.
Crown Estate Office.
Customs and Excise.
Data Protection Registrar.
Ministry of Defence.
Development Commission.
Department of Education and Science.

Central Bureau for Educational Visits and Exchanges.
Department of Employment.
Department of Energy.
Department of the Environment.
Equal Opportunities Commission.
Export Credits Guarantee Department.
Office of the Director General of Fair Trading.
British Film Institute.
Foreign and Commonwealth Office.
Forestry Commission.
Registry of Friendly Societies.
Office of the Director General of Gas Supply.
Health and Safety Commission.
Health and Safety Executive.
Department of Health and Social Security.
Highlands and Islands Development Board.
Historic Buildings and Monuments Commission for England.
Home Office.
Horserace Betting Levy Board.
Housing Corporation.
Central Office of Information.
Inland Revenue.
Intervention Board for Agricultural Produce.
Land Registry.
The following general lighthouse authorities—
(a) the Corporation of the Trinity House of Deptford Strond;
(b) the Commissioners of Northern Lighthouses.
The Lord Chancellor's Department.
Lord President of the Council's Office.
Management and Personnel Office.
Manpower Services Commission.
Medical Practices Committee.
Scottish Medical Practices Committee.
Museums and Galleries Commission.
National Debt Office.
Trustees of the National Heritage Memorial Fund.
Department for National Savings.
Nature Conservancy Council.
Commission for the New Towns.
Development corporations for new towns.
Northern Ireland Court Service.
Northern Ireland Office.
Ordnance Survey.
Office of Population Censuses and Surveys.
Registrar of Public Lending Right.
Public Record Office.
Scottish Record Office.
Commission for Racial Equality.
Red Deer Commission.
Department of the Registers of Scotland.
General Register Office, Scotland.
Agricultural and Food Research Council.
Economic and Social Research Council.

Medical Research Council.
Natural Environment Research Council.
Science and Engineering Research Council.
Residuary Bodies.
Royal Mint.
Scottish Courts Administration.
Scottish Office.
Council for Small Industries in Rural Areas.
Central Council for Education and Training in Social Work.
Sports Council.
Scottish Sports Council.
Sports Council for Wales.
Stationery Office.
Office of the Director General of Telecommunications.
English Tourist Board.
Scottish Tourist Board.
Wales Tourist Board.
Board of Trade.
Department of Trade and Industry.
Agricultural Training Board.
Clothing and Allied Products Industry Training Board.
Construction Industry Training Board.
Engineering Industry Training Board.
Hotel and Catering Industry Training Board.
Plastics Processing Industry Training Board.
Road Transport Industry Training Board.
Department of Transport.
Treasury.
Treasury Solicitor.
Urban development corporations.
Development Board for Rural Wales.
Welsh Office.

Note Schedule printed as substituted by the Parliamentary and Health Service Commissioners Act 1987,Sch. 1, with notes to the Schedule omitted. See *ibid*. for these notes.

Section 5

SCHEDULE 3
MATTERS NOT SUBJECT TO INVESTIGATION

1. Action taken in matters certified by a Secretary of State or other Minister of the Crown to affect relations or dealings between the Government of the United Kingdom and any other Government or any international organisation of States or Governments.

2. Action taken, in any country or territory outside the United Kingdom, by or on behalf of any officer representing or acting under the authority of Her Majesty in respect of the United Kingdom, or any other officer of the Government of the United Kingdom [other than action which is taken by an officer (not being an honorary consular officer) in the exercise of a consular function on behalf of the Government of the United Kingdom and which is so taken in relation to a citizen of the United Kingdom and Colonies who has the right of abode in the United Kingdom].

3. Action taken in connection with the administration of the goverment of any country or territory outside the United Kingdom which forms part of Her Majesty's dominions or in which Her Majesty has jurisdiction.

4. Action taken by the Secretary of State under the Extradition Act 1870 or the Fugitive Offenders Act 1881.

5. Action taken by or with the authority of the Secretary of State for the purposes of investigating crime or of protecting the security of the State, including action so taken with respect to passports.

6. The commencement or conduct of civil or criminal proceedings before any court of law in the United Kingdom, of proceedings at any place under the Naval Discipline Act 1957, the Army Act 1955 or the Air Force Act 1955, or of proceedings before any international court or tribunal.

7. Any exercise of the prerogative of mercy or of the power of a Secretary of State to make a reference in respect of any person to the Court of Appeal, the High Court of Justiciary or the Courts-Martial Appeal Court.

8. Action taken on behalf of the Minister of Health or the Secretary of State by a [Regional Health Authority, an Area Health Authority, [a District Health Authority], a special health authority, [except the [Rampton Hospital board], [the Broadmoor Hospital Board and the Moss Side and Park Lane Hospitals Board]] a Family Practitioner Comittee, [a Health Board or the Common Services Agency for the Scottish Health Service], or by the Public Health Laboratory Service Board.

9. Action taken in matters relating to contractual or other commercial transactions, whether within the United Kingdom or elsewhere, being transactions of a government department or authority to which this Act applies or of any such authority or body as is mentioned in paragraph (a) or (b) of subsection (1) of section 6 of this Act and not being transactions for or relating to—

(a) the acquisition of land compulsorily or in circumstances in which it could be acquired compulsorily;

(b) the disposal as surplus of land acquired compulsorily or in such circumstances as aforesaid.

10. (1) Action taken in respect of appointments or removals, pay, discipline, superannuation or other personnel matters, in relation to—

(a) service in any of the armed forces of the Crown, including reserve and auxiliary and cadet forces;

(b) service in any office or employment under the Crown or under any authority [(to which this Act applies)]; or

(c) service in any office or employment, or under any contract for services, in respect of which power to take action, or to determine or approve the action to be taken, in such matters is vested in Her Majesty, any Minister of the Crown or any such authority as aforesaid.

[(2) Sub-paragraph (1)(c) above shall not apply to any action (not otherwise excluded from investigation by this Schedule) which is taken by the Secretary of State in connection with—

(a) the provision of information relating to the terms and conditions of any employment covered by an agreement entered into by him under section 12(1) of the Overseas Development and Cooperation Act 1980 or

(b) the provision of any allowance, grant or supplement or any benefit (other than those relating to superannuation) arising from the designation of any person in accordance with such an agreement.]

11. The grant of honours, awards or privileges within the gift of the Crown, including the grant of Royal Charters.

FIREARMS ACT 1968
(1968, c. 27)

An Act to consolidate the Firearms Acts 1937 and 1965, the Air Guns and Shot Guns, etc, Act 1962, Part V of the Criminal Justice Act 1967 and certain enactments amending the Firearms Act 1937

[30 May 1968]

Territorial extent England and Wales, Scotland

*****

PART III
LAW ENFORCEMENT AND PUNISHMENT OF OFFENCES

46 Power of search with warrant

(1) If a justice of the peace or, in Scotland, the sheriff or any magistrate (by whatever name called) officiating under the provisions of a general or local Police Act, is satisfied by information on oath that there is reasonable ground for suspecting that an offence relevant for the purposes of this section has been, is being, or is about to be committed, he may grant a search warrant authorising a constable . . .

(a) to enter at any time any premises or place named in the warrant, if necessary by force, and to search the premises or place and every person found there;

(b) to seize and detain any firearm or ammunition which he may find on the premises or place, or on any such person, in respect of which or in connection with which he has reasonable ground for suspecting that an offence relevant for the purposes of this section has been, is being or is about to be committed; and

(c) if the premises are those of a registered firearms dealer, to examine any books relating to the business.

(2) The offences relevant for the purposes of this section are all offences under this Act except an offence under section 22(3) or an offence relating specifically to air weapons.

47 Powers of constables to stop and search

(1) A constable may require any person whom he has reasonable cause to suspect—

(a) of having a firearm, with or without ammunition, with him in a public place; or

(b) to be committing or about to commit, elsewhere than in a public place, an offence relevant for the purposes of this section,

to hand over the firearm or any ammunition for examination by the constable.

(2) It is an offence for a person having a firearm or ammunition with him to fail to hand it over when required to do so by a constable under subsection (1) of this section.

(3) If a constable has reasonable cause to suspect a person of having a firearm with him in a public place, or to be committing or about to commit, elsewhere than in a public place, an offence relevant for the purposes of this section, the constable may search that person and may detain him for the purpose of doing so.

(4) If a constable has reasonable cause to suspect that there is a firearm in a vehicle in a public place, or that a vehicle is being or is about to be used in connection with the commission of an offence relevant for the purposes of this section elsewhere than in a public place, he may search the vehicle and for that purpose require the person driving or in control of it to stop it.

(5) For the purpose of exercising the powers conferred by this section a constable may enter any place.

(6) The offences relevant for the purpose of his section are those under sections 18(1) and (2) and 20 of this Act.

48 Production of certificates

(1) A constable may demand, from any person whom he believes to be in possession of a firearm or ammunition to which section 1 of this Act applies, or of a shot gun, the production of his firearm certificate or, as the case may be, his shot gun certificate.

(2) If a person upon whom a demand is made under this section fails to produce the certificate or to permit the constable to read it, or to show that he is entitled by virtue of this Act to have the firearm, ammunition or shot gun in his possession without holding a certificate, the constable may seize and detain the firearm, ammunition or shot gun and may require the person to declare to him immediately his name and address.

(3) If under this section a person is required to declare to a constable his name and address, it is an offence for him to refuse to declare it or to fail to give his true name and address.

* * * * *

THEATRES ACT 1968
(1968, c. 54)

An Act to abolish censorship of the theatre and to amend the law in respect of theatres and theatrical performances [26 July 1968]

Territorial extent England and Wales, Scotland

Abolition of censorship of the theatre

1 Abolition of censorship of the theatre

(1) The Theatres Act 1843 is hereby repealed; and none of the powers which were exercisable thereunder by the Lord Chamberlain of Her Majesty's Household shall be exercisable by or on behalf of Her Majestyby virtue of Her royal prerogative.

(2) In granting, renewing or transferring any licence under this Act for the use of any premises for the public performance of plays or in varying any of the terms, conditions or restrictions on or subject to which any such licence is held, the licensing authority shall not have power to impose any term, condition or restriction as to the nature of the plays which may be performed under the licence or as to the manner of performing plays thereunder:

Provided that nothing in this subsection shall prevent a licensing authority from imposing any term, condition or restriction which they consider necessary in the interests of physical safety or health or any condition regulating or prohibiting the giving of an exhibition, demonstration or performance of hypnotism within the meaning of the Hypnotism Act 1952.

Provisions with respect to performances of plays

2 Prohibition of presentation of obscene performances of plays

(1) For the purposes of this section a performance of a play shall be deemed to be obscene if, taken as a whole, its effect was such as to tend to deprave and corrupt persons who were likely, having regard to all relevant circumstances, to attend it.

(2) Subject to sections 3 and 7 of this Act, if an obscene performance of a play is given, whether in public or private, any person who (whether for gain or not) presented or directed that performance shall be liable—

(a) on summary conviction, to a fine not exceeding [level 5 on the standard scale] or to imprisonment for a term not exceeding six months;

(b) on conviction on indictment, to a fine or to imprisonment for a term not exceeding three years, or both.

(3) A prosecution on indictment for an offence under this section shall not be commenced more than two years after the commission of the offence.

(4) No person shall be proceeded against in respect of a performance of a play or anything said or done in the course of such a performance—

(a) for an offence at common law where it is of the essence of the offence that the performance or, as the case may be, what was said or done was obscene, indecent, offensive, disgusting or injurious to morality;

. . .

and no person shall be proceeded against for an offence at common law of conspiring to corrupt public morals, or to do any act contrary to public morals or decency, in respect of an agreement to present or give a performance of a play, or to cause anything to be said or done in the course of such a performance.

3 Defence of public good

(1) A person shall not be convicted of an offence under section 2 of this Act if it is proved that the giving of the performance in question was justified as being for the public good on the ground that it was in the interests of drama, opera, ballet or any other art, or of literature or learning.

(2) It is hereby declared that the opinion of experts as to the artistic, literary or other merits of a performance of a play may be admitted in any proceedings for an offence under section 2 of this Act either to establish or negative the said ground.

4 Amendment of law of defamation

(1) For the purposes of the law of libel and slander (including the law of criminal libel so far as it relates to the publication of defamatory matter) the publication of words in the course of a performance of a play shall, subject to section 7 of this Act, be treated as publication in permanent form.

(2)-(4) * * * * *

5 . . . [Repealed by the Public Order Act 1986].

6 Provocation of breach of peace by means of public performance of a play

(1) Subject to section 7 of this Act, if there is given a public performance of a play involving the use of threatening, abusive or insulting words or behaviour, any person who (whether for gain or not) presented or directed that performance shall be guilty of an offence under this section if—

(a) he did so with intent to provoke a breach of the peace; or

(b) the performance, taken as a whole, was likely to occasion a breach of the peace.

(2) A person guilty of an offence under this section shall be liable [on summary conviction to a fine not exceeding [level 5 on the standard scale] or to imprisonment for a period not exceeding six months or both].

7 Exceptions for performances given in certain circumstances

(1) Nothing in sections 2 to 4 of this Act shall apply in relation to a performance of a play given on a domestic occasion in a private dwelling.

(2) Nothing in sections 2 to 6 of this Act shall apply in relation to a performance of a play given solely or primarily for one or more of the following purposes, that is to say—

(a) rehearsal; or

(b) to enable—

(i) a record or cinematograph film to be made from or by means of the performance; or

(ii) the performance to be broadcast; or

(iii) the performance to be [included in a cable programme service which is or does not require to be licensed];

but in any proceedings for an offence under section 2 . . . or 6 of this Act alleged to have been committd in respect of a performance of a play or an offence at common law alleged to have been committed in England and Wales by the publication of defamatory matter in the course of a performance of a play, if it is proved that the performance was attended by persons other than persons directly connected with the giving of the performance or the doing in relation thereto of any of the things mentioned in paragraph (b) above, the performance shall be taken not to have been solely or primarily for one or more of the said purposes unless the contrary is shown.

(3) * * * * *

8 Restriction on institution of proceedings

Proceedings for an offence under section 2 . . . or 6 of this Act or an offence at common law committed by the publication of defamatory matter in the course of a performance of a play shall not be instituted in England and Wales except by or with the consent of the Attorney-General.

9 Script as evidence of what was performed

(1) Where a performance of a play was based on a script, then, in any proceedings for an offence under section 2 . . . or 6 of this Act alleged to have been committed in respect of that performance—

(a) an actual script on which that performance was based shall be admissible as evidence of what was performed and of the manner in which the performance or any part of it was given; and

(b) if such a script is given in evidence on behalf of any party to the proceedings then, except in so far as the contrary is shown, whether by evidence given on behalf of the same or any other party, the performance shall be taken to have been given in accordance with that script.

(2) In this Act "script", in relation to a performance of a play, means the text of the play (whether expressed in words or in musical or other notation) together with any stage or other directions for its performance, whether contained in a single document or not.

* * * * *

FOREIGN COMPENSATION ACT 1969
(1969, c. 20)

An Act to make provision with respect to certain property (including the proceeds thereof and any income or other property accruing therefrom) of persons formerly resident or carrying on business in Estonia, Latvia, Lithuania or a part of Czechoslovakia, Finland, Poland or Rumania which has been ceded to the Union of Soviet Socialist Republics, and to amend the Foreign Compensation Act 1950 [16 May 1969]

Territorial extent United Kingdom

* * * * *

3 Determination of the Foreign Compensation Commission and appeals against such determinations

(1) The Foreign Compensation Commission shall have power to determine any question as to the construction or interpretation of any provision of an Order in Council under section 3 of the Foreign Compensation Act 1950 with respect to claims falling to be determined by them.

(2) Subject to subsection (4) below, the Commission shall, if so required by a person mentioned in subsection (6) below who is aggrieved by any determination of the Commission on any question of law relating to the jurisdiction of the Commission or on any question mentioned in subsection (1) above, state and sign a case for the decision of the Court of Appeal.

(3) In this section "determination" includes a determination which under rules under section 4(2) of the Foreign Compensation Act 1950 (rules of procedure) is a provisional determination, and anything which purports to be a determination.

(4) Where the Court of Appeal decide a question on a case stated and signed by the Commission on a provisional determination in any proceedings, subsection (2) above shall not require the Commission to state and sign a case on a final determination by them of that question in those proceedings.

(5) Any person mentioned in subsection (6) below may, with a view to requiring the Commission to state and sign a case under this section, request the Commission to furnish a written statement of the reasons for any determination of theirs, but the Commission shall not be obliged to state the reasons for any determination unless it is given on a claim in which a question mentioned in subsection (2) above arises.

(6) The person who may make a request under subsection (5) above or a requirement under subsection (2) above in relation to any claim are the claimant and any person appointed by the Commission to represent the interests of any fund out of which the claim would, if allowed, be met.

(7) * * * * *

(8) Notwithstanding anything in section 3 of the Appellate Jurisdiction Act 1876 (right of appeal to the House of Lords from decisions of the Court of Appeal), no appeal shall lie to the House of Lords from a decision of the Court of Appeal on an appeal under this section.

(9) Except as provided by subsection (2) above and subsection (10) below, no determination by the Commission on any claim made to them under the Foreign Compensation Act 1950 shall be called in question in any court of law.

(10) Subsection (9) above shall not affect any right of any person to bring proceedings questioning any determination of the Commission on the ground that it is contrary to natural justice.

(11) Subsection (2) to (10) above shall not apply to a determination of the Commission of which notice was sent by them before the passing of this Act.

(12) Section 4(4) of the Foreign Compensation Act 1950 (which makes provision corresponding to subsection (9) above) shall not apply to a determination of the Commission of which notice is sent by them after the passing of this Act.

* * * * *

GENOCIDE ACT 1969
(1969, c. 12)

An Act to give effect to the Convention on the Prevention and Punishment of the Crime of Genocide [27 March 1969]

Territorial extent United Kingdom

1 Genocide

(1) A person commits an offence of genocide if he commits any act falling within the definition of "genocide" in Article II of the Genocide Convention as set out in the Schedule to this Act.

(2) A person guilty of an offence of genocide shall on conviction on indictment—

(a) if the offence consists of the killing of any person, be sentenced to imprisonment for life;

(b) in any other case, be liable to imprisonment for a term not exceeding fourteen years.

(3) Proceedings for an offence of genocide shall not be instituted in England or Wales except by or with the consent of the Attorney General and shall not be instituted in Northern Ireland except by or with the consent of the Attorney General for Northern Ireland.

(4)-(7) . . .

2 Extradition and evidence for foreign courts

(1) There shall be deemed to be included—

(a) in the list of extradition crimes contained in Schedule 1 to the Extradition Act 1870; and

(b) among the descriptions of offences set out in Schedule 1 to the Fugitive Offenders Act 1967,

any offence of genocide and (so far as not so included by virtue of the foregoing) any . . . conspiracy to commit such an offence and any direct and public incitement to commit such an offence.

(2) *****

(3) It shall not be an objection to any proceedings taken against a person by virtue of the preceding provisions of this section that under the law in force at the time when and in the place where he is alleged to have committed the act of which he is accused or of which he was convicted he could not have been punished therefor.

TAXES MANAGEMENT ACT 1970
(1970, c. 9)

An Act to consolidate certain of the enactments relating to income tax, capital gains tax and corporation tax, including certain enactments relating also to other taxes [12 March 1970]

Territorial extent United Kingdom

Note The sections printed here were added by the Finance Act 1976, Sch. 6.

*****

20C Entry with warrant to obtain documents

(1) If the appropriate judicial authority is satisfied on information on oath given by an officer of the Board that—

(a) there is reasonable ground for suspecting that an offence involving any form of fraud in connection with, or in relation to, tax has been committed and that evidence of it is to be found on premises specified in the information; and

(b) in applying under this section, the officer acts with the approval of the Board given in relation to the particular case,

the authority may issue a warrant in writing authorising an officer of the Board to enter the premises, if necessary by force, at any time within 14 days from the time of issue of the warrant, and search them.

(2) Section 4A of the Inland Revenue Regulation Act 1890 (Board's functions to be exercisable by an officer acting under their authority) does not apply to the giving of Board approval under this section.

(3) On entering the premises with a warrant under this section, the officer may seize and remove any things whatsoever found there which he has reasonable cause to believe may be required as evidence for the purposes of proceedings in respect of such an offence as is mentioned in subsection (1) above.

But this does not authorise the seizure and removal of documents in the possession of a barrister, advocate or solicitor with respect to which a claim to professional privilege could be maintained.

(4) Where entry to premises has been made with a warrant under this section, and the officer making the entry has seized any things under the authority of the warrant, he shall, if so requested by a person showing himself either—

(a) to be the occupier of the premises; or

(b) to have had the possession or custody of those things immediately before the seizure,

provided that person with a list of them.

(5) Where documents are seized which relate to any business, and it is shown that access to them is required for the continued conduct of the business, the officer who has seized them shall afford reasonable access to the documents to the person carrying on the business.

20D Interpretation of ss. 20 to 20C

(1) For the purposes of section 20A and 20C above, "the appropriate judicial authority" is—

(a) in England and Wales, a Circuit judge;
(b) in Scotland, a Sheriff; and
(c) in Northern Ireland, a county court judge.

(2), (3) * * * * *

* * * * *

COURTS ACT 1971
(1971, c. 23)

An Act to make further provision as respects the Supreme Court and county courts, judges and juries, to establish a Crown Court as part of the Supreme Court to try indictments and exercise certain other jurisdiction, to abolish courts of assize and certain other courts and to deal with their jurisdiction and other consequential matters, and to amend in other respects the law about courts and court proceedings [12 May 1971]

Teritorial extent England and Wales

1-15 . . . [Repealed by the Supreme Court Act 1981].

PART III
JUDGES

16 Appointment of Circuit Judges

(1) Her Majesty may from time to time appoint as Circuit judges, to serve in the Crown Court and county courts and to carry out such other judicial functions as may be conferred on them under this or any other enactment, such qualified persons as may be recommended to Her by the Lord Chancellor.

(2) The maximum number of Circuit judges shall be such as may be determined from time to time by the Lord Chancellor with the concurrence of the Minister for the Civil Service.

(3) No person shall be qualified to be appointed a Circuit judge unless he is a barrister of at least ten years' standing or a Recorder who has held that office for at least [three] years.

(4) Before recommending any person to Her Majesty for appointment as a Circuit judge, the Lord Chancellor shall take steps to satisfy himself that that person's health is satisfactory.

(5) * * * * *

17 Retirement, removal and disqualifications of Circuit judges

(1) Subject to subsections (2) to (4) below, a Circuit judge shall vacate his office at the end of the completed year of service in which he attains the age of seventy-two.

(2) Where the Lord Chancellor considers it desirable in the public interest to retain a Circuit judge in office after the time at which he would otherwise retire in accordance with subsection (1) above, he may from time to time authorise the continuance in office of that judge until such date, not being later than the date on which the judge attains the age of seventy-five, as he thinks fit.

(3) For the purposes of subsection (1) above a person who becomes a Circuit judge by virtue of any provision of paragraph 1 of Schedule 2 to this Act shall be treated as completing a year of service on the anniversary of his appointment to the office by virtue of which he becomes a Circuit judge.

(4) The Lord Chancellor may, if he thinks fit, remove a Circuit judge from office on the ground of incapacity or misbehaviour.

(5) . . .

(6) So long as he holds office as such, no Circuit judge shall practise as a barrister, or act for any remuneration to himself as arbitrator or referee, or be directly or indirectly concerned as a conveyancer, notary public or solicitor.

* * * * *

IMMIGRATION ACT 1971
(1971, c. 77)

An Act to amend and replace the present immigration laws, to make certain related changes in the citizenship law and enable help to be given to those wishing to return abroad, and for purposes connected therewith [28 October 1971]

Teritorial extent United Kingdom

Note This Act is printed as extensively amended by the British Nationality Act 1981.

PART I
REGULATION OF ENTRY INTO AND STAY IN UNITED KINGDOM

1 General principles

(1) All those who are in this Act expressed to have the right of abode in the United Kingdom shall be free to live in, and to come and go into and from, the United Kingdom without let or hindrance except such as may be required under and in accordance with this Act to enable their right to be established or as may be otherwise lawfully imposed on any person.

(2) Those not having that right may live, work and settle in the United Kingdom by permission and subject to such regulation and control of their entry into, stay in and departure from the United Kingdom as is imposed by this Act; and indefinite leave to enter or remain in the United Kingdom shall, by virtue of this provision, be treated as having been given under this Act to those in the United Kingdom at its coming into force, if they are then settled there (and not exempt under this Act from the provisions relating to leave to enter or remain).

(3) Arrival in and departure from the United Kingdom on a local journey from or to any of the Islands (that is to say, the Channel Islands and Isle of Man) or the Republic of Ireland shall not be subject to control under this Act, nor shall a person require leave to enter the United Kingdom on so arriving, except in so far as any of those places is for any purpose excluded from this subsection under the powers conferred by this Act; and in this Act the United Kingdom and those places, or such of them as are not so excluded, are collectively referred to as "the common travel area".

(4) The rules laid down by the Secretary of State as to the practice to be followed in the administration of this Act for regulating the entry into and stay in the United Kingdom of persons not having the right of abode shall include provision for admitting (in such cases and subject to such restrictions as may be provided by the rules, and subject or not to conditions as to length of stay or otherwise) persons coming for the purpose of taking employment, or for purposes of study, or as visitors, or as dependants of persons lawfully in or entering the United Kingdom.

(5) The rules shall be so framed that Commonwealth citizens settled in the United Kingdom at the coming into force of this Act and their wives and children are not, by virtue of anything in the rules, any less free to come into and go from the United Kingdom than if this Act had not been passed.

[2 Statement of right of abode in United Kingdom

(1) A person is under this Act to have the right of abode in the United Kingdom if—

(a) he is a British citizen; or

(b) he is a Commonwealth citizen who—

(i) immediately before the commencement of the British Nationality Act 1981 was a Commonwealth citizen having the right of abode in the United Kingdom by virtue of section 2(1)(d) or section 2(2) of this Act as then in force; and

(ii) has not ceased to be a Commonwealth citizen in the meanwhile.

(2) In relation to Commonwealth citizens who have the right of abode in the United Kingdom by virtue of subsection (1)(b) above, this Act, except this section and sections 3(9) and (9A), 5(2) and 13(3), shall apply as if they were British citizens; and in this Act (except as aforesaid) "British citizen" shall be construed accordingly.]

Note Sections 2(1) and 2(2) as in force prior to the commencement of the 1981 Act provided as follows:

(1) A person is under this Act to have the right of abode in the United Kingdom if—

(a) he is a citizen of the United Kingdom and Colonies who has that citizenship by his birth, adoption, naturalisation or (except as mentioned below) registration in the United Kingdom or in any of the Islands; or

(b) he is a citizen of the United Kingdom and Colonies born to or legally adopted by a parent who had that citizenship at the time of the birth or adoption, and the parent either—

(i) then had that citizenship by his birth, adoption, naturalisation or (except as mentioned below) registration in the United Kingdom or in any of the Islands; or

(ii) had been born to or legally adopted by a parent who at the time of that birth or adoption so had it; or

(c) he is a citizen of the United Kingdom and Colonies who has at any time been settled in the United Kingdom and Islands and had at that time (and while such a citizen) been ordinarily resident there for the last five years or more; or

(d) he is a Commonwealth citizen born to or legally adopted by a parent who at the time of the birth or adoption had citizenship of the United Kingdom and Colonies by his birth in the United Kingdom or in any of the Islands.

(2) A woman is under this Act also to have the right of abode in the United Kingdom if she is a Commonwealth citizen and either—

(a) is the wife of any such citizen of the United Kingdom and Colonies as is mentioned in subsection (1)(a), (b) or (c) above or any such Commonwealth citizen as is mentioned in subsection (1)(d); or

(b) has at any time been the wife—

(i) of a person then being such a citizen of the United Kingdom and Colonies or Commonwealth citizen; or

(ii) of a British subject who but for his death would on the date of commencement of the British Nationality Act 1948 have been such a citizen of the United Kingdom and Colonies as is mentioned in subsection (1)(a) or (b);

but in subsection (1)(a) and (b) above references to registration as a citizen of the United Kingdom and Colonies shall not, in the case of a woman, include registration after the passing of this Act under or by virtue of section 6(2) (wives) of the British Nationality Act 1948 unless she is so registered by virtue of her marriage to a citizen of the United Kingdom and Colonies before the passing of this Act."

3 General provisions for regulation and control

(1) Except as otherwise provided by or under this Act, where a person is not [a British citizen]—

(a) he shall not enter the United Kingdom unless given leave to do so in accordance with this Act;

(b) he may be given leave to enter the United Kingdom (or, when already there, leave to remain in the United Kingdom) either for a limited or for an indefinite period;

(c) if he is given a limited leave to enter or remain in the United Kingdom, it may be given subject to conditions restricting his employment or occupation in the United Kingdom, or requiring him to register with the police, or both.

(2) The Secretary of State shall from time to time (and as soon as may be) lay before Parliament statements of the rules, or of any changes in the rules, laid down by him as to

the practice to be followed in the administration of this Act for regulating the entry into and stay in the United Kingdom of persons required by this Act to have leave to enter, including any rules as to the period for which leave is to be given and the conditions to be attached in different circumstances; and section 1(4) above shall not be taken to require uniform provision to be made by the rules as regards admission of persons for a purpose or in a capacity specified in section 1(4) (and in particular, for this as well as other purposes of this Act, account may be taken of citizenship or nationality).

If a statement laid before either House of Parliament under this subsection is disapproved by a resolution of that House passed within the period of forty days beginning with the date of laying (and exclusive of any period during which Parliament is dissolved or prorogued or during which both Houses are adjourned for more than four days), then the Secretary of State shall as soon as may be make such changes or further changes in the rules as appear to him to be required in the circumstances, so that the statement of those changes be laid before Parliament at least by the end of the period of forty days beginning with the date of the resolution (but exclusive as aforesaid).

(3) In the case of a limited leave to enter or remain in the United Kingdom,—

(a) a person's leave may be varied, whether by restricting, enlarging or removing the limit on its duration, or by adding, varying or revoking conditions, but if the limit on its duration is removed, any conditions attached to the leave shall cease to apply; and

(b) the limitation on and any conditions attached to a person's leave may be imposed (whether originally or on a variation) so that they will, if not superseded, apply also to any subsequent leave he may obtain after an absence from the United Kingdom within the period limited for the duration of the earlier leave.

(4) A person's leave to enter or remain in the United Kingdom shall lapse on his going to a country or territory outside the common travel area (whether or not he lands there), unless within the period for which he had leave he returns to the United Kingdom in circumstances in which he is not required to obtain leave to enter; but, if he does so return, his previous leave (and any limitation on it or conditions attached to it) shall continue to apply.

(5) A person who is not [a British citizen] shall be liable to deportation from the United Kingdom—

(a) if, having only a limited leave to enter or remain, he does not observe a condition attached to the leave or remains beyond the time limited by the leave; or

(b) if the Secretary of State deems his deportation to be conducive to the public good; or

(c) if another person to whose family he belongs is or has been ordered to be deported.

(6) Without prejudice to the operation of subsection (5) above, a person who is not [a British citizen] shall also be liable to deportation from the United Kingdom if, after he has attained the age of seventeen, he is convicted of an offence for which he is punishable with imprisonment and on his conviction is recommended for deportation by a court empowered by this Act to do so.

(7) Where it appears to Her Majesty proper so to do by reason of restrictions or conditions imposed on [British citizens, British Dependent Territories citizens or British Overseas citizens] when leaving or seeking to leave any country or the territory subject to the government of any country, Her Majesty may by Order in Council make provision for prohibiting persons who are nationals or citizens of the country and are not [British citizens] from embarking in the United Kingdom, or from doing so elsewhere than at a port of exit, or for imposing restrictions or conditions on them when embarking or about to embark in the United Kingdom; and Her Majesty may also make provision by Order in Council to enable those who are not [British citizens] to be, in such cases as may be prescribed by the Order, prohibited in the interests of safety from so embarking on a ship or aircraft specified or indicated in the prohibition.

Any Order in Council under this subsection shall be subject to annulment in pursuance of a resolution of either House of Parliament.

(8) When any question arises under this Act whether or not a person is [a British citizen], or is entitled to any exemption under this Act, it shall lie on the person asserting it to prove that he is.

[(9) A person within this subsection seeking to enter the United Kingdom and claiming to have the right of abode there shall prove that he has that right by means of such certificate of entitlement as may be specified in the immigration rules, unless—

(a) he claims to be a British citizen and produces (or is present when there is produced) a United Kingdom passport describing him as such a citizen or a United Kingdom passport describing him as a citizen of the United Kingdom and Colonies having the right of abode in the United Kingdom; or

(b) in the case of a woman falling within subsection (9A)(b) below who claims to be a British citizen as here mentioned by virtue of section 2(2) of this Act as in force immediately before the commencement of the British Nationality Act 1981, she shows that immediately before that commencement she—

(i) was a citizen of the United Kingdom and Colonies; and

(ii) has the right of abode in the United Kingdom by virtue of section 2(2) of this Act, as then in force, apart from any reference therein to section 2(1)(c) or (d) as then in force.

(9A) A person is within subsection (9) above if—

(a) he is not a British citizen; or

(b) he claims to be a British citizen by virtue of section 11(1) of the British Nationality Act 1981 on the ground that immediately before the commencement of that Act he had the right of abode in the United Kingdom by virtue of section 2(1)(c) or section 2(2) of this Act, as then in force.]

4, 5 *****

6 Recommendations by court for deportation

(1) Where under section 3(6) above a person convicted of an offence is liable to deportation on the recommendation of a court, he may be recommended for deportation by any court having power to sentence him for the offence unless the court commits him to be sentenced or further dealt with for that offence by another court:

. . . . .

(2)-(4) *****

(4) Where a court recommends or purports to recommend a person for deportation, the validity of the recommendation shall not be called in question except on an appeal against the recommendation or against the conviction on which it is made; but—

. . . the recommendation shall be treated as a sentence for the purpose of any . . . enactment providing an appeal against sentence; . . .

(6), (7) *****

7 Exemption from deportation for certain existing residents

(1) Notwithstanding anything in section 3(5) or (6) above but subject to the provisions of this section, a Commonwealth citizen or citizen of the Republic of Ireland who was such a citizen at the coming into force of this Act and was then ordinarily resident in the United Kingdom—

(a) shall not be liable to deportation under section 3(5)(b) if at the time of the Secretary of State's decision he had at all times since the coming into force of this Act been ordinarily resident in the United Kingdom and Islands; and

(b) shall not be liable to deportation under section 3(5)(a), (b) or (c) if at the time of the Secretary of State's decision he had for the last five years been ordinarily resident in the United Kingdom and Islands; and

(c) shall not on conviction of an offence be recommended for deportation under section 3(6) if at the time of the conviction he had for the last five years been ordinarily resident in the United Kingdom and Islands.

(2) A person who has at any time become ordinarily resident in the United Kingdom or in any of the Islands shall not be treated for the purposes of this section as having ceased to be so by reason only of his having remained there in breach of the immigration laws.

(3) The "last five years" before the material time under subsection (1)(b) or (c) above is to be taken as a period amounting in total to five years exclusive of any time during which the person claiming exemption under this section was undergoing imprisonment or detention by virtue of a sentence passed for an offence on a conviction in the United Kingdom and Islands, and the period for which he was imprisoned or detained by virtue of the sentence amounted to six months or more.

(4), (5) * * * * *

* * * * *

PART II
APPEALS

The appellate authorities

12 Immigration Appeal Tribunal and adjudicators

The Immigration Appeal Tribunal and adjudicators provided for by the Immigration Appeals Act 1969 shall continue for purposes of this Act, and—

(a) members of the Tribunal shall continue to be appointed by the Lord Chancellor and adjudicators by the Secretary of State; and

(b) the provisions of Schedule 1 to that Act shall continue to apply, as set out in Schedule 5 to this Act with the required adaptation of references to that Act, but with the substitution also of references to the Minister for the Civil Service for references to the Treasury.

Appeals to adjudicator or Tribunal in first instance

13 Appeals against exclusion from United Kingdom

(1) Subject to the provisions of this Part of this Act, a person who is refused leave to enter the United Kingdom under this Act may appeal to an adjudicator against the decision that he requires leave or against the refusal.

(2) Subject to the provisions of this Part of this Act, a person who, on an application duly made, is refused a [certificate of entitlement] or an entry clearance may appeal to an adjudicator against the refusal.

(3) [A person within section 3(9) above who does not hold a certificate of entitlement shall not be entitled to appeal on the ground that he has the right of abode in the United Kingdom against a decision that he requires leave to enter the United Kingdom unless—

(a) he claims to be a British citizen and produces (or is present when there is produced) a United Kingdom passport describing him as such a citizen or a United Kingdom passport describing him as a citizen of the United Kingdom and Colonies having the right of abode in the United Kingdom; or

(b) in the case of such a woman as is mentioned in paragraph (b) or section 3(9) above, she shows that immediately before the commencement of the British Nationality Act 1981 she satisfied the conditions specified in sub-paragraphs (i) and (ii) of that paragraph;]

and a person shall not be entitled to appeal against a refusal of leave to enter so long as he is in the United Kingdom, unless he was refused leave at a port of entry and at a time when he held a current entry clearance or was a person named in a current work permit.

(4) An appeal against a refusal of leave to enter shall be dismissed by the adjudicator if he is satisfied that the appellant was at the time of the refusal an illegal entrant, and an appeal against a refusal of an entry clearance shall be dismissed by the adjudicator if he is

satisfied that a deportation order was at the time of the refusal in force in respect of the appellant.

(5) A person shall not be entitled to appeal against a refusal of leave to enter, or against a refusal of an entry clearance, if the Secretary of State certifies that directions have been given by the Secretary of State (and not by a person acting under his authority) for the appellant not to be given entry to the United Kingdom on the ground that his exclusion is conducive to the public good, or if the leave to enter or entry clearance was refused in obedience to any such directions.

14 Appeals against conditions

(1) Subject to the provisions of this Part of this Act, a person who has a limited leave under this Act to enter or remain in the United Kingdom may appeal to an adjudicator against any variation of the leave (whether as regards duration or conditions), or against any refusal to vary it; and a variation shall not take effect so long as an appeal is pending under this subsection against the variation, nor shall an appellant be required to leave the United Kingdom by reason of the expiration of his leave so long as his appeal is pending under this subsection against a refusal to enlarge or remove the limit on the duration of the leave.

(2) * * * * *

(3) A person shall not be entitled to appeal under subsection (1) above against any variation of his leave which reduces its duration, or against any refusal to enlarge or remove the limit on its duration, if the Secretary of State certifies that the appellant's departure from the United Kingdom would be conducive to the public good, as being in the interest of national security or of the relations between the United Kingdom and any other country or for other reasons of a political nature, or the decision questioned by the appeal was taken on that ground by the Secretary of State (and not by a person acting under his authority).

(4) A person shall not be entitled to appeal under subsection (1) above against any variation made by statutory instrument, or against any refusal of the Secretary of State to make a statutory instrument.

15 Appeals in respect of deportation orders

(1) Subject to the provisions of this Part of this Act, a person may appeal to an adjudicator against—

(a) a decision of the Secretary of State to make a deportation order against him by virtue of section 3(5) above; or

(b) a refusal by the Secretary of State to revoke a deportation order made against him.

(2) A deportation order shall not be made against a person by virtue of section 3(5) above so long as an appeal may be brought against the decision to make it nor, if such an appeal is duly brought, so long as the appeal is pending; but, in calculating the period of eight weeks limited by section 5(3) above for making a deportation order against a person as belonging to the family of another person, there shall be disregarded any period during which there is pending an appeal against the decision to make it.

(3) A person shall not be entitled to appeal against a decision to make a deportation order against him if the ground of the decision was that his deportation is conducive to the public good as being in the interests of national security or of the relations between the United Kingdom and any other country or for other reasons of a political nature.

(4) A person shall not be entitled to appeal under this section against a refusal to revoke a deportation order, if the Secretary of State certifies that the appellant's exclusion from the United Kingdom is conducive to the public good or if revocation was refused on that ground by the Secretary of State (and not by a person acting under his authority).

(5) A person shall not be entitled to appeal under this section against a refusal to revoke a deportation order so long as he is in the United Kingdom, whether because he has

not complied with the requirement to leave or because he has contravened the prohibition on entering.

(6) * * * * *

(7) An appeal under this section shall be to the Appeal Tribunal in the first instance, instead of to an adjudicator, if—

(a) it is an appeal against a decision to make a deportation order and the ground of the decision was that the deportation of the appellant is conducive to the public good; or

(b) it is an appeal against a decision to make a deportation order against a person as belonging to the family of another person, or an appeal against a refusal to revoke a deportation order so made; or

(c) there is pending a related appeal to which paragraph (b) above applies.

(8), (9) * * * * *

16 * * * * *

17 Appeals against removal on objection to destination

(1) Subject to the provisions of this Part of this Act, where directions are given under this Act for a person's removal from the United Kingdom either—

(a) on his being refused leave to enter; or

(b) on a deportation order being made against him; or

(c) on his having entered the United Kingdom in breach of a deportation order;

he may appeal to an adjudicator against the directions on the ground that he ought to be removed (if at all) to a different contry or territory specified by him.

(2) Where a person appeals under section 13(1) above on being refused leave to enter the United Kingdom, and either—

(a) before he does so, directions have been given for his removal from the United Kingdom to any country or territory; or

(b) before or after he does so, the Secretary of State or an immigration officer serves on him notice that any directions which may be given for his removal by virtue of the refusal will be for his removal to a country or territory or one of several countries or territories specified in the notice;

then he may on that appeal object to the country or territory to which he would be removed in pursuance of the directions, or to that specified in the notice (or to one or more of those specified), and claim that he ought to be removed (if at all) to a different country or territory specified by him.

(3) Where a person appeals under section 15 above against a decision to make a deportation order against him, and before or after he does so the Secretary of State serves on him notice that any directions which may be given for his removal by virtue of the deportation order will be for his removal to a country or territory or one of several countries or territories specified in the notice, then he may on the appeal object to the country or territory specified in the notice (or to one or more of those specified), and claim that he ought to be removed (if at all) to a different country or territory specified by him.

(4) Where by virtue of subsection (2) or (3) above a person is able to object to a country or territory on an appeal under section 13(1) or 15, and either he does not object to it on that appeal or his objection to it on that appeal is not sustained, then he shall not be entitled to appeal under this section against any directions subsequently given by virtue of the refusal or order in question, if their effect will be his removal to that country or territory.

(5) A person shall not be entitled to appeal under this section against any directions given on his being refused leave to enter the United Kingdom, unless either he is also appealing under section 13(1) against the decision that he requires leave to enter or he was refused leave at a port of entry and at a time when he held a current entry clearance or was a person named in a current work permit.

18 * * * * *

19 Determination of appeals by adjudicators

(1) Subject to sections 13(4) and 16(4) above, and to any restriction on the grounds of appeal, an adjudicator on an appeal to him under this Part of this Act—

(a) shall allow the appeal if he considers—

(i) that the decision or action against which the appeal is brought was not in accordance with the law or with any immigration rules applicable to the case; or

(ii) where the decision or action involved the exercise of a discretion by the Secretary of State or an officer, that the discretion should have been exercised differently; and

(b) in any other case, shall dismiss the appeal.

(2) For the purposes of subsection (1)(a) above the adjudicator may review any determination of a question of fact on which the decision or action was based; and for the purposes of subsection (1)(a)(ii) no decision or action which is in accordance with the immigration rules shall be treated as having involved the exercise of a discretion by the Secretary of State by reason only of the fact that he has been requested by or on behalf of the appellant to depart, or to authorise any officer to depart, from the rules and has refused to do so.

(3), (4) * * * * *

Appeals from adjudicator to Tribunal, and review of decisions

20 Appeal to Tribunal from determination of adjudicator

(1) Subject to any requirement of rules of procedure as to leave to appeal, any party to an appeal to an adjudicator may, if dissatisfied with his determination thereon, appeal to the Appeal Tribunal, and the Tribunal may affirm the determination or make any other determination which could have been made by the adjudicator.

(2), (3) * * * * *

21-23 * * * * *

PART III
CRIMINAL PROCEEDINGS

24 Illegal entry and similar offences

(1) A person who is not [a British citizen] shall be guilty of an offence punishable on summary conviction with a fine of not more than [level 4 on the standard scale] or with imprisonment for not more than six months, or with both, in any of the following cases:—

(a) if contrary to this Act he knowingly enters the United Kingdom in breach of a deportation order or without leave;

(b) if, having only a limited leave to enter or remain in the United Kingdom, he knowingly either—

(i) remains beyond the time limited by the leave; or

(ii) fails to observe a condition of the leave;

(c) if, having lawfully entered the United Kingdom without leave by virtue of section 8(1) above, he remains without leave beyond the time allowed by section 8(1);

(d) if, without reasonable excuse, he fails to comply with any requirement imposed on him under Schedule 2 to this Act to report to a medical officer of health, or to attend, or submit to a test or examination, as required by such an officer;

(e) if, without reasonable excuse, he fails to observe any restriction imposed on him under Schedule 2 or 3 to this Act as to residence or as to reporting to the police or to an immigration officer;

(f) if he disembarks in the United Kingdom from a ship or aircraft after being placed on board under Schedule 2 or 3 to this Act with a view to his removal from the United Kingdom;

(g) if he embarks in contravention of a restriction imposed by or under an Order in Council under section 3(7) of this Act.

(2) A constable or immigration officer may arrest without warrant anyone who has, or whom he, with reasonable cause, suspects to have, committed or attempted to commit an offence under this section other than an offence under subsection (1)(d) above.

(3), (4) *****

25-32 *****

PART IV
SUPPLEMENTARY

33 Interpretation

(1) For purposes of this Act, except in so far as the context otherwise requires—

*****

"entrant" means a person entering or seeking to enter the United Kingdom, and "illegal entrant" means a person unlawfully entering or seeking to enter in breach of a deportation order or of the immigration laws, and includes also a person who has so entered;

"entry clearance" means a visa, entry certificate or other document which, in accordance with the immigration rules, is to be taken as evidence of a person's eligibility, though not [a British citizen], for entry into the United Kingdom (but does not include a work permit);

"immigration laws" means this Act and any law for purposes similar to this Act which is for the time being or has (before or after the passing of this Act) been in force in any part of the United Kingdom and Islands;

"immigration rules" means the rules for the time being laid down as mentioned in section 3(2) above;

*****

"limited leave" and "indefinite leave" mean respectively leave under this Act to enter or remain in the United Kingdom which is, and one which is not, limited as to duration;

"settled" shall be construed in accordance [with subsection (2A) below];

*****

"work permit" means a permit indicating, in accordance with the immigration rules, that a person named in it is eligible, though not [a British citizen], for entry into the United Kingdom for the purpose of taking employment.

(2) It is hereby declared that, except as otherwise provided in this Act, a person is not to be treated for the purposes of any provision of this Act as ordinarily resident in the United Kingdom or in any of the Islands at a time when he is there in breach of the immigration laws.

[(2A) Subject to section 8(5) above, references to a person being settled in the United Kingdom are references to his being ordinarily resident there without being subject under the immigration laws to any restriction on the period for which he may remain.]

(3), (4) *****

(5) This Act shall not be taken to supersede or impair any power exercisable by Her Majesty in relation to aliens by virtue of Her prerogative.

34-37 *****

MISUSE OF DRUGS ACT 1971
(1971, c. 38)

An Act to make new provision with respect to dangerous or otherwise harmful drugs and related matters, and for purposes connected therewith [27 May 1971]

Territorial extent United Kingdom

* * * * *

Law enforcement and punishment of offences

23 Powers to search and obtain evidence

(1) A constable or other person authorised in that behalf by a general or special order of the Secretary of State (or in Northern Ireland either of the Secretary of State or the Ministry of Home Affairs for Northern Ireland) shall, for the purposes of the execution of this Act, have power to enter the premises of a person carrying on business as a producer or supplier of any controlled drugs and to demand the production of, and to inspect, any books or documents relating to dealings in any such drugs and to inspect any stocks of any such drugs.

(2) If a constable has reasonable grounds to suspect that any person is in possession of a controlled drug in contravention of this Act or of any regulations made thereunder, the constable may—

(a) search that person, and detain him for the purpose of searching him;

(b) search any vehicle or vessel in which the constable suspects that the drug may be found, and for that purpose require the person in control of the vehicle or vessel to stop it;

(c) seize and detain, for the purposes of proceedings under this Act, anything found in the course of the search which appears to the constable to be evidence of an offence under this Act.

In this subsection "vessel" includes a hovercraft within the meaning of the Hovercraft Act 1968; and nothing in this subsection shall prejudice any power of search or any power to seize or detain property which is exercisable by a constable apart from this subsection.

(3) If a justice of the peace (or in Scotland a justice of the peace, a magistrate or a sheriff) is satisfied by information on oath that there is reasonable ground for suspecting—

(a) that any controlled drugs are, in contravention of this Act or of any regulations made thereunder, in the possession of a person on any premises; or

(b) that a document directly or indirectly relating to, or connected with, a transaction or dealing which was, or an intended transaction or dealing which would if carried out be, an offence under this Act, or in the case of a transaction or dealing carried out or intended to be carried out in a place outside the United Kingdom, an offence against the provision of a corresponding law in force in that place, is in the possession of a person on any premises,

he may grant a warrant authorising any constable acting for the police area in which the premises are situated at any time or times within one month from the date of the warrant, to enter, if need be by force, the premises named in the warrant, and to search the premises and any person found therein and, if there is reasonable ground for suspecting that an offence under this Act has been committed in relation to any controlled drugs found on the premises or in the possession of any such persons, or that a document so found is such a document as is mentioned in paragraph (b) above, to seize and detain those drugs or that document, as the case may be.

(4) A person commits an offence if he—

(a) intentionally obstructs a person in the exercise of his powers under this section; or

(b) conceals from a person acting in the exercise of his powers under subsection (1) above any such books, documents, stocks or drugs as are mentioned in that subsection; or

(c) without reasonable excuse (proof of which shall lie on him) fails to produce any such books or documents as are so mentioned where their production is demanded by a person in the exercise of his powers under that subsection.

*****

TRIBUNALS AND INQUIRIES ACT 1971
(1971, c. 62)

An Act to consolidate the Tribunals and Inquiries Acts 1958 and 1966 as amended

[27 July 1971]

Territorial extent United Kingdom

The Council on Tribunals and its functions

1 Council on Tribunals

(1) There shall continue to be a council entitled the Council on Tribunals (being the council constituted by the Tribunals and Inquiries Act 1958)—

(a) to keep under review the constitution and working of the tribunals specified in Schedule 1 to this Act (being the tribunals constituted under or for the purposes of the statutory provisions specified in that Schedule) and, from time to time, to report on their constitution and working;

(b) to consider and report on such particular matters as may be referred to the Council under this Act with respect to tribunals other than the ordinary courts of law, whether or not specified in Schedule 1 to this Act, or any such tribunal;

(c) to consider and report on such matters as may be referred as aforesaid, or as the Council may determine to be of special importance, with respect to administrative procedures involving, or which may involve, the holding by or on behalf of a Minister of a statutory inquiry, or any such procedure.

(2) Nothing in this section shall authorise or require the Council to deal with any matter with respect to which the Parliament of Northern Ireland has power to make laws.

2 Composition of the Council and the Scottish Committee

(1) Subject to subsection (3) of this section the Council on Tribunals (in this Act referred to as "the Council") shall consist of not more than fifteen nor less than ten members appointed by the Lord Chancellor and the Secretary of State, and one of the members shall be so appointed to be chairman of the Council.

(2) There shall be a Scottish Committee of the Council (in this Act referred to as "the Scottish Committee") which, subject to subsection (3) of this section, shall consist of—

(a) either two or three members of the Council designated by the Secretary of State; and

(b) either three or four persons, not being members of the Council, appointed by the Secretary of State;

and the Secretary of State shall appoint one of the members of the Scottish Committee (being a member of the Council) to be chairman of the Scottish Committee.

(3) In addition to the persons appointed or designated as aforesaid, the Parliamentary Commissioner for Administration shall, by virtue of his office, be a member of the Council and of the Scottish Committee.

(4) In appointing members of the Council regard shall be had to the need for representation of the interests of persons in Wales.

3, 4 *****

5 Recommendations of Council as to appointment of members of tribunals

(1) Without prejudice to the generality of section 1(1)(a) of this Act, the Council may make to the appropriate Minister general recommendations as to the making of appointments to membership of any such tribunals as are specified in Schedule 1 to this Act or of panels constituted for the purposes of any such tribunals; and (without prejudice, however, to any statutory provisions having effect with respect to such appointments) the appropriate Minister shall have regard to recommendations under this section.

(2) In this section "the appropriate Minister" means, in relation to appointments of any description, the Minister making the appointments or, if they are not made by a Minister, the Minister in charge of the government department concerned with the tribunals in question.

(3) * * * * *

8 Concurrence required for removal of members of certain tribunals

(1) Subject to subsection (2) of this section, no power of a Minister other than the Lord Chancellor to terminate a person's membership of any such tribunal as is specified in Schedule 1 to this Act, or of a panel constituted for the purposes of any such tribunal, shall be exercisable except with the consent of—

(a) the Lord Chancellor, the Lord President of the Court of Session and the Lord Chief Justice of Northern Ireland, if the tribunal sits in all parts of the United Kingdom;

(b) the Lord Chancellor and the Lord President of the Court of Session, if the tribunal sits in all parts of Great Britain;

(c) the Lord Chancellor and the Lord Chief Justice of Northern Ireland, if the tribunal sits both in England and Wales and in Northern Ireland;

(d) the Lord Chancellor, if the tribunal does not sit outside England and Wales;

(e) the Lord President of the Court of Session, if the tribunal sits only in Scotland;

(f) the Lord Chief Justice of Northern Ireland, if the tribunal sits only in Northern Ireland.

(2), (3) * * * * *

9 * * * * *

10 Procedural rules for tribunals

(1) No power of a Minister, the Lord President of the Court of Session, [the Commissioners of Inland Revenue, the Commissioners of Customs and Excise or the Foreign Compensation Commission] to make, approve, confirm or concur in procedural rules for any such tribunal as is specified in Schedule 1 to this Act shall be exercisable except after consultation with the Council.

(2), (3) * * * * *

11 Procedure in connection with statutory inquiries

(1) The Lord Chancellor, after consultation with the Council, may make rules regulating the procedure to be followed in connection with statutory inquiries held by or on behalf of Ministers; and different provision may be made by any such rules in relation to different classes of such inquiries.

(2)-(4) * * * * *

12 Reasons to be given for decisions of tribunals and Ministers

(1) Subject to the provisions of this section, where—

(a) any such tribunal as is specified in Schedule 1 to this Act gives any decision; or

(b) any Minister notifies any decision taken by him after the holding by him or on his behalf of a statutory inquiry, or taken by him in a case in which a person concerned could (whether by objecting or otherwise) have required the holding as aforesaid of a statutory inquiry, it shall be the duty of the tribunal or Minister to furnish a statement, either written or oral, of the reasons for the decision if requested, on or before the giving or notification of the decision, to state the reasons.

(2) The said statement may be refused, or the specification of the reasons restricted, on grounds of national security, and the tribunal or Minister may refuse to furnish the statement to a person not primarily concerned with the decision if of opinion that to furnish it would be contrary to the interests of any person primarily concerned.

(3), (4) * * * * *

(5) Any statement of the reasons for such a decision as is mentioned in paragraph (a) or (b) of subsection (1) of this section, whether given in pursuance of that subsection or of any other statutory provisions, shall be taken to form part of the decision and accordingly to be incorporated in the record.

(6) * * * * *

13 * * * * *

14 Extension of supervisory powers of superior courts

(1) As respects England and Wales or Northern Ireland, any provision in an Act passed before 1st August 1958 that any order or determination shall not be called into question in any court, or any provision in such an Act which by similar words excludes any of the powers of the High Court, shall not have effect so as to prevent the removal of the proceedings into the High Court by order of certiorari or to prejudice the powers of the High Court to make orders of mandamus:

Provided that this subsection, so far as it relates to the High Court in Northern Ireland, shall not affect any provision in its application to a matter with respect to which the Parliament of Northern Ireland has power to make laws.

(2) As respects Scotland, any provision in an Act passed before 1st August 1958 that any order or determination shall not be called into question in any court, or any provision in such an Act which by similar words excludes any jurisdiction which the Court of Session would otherwise have to entertain an application for reduction or suspension of any order or determination, or otherwise to consider the validity of any order or determination, shall not have effect so as to prevent the exercise of any such jurisdiction.

(3) Nothing in this section shall . . . apply to any order or determination of a court of law or where an Act makes special provision for application to the High Court or the Court of Session within a time limited by the Act.

15-20 * * * * *

EUROPEAN COMMUNITIES ACT 1972
(1972, c. 68)

An Act to make provision in connection with the enlargement of the European Communities to include the United Kingdom, together with (for certain purposes) the Channel Islands, the Isle of Man and Gibraltar [17 October 1972]

Territorial extent United Kingdom

PART I
GENERAL PROVISIONS

1 Short title and interpretation

(1) This Act may be cited as the European Communities Act 1972.

(2) In this Act . . .

"the Communities" means the European Economic Community, the European Coal and Steel Community and the European Atomic Energy Community;

"the Treaties" or "the Community Treaties" means, subject to subsection (3) below, the pre-accession treaties, that is to say, those described in Part I of Schedule 1 to this Act, taken with—

* * * * * [full list omitted]

and any expression defined in Schedule 1 to this Act has the meaning there given to it.

(3) If Her Majesty by Order in Council declares that a treaty specified in the Order is to be regarded as one of the Community Treaties as herein defined, the Order shall be conclusive that it is to be so regarded; but a treaty entered into by the United Kingdom after the 22nd January 1972, other than a pre-accession treaty to which the United Kingdom accedes on terms settled on or before that date, shall not be so regarded unless it is so specified, nor be so specified unless a draft of the Order in Council has been approved by resolution of each House of Parliament.

(4) For purposes of subsections (2) and (3) above, "treaty" includes any international agreement, and any protocol or annex to a treaty or international agreement.

2 General implementation of Treaties

(1) All such rights, powers, liabilities, obligations and restrictions from time to time created or arising by or under the Treaties, and all such remedies and procedures from time to time provided for by or under the Treaties, as in accordance with the Treaties are without further enactment to be given legal effect or used in the United Kingdom shall be recognised and available in law, and be enforced, allowed and followed accordingly; and the expression "enforceable Community right" and similar expressions shall be read as referring to one to which this subsection applies.

(2) Subject to Schedule 2 to this Act, at any time after its passing Her Majesty may by Order in Council, and any designated Minister or department may by regulations, make provision—

(a)for the purpose of implementing any Community obligation of the United Kingdom, or enabling any such obligation to be implemented, or of enabling any rights enjoyed or to be enjoyed by the United Kingdom under or by virtue of the Treaties to be exercised; or

(b) for the purpose of dealing with matters arising out of or related to any such obligation or rights or the coming into force, or the operation from time to time, of subsection (1) above;

and in the exercise of any statutory power or duty, including any power to give directions or to legislate by means of orders, rules, regulations or other subordinate instrument, the person entrusted with the power or duty may have regard to the objects of the Communities and to any such obligation or rights as aforesaid.

In this subsection "designated Minister or Department" means such Minister of the Crown or government department as may from time to time be designated by Order in Council in relation to any matter or for any purpose, but subject to such restrictions or conditions (if any) as may be specified by the Order in Council.

(3) There shall be charged on and issued out of the Consolidated Fund or, if so determined by the Treasury, the National Loans Fund the amounts required to meet any Community obligation to make payments to any of the Communities or member States, or any Community obligation in respect of contributions to the capital or reserves of the European Investment Bank or in respect of loans to the Bank, or to redeem any notes or obligations issued or created in respect of any such Community obligation; and, except as otherwise provided by or under any enactment,—

(a) any other expenses incurred under or by virtue of the Treaties or this Act by any Minister of the Crown or government department may be paid out of moneys provided by Parliament; and

(b) any sums received under or by virtue of the Treaties or this Act by any Minister of the Crown or government department, save for such sums as may be required for disbursements permitted by any other enactment, shall be paid into the Consolidated Fund or, if so determined by the Treasury, the National Loans Fund.

(4) The provision that may be made under subsection (2) above includes, subject to Schedule 2 to this Act, any such provision (of any such extent) as might be made by Act of Parliament, and any enactment passed or to be passed, other than one contained in this Part of this Act, shall be construed and have effect subject to the foregoing provisions of this section; but, except as may be provided by any Act passed after this Act, Schedule 2 shall have effect in connection with the powers conferred by this and the following sections of this Act to make Orders in Council and regulations.

(5), (6) *****

3 Decisions on, and proof of, Treaties and Community instruments, etc

(1) For the purposes of all legal proceedings any question as to the meaning or effect of any of the Treaties, or as to the validity, meaning or effect of any Community instrument, shall be treated as a question of law (and, if not referred to the European Court, be for determination as such in accordance with the principles laid down by and any relevant decision of the European Court).

(2) Judicial notice shall be taken of the Treaties, of the Official Journal of the Communities and of any decision of, or expression of opinion by, the European Court on any such question as aforesaid; and the Official Journal shall be admissible as evidence of any instrument or other act thereby communicated of any of the Communities or of any Community institution.

(3), (4), (5) *****

*****

Section 2

SCHEDULE 2

PROVISIONS AS TO SUBORDINATE LEGISLATION

1.—(1) The powers conferred by section 2(2) of this Act to make provision for the purposes mentioned in section 2(2)(a) and (b) shall not include power—

(a) to make any provision imposing or increasing taxation; or

(b) to make any provision taking effect from a date earlier than that of the making of the instrument containing the provision; or

(c) to confer any power to legislate by means of orders, rules regulations or other subordinate instrument, other than rules of procedure for any court or tribunal; or

(d) to create any new criminal offence punishable with imprisonment for more than two years or punishable on summary conviction with imprisonment for more than three months or with a fine of more than [level 5 on the standard scale] (if not calculated on a daily basis) or with a fine of more than [£100 a day].

(2) Sub-paragraph (1)(c) above shall not be taken to preclude the modification of a power to legislate conferred otherwise than under section 2(2), or the extension of any such power to purposes of the like nature as those for which it was conferred; and a power to give directions as to matters of administration is not to be regarded as a power to legislate within the meaning of sub-paragraph (1)(c).

2.—(1) Subject to paragraph 3 below, where a provision contained in any section of this Act confers power to make regulations (otherwise than by modification or extension of an existing power), the power shall be exercisable by statutory instrument.

(2) Any statutory instrument containing an Order in Council or regulations made in the exercise of a power so conferred, if made without a draft having been approved by resolution of each House of Parliament, shall be subject to annulment in pursuance of a resolution of either House.

LOCAL GOVERNMENT ACT 1972
(1972, c. 70)

An Act to make provision with respect to local government and the functions of local authorities in England and Wales; to amend Part II of the Transport Act 1968; to confer rights of appeal in respect of decisions relating to licences under the Home Counties (Music and Dancing) Licensing Act 1926; to make further provision with respect to magistrates' courts committees; to abolish certain inferior courts of record; and for connected purposes [26 October 1972]

Territorial extent England and Wales

* * * * *

PART V
GENERAL PROVISIONS AS TO MEMBERS AND PROCEEDINGS OF LOCAL AUTHORITIES

Restrictions on voting

94 Disability of members of authorities for voting on account of interest in contracts, etc

(1) Subject to the provisions of section 97 below, if a member of a local authority has any pecuniary interest, direct or indirect, in any contract, proposed contract or other matter, and is present at a meeting of the local authority at which the contract or other matter is the subject of consideration, he shall at the meeting and as soon as practicable after its commencement disclose the fact and shall not take part in the consideration or discussion of the contract or other matter or vote on any question with respect to it.

(2) If any person fails to comply with the provisions of subsection (1) above he shall for each offence be liable on summary conviction to a fine not exceeding [level 4 on the standard scale] unless he proves that he did not know that the contract, proposed contract or other matter in which he had a pecuniary interest was the subject of consideration at that meeting.

(3) A prosecution for an offence under this section shall not be instituted except by or on behalf of the Director of Public Prosecutions.

(4), (5) * * * * *

95 Pecuniary interests for purposes of section 94

(1) For the purposes of section 94 above a person shall be treated, subject to the following provisions of this section and to section 97 below, as having indirectly a pecuniary interest in a contract, proposed contract or other matter, if—

(a) he or any nominee of his is a member of a company or other body with which the contract was made or is proposed to be made or which has a direct pecuniary interest in the other matter under consideration; or

(b) he is a partner, or is in the employment, of a person with whom the contract was made or is proposed to be made or who has a direct pecuniary interest in the other matter under consideration.

(2) Subsection (1) above does not apply to membership of or employment under any public body, and a member of a company or other body shall not by reason only of his membership be treated as having an interest in any contract, proposed contract or other matter if he has no beneficial interest in any securities of that company or other body.

(3) In the case of married persons living together the interest of one spouse shall, if known to the other, be deemed for the purpose of section 94 above to be also an interest of the other.

96 General notices and recording of disclosures for purposes of section 94

(1) A general notice given in writing to the proper officer of the authority by a member thereof to the effect that he or his spouse is a member or in the employment of a

specified company or other body, or that he or his spouse is a partner or in the employment of a specified person, or that he or his spouse is the tenant of any premises owned by the authority, shall, unless and until the notice is withdrawn, be deemed to be a sufficient disclosure of his interest in any contract, proposed contract or other matter relating to that company or other body or to that person or to those premises which may be the subject of consideration after the date of the notice.

(2) The proper officer of the authority shall record in a book to be kept for the purpose particulars of any disclosure made under section 94 above and of any notice given under this section, and the book shall be open at all reasonable hours to the inspection of any member of the local authority.

97-100 * * * * *

[PART VA
ACCESS TO MEETINGS AND DOCUMENTS OF CERTAIN AUTHORITIES, COMMITTEES AND SUB-COMMITEES

Note This Part was added by the Local Government (Access to Information) Act 1985.

100A Admission to meetings of principal councils

(1) A meeting of a principal council shall be open to the public except to the extent that they are excluded (whether during the whole or part of the proceedings) under subsection (2) below or by resolution under subsection (4) below.

(2) The public shall be excluded from a meeting of a principal council during an item of business whenever it is likely, in view of the nature of the business to be transacted or the nature of the proceedings, that, if members of the public were present during that item, confidential information would be disclosed to them in breach of the obligation of confidence; and nothing in this Part shall be taken to authorise or require the disclosure of confidential information in breach of the obligation of confidence.

(3) For the purposes of subsection (2) above, "confidential information" means—

(a) information furnished to the council by a Government department upon terms (however expressed) which forbid the disclosure of the information to the public; and

(b) information the disclosure of which to the public is prohibited by or under any enactment or by the order of a court;

and, in either case, the reference to the obligation of confidence is to be construed accordingly.

(4) A principal council may by resolution exclude the public from a meeting during an item of business whenever it is likely, in view of the nature of the business to be transacted or the nature of the proceedings, that if members of the public were present during that item there would be disclosure to them of exempt information, as defined in section 100I below.

(5), (6) * * * * *

(7) Nothing in this section shall require a principal council to permit the taking of photographs of any proceedings, or the use of any means to enable persons not present to see or hear any proceedings (whether at the time or later), or the making of any oral report on any proceedings as they take place.

(8) This section is without prejudice to any power of exclusion to supress or prevent disorderly conduct or other misbehaviour at a meeting.

[100B Access to agenda and connected reports

(1) Copies of the agenda for a meeting of a principal council and, subject to subsection (2) below, copies of any report for the meeting shall be open to inspection by members of the public at the offices of the council in accordance with subsection (3) below.

(2) If the proper officer thinks fit, there may be excluded from the copies of reports provided in pursuance of subsection (1) above the whole of any report which, or any part

which, relates only to items during which, in his opinion, the meeting is likely not to be open to the public.

(3) Any document which is required by subsection (1) above to be open to inspection shall be so open at least three clear days before the meeting, except that—

(a) where the meeting is convened at shorter notice, the copies of the agenda and reports shall be open to inspection from the time the meeting is convened, and

(b) where an item is added to an agenda copies of which are open to inspection by the public, copies of the item (or of the revised agenda), and the copies of any report for the meeting relating to the item, shall be open to inspection from the time the item is added to the agenda;

but nothing in this subsection requires copies of any agenda, item or report to be open to inspection by the public until copies are available to members of the council.

(4) An item of business may not be considered at a meeting of a principal council unless either—

(a) a copy of the agenda including the item (or a copy of the item) is open to inspection by members of the public in pursuance of subsection (1) above for at least three clear days before the meeting or, where the meeting is convened at shorter notice, from the time the meeting is convened; or

(b) by reason of special circumstances, which shall be specified in the minutes, the chairman of the meeting is of the opinion that the item should be considered at the meeting as a matter of urgency.

(5)-(8) *****

[100C Inspection of minutes and other documents after meetings

(1) After a meeting of a principal council the following documents shall be open to inspection by members of the public at the offices of the council until the expiration of the period of six years beginning with the date of the meeting, namely—

(a) the minutes, or a copy of the minutes, of the meeting, excluding so much of the minutes of proceedings during which the meeting was not open to the public as discloses exempt information;

(b) where applicable, a summary under subsection (2) below;

(c) a copy of the agenda for the meeting; and

(d) a copy of so much of any report for the meeting as relates to any item during which the meeting was open to the public.

(2) *****

[100D Inspection of background papers

(1) Subject, in the case of section 100C(1), to subsection (2) below, if and so long as copies of the whole or part of a report for a meeting of a principal council are required by sectin 100B(1) or 100C(1) above to be open to inspection by members of the public—

(a) copies of a list, compiled by the proper officer, of the background papers for the report or the part of the report, and

(b) at least one copy of each of the documents included in that list,

shall also be open to their inspection at the offices of the council.

(2) Subsection (1) above does not require a copy of the list, or of any document included in the list, to be open to inspection after the expiration of the period of four years beginning with the date of the meeting.

(3)-(5) *****

[100E Application to committees and sub-committees

(1) Sections 100A to 100D above shall apply in relation to a committee or sub-committee of a principal council as they apply in relation to a principal council.

(2)-(4) *****

100F *****

[100G Principal councils to publish additional information

(1) A principal council shall maintain a register stating—

(a) the name and address of every member of the council for the time being and the ward or division which he represents; and

(b) the name and address of every member of each committee or sub-committee of the council for the time being.

(2) A principal council shall maintain a list—

(a) specifying those powers of the council which, for the time being, are exercisable from time to time by officers of the council in pursuance of arrangements made under this Act or any other enactment for their discharge by those officers; and

(b) stating the title of the officer by whom each of the powers so specified is for the time being so exercisable;

but this subsection does not require a power to be specified in the list if the arrangements for its discharge by the officer are made for a specified period not exceeding six months.

(3), (4) *****]

PART VI
DISCHARGE OF FUNCTIONS

101 Arrangements for discharge of functions by local authorities

(1) Subject to any express provision contained in this Act or any Act passed after this Act, a local authority may arrange for the discharge of any of their functions—

(a) by a committee, a sub-committee or an officer of the authority; or

(b) by any other local authority.

(2) Where by virtue of this section any functions of a local authority may be discharged by a committee of theirs, then, unless the local authority otherwise direct, the committee may arrange for the discharge of any of those functions by a sub-committee or an officer of the authority and where by virtue of this section any functions of a local authority may be discharged by a sub-committee of the authority, then, unless the local authority or the committee otherwise direct, the sub-committee may arrange for the discharge of any of those functions by an officer of the authority.

(3) Where arrangements are in force under this section for the discharge of any functions of a local authority by another local authority, then, subject to the terms of the arrangements, that other authority may arrange for the discharge of those functions by a committee, sub-committee or officer of theirs and subsection (2) above shall apply in relation to those functions as it applies in relation to the functions of that other authority.

(4) Any arrangements made by a local authority or committee under this section for the discharge of any functions by a committee, sub-committee, officer or local authority shall not prevent the authority or committee by whom the arrangements are made from exercising those functions.

(5) Two or more local authorities may discharge any of their functions jointly and, where arrangements are in force for them to do so,—

(a) they may also arrange for the discharge of those functions by a joint committee of theirs or by an officer of one of them and subsection (2) above shall apply in relation to those functions as it applies in relation to the functions of the individual authorities; and

(b) any enactment relating to those functions or the authorities by whom or the areas in respect of which they are to be discharged shall have effect subject to all necessary modifications in its application in relation to those functions and the authorities by whom and the areas in respect of which (whether in pursuance of the arrangements or otherwise) they are to be discharged.

(6) A local authority's functions with respect to levying, or issuing a precept for, a rate or borrowing money shall be discharged only by the authority.

*****

PART XI
GENERAL PROVISIONS AS TO LOCAL AUTHORITIES

Legal proceedings

222 Power of local authorities to prosecute or defend legal proceedings

(1) Where a local authority consider it expedient for the promotion or protection of the interests of the inhabitants of their area—

(a) they may prosecute or defend or appear in any legal proceedings and, in the case of civil proceedings, may institute them in their own name, and

(b) they may, in their own name, make representations in the interests of the inhabitants at any public inquiry held by or on behalf of any Minister or public body under any enactment.

(2) In this section "local authority" includes the Common Council.

* * * * *

Byelaws

235 Power of councils to make byelaws for good rule and government and suppression of nuisances

(1) The council of a district and the council of a London borough may make byelaws for the good rule and government of the whole or any part of the district or borough, as the case may be, and for the prevention and suppression of nuisances therein.

(2) The confirming authority in relation to byelaws made under this section shall be the Secretary of State.

(3) Byelaws shall not be made under this section for any purpose as respects any area if provision for that purpose as respects that area is made by, or is or may be made under, any other enactment.

236 Procedure, etc, for byelaws

(1) Subject to subsection (2) below, the following provisions of this section shall apply to byelaws to be made by a local authority under this Act [and to byelaws made by a local authority, a metropolitan county passenger transport authority or the Inner London Education Authority under any other enactment conferring on the authority] a power to make byelaws and for which specific provision is not otherwise made.

(2) This section shall not apply to byelaws made by statutory water undertakers under section 17 or 18 of the Water Act 1945 or by the Civil Aviation Authority under [section 29 of the Civil Aviation Act 1982].

(3) The byelaws shall be made under the common seal of the authority, or, in the case of byelaws made by a parish or community council not having a seal, under the hands and seals of two members of the council, and shall not have effect until they are confirmed by the confirming authority.

(4) At least one month before application for conformation of the byelaws is made, notice of the intention to apply for confirmation shall be given in one or more local newspapers circulating in the area to which the byelaws are to apply.

(5) For at least one month before application for confirmation is made, a copy of the byelaws shall be deposited at the offices of the authority by whom the byelaws are made, and shall at all reasonable hours be open to public inspection without payment.

(6) The authority by whom the byelaws are made shall, on application, furnish to any person a copy of the byelaws, or of any part thereof on payment of such sum, not exceeding 10p for every hundred words contained in the copy, as the authority may determine.

(7) The confirming authority may confirm, or refuse to confirm, any byelaw submitted under this section for confirmation, and may fix the date on which the byelaw is to come into operation and if no date is so fixed the byelaw shall come into operation at the expiration of one month from the date of its confirmation.

(8) A copy of the byelaws, when confirmed, shall be printed and deposited at the offices of the authority by whom the byelaws are made, and shall at all reasonable hours be open to public inspection without pyament, and a copy thereof shall, on application, be furnished to any person on payment of such sum, not exceeding 20p for every copy, as the authority may determine.

(9), (10) * * * * *

(11) In this section the expression "the confirming authority" means the authority or person, if any, specified in the enactment (including any enactment in this Act) under which the byelaws are made, or in any enactment incorporated therein or applied thereby, as the authority or person by whom the byelaws are to be confirmed, or if no authority or person is so specified, means the Secretary of State.

* * * * *

[SCHEDULE 12A
ACCESS TO INFORMATION: EXEMPT INFORMATION

PART I
DESCRIPTIONS OF EXEMPT INFORMATION

1. Information relating to a particular employee, former employee or applicant to become an employee of, or a particular office-holder, former office-holder or applicant to become an office-holder under, the authority.

2. Information relating to a particular employee, former employee or applicant to become an employee of, or a particular officer, former officer or applicant to become an officer appointed by—

(a) a magistrates' court committee, within the meaning of section 19 of the Justices of the Peace Act 1979; or

(b) a probation committee appointed under paragraph 2 of Schedule 3 to the Powers of Criminal Courts Act 1973.

3. Information relating to any particular occupier or former occupier of, or applicant for accommodation provided by or at the expense of the authority.

4. Information relating to any particular applicant for, or recipient or former recipient of, any service provided by the authority.

5. Information relating to any particular applicant for, or recipient or former recipient of, any financial assistance provided by the authority.

6. Information relating to the adoption, care, fostering or education of any particular child.

7. Information relating to the financial or business affairs of any particular person (other than the authority).

8. The amount of any expenditure proposed to be incurred by the authority under any particular contract for the acquisition of property or the supply of goods or services.

9. Any terms proposed or to be proposed by or to the authority in the course of negotiations for a contract for the acquisition or disposal of property or the supply of goods or services.

10. The identity of the authority (as well as of any other person, by virtue of paragraph 7 above) as the person offering any particular tender for a contract for the supply of goods or services.

11. Information relating to any consultations or negotiations, or contemplated consultations or negotiations, in connection with any labour relations matter arising between the authority or a Minister of the Crown and employees of, or office-holders under, the authority.

12. Any instructions to counsel and any opinion of counsel (whether or not in connection with any proceedings) and any advice received, information obtained or action to be taken in connection with—

(a) any legal proceedings by or against the authority, or

(b) the determination of any matter affecting the authority,

(whether, in either case, proceedings have been commenced or are in contemplation).

13. Information which, if disclosed to the public, would reveal that the authority proposes—

(a) to give under any enactment a notice under or by virtue of which requirements are imposed on a person; or

(b) to make an order or direction under any enactment.

14. Any action taken or to be taken in connection with the prevention, investigation or prosecution of crime.

15. The identity of a protected informant.]

* * * * *

ROAD TRAFFIC ACT 1972
(1972, c. 20)

An Act to consolidate certain enactments relating to road traffic with amendments to give effect to recommendation sof the Law Commission and the Scottish Law Commission [30 March 1972]

Territorial extent England and Wales, Scotland

* * * * *

PART VII
MISCELLANEOUS AND GENERAL

Furnishing of information and production of documents

159 Power of police to stop vehicles

A person driving a motor vehicle on a road and a person riding a cycle, not being a motor vehicle, on a road shall stop the same on being so required by a constable in uniform, and if he fails to do so he shall be guilty of an offence.

160 * * * * *

161 Power of constables to require production of driving licences and in certain cases statement of date of birth

(1) Any such person as follows, that is to say,—

(a) a person driving a motor vehicle on a road, or

(b) a person whom a constable has reasonable cause to believe to have been the driver of a motor vehicle at a time when an accident occurred owing to its presence on a road, or

(c) a person whom a constable has reasonable cause to believe to have committed an offence in relation to the use of a motor vehicle on a road, or

(d) a person who supervises the holder of a provisional licence granted under Part III of this Act while the holder is driving a motor vehicle on a road or whom a constable has reasonable cause to believe was supervising the holder of such a licence while driving at a time when an offence is suspected of having been committed by the said holder in relation to the use of the vehicle on a road,

shall, on being so required by a constable, produce for examination his licence to drive a motor vehicle granted under Part III of this Act, so as to enable the constable to ascertain the name and address of the holder of the licence, the date of issue, and the authority by which it was issued; and shall in presecribed circumstances, on being so required by the constable, state his date of birth.

(2), (3), (3A) * * * * *

(4) If a person required under the foregoing provisions of this section to produce a licence or state his date of birth to a constable fails to do so he shall [subject to sub-section (4A)] be guilty of an offence; . . . [in respect of a failure to produce his licence].

[(4A) In proceedings against any person for the offence of failing to produce a licence it shall be a defence for him to show that—

(a) within seven days after the production of his licence was required he produced it at such police station as may have been specified by him at the time its production was required; or

(b) he produced it in person there as soon as was reasonable practicable; or

(c) it was not reasonably practicable for him to produce it there before the day on which the proceedings were commenced;

and for the purposes of this subsection the laying of the information or, in Scotland, the service of the complaint on the accused shall be treated as the commencement of the proceedings.]

(5), (6) *****

162 Power of constables to obtain names and addresses of drivers, and others, and to require production of evidence of insurance or security and test certificates

(1) Any such person as follows, that is to say,—

(a) a person driving on a road a motor vehicle (other than an invalid carriage), or

(b) a person whom a constable has reasonable cause to believe to have been the driver of a motor vehicle (other than an invalid carriage) at a time when an accident occurred owing to its presence on a road, or

(c) a person whom a constable has reasonable cause to believe to have committed an offence in relation to the use on a road of a motor vehicle (other than an invalid carriage), shall, on being so required by a constable, give his name and address and the name and address of the owner of the vehicle and produce for examination—

(i) the relevant certificate of insurance or certificate of security within the meaning of Part VI of this Act, or such other evidence that the vehicle is not or was not being driven in contravention of section 143 thereof as may be prescribed by regulations made by the Secretary of State,

(ii) in relation to a vehicle to which section 44 of this Act applies, a test certificate issued in respect thereof as mentioned in subsection (1) of that section, and

(iii) in relation to a goods vehicle the use of which on a road without a plating certificate, [or] goods vehicle test certificate . . . is an offence under section 46(1) or (2) . . . of this Act, any such certificate issued in respect of that vehicle or any trailer drawn by it,

and if he fails to do so he shall, subject to subsection (2) below, be guilty of an offence.

(2) A person shall not be convicted of an offence under subsection (1) above by reason only of failure to produce any certificate or other evidence to a constable [if in proceedings against him for the offence he shows that—

(a) within seven days after the date on which the production of the certificate or other evidence was required it was produced at such police station as may have been specified by him at the time when its production was required; or

(b) it was produced there as soon as was reasonably practicable; or

(c) it was not reasonably practicable for it to be produced there before the day on which the proceedings were commenced;

and for the purposes of this subsection the laying of the information or, in Scotland, the service of the complaint on the accused shall be treated as the commencement of the proceedings.]

(3), (4) *****

*****

NORTHERN IRELAND CONSTITUTION ACT 1973
(1973, c. 36)

An Act to make new provision for the government of Northern Ireland [18 July 1973]

Territorial extent United Kingdom

PART I
PRELIMINARY

Status of Northern Ireland

1 Status of Northern Ireland as part of United Kingdom
It is hereby declared that Northern Ireland remains part of Her Majesty's dominions and of the United Kingdom, and it is hereby affirmed that in no event will Northern Ireland or any part of it cease to be part of Her Majesty's dominions and of the United Kingdom without the consent of the majority of the people of Northern Ireland voting in a poll held for the purposes of this section in accordance with Schedule 1 to this Act.

* * * * *

LOCAL GOVERNMENT ACT 1974
(1974, c. 7)

An Act to make further provision, in relation to England and Wales, with respect to the payment of grants to local authorities, rating and valuation, borrowing and lending by local authorities and the classification of highways; to extend the powers of the Countryside Commission to give financial assistance; to provide for the establishment of Commissions for the investigation of administrative action taken by or on behalf of local and other authorities; to restrict certain grants under the Transport Act 1968; to provide for the removal or relaxation of certain statutory controls affecting local government activities; to make provision in relation to the collection of sums by local authorities on behalf of water authorities; to amend section 259(3) of the Local Government Act 1972 and to make certain minor amendments of or consequential on that Act; and for connected purposes [8 February 1974]

Territorial extent England and Wales

PART III
LOCAL GOVERNMENT ADMINISTRATION

23 The Commissions for Local Administration

(1) For the purpose of conducting investigations in accordance with this Part of this Act, there shall be—

(a) a body of commissioners to be known as the Commission for Local Administration in England, and

(b) a body consisting of two or more commissioners to be known as the Commission for Local Administration in Wales.

(2) The Parliamentary Commissioner shall be a member of each of the Commissions.

(3) In the following provisions of this Part of this Act the expression "Local Commissioner" means a person, other than the Parliamentary Commissioner, who is a member of one of the Commissions.

(4) Appointments to the office of Local Commissioner shall be made by Her Majesty on the recommendation of the Secretary of State after consultation with the appropriate representative body, and a person so appointed shall, subject to subsection (6) below, hold office during good behaviour.

(5) Local Commissioners may be appointed to serve either as full-time commissioners or as part-time commissioners.

(6) A Local Commissioner may be relieved of office by Her Majesty at his own request or may be removed from office by Her Majesty on grounds of incapacity or misbehaviour, and shall in any case vacate office on completing the year of service in which he attains the age of sixty-five years.

(7) The Secretary of State shall designate two of the Local Commissioners for England as chairman and vice-chairman respectively of the Commission for Local Administration in England and, in the event of there being more than one Local Commissioner for Wales, shall designate one of them as chairman of the Commission for Local Administration in Wales.

(8) The Commission for Local Administration in England shall divide England into areas and shall provide, in relation to each area, for one or more of the Local Commissioners to be responsible for the area; and where the Commission for Local Administration in Wales consist of more than one Local Commissioner they may, if they think fit, act in a similar way in Wales.

A Local Commissioner may, by virtue of this Subsection, be made responsible for more than one area.

(9)-(13) * * * * *

24 Bodies representing authorities to which Part III applies

(1) The Secretary of State shall by order designate bodies to be called respectively "the representative body for England" and "the representative body for Wales".

(2) The said representative bodies shall be bodies appearing to the Secretary of State to represent authorities in England to which this Part of this Act applies, or as the case may be such authorities in Wales.

(3) An order made under subsection (1) above may be varied or revoked by a subsequent order so made, and shall be contained in a statutory instrument subject to annulment in pursuance of a resolution of either House of Parliament.

(4) For the year ending on 31st March 1975, and for each subsequent financial year, each of the Commissions shall prepare a general report on the discharge of their functions and shall submit it to the appropriate representative body.

(5) The report shall be submitted as soon as may be after the Commission have received the reports for the year from Local Commissioners under section 23(11) above, and each Commission shall submit copies of those reports, together with their own report.

(6) Each representative body shall arrange for the publication of the reports submitted to them under the preceding provisions of this section.

(7) In transmitting to local authorities recommendations or conclusions conveyed by either of the Commissions (in accordance with section 23(12) above) the representative body concerned may make such comments on those recommendations or conclusions as they think appropriate.

(8) Where, in accordance with subsection (6) above, a representative body arrange for the publication of a report submitted to them under subsection (4) above, they may also arrange for the report to be published with an annex containing such comments on the report as they think appropriate.

(7)-(10) * * * * *

25 Authorities subject to investigation

(1) This Part of this Act applies to—

(a) any local authority,

[(aa) the Land Authority for Wales . . .],

(b) any joint board the constituent authorities of which are all local authorities,

[(c) any joint authority established by Part IV of the Local Government Act 1985;

(ca) any other police authority, except the Secretary of State;

(cb) the Inner London Education Authority; and]

(d) any water authority within the meaning of the Water Act 1973.

(2) Her Majesty may by Order in Council provide that this Part of this Act shall also apply, subject to any modifications or exceptions specified in the Order, to any authority specified in the Order, being an authority which is established by or under an Act of Parliament, and which has power to levy a rate, or to issue a precept.

(3)-(5) * * * * *

26 Matters subject to investigation

(1) Subject to the provisions of this Part of this Act where a written complaint is made by or on behalf of a member of the public who claims to have sustained injustice in consequence of maladministration in connection with action taken by or on behalf of an authority to which this Part of this Act applies, being action taken in the exercise of administrative functions of that authority, a Local Commissioner may investigate that complaint.

(2) A complaint shall not be entertained under this Part of this Act unless—

(a) it is made in writing to a member of the authority, or of any other authority concerned, specifying the action alleged to constitute maladministration, and

(b) it is referred to the Local Commissioner, with the consent of the person aggrieved, or of a person acting on his behalf, by that member, or by any other person who is a member of any authority concerned, with a request to investigate the complaint.

(3) If the Local Commissioner is satisfied that any member of any authority concerned has been requested to refer the complaint to a Local Commissioner, and has not done so, the Local Commissioner may, if he thinks fit, dispense with the requirements in subsection (2)(b) above.

(4) A complaint shall not be entertained unless it was made to a member of any authority concerned within twelve months from the day on which the person aggrieved first had notice of the matters alleged in the complaint, but a Local Commissioner may conduct an investigation pursuant to a complaint not made within that period if he considers that there are special circumstances which make it proper to do so.

(5) Before proceeding to investigate a complaint, a Local Commissioner shall satisfy himself that the complaint has been brought, by or on behalf of the person aggrieved, to the notice of the authority to which the complaint relates and that that authority has been afforded a reasonable opportunity to investigate, and reply to, the complaint.

(6) A local Commissioner shall not conduct an investigation under this Part of this Act in respect of any of the following matters, that is to say,—

(a) any action in respect of which the person aggrieved has or had a right of appeal, reference or review to or before a tribunal constituted by or under any enactment;

(b) any action in respect of which in the person aggrieved has or had a right of appeal to a Minister of the Crown; or

(c) any action in respect of which the person aggrieved has or had a remedy by way of proceedings in any court of law:

Provided that a Local Commissioner may conduct an investigation notwithstanding the existence of such a right or remedy if satisfied that in the particular circumstances it is not reasonable to expect the person aggrieved to resort or have resorted to it.

(7) A Local Commissioner shall not conduct an investigation in respect of any action which in his opinion affects all or most of the inhabitants of the area of the authority concerned.

(8) Without prejudice to the preceding provisions of this section, a Local Commissioner shall not conduct an investigation under this Part of this Act in respect of any such action or matter as is described in Schedule 5 to this Act.

(9) Her Majesty may by Order in Council amend the said Schedule 5 so as to exclude from the provisions of that Schedule such actions or matters as may be described in the Order; and any Order made by virtue of this subsection shall be subject to annulment in pursuance of a resolution of either House of Parliament.

(10) In determining whether to initiate, continue or discontinue an investigation, a Local Commissioner shall, subject to the proceeding provisions of this section, act at discretion; and any question whether a complaint is duly made under this Part of this Act shall be determined by the Local Commissioner.

(11), (12) * * * * *

27 Provisions relating to complaints

(1) A complaint under this Part of this Act may be made by any individual, or by any body of persons whether incorporated or not, not being—

(a) a local authority or other authority or body constituted for purposes of the public service or of local government, or for the purposes of carrying on under national ownership any industry or undertaking or part of an industry or undertaking;

(b) any other authority or body whose members are appointed by Her Majesty or any Minister of the Crown or government department, or whose revenues consist wholly or mainly of moneys provided by Parliament.

(2) * * * * *

28 Procedure in respect of investigations

(1) Where a Local Commissioner proposes to conduct an investigation pursuant to a complaint, he shall afford to the authority concerned, and to any person who is alleged in the complaint to have taken or authorised the action complained of, an opportunity to comment on any allegations contained in the complaint.

(2) Every such investigation shall be conducted in private, but except as aforesaid the procedure for conducting an investigation shall be such as the Local Commissioner considers appropriate in the circumstances of the case; and without prejudice to the generality of the preceding provision the Local Commissioner may obtain information from such persons and in such manner, and make such inquiries as he thinks fit, and may determine whether any person may be represented (by counsel or solicitor or otherwise) in the investigation.

(3) * * * * *

(4) The conduct of an investigation under this Part of this Act shall not affect any action taken by the authority concerned, or any power or duty of that authority to take further action with respect to any matters subject to the investigation.

29 Investigations: further provisions

(1) For the purposes of an investigation under this Part of this Act a Local Commissioner may require any member or officer of the authority concerned, or any other person who in his opinion is able to furnish information or produce documents relevant to the investigation, to furnish any such information or produce any such documents.

(2) For the purposes of any such investigation a Local Commissioner shall have the same powers as the High Court in respect of the attendance and examination of witnesses, and in respect of the production of documents.

(3) A Local Commissioner may, under subsection (1) above, require any person to furnish information concerning communications between the authority concerned and any Government department, or to produce any correspondence or other documents forming part of any such written communications.

(4) No obligation to maintain secrecy or other restriction upon the disclosure of information obtained by or furnished to persons in Her Majesty's service, whether imposed by any enactment or by any rule of law, shall apply to the disclosure of information in accordance with subsection (3) above; and where that subsection applies the Crown shall not be entitled to any such privilege in respect of the production of documents or the giving of evidence as is allowed by law in legal proceedings.

(5)-(10) * * * * *

30 Reports on investigations

(1) In any case where a Local Commissioner conducts an investigation, or decides not to conduct an investigation, he shall send a report of the results of the investigation, or as the case may be a statement of his reasons for not conducting an investigation—

(a) to the person, if any, who referred the complaint to the Local Commissioner in accordance with section 26(2) above, and

(b) to the complainant, and

(c) to the authority concerned, and to any other authority or person who is alleged in the complaint to have taken or authorised the action complained of.

(2), (2A) * * * * *

(3) Apart from identifying the authority or authorities concerned the report shall not—

(a) mention the name of any person, or

(b) contain any particulars which, in the opinion of the Local Commissioner, are likely to identify any person and can be omitted without impairing the effectiveness of the report,

unless, after taking into account the public interest as well as the interests of the complainant and of persons other than the complainant, the Local Commissioner considers it necessary to mention the name of that person or to include in the report any such particulars.

(4) Subject to the provisions of subsection (7) below, the authority concerned shall for a period of three weeks make copies of the report available for inspection by the public without charge at all reasonable hours at one or more of their offices; and any person shall be entitled to take copies of, or extracts from, the report when so made available.

(5) Not later than one week after the report is received by the authority concerned, the proper officer of the authority shall give public notice, by advertisement in newspapers and such other ways as appear to him appropriate, that the report will be available for inspection as provided by subsection (4) above, and shall specify the date, being a date after the giving of the public notice, from which the period of three weeks will begin.

(6) * * * * *

(7) The Local Commissioner may, if he thinks fit after taking into account the public interest as well as the interests of the complainant and of persons other than the complainant, direct that a report specified in the direction shall not be subject to the provisions of subsections (4) and (5) above about its publication.

31 Reports on investigations: further provisions

(1) If in the opinion of the Local Commissioner, as set out in the report, injustice has been caused to the person aggrieved in consequence of maladministration, the report shall be laid before the authority concerned, and it shall be the duty of that authority to consider the report, and to notify the Local Commissioner of the action which the authority have taken, or propose to take.

(2) If the Local Commissioner—

(a) does not receive any such notification within a reasonable time; or

(b) is not satisfied with the action which the authority concerned have taken; or

(c) does not within a reasonable time receive confirmation from the authority concerned that they have taken action, as proposed, to the satisfaction of the Local Commissioner,

he shall make a further report setting out those facts; and section 30 above shall apply, with any necessary modifications, to that further report.

[(3) In any case where—

(a) a report is laid before an authority under subsection (1) above, and

(b) on consideration of the report, it appears to the authority that a payment should be made to, or some other benefit should be provided for, a person who has suffered injustice in consequence of maladministration referred to in the report, the authority may incur such expenditure as appears to them to be appropriate in making such a payment or providing such a benefit.]

32, 33 *****

34 Interpretation of Part III

(1), (2) *****

(3) It is hereby declared that nothing in this Part of this Act authorises or requires a Local Commissioner to question the merits of a decision taken without maladministration by an authority in the exercise of a discretion vested in that authority.

*****

Section 26

SCHEDULE 5

MATTERS NOT SUBJECT TO INVESTIGATION

1. The commencement or conduct of civil or criminal proceedings before any court of law.

2. Action taken by any authority in connection with the investigation or prevention of crime.

3.—(1) Action taken in matters relating to contractual or other commercial transactions of any authority to which Part III of this Act applies, including transactions falling within sub-paragraph (2) below but excluding transactions falling within sub-paragraph (3) below.

(2) The transactions mentioned in sub-paragraph (1) above as included in the matters which, by virtue of that sub-paragraph, are not subject to investigation are all transactions of an authority to which Part III of this Act applies relating to the operation of public passenger transport, the carrying on of a dock or harbour undertaking, the provision of entertainment, or the provision and operation of industrial establishments and of markets.

(3) The transactions mentioned in sub-paragraph (1) above as not included in those matters are—

(a) transactions for or relating to the acquisition or disposal of land; and

(b) all transactions (not being transactions falling within sub-paragraph (2) above) in the discharge of functions exercisable under any public general Act, other than those required for the procurement of the goods and services necessary to discharge those functions.

4. Action taken in respect of appointments or removals, pay, discipline, superannuation or other personnel matters.

5.—(1) Any action taken by a local education authority in the exercise of functions under section 23 of the Education Act 1944 [or sections 17 to 19 of the Education (No 2) Act 1986] (secular instruction in county schools and in voluntary schools).

(2) Any action concerning—

(a) the giving of instruction, whether secular or religious, or

(b) conduct, curriculum, internal organisation, management or discipline, whether—

(i) in any school maintained by the authority, or

(ii) in any college of education or establishment of further education maintained by the authority.

NORTHERN IRELAND ACT 1974
(1974, c. 28)

An Act to provide for the dissolution of the existing Northern Ireland Assembly and its prorogation until dissolution; to make temporary provision for the government of Northern Ireland; to provide for the election and holding of a Constitutional Convention in Northern Ireland; and for purposes connected with those matters [17 July 1974]

Territorial extent Northern Ireland

1 Dissolution and prorogation of existing Assembly and temporary provision for government of Northern Ireland

(1) Her Majesty may by Order in Council dissolve the Assembly elected under the Northern Ireland Assembly Act 1973; and subsection (7) of section 27 of the Northern Ireland Constitution Act 1973 (power to appoint day for new elections etc) shall have effect on the dissolution of that Assembly under this section as if it had been dissolved by Her Majesty under subsection (5) of that section.

(2) . . .

(3) The provisions of Schedule 1 to this Act shall have effect with respect to the exercise of legislative, executive and other functions in relation to Northern Ireland during the interim period specified by or under subsection (4) below.

(4) The interim period shall be the period of one year beginning with the passing of this Act but the Secretary of State may by order direct that it shall continue until a date after, or end on a date earlier than, the date on which it would otherwise expire (whether by virtue of this subsection or of a previous order thereunder).

(5) No order under subsection (4) above shall provide for the interim period to continue until a date more than one year after the date on which it would otherwise expire.

(6) The power to make an order under subsection (4) above shall be exercisable by statutory instrument; and no order shall be made under that subsection unless a draft of it has been approved by resolution of each House of Parliament.

2 . . .

Section 1(3) SCHEDULE 1

TEMPORARY PROVISION FOR GOVERNMENT OF NORTHERN IRELAND

Legislative functions

1.—(1) During the interim period—

(a) no Measure shall be passed by the Assembly; and

(b) Her Majesty may by Order in Council make laws for Northern Ireland, and in particular, provision for any matter for which the Constitution Act authorises or requires provision to be made by Measure.

(2) No recommendation shall be made to Her Majesty to make any Order in Council under this paragraph containing a provision in relation to which the Secretary of State would be precluded by section 5(1) of the Constitution Act from giving his consent if it were contained in a proposed Measure.

(3) The power to make an Order in Council under this paragraph includes power to vary or revoke a previous Order made thereunder.

(4) No recommendation shall be made to Her Majesty to make an Order in Council under this paragraph unless either—

(a) a draft of the Order has been approved by resolution of each House of Parliament; or

(b) the Order declares that it has been made to appear to Her Majesty that by reason of urgency the Order requires to be made without a draft having been so approved.

(5) Any Order in Council under this paragraph, other than an Order of which a draft has been approved by resolution of each House of Parliament, shall be laid before Parliament after being made and, if at the end of the period of forty days after the date on which it is made the Order has not been approved by resolution of each House, shall then cease to have effect (but without prejudice to anything previously done under the Order or to the making of a new Order).

(6) In reckoning the period mentioned in sub-paragraph (5) above no account shall be taken of any time during which Parliament is dissolved or prorogued or during which both Houses are adjourned for more than four days.

(7) References to Measures in any enactment or instrument (whether passed or made before or after the passing cf this Act) shall, so far as the context permits, be deemed to include references to Orders in Council under this paragraph.

(8) Orders in Council under this paragraph may be omitted from any annual edition of statutory instruments required to be prepared under regulations made by virtue of section 8 of the Statutory Instrtuments Act 1946.

* * * * *

TRADE UNION AND LABOUR RELATIONS ACT 1974
(1974, c. 52)

An Act to repeal the Industrial Relations Act 1971; to make provision with respect to the law relating to trade unions, employers' associations, workers and employers, including the law relating to unfair dismissal, and with respect to the jurisdiction and procedure of industrial tribunals; and for connected purposes [31 July 1974]

Territorial extent England and Wales, Scotland

* * * * *

Restrictions on legal liability and legal proceedings

[15 Peaceful picketing

(1) It shall be lawful for a person in contemplation or furtherance of a trade dispute to attend—

(a) at or near his own place of work, or

(b) if he is an official of a trade union, at or near the place of work of a member of that union whom he is accompanying and whom he represents,

for the purpose only of peacefully obtaining or communicating information, or peacefully persuading any person to work or abstain from working.

(2) If a person works or normally works—

(a) otherwise than at any one place, or

(b) at a place the location of which is such that attendance there for a purpose mentioned in subsection (1) above is impracticable,

his place of work for the purposes of that subsection shall be any premises of his employer from which he works or from which his work is administered.

(3) In the case of a worker who is not in employment

[where—

(a) his] last employment was terminated in connection with a trade dispute [or

(b) the termination of his employment was one of the circumstances giving rise to a trade dispute,]

subsection (1) above shall in relation to that dispute have effect as if any reference to his place of work were a reference to his former place of work.]

(4) * * * * *

Note This section is printed as substituted by the Employment Act 1980, s. 16(1) and further amended by the Employment Act 1982.

* * * * *

CRIMINAL PROCEDURE (SCOTLAND) ACT 1975
(1975, c. 21)

An Act to consolidate certain enactments relating to criminal procedure in Scotland

[8 May 1975]

Territorial extent Scotland

PART I
SOLEMN PROCEDURE

Jurisdiction

* * * * *

9 Instructions by Lord Advocate as to reporting offences
The Lord Advocate may from time to time issue instructions to a chief constable with regard to the reporting, for consideration of the question of prosecution, of offences alleged to have been committed within the area of such chief constable, and it shall be the duty of a chief constable to whom any such instruction is issued to secure compliance therewith.

10 Intimation of proceedings in High Court to Lord Advocate
In any proceedings in the High Court (other than a proceeding to which the Lord Advocate or a procurator fiscal is a party) it shall be competent for the court to order intimation of such proceedings to the Lord Advocate.

11 Procedure after intimation
On intimation being made to the Lord Advocate of a proceeding in the High Court under section 10 of this Act, the Lord Advocate shall be entitled to appear and be heard in such proceeding.

PROCEDURE PRIOR TO TRIAL

Arrest, Judicial Examination, Custody, Bail, Etc.

18 Power of constable to take offenders into custody
(1) Without prejudice to any other powers of arrest, any constable may take into custody, without warrant—

(a) any person who within his view commits any of the offences mentioned in Schedule 1 to this Act, if the constable does not know and cannot ascertain his name and address;

(b) any person who has committed, or whom he has reason to believe to have committed, any of the offences mentioned in Schedule 1 to this Act, if the constable does not know and cannot ascertain his name and address or has reasonable ground for believing that he will abscond.

[(2) Where a person has been arrested under this section, the officer in charge of a police station may—

(a) liberate him upon a written undertaking, signed by him and certified by the said officer, in terms of which that person undertakes to appear at a specified court at a specified time; or

(b) liberate him without any such undertaking; or

(c) refuse to liberate him; and such refusal and the detention of that person until his case is tried in the usual form shall not subject the officer to any claim whatsoever.

(3) A person in breach of an undertaking given by him under subsection (2)(a) above without reasonable excuse shall be guilty of an offence and liable to the following penalties—

(a) a fine not exceeding [level 4 on the standard scale]; and

(b) imprisonment for a period not exceeding 3 months.

(4) The penalties provided for in subsection (3) above may be imposed in addition to any other penalty which it is competent for the court to impose, notwithstanding that the total of penalties imposed may exceed the maximum penalty which it is competent to impose in respect of the original offence.

(5) In any proceedings relating to an offence under this section, a writing, purporting to be such an undertaking as is mentioned in subsection (2)(a) above and bearing to be signed and certified, shall be sufficient evidence of the terms of the undertaking given by the arrested person.]

19 Prisoners before examination to have access to solicitor

(1) Where any person has been arrested on any criminal charge, such person shall be entitled immediately upon such arrest

[(a)] to have intimation sent to a solicitor that his professional assistance is required by such person, and informing him of the place to which such person is to be taken for examination [and

(b) to be told what rights there are under paragraph (a) above and subsections (2) and (3) below.]

(2) Such solicitor shall be entitled to have a private interview with the person accused before he is examined on declaration, and to be present at such examination.

(3) It shall be in the power of the sheriff or justice to delay such examination for a period not exceeding 48 hours from and after the time of such person's arrest, in order to allow time for the attendance of such solicitor.

20 Accused at examination need not emit a declaration

(1) Where the accused is brought before the sheriff for examination on any charge and he or his solicitor intimates that he does not desire to emit a declaration in regard to such charge, it shall be unnecessary to take a declaration, and [subject to section 20A of this Act] the accused may be committed for further examination or until liberated in due course of law without a declaration being taken.

(2) Where the accused does not desire to emit a declaration as aforesaid, that fact shall be recorded in the warrant of committal.

(3) The foregoing provisions of this section shall not prejudice the right of the accused subsequently to emit a declaration on intimating to the prosecutor his desire to do so; [and that declaration shall be taken in further examination.]

[(3A) An accused person may, where subsequent to examination (or further examination) on any charge the prosecutor desires to question him as regards an extrajudicial confession (whether or not a full admission) allegedly made by him, to or in the hearing of an officer of police, which is relevant to the charge and as regards which he has not previously been examined, be brought before the sheriff for further examination.

(3B) Where the accused is brought before the sheriff for further examination it shall be in the power of the sheriff to delay that examination for a period not exceeding 24 hours in order to allow time for the attendance of the accused's solicitor.

(3C) Any proceedings before the sheriff in examination or further examination shall be conduct in chambers and without the presence of any co-accused.]

(4) * * * * *

[20A Accused at examination may be questioned by prosecutor

(1) Subject to the following provisions of this section, an accused on being brought before the sheriff for examination on any charge (whether that examination is the first examination or a further examination) may be questioned by the prosecutor in so far as such questioning is directed towards eliciting any denial, explanation, justification or comment which the accused may have as regards—

(a) matters averred in the charge:

Provided that the particular aims of a line of questions under this paragraph shall be to determine—

(i) whether any account which the accused can give ostensibly discloses a category of defence (as for example alibi, incrimination, or the consent of an alleged victim); and

(ii) the nature and particulars of that defence;

(b) the alleged making by the accused, to or in the hearing of an officer of police, of an extrajudicial confession (whether or not a full admission) relevant to the charge:

Provided that questions under this paragraph may only be put if the accused has, before the examination, received from the prosecutor or from an officer of police a written record of the confession allegedly made; or

(c) what is said in any declaration emitted in regard to the charge by the accused at the examination.

(2) The prosecutor shall, in framing questions in exercise of his power under subsection (1) above, have regard to the following principles—

(a) the questions should not be designed to challenge the truth of anything said by the accused;

(b) there should be no reiteration of a question which the accused has refused to answer at the examination; and

(c) there should be no leading questions;

and the sheriff shall ensure that all questions are fairly put to, and understood by, the accused.

(3) The accused, where he is represented by a solicitor at the judicial examination, shall be told by the sheriff that he may consult that solicitor before answering any question.

(4) With the permission of the sheriff, the solicitor for the accused may ask the accused any question the purpose of which is to clarify any ambiguity in an answer given by the accused to the prosecutor at the examination or to give the accused an opportunity to answer any question which he has previously refused to answer.

(5) An accused may decline to answer a question under subsection (1) above; and, where he is subsequently tried on the charge mentioned in that subsection or on any other charge arising out of the circumstances which gave rise to the charge so mentioned, his having so declined may be commented upon by the prosecutor, the judge presiding at the trial, or any co-accused, only where and in so far as the accused (or any witness called on his behalf) in evidence avers something which could have been stated appropriately in answer to that question.

(6) The procedure in relation to examination under this section shall be prescribed by Act of Adjournal under this Act.]

Note This section and the one following were added by the Criminal Justice (Scotland) Act 1980, s. 6.

[20B Record to be made of proceedings at examination

(1) The prosecutor shall provide for a *verbatim* record to be made by a shorthand writer of all questions to and answers and declarations by, the accused in examination, or further examination, under sections 20 and 20A of this Act.

(2) The shorthand writer shall sign the transcript of the notes taken by him and shall certify that it is a complete and accurate record of the said questions, answers and declarations; and, subject to subsection (4) below, it shall for all purposes be so deemed.

(3)-(9) * * * * *

169 Restrictions on report of proceedings involving persons under 16

(1) No newspaper report of any proceedings in a court shall reveal the name, address or school, or include any particulars calculated to lead to the identification, of any person under the age of 16 years concerned in the proceedings, either—

(a) as being a person against or in respect of whom the proceedings are taken; or

(b) as being a witness therein;

nor shall any picture which is, or includes, a picture of a person under the age of 16 years so concerned in the proceedings be published in any newspaper in a context relevant to the proceedings:

Provided that, in any case—

(i) where the person is concerned in the proceedings as a witness only and no one against whom the proceedings are taken is under the age of 16 years, the foregoing provisions of this subsection shall not apply unless the court so directs;

(ii) the court may at any stage of the proceedings if satisfied that it is in the public interest so to do, direct that the requirements of this section (including such requirements as applied by a direction under paragraph (i) above) shall be dispensed with to such extent as the court may specify;

(iii) the Secretary of State may, after completion of the proceedings, if so satisfied by order dispense with the said requirements to such extent as may be specified in the order.

(2) This section shall, with necessary modifications, apply in relation to sound and television broadcasts [and any programme included in a cable programme service] as it applies in relation to newspapers.

(3) A person who publishes matter in contravention of this section shall be guilty of an offence and liable on summary conviction to a fine not exceeding [level 5 on the standard scale].

(4) In this section, references to a court shall not include a court in England, Wales or Northern Ireland.

* * * * *

Note Sections 294 and 374 make substantially the same provisions in relation to summary procedure as ss. 18 and 169 for solemn procedure.

Sections 14, 18, 62, 143, 167, 171, 294, 313, 323, 331, 348, 363, 364 and 368

SCHEDULE 1

OFFENCES AGAINST CHILDREN UNDER THE AGE OF 17 YEARS TO WHICH SPECIAL PROVISIONS APPLY

(a) Any offence under the Criminal Law Amendment Act 1885.

(b) Any offence in respect of a child under the age of 17 years which constitutes the crime of incest.

(c) Any offence under section 12, 13, 14, 15, 22 or 33 of the Children and Young Persons (Scotland) Act 1937.

(d) Any other offence involving bodily injury to a child under the age of 17 years.

HOUSE OF COMMONS DISQUALIFICATION ACT 1975
(1975, c. 24)

An Act to consolidate certain enactments relating to disqualification for membership of the House of Commons [8 May 1975]

Territorial extent United Kingdom

1 Disqualification of holders of certain offices and places

(1) Subject to the provisions of this Act, a person is disqualified for membership of the House of Commons who for the time being—

(a) holds any of the judicial offices specified in Part I of Schedule 1 to this Act;

(b) is employed in the civil service of the Crown, whether in an established capacity or not, and whether for the whole or part of his time;

(c) is a member of any of the regular armed forces of the Crown or the Ulster Defence Regiment;

(d) is a member of any police force maintained by a police authority;

(e) is a member of the legislature of any country or territory outside the Commonwealth; or

(f) holds any office described in Part II or Part III of Schedule 1.

(2), (3) * * * * *

(4) Except as provided by this Act, a person shall not be disqualified for membership of the House of Commons by reason of his holding an office or place of profit under the

Crown or any other office or place; and a person shall not be disqualified for appointment to or for holding any office or place by reason of his being a member of that House.

2 Ministerial offices

(1) Not more than ninety-five persons being the holders of offices specified in Schedule 2 to this Act (in this sectin referred to as Ministerial offices) shall be entitled to sit and vote in the House of Commons at any one time.

(2) If at any time the number of members of the House of Commons who are holders of Ministerial offices exceeds the number entitled to sit and vote in that House under subsection (1) above, none except any who were both members of that House and holders of Ministerial offices before the excess occurred shall sit or vote therein until the number has been reduced, by death, resignation or otherwise, to the number entitled to sit and vote as aforesaid.

(3) A person holding a Ministerial office is not disqualified by this Act by reason of any office held by him ex officio as the holder of that Ministerial office.

3 Reserve and Auxiliary Forces etc. * * * * *

4 Stewardship of Chiltern Hundreds, etc.

For the purposes of the provisions of this Act relating to the vacation of the seat of a member of the House of Commons who becomes disqualified by this Act for membership of that House, the office of steward or bailiff of Her Majesty's three Chiltern Hundreds of Stoke, Desborough and Burnham, or of the Manor of Northstead, shall be treated as included among the offices described in Part III of Schedule 1 to this Act.

5 Power to amend Schedule 1

(1) If at any time it is resolved by the House of Commons that Schedule 1 to this Act be amended, whether by the addition or omission of any office or the removal of any office from one Part of the Schedule to another, or by altering the description of any office specified therein, Her Majesty may by Order in Council amend that Schedule accordingly.

(2) * * * * *

6 Effects of disqualification and provision for relief

(1) Subject to any order made by the House of Commons under this section,—

(a) if any person disqualified by this Act for membership of that House, or for membership for a particular constituency, is elected as a member of that House, or as a member for that constituency, as the case may be, his election shall be void; and

(b) if any person being a member of that House becomes disqualified by this Act for membership for the constituency for which he is sitting, his seat shall be vacated.

(2) If, in a case falling or alleged to fall within subsection (1) above, it appears to the House of Commons that the grounds of disqualification or alleged disqualification under this Act which subsisted or arose at the material time have been removed, and that it is otherwise proper so to do, that House may by order direct that any such disqualification incurred on those grounds at that time shall be disregarded for the purposes of this section.

(3), (4) * * * * *

7 Jurisdiction of Privy Council as to disqualification

(1) Any person who claims that a person purporting to be a member of the House of Commons is disqualified by this Act, or has been so disqualified at any time since his election, may apply to Her Majesty in Council, in accordance with such rules as Her Majesty in Council may prescribe, for a declaration to that effect.

(2) Section 3 of the Judicial Committee Act 1833 (reference to the Judicial Committee of the Privy Council of appeals to Her Majesty in Council) shall apply to any application under this section as it applies to an appeal to Her Majesty in Council from a court.

(3)-(5) * * * * *

8, 9 *****

10 Savings as to disqualification of priests in holy orders etc.

Nothing in this Act shall be construed as affecting the enactments relating to the disqualification for membership of the House of Commons of priests in holy orders or ministers of any religious denomination.

*****

Section 2

SCHEDULE 2
MINISTERIAL OFFICE

Prime Minister and First Lord of the Treasury.
Lord President of the Council.
Lord Privy Seal.
Chancellor of the Duchy of Lancaster.
Paymaster General.
President of the Board of Trade.
Secretary of State.
Chancellor of the Exchequer.
Minister of Agriculture, Fisheries and Food.
Minister of State.
Chief Secretary to the Treasury.
Minister in charge of a public department of Her Majesty's Government in the United Kingdom (if not within the other provisions of this Schedule).
Attorney General.
Lord Advocate.
Solicitor General.
Solicitor General for Scotland.
Parliamentary Secretary to the Treasury.
Financial Secretary to the Treasury.
Parliamentary Secretary in a Government Department other than the Treasury, or not in a department.
Junior Lord of the Treasury.
Treasurer of Her Majesty's Household.
Comptroller of Her Majesty's Household.
Vice-Chamberlain of Her Majesty's Household.
Assistant Government Whip.

MINISTERIAL AND OTHER SALARIES ACT 1975
(1975, c. 27)

An Act to consolidate the enactments relating to the salaries of Ministers and Opposition Leaders and Chief Whips and to other matters connected therewith [8 May 1975]

Territorial extent United Kingdom

1 Salaries

(1) Subject to the provisions of this Act—

(a) there shall be paid to the holder of any Ministerial office specified in Schedule 1 to this Act such salary as is provided for by that Schedule; and

(b) there shall be paid to the Leaders and Whips of the Opposition such salaries as are provided for by Schedule 2 to this Act.

(2) There shall be paid to the Lord Chancellor a salary (which shall be charged on and paid out of the Consolidated Fund of the United Kingdom) at such rate as together with the salary payable to him as Speaker of the House of Lords will amount to [£83,000] a year, but

so that the salary payable to a Lord Chancellor under this subsection shall be abated by the amount of any pension payable to him in respect of any public office in the United Kingdom or elsewhere to which he had previously been appointed or elected.

(3) There shall be paid to the Speaker of the House of Commons a salary (which shall be charged on and paid out of the Consolidated Fund of the United Kingdom) of [£34,875] a year; and on a dissolution of Parliament the Speaker of the House of Commons at the time of the dissolution shall for this purpose be deemed to remain Speaker until a Speaker is chosen by the New Parliament.

(4), (5) * * * * *

2 Opposition Leaders and Whips

(1) In this Act "Leader of the Opposition" means, in relation to either House of Parliament, that Member of that House who is for the time being the Leader in that House of the party in opposition to Her Majesty's Government having the greatest numerical strength in the House of Commons; and "Chief Opposition Whip" means, in relation to either House of Parliament, the person for the time being nominated as such by the Leader of the Opposition in that House; and "Assistant Opposition Whip", in relation to the House of Commons, means a person for the time being nominated as such, and to be paid as such, by the Leader of the Opposition in the House of Commons.

(2) If any doubt arises as to which is or was at any material time the party in opposition to Her Majesty's Government having the greatest numerical strength in the House of Commons, or as to who is or was at any material time the leader in that House of such a party, the question shall be decided for the purposes of this Act by the Speaker of the House of Commons, and his decision, certified in writing under his hand, shall be final and conclusive.

(3) If any doubt arises as to who is or was at any material time the Leader in the House of Lords of the said party, the question shall be decided for the purposes of this Act by the Lord Chancellor, and his decision, certified in writing under his hand, shall be final and conclusive.

3 * * * * *

4 Interpretation

(1) In this Act—

"Junior Lord of the Treasury" means any Lord Commissioner of the Treasury other than the First Lord and the Chancellor of the Exchequer;

"Minister of State" and "Parliamentary Secretary" have the same meanings as in the House of Commons Disqualification Act 1975.

(2) * * * * *

* * * * *

MINISTERS OF THE CROWN ACT 1975
(1975, c. 26)

An Act to consolidate the enactments relating to the redistribution of functions between Ministers of the Crown, the alteration of the style and title of such Ministers and certain other provisions about such Ministers [8 May 1975]

Territorial extent United Kingdom

1 Power by Order in Council to transfer functions of Ministers

(1) Her Majesty may by Order in Council—

(a) provide for the transfer to any Minister of the Crown of any functions previously exercisable by another Minister of the Crown;

(b) provide for the dissolution of the government department in the charge of any Minister of the Crown and the transfer to or distribution among such other Minister or Ministers of the Crown as may be specified in the Order of any functions previously exercisable by the Minister in charge of that department;

(c) direct that functions of any Minister of the Crown shall be exercisable concurrently with another Minister of the Crown, or shall cease to be so exercisable.

(2) An Order in Council under this section may contain such incidental, consequential and supplemental provisions as may be necessary or expedient for the purpose of giving full effect to the Order, including provisions—

(a) for the transfer of any property, rights and liabilities held, enjoyed or incurred by any Minister of the Crown in connection with any functions transferred or distributed;

(b) for the carrying on and completion by or under the authority of the Minister to whom any functions are transferred of anything commenced by or under the authority of a minister of the Crown before the date when the Order takes effect;

(c) for such adaptations of the enactments relating to any functions transferred as may be necessary to enable them to be exercised by the Minister to whom they are transfered and his officers;

(d) for making in the enactments regulating the number of offices in respect of which salaries may be paid or in section 2 of, and Schedule 2 to, the House of Commons Disqualification Act 1975 (which regulate the number of office holders who may be elected, and sit and vote, as members of the House of Commons), such modifications as may be expedient by reason of any transfer of functions or dissolution of a Department effected by the Order;

(e) for the substitution of the Minister to whom functions are transferred for any other Minister of the Crown in any instrument, contract, or legal proceedings made or commenced before the date when the Order takes effect.

(3) No modifications shall be made by virtue of paragraph (d) of subsection (2) above, in any of the enactments mentioned in that paragraph, so as to increase the amount of any salary which may be paid, or the aggregate number of persons to whom salaries may be paid, under those enactments or the aggregate number of persons capable thereunder of sitting and voting as Members of the House of Commons.

(4) Where by any Order made under this section provision is made for the transfer of functions in respect of which any Minister may sue or be sued by virtue of any enactment, the Order shall make any provision which may be required for enabling the Minister to whom those functions are transferred to sue or be sued in like manner.

2, 3 * * * * *

4 Change of title of Ministers

If Her Majesty is pleased by Order in Council to direct that any change shall be made in the style and title of a Minister of the Crown, the Order may contain provisions substituting the new style and title—

(a) in the enactments (including those mentioned in section 1(2)(d) above) relating to the Minister;

(b) in any instrument, contract, or legal proceedings made or commenced before the date when the Order takes effect.

5 Supplementary provisions as to Orders

(1) No Order in Council which provides for the dissolution of a government department shall be made under this Act unless, after copies of the draft thereof have been laid before Parliament, each House presents an Address to Her Majesty praying that the Order be made.

(2) An Order in Council under this Act, not being an Order made in pursuance of such an Address as aforesaid, shall be laid before Parliament and shall be subject to annulment in pursuance of a resolution of either House of Parliament.

(3), (4) * * * * *

(5) Nothing in this Act shall prejudice any power exercisable by virtue of the prerogative of the Crown in relation to the functions of Ministers of the Crown.

(6) * * * * *

* * * * *

SEX DISCRIMINATION ACT 1975
(1975, c. 65)

An Act to render unlawful certain kinds of sex discrimination and discrimination on the ground of marriage, and establish a Commission with the function of working towards the elimination of such discrimination and promoting equality of opportunity between men and women generally; and for related purposes [12 November 1975]

Territorial extent England and Wales, Scotland

* * * * *

PART V
GENERAL EXCEPTIONS FROM PARTS II TO IV

52 Acts safeguarding national security

(1) Nothing in Parts II to IV shall render unlawful an act done for the purpose of safeguarding national security.

(2) A certificate purporting to be signed by or on behalf of a Minister of the Crown and certifying that an act specified in the certificate was done for the purpose of safeguarding national security shall be conclusive evidence that it was done for that purpose.

(3) A document purporting to be a certificate such as is mentioned in subsection (2) shall be received in evidence and, unless the contrary is proved, shall be deemed to be such a certificate.

* * * * *

RACE RELATIONS ACT 1976
(1976, c. 74)

An Act to make fresh provision with respect to discrimination on racial grounds and relations between people of different racial groups; and to make in the Sex Discrimination Act 1975 amendments for bringing provisions in that Act relating to its administration and enforcement into conformity with the corresponding provisons in this Act [22 November 1976]

Territorial extent England and Wales, Scotland

* * * * *

PART VI
GENERAL EXEMPTIONS FROM PARTS II TO IV

42 Acts safeguarding national security

Nothing in Parts II to IV shall render unlawful an act done for the purpose of safeguarding national security.

PART VIII
ENFORCEMENT

Evidence

69 Evidence

(1) *****

(2) In any proceedings under this ACt a certificate signed by or on behalf of a Minister of the Crown and certifying—

(a) that any arrangements or conditions specified in the certificate were made, approved or imposed by a Minister of the Crown and were in operation at a time or throughout a period so specified; or

(b) that an act specified in the certificate was done for the purpose of safeguarding national security,

shall be conclusive evidence of the matters certified.

(3) A document purporting to be a certificate such as is mentioned in subsection (2) shall be received in evidence and, unless the contrary is proved, shall be deemed to be such a certificate.

70 . . .

PART X
SUPPLEMENTAL

71 Local Authorities: general statutory duty

Without prejudice to their obligation to comply with any other provision of this Act, it shall be the duty of every local authority to make appropriate arangements with a view to securing that their various functions are carried out with due regard to the need—

(a) to eliminate unlawful racial discrimination; and

(b) to promote equality of opportunity and good relations, between persons of different racial groups;

[and in this section "local authority" includes the Inner London Education Authority and a joint authority established by Part IV of the Local Government Act 1985.]

*****

CRIMINAL LAW ACT 1977
(1977, c. 45)

An Act to amend the law of England and Wales with respect to criminal conspiracy; to make new provision in that law, in place of the provisions of the common law and the Statutes of Forcible Entry, for restricting the use or threat of violence for securing entry into any premises and for penalising unauthorised entry or remaining on premises in certain circumstances; otherwise to amend the criminal law, including the law with respect to the administration of criminal justice; to provide for the alteration of certain pecuniary and other limits; to amend section 9(4) of the Administration of Justice Act 1973, the Legal Aid Act 1974, the Rabies Act 1974 and the Diseases of Animals (Northern Ireland) Order 1975 and the law about juries and coroners' inquests; and for conencted purposes [29 July 1977]

Territorial extent England and Wales

PART I
CONSPIRACY

1 The offence of conspiracy

[(1) Subject to the following provisions of this Part of this Act, if a person agrees with any other person or persons that a course of conduct shall be pursued which, if the agreement is carried out in accordance with their intentions, either—

(a) will necessarily amount to or involve the commission of any offence or offences by one or more of the parties to the agreement, or

(b) would do so but for the existence of facts which render the commission of the offence or any of the offences impossible,

he is guilty of conspiracy to commit the offence in question.]

(2) Where liability for any offence may be incurred without knowledge on the part of the person committing it of any particular fact or circumstances necessary for the commission of the offence, a person shall nevertheless not be guilty of conspiracy to commit that offence by virtue of subsection (1) above unless he and at least one other party to the agreement intend or know that the fact or circumstances shall or will exist at the time when the conduct constituting the offence is to take place.

(3) Where in pursuance of any agreement the acts in question in relation to any offence are to be done in contemplation or furtherance of a trade dispute (within the meaning of the Trade Union and Labour Relations Act 1974) that offence shall be disregarded for the purposes of subsection (1) above provided that it is a summary offence which is not punishable with imprisonment.

(4) * * * * *

5 Abolitions, savings, transitional provisions, consequential amendment and repeals

(1) Subject to the following provisions of this section, the offence of conspiracy at common law is hereby abolished.

(2) Subsection (1) above shall not affect the offence of conspiracy at common law so far as relates to conspiracy to defraud, . . .

(3) Subsection (1) above shall not affect the offence of conspiracy at common law if and in so far as it may be committed by entering into an agreement to engage in conduct which—

(a) tends to corrupt public morals or outrages public decency; but

(b) would not amount to or involve the commission of an offence if carried out by a single person otherwise than in pursuance of an agreement.

(4)-(9) * * * * *

(10), (11) . . .

* * * * *

EMPLOYMENT PROTECTION (CONSOLIDATION) ACT 1978
(1978, c. 44)

An Act to consolidate certain enactments relating to rights of employees arising out of their employment; and certain enactments relating to the insolvency of employers; to industrial tribunals; to recoupment of certain benefits; to conciliation officers; and to the Employment Appeal Tribunal [31 July 1978]

Territorial extent England and Wales, Scotland

* * * * *

PART IX
MISCELLANEOUS AND SUPPLEMENTAL

Crown employment

138 Application of Act to Crown employment

(1) Subject to the following provisions of this section, Parts I (so far as it relates to itemised pay statements), II, III . . ., V, VIII and this Part and section 53 shall have effect in relation to Crown employment and to persons in Crown employment as they have effect in relation to other employment and to other employees.

(2) In this section, subject to subsection (3) to (5), "Crown employment" means employment under or for the purposes of a government department or any officer or body exercising on behalf of the Crown functions conferred by any enactment.

(3) This section does not apply to service as a member of the naval, military or air forces of the Crown, . . ., but does apply to employment by any association established for the purposes of [Part VI of the Reserve Forces Act 1980].

(4) For the purposes of this section, Crown employment does not include any employment in respect of which there is in force a certificate issued by or on behalf of a Minister of the Crown certifying that employment of a description specified in the certificate, or the employment of a particular person so specified, is (or, at a time specified in the certificate, was) required to be excepted from this section for the purpose of safeguarding national security; and any document purporting to be a certificate so issued shall be received in evidence and shall, unless the contrary is proved, be deemed to be such a certificate.

(5), (6) * * * * *

(7) For the purposes of the application of the provisions of this Act in relation to Crown employment in accordance with subsection (1)—

(a) any reference to an employee shall be construed as a reference to a person in Crown employment;

(b) any reference to a contract of employment shall be construed as a reference to the terms of employment of a person in Crown employment;

(c) any reference to dismissal shall be construed as a reference to the termination of Crown employment;

(d) any reference to redundancy shall be construed as a reference to the existence of such circumstances as, in accordance with any arrangements for the time being in force as mentioned in section 111(3), are treated as equivalent to redundancy in relation to Crown employment;

(e) the reference in paragraph 1(5)(c) of Schedule 9 to a person's undertaking or any undertaking in which he works shall be construed as a reference to the national interest; and

(f) any other reference to an undertaking shall be constrtued, in relation to a Minister of the Crown, as a reference to his functions or (as the context may require) to the department of which he is in charge and, in relation to a government department, officer or body, shall be construed as a reference to the functions of the department, officer or body or (as the context may require) to the department, officer or body.

(8) Where the terms of employment of a person in Crown employment restrict his right to take part in—

(a) certain political activities; or

(b) activities which may conflict with his official functions,

nothing in section 29 shall require him to be allowed time of work for public duties connected with any such activities.

* * * * *

EUROPEAN ASSEMBLY ELECTIONS ACT 1978
(1978, c. 10)

An Act to make provision for and in connection with the election of representatives to the Assembly of the European Communities, and to prevent any treaty providing for any increase in the powers of the Assembly from being ratified by the United Kingdom unless approved by Act of Parliament

[5 May 1978]

Territorial extent United Kingdom

Note References to the Assembly should now be read as references to the Parliament: European Communities (Amendment) Act 1986, s. 3(1).

1 Election of representatives to the European Assembly
The representatives of the people of the United Kingdom in the Assembly of the European Communities . . . shall be elected in accordance with this Act.

2 Number of representatives
The number of representatives to the Assembly to be elected in the United Kingdom shall be 81; and of those representatives—
(a) 66 shall be elected in England;
(b) 8 shall be elected in Scotland;
(c) 4 shall be elected in Wales; and
(d) 3 shall be elected in Northern Ireland.

3 Method of election
Assembly elections shall be held and conducted in accordance with the provisions of Schedule 1 to this Act (with Schedule 2) under the simple majority system (for Great Britain) and the single transferable vote system (for Nothern Ireland).

4, 5 * * * * *

6 Parliamentary approval of treaties increasing Assembly's powers
(1) No treaty which provides for any increase in the powers of the Assembly shall be ratified by the United Kingdom unless it has been approved by an Act of Parliament.
(2) In this section "treaty" includes any international agreement, and any protocol or annex to a treaty or international agreement.

Note Section 3(4) of the European Communities (Amendment) Act 1986 provides that for the purposes of this section the Single European Act is approved.

* * * * *

NORTHERN IRELAND (EMERGENCY PROVISIONS) ACT 1978
(1978, c. 5)

An Act to consolidate, with certain exceptions, the Northern Ireland (Emergency Provisions) Act 1973, the Northern Ireland (Young Persons) Act 1974 and the Northern Ireland (Emergency Provisions) (Amendment) Act 1975 [23 March 1978]

Territorial extent Northern Ireland

Note This Act is printed with extensive amendments made by the Northern Ireland (Emergency Provisions) Act 1987.

14 Powers of arrest of members of Her Majesty's forces
(1) A member of Her Majesty's forces on duty may arrest without warrant, and detain for not more than four hours, a person who [he has reasonable grounds to suspect is committing, has committed or is about to commit any offence].
(2) A person effecting an arrest under this section complies with any rule of law requiring him to state the ground of arrest if he states that he is effecting the arrest as a member of Her Majesty's forces.
(3) For the purpose of arresting a person under this section a member of Her Majesty's forces may enter and search any premises or other place—
(a) where that person is, or
(b) [if there are reasonable grounds for suspecting that that person is a terrorist or has committed an offence involving the use or possession of an explosive substance or firearm, where there are reasonable grounds for suspecting him to be.]

15-17 * * * * *

18 Power to stop and question

Any member of Her Majesty's forces on duty or any constable may stop and question any person for the purpose of ascertaining—

(a) that person's identity and movements;

(b) what he knows concerning any recent explosion or any other [recent] incident endangering life or concerning any person killed or injured in any such explosion or incident; or

(c) any one or more of the matters referred to in paragraphs (a) and (b) above.

(2) Any person who—

(a) fails to stop when required to do so under this section, or

(b) refuses to answer, or fails to answer to the best of his knowledge and ability, any question addressed to him under this section,

shall be liable on summary conviction to [a fine not exceeding level 5 on the standard scale.]

19-21 * * * * *

PART III

OFFENCES AGAINST PUBLIC SECURITY AND PUBLIC ORDER

22 Unlawful collection, etc of information

(1) No person shall, without lawful authority or reasonable excuse (the proof of which lies on him)—

(a) collect, record, publish, communicate or attempt to elicit any information with respect to any person to whom this paragraph applies which is of such a nature as is likely to be useful to terrorists;

(b) collect or record any information which is of such a nature as is likely to be useful to terrorists in planning or carrying out any act of violence; or

(c) have in his possession any record of or document containing any such information as is mentioned in paragraph (a) or (b) above.

(2) Subsection (1)(a) above applies to any of the following persons, that is to say—

(a) any constable or member of Her Majesty's forces;

(b) any person holding judicial office;

(c) any officer of any court; . . .

(d) any person employed for the whole of his time in the prison service in Northern Ireland; and

[(e) any person who has at any time been a person falling within any of the preceding paragraphs.]

(3) In subsection (1) above any reference to recording information includes a reference to recording it by means of photography or by any other means.

(4) If any person contravenes this section, he shall be liable—

(a) on summary conviction, to imprisonment for a term not exceeding six months or to a fine not exceeding [level 5 on the standard scale], or both;

(b) on conviction on indictment, to imprisonment for a term not exceeding ten years or a fine, or both.

(5) The court by or before which a person is convicted of an offence under this section may order the forfeiture of any record or document mentioned in subsection (1) above which is found in his possession.

(6) * * * * *

23 * * * * *

24 Failure to disperse when required to do so

(1) Where any commissioned officer of Her Majesty's forces or any officer of the Royal Ulster Constabulary not below the rank of chief inspector is of opinion that any assembly of three or more persons—

(a) may lead to a breach of the peace or public disorder; or

(b) may make undue demands on the police or Her Majesty's forces,

he, or any member of those forces on duty or any constable, may order the person constituting the assemby to disperse forthwith.

(2) Where an order is given under this section with respect to an assembly, any person who thereafter joins or remains in the assembly or otherwise fails to comply with the order shall be liable on summary conviction to imprisonment for a term not exceeding six months or to a fine not exceeding [level 5 on the standard scale], or both.

* * * * *

PROTECTION OF CHILDREN ACT 1978
(1978, c. 37)

An Act to prevent the exploitation of children by making indecent photographs of them; and to penalise the distribution, showing and advertisement of such indecent photographs

[20 July 1978]

Territorial extent England and Wales

1 Indecent photographs of children

(1) It is an offence for a person—

(a) to take, or permit to be taken, any indecent photograph of a child (meaning in this Act a person under the age of 16); or

(b) to distribute or show such indecent photographs; or

(c) to have in his possession such indecent photographs, with a view to their being distributed or shown by himself or others; or

(d) to publish or cause to be published any advertisement likely to be understood as conveying that the advertiser distributes or shows such indecent photographs, or intends to do so.

(2) For purposes of this Act, a person is to be regarded as distributing an indecent photograph if he parts with possession of it to, or exposes or offers it for acquisition by, another person.

(3) Proceedings for an offence under this Act shall not be instituted except by or with the consent of the Director of Public Prosecutions.

(4) Where a person is charged with an offence under subsection (1)(b) or (c), it shall be a defence for him to prove—

(a) that he had a legitimate reason for distributing or showing the photographs or (as the case may be) having them in his possession; or

(b) that he had not himself seen the photographs and did not know, nor had any cause to suspect, them to be indecent.

(5), (6) * * * * *

2 Evidence

(1), (2) . . .

(3) In proceedings under this Act a person is to be taken as having been a child at any material time if it appears from the evidence as a whole that he was then under the age of 16.

3 * * * * *

4 Entry, search and seizure

(1) The following applies where a justice of the peace is satisfied by information on oath, laid by or on behalf of the Director of Public Prosecutions or by a constable, that there is reasonable ground for suspecting that, in any premises in the petty sessions area for which he acts, there are indecent photographs of children and that such photographs—

(a) are or have been taken there; or

(b) are or have been shown there, or are kept there with a view to their being distributed or shown.

(2) The justice may issue a warrant under his hand authorising any constable to enter (if need be by force) and search the premises within fourteen days from the date of the warrant, and to seize and remove any articles which he believes (with reasonable cause) to be or include indecent photographs of children taken or shown on the premises, or kept there with a view to their being distributed or shown.

(3) Articles seized under the authority of the warrant, and not returned to the occupier of the premises, shall be brought before a justice of the peace acting for the same petty sessions area as the justice who issued the warrant.

(4) * * * * *

5 * * * * *

6 Punishments

(1) Offences under this Act shall be punishable either on conviction on indictment or on summary conviction.

(2) A person convicted on indictment of any offence under this Act shall be liable to imprisonment for a term of not more than three years, or to a fine or to both.

(3) A person convicted summarily of any offence under this Act shall be liable—

(a) to imprisonment for a term not exceeding six months; or

(b) to a fine not exceeding the prescribed sum for the purposes of [section 32 of the Magistrates' Courts Act 1980] (punishment on summary conviction of offences triable either way: £1,000 or other sum substituted by order under that Act), or to both.

7, 8, 9 * * * * *

SUPPRESSION OF TERRORISM ACT 1978
(1978, c. 26)

An Act to give effect to the European Convention on the Suppression of Terrorism; to amend the law relating to the extradition of criminals and the obtaining of evidence for criminal proceedings outside the United Kingdom; to confer jurisdiction in respect of certain offences committed outside the United Kingdom; and for connected purposes [30 June 1978]

Territorial extent United Kingdom

1 Cases in which certain offences are not to be regarded as of a political character

(1) This section applies to any offence of which a person is accused or has been convicted outside the United Kingdom if the act constituting the offence, or the equivalent act, would, if it took place in any part of the United Kingdom or, in the case of an extra-territorial offence, in corresponding circumstances outside the United Kingdom, constitute one of the offences listed in Schedule 1 to this Act.

(2) For the purposes mentioned in subsection (3) below—

(a) no offence to which this section applies shall be regarded as an offence of a political character; and

(b) no proceedings in respect of an offence to which this section applies shall be regarded as a criminal matter of a political character or as criminal proceedings of a political character.

(3) Those purposes are—

(a) the purposes of the Extradition Act 1870 in relation to any requisition for the surrender of a fugitive criminal made on behalf of a convention country after the coming into force of this paragraph;

(b) the purposes of the Fugitive Offenders Act 1967 in relation to any request for the return of a person under the Act made on behalf of a convention country after the coming into force of this paragraph;

(c) the purposes of the Backing of Warrants (Republic of Ireland) Act 1965 in relation to any warrant issued in the Republic of Ireland to which this paragraph applies by virtue of an order under subsection (4) below; and

(d) the purposes of section 5 of the Extradition Act 1873 (evidence for foreign criminal matters) and section 5 of the Evidence (Proceedings in Other Jurisdictions) Act 1975 (evidence for criminal proceedings outside the United Kingdom) in relation to—

(i) any criminal proceedings instituted in a convention country (not being the Republic of Ireland) after the coming into force of this sub-paragraph; and

(ii) any criminal proceedings in the Republic of Ireland to which this sub-paragraph applies by virtue of an order under subsection (4) below.

(4), (5) * * * * *

2 Restrictions on return of criminal under Extradition Act 1870, or to Republic of Ireland, in certain cases

(1) In relation to any requisition for the surrender of a fugitive criminal made as mentioned in section 1(3)(a) above in respect of an offence to which section 1 above applies, the Extradition Act 1870 shall have effect as if at the end of paragraph (1) of section 3 (which prohibits the surrender of a criminal if he proves as there mentioned that the requisition for his surrender has in fact been made with a view to try or punish him for an offence of a political character) there were added the words "or with a view to try or punish him on account of his race, religion, nationality, or political opinions, or that he might, if surrendered, be prejudiced at his trial or punished, detained or restricted in his personal liberty by reason of his race, religion, nationality or political opinions:".

(2) * * * * *

3 * * * * *

4 Jurisdiction in respect of offences committed outside United Kingdom

(1) If a person, whether a citizen of the United Kingdom and Colonies or not, does in a convention country any act which, if he had done it in a part of the United Kingdom, would have made him guilty in that part of the United Kingdom of—

(a) an offence mentioned in paragraph 1, 2, 4, 5, 10, 11, [11B,] 12, 13, 14 or 15 of Schedule 1 to this Act; or

(b) an offence of attempting to commit any offence so mentioned,

he shall, in that part of the United Kingdom, be guilty of the offence or offences aforesaid of which the act would have made him guilty if he had done it there.

(2) * * * * *

(3) If a person who is a national of a convention country but not a citizen of the United Kingdom and Colonies does outside the United Kingdom and that convention country any act which makes him in that convention country guilty of an offence and which, if he had been a citizen of the United Kingdom and Colonies, would have made him in any part of the United Kingdom guilty of an offence mentioned in paragraph 1, 2 or 13 of Schedule 1 to this Act, he shall, in any part of the United Kingdom, be guilty of the offence or offences aforesaid of which the act would have made him guilty if he had been such a citizen.

(4) Proceedings for an offence which [(disregarding the provisions of the Internationally Protected Persons Act 1978)] would not be an offence apart from this section shall not be instituted—

(a) in Northern Ireland, except by or with the consent of the Attorney General for Northern Ireland; or

(b) in England and Wales, except by or with the consent of the Attorney General;

and references to a consent provision in Article 7(3) to (5) of the Prosecution of Offences (Northern Ireland) Order 1972 (which relates to consents to prosecutions) shall include so much of this subsection as precedes paragraph (b).

(5)-(7) * * * * *

5 Power to apply provisions of Act to non-convention countries

(1) In the case of any country which, not being a convention country, is either—

(a) a designated Commonwealth country within the meaning of the Fugitive Offenders Act 1967; or

(b) a foreign state with which there is in force an arrangement of the kind described in section 2 of the Extradition Act 1870 with respect to the surrender to that state of fugitive criminals; or

(c) a United Kingdom dependency within the meaning of the Fugitive Offenders Act 1967,

the Secretary of State may by order direct—

(i) in the case of a country within paragraph (a) or (b) above, that all or any of the provisions of this Act which would, apart from this section, apply only in relation to convention countries shall apply in relation to that country (subject to such exceptions, if any, as may be specified in the order) as they apply in relation to a covention country; or

(ii) in the case of a country within paragraph (c) above, that the provisions of section 4 above shall so apply in relation to that country;

and while such an order is in force in the case of any country, the provisions in question shall apply in relation to it accordingly.

(2) The Secretary of State may, at any time when the Republic of Ireland is not a convention country, by order direct that section 4 above shall apply in relation to the Republic as if it were a convention country; and while such an order is in force, that section shall apply in relation to the Republic accordingly.

(3) An order under subsection (2) above shall, unless previously revoked, cease to have effect if the Republic of Ireland subsequently becomes a convention country.

* * * * *

Sections 1, 4

SCHEDULE 1
LIST OF OFFENCES

Common law offences

1. Murder.
2. Manslaughter or culpable homicide.
3. Rape.
4. Kidnapping, abduction or plagium.
5. False imprisonment.
6. Assault occasioning actual bodily harm or causing injury.
7. Wilful fire-raising.

Offences against the person

8. An offence under any of the following provisions of the Offences against the Person Act 1861—

(a) section 18 (wounding with intent to cause grievous bodily harm);

(b) section 20 (causing grievous bodily harm);

(c) section 21 (attempting to choke etc. in order to commit or assist in the committing of any indictable offence);

(d) section 22 (using chloroform etc. to commit or assist in the committing of any indictable offence);

(e) section 23 (maliciously administering poison etc. so as to endanger life or inflict grievous bodily harm);

(f) section 24 (maliciously administering poison etc. with intent to injure etc.);

(g) section 48 (rape).

9. An offence under section 1 of the Sexual Offences Act 1956 (rape).

Abduction

10. An offence under any of the following provisions of the Offences against the Person Act 1861—

(a) section 55 (abduction of unmarried girl under 16);

(b) section 56 (child-stealing or receiving stolen child).

11. An offence under section 20 of the Sexual Offences Act 1956 (abduction of unmarried girl under 16).

[*Taking of hostages*

11A. An offence under the Taking of Hostages Act 1982.]

[11B. An offence under section 2 of the Child Abduction Act 1984 (abduction of child by person other than parent etc.) or any corresponding provision in force in Northern Ireland.]

Explosives

12. An offence under any of the following provisions of the Offences against the Person Act 1861—

(a) section 28 (causing bodily injury by gunpowder);

(b) section 29 (causing gunpowder to explode etc. with intent to do grievous bodily harm).

(c) section 30 (placing gunpowder near a building etc. with intent to cause bodily injury).

13. An offence under any of the following provisions of the Explosive Substances Act 1883—

(a) section 2 (causing explosion likely to endanger life or property);

(b) section 3 (doing any act with intent to cause such an explosion, conspiring to cause such an explosion, or making or possessing explosive with intent to endanger life or property).

Firearms

14. The following offences under the Firearms Act 1968—

(a) an offence under section 16 (possession of firearm with intent to injure);

(b) an offence under subsection (1) of section 17 (use of firearm or imitation firearm to resist arrest) involving the use or attempted use of a firearm within the meaning of that section.

15. The following offences under the [Firearms (Northern Ireland) Order 1981]

(a) an offence under [Article 17] consisting of a person's having in his possession any firearm or ammunition (within the meaning of [that Article]) with intent by means thereof to endanger life, or to enable another person by means thereof to endanger life;

(b) an offence under [paragraph (1) of Article 18] (use of firearm or imitation firearm to resist arrest) involving the use or attempted use of a firearm within the meaning of [that Article].

Offences against property

16. An offence under section 1(2) of the Criminal Damage Act 1971 (destroying or damaging property intending to endanger life or being reckless as to danger to life).

17. An offence under Article 3(2) of the Criminal Damage (Northern Ireland) Order 1977 (destroying or damaging property intending to endanger life or being reckless as to danger to life).

Offences in relation to aircraft

[18. An offence under Part I of the Aviation Security Act 1982 (other than an offence under section 4 or 7 of that Act.]

Attempts

20. An offence of attempting to commit any offence mentioned in a preceding paragraph of this Schedule.

* * * * *

JUSTICES OF THE PEACE ACT 1979
(1979, c. 55)

An Act to consolidate certain enactments relating to justices of the peace (including stipendiary magistrates), justices' clerks and the administrative and financial arrangements for magistrates' courts, and to matters connected therewith, with amendments to give effect to recommendations of the Law Commission [6 December 1979]

Territorial extent England and Wales

PART I
GENERAL

* * * * *

Justices other than stipendiary magistrates

6 Appointment and removal of justices of the peace

(1) Subject to the following provisions of this Act, justices of the peace of any commission area shall be appointed [by the Lord Chancellor by instrument on behalf and in the name of Her Majesty], and a justice so appointed may be removed from office in like manner.

(2) The preceding subsection does not apply to stipendiary magistrates and shall be without prejudice to the position of the Lord Mayor and aldermen as justices for the City of London by virtue of the charters of the City.

* * * * *

Stipendiary magistrates other than metropolitan stipendiary magistrates

13 Appointment and removal of stipendiary magistrates

(1) It shall be lawful for Her Majesty to appoint a barrister or solicitor of not less than seven years' standing to be, during Her Majesty's pleasure, a whole-time stipendiary magistrate in any commission area or areas outside the inner London area and the City of London, and to appoint more than one such magistrate in the same area or areas.

(2) A person so appointed to be a magistrate in any commission area shall by virtue of his office be a justice of a peace for that area.

(3) Any appointment of a stipendiary magistrate under this section shall be of a person recommended to Her Majesty by the Lord Chancellor, and a stipendiary magistrate appointed under this section shall not be removed from office except on the Lord Chancellor's recommendation.

(4) The number of stipendiary magistrates appointed under this section shall not at any time exceed forty or such larger number as Her Majesty may from time to time by Order in Council specify.

(5) Her Majesty shall not be recommended to make an Order in Council under subsection (4) above unless a draft of the Order has been laid before Parliament and approved by resolution of each House.

* * * * *

PART V
PROTECTION OF JUSTICES AND INDEMNIFICATION OF JUSTICES AND JUSTICES' CLERKS

44 Acts done within jurisdiction

If apart from this section any action lies against a justice of the peace for an act done by him in the execution of his duty as such a justice, with respect to any matter within his jurisdiction as such a justice, the action shall be as for a tort, in the nature of an action on the case; and—

(a) in the statement or particulars of claim it shall be expressly alleged that the act in question was done maliciously and without reasonable and probable cause, and

(b) if that allegation is not proved at the trial of the action, judgment shall be given for the defendant, if it is in the High Court, or, if it is in the county court, the plaintiff shall be non-suited or judgment shall be given for the defendant.

45 Acts outside or in excess of jurisdiction

(1) This section applies—

(a) to any act done by a justice of the peace in a matter in respect of which by law he does not have jurisdiction or in which he has exceeded his jurisdiction, and

(b) to any act done under any conviction or order made or warrant issued by a justice of the peace in any such matter;

and in the following provisions of this section "the justice", in relation to any act falling within paragraph (a) above, means the justice of the peace by whom it is done, and, in relation to a conviction, order or warrant falling within paragraph (b) above, means the justice of the peace by whom the conviction or order is made or the warrant issued.

(2) Any person injured by an act to which this section applies may maintain an action against the justice without making any allegation in his statement or particulars of claim that the act complained of was done maliciously and without reasonable and probable cause.

(3) In respect of any act done under any such conviction or order as is mentioned in subsection (1)(b) above no action shall be brought against the justice until the conviction or order has been quashed, either on appeal or upon application to the High Court.

46 Warrant granted on a conviction or order made by another justice

Where a conviction or order is made by a justice or justices of the peace, and another justice, in good faith and without collusion, grants a warrant of distress or warrant of commitment thereon, no action shall be brought against the justice who granted the warrant by reason of any defect in the conviction or order, or for any want of jurisdiction in the justice or justices who made it, but the action (if any) shall be brought against the justice or justices who made the conviction or order.

47 Exercise of discretionary powers

Where by an enactment a discretionary power is given to a justice of the peace, no action shall be brought against the justice by reason of the manner in which he exercises his discretion in the execution of the power.

* * * * *

53 Indemnification of justices and justices' clerks

(1) Subject to the provisions of this section and of section 54 below, a justice of the peace or justices' clerk may be indemnified out of local funds in respect of—

(a) any costs reasonably incurred by him in or in connection with proceedings against him in respect of anything done or omitted in the exercise or purported exercise of the duty of his office, or in taking steps to dispute any claim which might be made in such proceedings;

(b) any damages awarded against him or costs ordered to be paid by him in any such proceedings; or

(c) any sums payable by him in connection with a reasonable settlement of any such proceedings or claim;

and shall be entitled to be so indemnified if, in respect of the matters giving rise to the proceedings or claim, he acted reasonably and in good faith.

(2)-(6) * * * * *

* * * * *

CRIMINAL JUSTICE (SCOTLAND) ACT 1980
(1980, c. 62)

An Act to make further provision as regards criminal justice in Scotland; and for connected purposes [13 November 1980]

Territorial extent Scotland

PART I
POLICE POWERS

1 Suspect or potential witness may be required by constable to identify himself

(1) Where a constable has reasonable grounds for suspecting that a person has committed or is committing an offence at any place, he may require—

(a) that person, if the constable finds him at that place or at any place where the constable is entitled to be, to give his name and address and may ask him for an explanation of the circumstances which have given rise to the constable's suspicion;

(b) any other person whom the constable finds at that place or at any place where the constable is entitled to be and who the constable believes has information relating to the offence, to give his name and address.

(2) The constable may require the person mentioned in paragraph (a) of subsection (1) above to remain with him while he (either or both)—

(a) verifies any name and address given by the person:

Provided that the constable shall exercise his power under this paragraph only where it appears to him that such verification can be obtained quickly;

(b) notes any explanation proffered by the person.

(3) A constable may use reasonable force to ensure that the person mentioned in paragraph (a) of subsection (1) above remains with him.

(4) A constable shall inform a person, when making a requirement of that person under—

(a) paragraph (a) of subsection (1) above, of his suspicion and of the general nature of the offence which he suspects that the person has committed or is committing;

(b) paragraph (b) of subsection (1) above, of his suspicion, of the general nature of the offence which he suspects has been or is being committed and that the reason for the requirement is that he believes the person has information relating to the offence;

(c) subsection (2) above, of why the person is being required to remain with him;

(d) either of the said subsections, that failure to comply with the requirement may constitute an offence.

(5) A person mentioned in—

(a) paragraph (a) of subsection (1) above who having been required—

(i) under that subsection to give his name and address; or

(ii) under subsection (2) above to remain with a constable,

fails, without reasonable excuse, to do so, shall be guilty of an offence and liable on summary conviction to a fine not exceeding [level 4 on the standard scale];

(b) paragraph (b) of the said subsection (1) who having been required under that subsection to give his name and address fails, without reasonable excuse, to do so shall be guilty of an offence and liable on summary conviction to a fine not exceeding [level 3 on the standard scale].

(6) A constable may arrest without warrant any person who he has reasonable grounds for suspecting has committed an offence under subsection (5) above.

2 Detention and questioning at police station

(1) Where a constable has reasonable grounds for suspecting that a person has committed or is committing an offence punishable by imprisonment, the constable may, for the purpose of facilitating the carrying out of investigations—

(a) into the offence; and

(b) as to whether criminal proceedings should be instigated against the person,

detain that person and take him as quickly as is reasonably practicable to a police station or other premises and, subject to the following provisions of this section, the detention may continue there.

(2) Detention under subsection (1) above shall be terminated not more than six hours after it begins or (if earlier)—

(a) when the person is arrested; [or

(aa) when he is detained in pursuance of any other enactment or subordinate instrument;] or

(b) where there are no longer such grounds as are mentioned in the said subsection (1);

and when a person has been detained under subsection (1) above [he shall be informed immediately upon the termination of his detention in accordance with this subsection] that his detention has been terminated.

(3) Where a person has been released at the termination of a period of detention under subsection (1) above he shall not thereafter be detained, under that subsection, on the same grounds or on any grounds arising out of the same circumstances.

[(3A) Where a person has previously been detained in pursuance of any other enactment or subordinate instrument, he may not be detained under subsection (1) above on the same grounds or on grounds arising from the same circumstances as those which led to his earlier detention.]

(4) At the time when a constable detains a person under subsection (1) above, he shall inform the person of his suspicion, of the general nature of the offence which he suspects has been or is being committed and of the reason for the detention; and there shall be recorded—

(a) the place where detention begins and the police station or other premises to which the person is taken;

(b) the general nature of the suspected offence;

(c) the time when detention under subsection (1) above begins and the time of the person's arrival at the police station or other premises;

(d) the time when the person is informed of his rights in terms of subsection (7) below and of subsection (1)(b) of section 3 of this Act and the identity of the constable so informing him;

(e) where the person requests such intimation to be sent as is specified in section 3(1)(b) of this Act, the time when such request is—

(i) made;

(ii) complied with; and

(f) the time of the person's departure from the police station or other premises or, where instead of being released he is arrested in respect of the alleged offence, the time of such arrest.

(5) Where a person is detained under subsection (1) above, a constable may—

(a) put questions to him in relation to the suspected offence:
Provided that this paragraph shall be without prejudice to any existing rule of law as regards the admissibility in evidence of any answer given;

(b) exercise the same powers of search as are avaialble following an arrest; and

(c) take fingerprints, palmprints and such other prints and impressions as the constable may, having regard to the circumstances of the suspected offence, reasonably consider appropriate:
Provided that the record of the prints and impressions so taken shall be destroyed immediately following a decision not to institute criminal proceedings against the person or on the conclusion of such proceedings otherwise than with a conviction or an order under section 182 or 383 (absolute discharge) or 183(1) or 384(1) (probation) of the 1975 Act.

(6) A constable may use reasonable force in exercising any power conferred by subsection (1), or by paragraph (b) or (c) or subsection (5), above.

(7) A person detained under subsection (1) above shall be under no obligation to answer any question other than to give his name and address, and a constable shall so inform him both on so detaining him and on arrival at the police station or other premises.

3 Right to have someone informed when arrested or detained

(1) Without prejudice to section 19 or 305 of the 1975 Act (intimation to solicitor following arrest), a person who, not being a person in respect of whose custody or detention subsection (3) below applies—

(a) has been arrested and is in custody in a police station or other premises, shall be entitled to have intimation of his custody and of the place where he is being held sent, to a person reasonably named by him;

(b) is being detained under section 2 of this Act in a police station or other premises, shall be entitled to have intimation of his detention and of the place where he is being detained sent, to a solicitor and to one other person reasonably named by him,
without delay or, where some delay is necessary in the interest of the investigation or the prevention of crime or the apprehension of offenders, with no more delay than is so necessary; and the person shall be informed of such entitlement—

(i) on arrival at the police station or other premises; or

(ii) where he is not arrested, or as the case may be detained, until after such arrival, on such arrest or detention.

(2) Where the person mentioned in paragraph (a) of subsection (1) above requests such intimation to be sent as is specified in that paragraph there shall be recorded the time when such request is—

(i) made;

(ii) complied with.

(3) Without prejudice to the said section 19 or 305, a constable shall, where a person who has been arrested and is in such custody as is mentioned in paragraph (a) of subsection (1) above or who is being detained as is mentioned in paragraph (b) of that subsection appears to him to be a child, send without delay such intimation as is mentioned in the said paragraph (a), or as the case may be paragraph (b), to that person's parent if known; and the parent—

(a) in a case were there is reasonable cause to suspect that he has been involved in the alleged offence in respect of which the person has been arrested or detained, may; and

(b) in any other case shall,

be permitted access to the person.

(4) The nature and extent of any access permitted under subsection (3) above shall be subject to any restriction essential for the furtherance of the investigation or the well-being of the person.

(5) In subsection (3) above—

(a) "child" means a person under 16 years of age; and

(b) "parent" includes guardian [and any person who has the actual custody of a child].

3A-3D *****

4 Search for offensive weapons

(1) Where a constable has reasonable grounds for suspecting that any person is carrying an offensive weapon and has committed or is committing an offence under section 1 of the Prevention of Crime Act 1953 (prohibition of carrying of offensive weapons in public) the constable may search that person without warrant, and detain him for such time as is reasonably required to permit the search to be carried out; and he shall inform the person of the reason for such detention.

(2) Any person who—

(a) intentionally obstructs a constable in the exercise of the constable's powers under subsection (1) above; or

(b) conceals from a constable acting in the exercise of the said powers an offensive weapon,

shall be guilty of an offence and liable on summary conviction to a fine not exceeding [level 4 on the standard scale].

(3) A constable may arrest without warrant any person who he has reason to believe has committed an offence under subsection (2) above.

(4) In this section, "offensive weapon" has the same meaning as in the said section 1.

*****

HIGHWAYS ACT 1980
(1980, c. 66)

An Act to consolidate the Highways Acts 1959 to 1971 and related enactments with amendments to give effect to recommendations of the Law Commission [13 November 1980]

Territorial extent England and Wales

*****

Obstruction of highways and streets

137 Penalty for wilful obstruction

(1) If a person, without lawful authority or excuse, in any way wilfully obstructs the free passage along a highway he is guilty of an offence and liable to a fine not exceeding [level 3 on the standard scale].

(2) . . .

*****

MAGISTRATES' COURTS ACT 1980
(1980, c. 43)

An Act to consolidate certain enactments relating to the jurisdiction of, and the practice and procedure before, magistrates' courts and the functions of justices' clerks, and to matters connected therewith, with amendments to give effect to recommendations of the Law Commission

[1 August 1980]

Territorial extent England and Wales

PART I
CRIMINAL JURISDICTION AND PROCEDURE

Jurisdiction to issue process and deal with charges

1 Issue of summons to accused or warrant for his arrest

(1) Upon an information being laid before a justice of the peace for an area to which this section applies that any person has, or is suspected of having, committed an offence,

the justice may, in any of the events mentioned in subsection (2) below, but subject to subsections (3) to (5) below,—

(a) issue a summons directed to that person requiring him to appear before a magistrates' court for the area to answer to the information, or

(b) issue a warrant to arrest that person and bring him before a magistrates' court for the area or such magistrates' court as is provided in subsection (5) below.

(2) *****

(3) No warrant shall be issued under this section unless the information is in writing and substantiated on oath.

(4) No warrant shall be issued under this section for the arrest of any person who has attained the age of 17 unless—

(a) the offence to which the warrant relates is an indictable offence or is punishable with imprisonment, or

(b) the person's address is not sufficiently established for a summons to be served on him.

(5)-(7) *****

(8) The areas to which this section applies are any county, any London commission area and the City of London.

*****

Committal proceedings

8 Restrictions on reports of committal proceedings

(1) Except as provided by subsections (2), (3) and (8) below, it shall not be lawful to publish in Great Britain a written report, or to broadcast [or include in a cable programme] in Great Britain a report, of any committal proceedings in England and Wales containing any matter other than that permitted by subsection (4) below.

(2) [Subject to subsection (2A) below] a magistrates' court shall, on an application for the purpose made with reference to any committal proceedings by the accused or one of the accused, as the case may be, order that subsection (1) above shall not apply to reports of those proceedings.

[(2A] Where in the case of two or more accused one of them objects to the making of an order under subsection (2) above, the court shall make the order if, and only if, it is satisfied, after hearing the representations of the accused, that it is in the interests of justice to do so.

(2B) An order under subsection (2) above shall not apply to reports of proceedings under subsection (2A) above, but any decision of the court to make or not to make such an order may be contained in reports published [broadcast or included in a cable programme] before the time authorised by subsection (3) below.]

(3) It shall not be unlawful under this section to publish [broadcast or include in a cable programme] a report of committal proceedings containing any matter other than that permitted by subsection (4) below—

(a) where the magistrates' court determines not to commit the accused, or determines to commit none of the accused, for trial, after it so determines;

(b) where the court commits the accused or any of the accused for trial, after the conclusion of his trial or, as the case may be, the trial of the last to be tried;

and where at any time during the inquiry the court proceeds to try summarily the case of one or more of the accused under section 25(3) or (7) below, while committing the other accused or one or more of the other accused for trial, it shall not be unlawful under this section to publish [broadcast or include in a cable programme] as part of a report of the summary trial, after the court determines to proceed as aforesaid, a report of so much of the committal proceedings containing any such matter as takes place before the determination.

(4) The following matters may be contained in a report of committal proceedings published [broadcast or included in a cable programme] without an order under subsection (2) above before the time authorised by subsection (3) above, that is to say—

(a) the identity of the court and the names of the examining justices;

(b) the names, addresses and occupations of the parties and witnesses and the ages of the accused and witnesses;

(c) the offence or offences, or a summary of them, with which the accused is or are charged;

(d) the names of counsel and solicitors engaged in the proceedings;

(e) any decision of the court to commit the accused or any of the accused for trial, and any decision of the court on the disposal of the case of any accused not committed;

(f) where the court commits the accused or any of the accused for trial, the charge or charges, or a summary of them, on which he is committed and the court to which he is committed;

(g) where the committal proceedings are adjourned, the date and place to which they are adjourned;

(h) any arrangements as to bail on committal or adjournment;

(i) whether legal aid was granted to the accused or any of the accused.

(5) If a report is published [broadcast or included in a cable programme] in contravention of this section, the following persons, that is to say—

(a) in the case of a publication of a written report as part of a newspaper or periodical, any proprietor, editor or publisher of the newspaper or periodical;

(b) in the case of a publication of a written report otherwise than as part of a newspaper or periodical, the person who publishes it;

(c) in the case of a broadcast of a report, any body corporate which transmits or provides the programme in which the report is broadcast and any person having functions in relation to the programme corresponding to those of the editor of a newspaper or periodical,

[(d) in the case of an inclusion of a report in a cable programme, any body corporate which spends or provides the programme and any person having functions in relation to the programme corresponding to those of an editor of a newspaper,]

shall be liable on summary conviction to a fine not exceeding [level 5 on the standard scale].

(6) Proceedings for an offence under this section shall not, in England and Wales, be instituted otherwise than by or with the consent of the Attorney-General.

(7) Subsection (1) above shall be in addition to, and not in derogation from, the provisions of any other enactment with respect to the publication of reports and proceedings of magistrates' and other courts.

(8), (9) * * * * *

PART VI
RECOGNIZANCES

Recognizances to keep the peace or be of good behaviour

115 Binding over to keep the peace or be of good behaviour

(1) The power of a magistrates' court on the complaint of any person to adjudge any other person to enter into a recognizance, with or without sureties, to keep the peace or to be of good behaviour towards the complaint shall be exercised by order on complaint.

(2) * * * * *

(3) If any person ordered by a magistrates' court under subsection (1) above to enter into a recognizance, with or without sureties, to keep the peace or to be of good behaviour fails to comply with the order, the court may commit him to custody for a period not exceeding 6 months or until he sooner complies with the order.

* * * * *

BRITISH NATIONALITY ACT 1981
(1981, c. 61)

An Act to make fresh provision about citizenship and nationality, and to amend the Immigration Act 1971 as regards the right of abode in the United Kingdom [30 October 1981]

Territorial extent United Kingdom

Note A new form of British Nationality, British National (Overseas), has been created by the Hong Kong (British Nationality) Order 1986 (SI 1986 No. 948) with effect from 1 July 1987. See the text of the Order for details. Amendments to this Act made by the Order consequent on this new category are incorporated in the text.

PART I
BRITISH CITIZENSHIP

Acquisition after commencement

1 Acquisition by birth or adoption

(1) A person born in the United Kingdom after commencement shall be a British citizen if at the time of the birth his father or mother is—

(a) a British citizen; or

(b) settled in the United Kingdom.

(2) A new-born infant who, after commencement, is found abandoned in the United Kingdom shall, unless the contrary is shown, be deemed for the purposes of subsection (1)—

(a) to have been born in the United Kingdom after commencement; and

(b) to have been born to a parent who at the time of the birth was a British citizen or settled in the United Kingdom.

(3) A person born in the United Kingdom after commencement who is not a British citizen by virtue of subsection (1) or (2) shall be entitled to be registered as a British citizen if, while he is a minor—

(a) his father or mother becomes a British citizen or becomes settled in the United Kingdom; and

(b) an application is made for his registration as a British citizen.

(4) A person born in the United Kingdom after commencement who is not a British citizen by virtue of subsection (1) or (2) shall be entitled, on an application for his registration as a British citizen made at any time after he has attained the age of ten years, to be registered as such a citizen if, as regards each of the first ten years of that person's life, the number of days on which he was absent from the United Kingdom in that year does not exceed 90.

(5) Where after commencement an order authorising the adoption of a minor who is not a British citizen is made by any court in the United Kingdom, he shall be a British citizen as from the date on which the order is made if the adopter or, in the case of a joint adoption, one of the adopters is a British citizen on that date.

(6) Where an order in consequence of which any person became a British citizen by virtue of subsection (5) ceases to have effect, whether on annulment or otherwise, the cesser shall not affect the status of that person as a British citizen.

(7) If in the special circumstances of any particular case the Secretary of State thinks fit, he may for the purposes of subsection (4) treat the person to whom the application relates as fulfilling the requirement specified in that subsection although, as regards any one or more of the first ten years of that person's life, the number of days on which he was absent from the United Kingdom in that year or each of the years in question exceeds 90.

(8) In this section and elsewhere in this Act "settled" has the meaning given by section 50.

2 Acquisition by descent

(1) A person born outside the United Kingdom after commencement shall be a British citizen if at the time of the birth his father or mother—

(a) is a British citizen otherwise than by descent; or

(b) is a British citizen and is serving outside the United Kingdom in service to which this paragraph applies, his or her recruitment for that service having taken place in the United Kingdom; or

(c) is a British citizen and is serving outside the United Kingdom in service under a Community institution, his or her recruitment for that service having taken place in a country which at the time of the recruitment was a member of the Communities.

(2) Paragraph (b) of subsection (1) applies to—

(a) Crown service under the government of the United Kingdom; and

(b) service of any description for the time being designated under subsection (3).

(3) For the purposes of this section the Secretary of State may by order made by statutory instrument designate any description of service which he considers to be closely associated with the activities outside the United Kingdom of Her Majesty's government in the United Kingdom.

(4) Any order made under subsection (3) shall be subject to annulment in pursuance of a resolution of either House of Parliament.

3 Acquisition by registration: minors

(1) If while a person is a minor an application is made for his registration as a British citizen, the Secretary of State may, if he thinks fit, cause him to be registered as such a citizen.

(2) A person born outside the United Kingdom shall be entitled, on an application for his registration as a British citizen made within the period of twelve months from the date of the birth, to be registered as such a citizen if the requirements specified in subsection (3) or, in the case of a person born stateless, the requirements specified in paragraphs (a) and (b) of that subsection, are fulfilled in the case of either that person's father or his mother ("the parent in question").

(3) The requirements referred to in subsection (2) are—

(a) that the parent in question was a British citizen by descent at the time of the birth; and

(b) that the father or mother of the parent in question—

(i) was a British citizen otherwise than by descent at the time of the birth of the parent in question; or

(ii) became a British citizen otherwise than by descent at commencement, or would have become such a citizen otherwise than by descent at commencement but for his or her death; and

(c) that, as regards some period of three years ending with a date not later than that date of the birth—

(i) the parent in question was in the United Kingdom at the beginning of that period; and

(ii) the number of days on which the parent in question was absent from the United Kingdom in the period does not exceed 270.

(4) If in the special circumstances of any particular case the Secretary of State thinks fit, he may treat subsection (2) as if the reference to twelve months were a reference to six years.

(5) A person born outside the United Kingdom shall be entitled, on an application for his registration as a British citizen made while he is a minor, to be registered as such a citizen if the following requirements are satisfied, namely—

(a) that at the time of that person's birth his father or mother was a British citizen by descent; and

(b) subject to subsection (6), that that person and his father and mother were in the United Kingdom at the beginning of the period of three years ending with the date of the application and that, in the case of each of them, the number of days on which the person in question was absent from the United Kingdom in that period does not exceed 270; and

(c) subject to subsection (6), that the consent of his father and mother to the registration has been signified in the prescribed manner.

(6) In the case of an application under subsection (5) of the registration of a person as a British citizen—

(a) if his father or mother died, or their marriage was terminated, on or before the date of the application, or his father and mother were legally separated on that date, the references to his father and mother in paragraph (b) of that subsection shall be read either as references to his father or as references to his mother;

(b) if his father or mother died on or before that date, the reference to his father and mother in paragraph (c) of that subsection shall be read as a reference to either of them; and

(c) if he was born illegitimate, all those references shall be read as references to his mother.

4 Acquisition by registration: British Dependent Territories citizens etc.

(1) This section applies to any person who is a British Dependent Territories citizen, [a British National [(Overseas),] a British Overseas citizen, a British subject under this Act or a British protected person.

(2) A person to whom this section applies shall be entitled, on an application for his registration as a British citizen, to be registered as such a citizen if the following requirements are satisfied in the case of that person, namely—

(a) subject to subsection (3), that he was in the United Kingdom at the beginning of the period of five years ending with the date of the application and that the number of days on which he was absent from the United Kingdom in that period does not exceed 450; and

(b) that the number of days on which he was absent from the United Kingdom in the period of twelve months so ending does not exceed 90; and

(c) that he was not at any time in the period of twelve months so ending subject under the immigration laws to any restriction on the period for which he might remain in the United Kingdom; and

(d) that he was not at any time in the period of five years so ending in the United Kingdom in breach of the immigration laws.

(3) So much of subsection (2)(a) as requires the person in question to have been in the United Kingdom at the beginning of the period there mentioned shall not apply in relation to a person who was settled in the United Kingdom immediately before commencement.

(4) If in the special circumstances of any particular case the Secretary of State thinks fit, he may for the purposes of subsection (2) do all or any of the following things, namely—

(a) treat the person to whom the application relates as fulfilling the requirement specified in subsection (2)(a) or subsection (2)(b), or both, although the number of days on which he was absent from the United Kingdom in the period there mentioned exceeds the number there mentioned;

(b) disregard any such restriction as is mentioned in subsection (2)(c), not being a restriction to which that person was subject on the date of the application;

(c) treat that person as fulfilling the requirement specified in subsection (2)(d) although he was in the United Kingdom in breach of the immigration laws in the period there mentioned.

(5) If, on an application for registration as a British citizen made by a person to whom this section applies, the Secretary of State is satisfied that the applicant has at any time

served in service to which this subsection applies, he may, if he thinks fit in the special circumstances of the applicant's case, cause him to be registered as such a citizen.

(6) Subsection (5) applies to—

(a) Crown service under the government of a dependent territory; and

(b) paid or unpaid service (not falling within paragraph (a)) as a member of any body established by law in a dependent territory members of which are appointed by or on behalf of the Crown.

5 Acquisition by registration: nationals for purposes of the Community treaties
A British Dependent Territories citizen who falls to be treated as a national of the United Kingdom for the purposes of the Community Treaties shall be entitled to be registered as a British citizen if an application is made for his registration as such a citizen.

6 Acquisition by naturalisation

(1) If, on an application for naturalisation as a British citizen made by a person of full age and capacity, the Secretary of State is satisfied that the applicant fulfils the requirements of Schedule 1 for naturalisation as such a citizen under this subsection, he may, if he thinks fit, grant to him a certificate of naturalisation as such a citizen.

(2) If, on an application for naturalisation as a British citizen made by a person of full age and capacity who on the date of the application is married to a British citizen, the Secretary of State is satisfied that the applicant fulfils the requirements of Schedule 1 for naturalisation as such a citizen under this subsection, he may, if he thinks fit, grant to him a certificate of naturalisation as such a citizen.

7-10 * * * * *

Acquisition at commencement

11 Citizens of UK and Colonies who are to become British citizens at commencement

(1) Subject to subsection (2), a person who immediately before commencement—

(a) was a citizen of the United Kingdom and Colonies; and

(b) had the right of abode in the United Kingdom under the Immigration Act 1971 as then in force,

shall at commencement become a British citizen.

(2) A person who was registered as a citizen of the United Kingdom and Colonies under section 1 of the British Nationality (No 2) Act 1964 (stateless persons) on the ground mentioned in subsection (1)(a) of that section (namely that his mother was a citizen of the United Kingdom and Colonies at the time when he was born) shall not become a British citizen under subsection (1) unless—

(a) his mother becomes a British citizen under subsection (1) or would have done so but for her death; or

(b) immediately before commencement he had the right of abode in the United Kingdom by virtue of section 2(1)(c) of the Immigration Act 1971 as then in force (settlement in United Kingdom, combined with five or more years' ordinary residence there as a citizen of the United Kingdom and Colonies).

(3) * * * * *

Renunciation and resumption

12 Renunciation

(1) If any British citizen of full age and capacity makes in the prescribed manner a declaration of renunciation of British citizenship, then, subject to subsection (3) and (4), the Secretary of State shall cause the declaration to be registered.

(2) On the registration of a declaration made in pursuance of this section the person who made it shall cease to be a British citizen.

(3) A declaration made by a person in pursuance of this section shall not be registered unless the Secretary of State is satisfied that the person who made it will after the

registration have or acquire some citizenship or nationality other than British citizenship; and if that person does not have any such citizenship or nationality on the date of registration and does not acquire some such citizenship or nationality within six months from that date, he shall be, and be deemed to have remained, a British citizen notwithstanding the registration.

(4) The Secretary of State may withhold registration of any declaration made in pursuance of this section if it is made during any war in which Her Majesty may be engaged in right of Her Majesty's government in the United Kingdom.

(5) For the purposes of this section any person who has been married shall be deemed to be of full age.

13, 14 * * * * *

PART II
BRITISH DEPENDENT TERRITORIES CITIZENSHIP

Acquisition after commencement

15 Acquisition by birth or adoption

(1) A person born in a dependent territory after commencement shall be a British Dependent Territories citizen if at the time of the birth his father or mother is—

(a) a British Dependent Territories citizen; or

(b) settled in a dependent territory.

(2) A new-born infant who, after commencement, is found abandoned in a dependent territory shall, unless the contrary is shown, be deemed for the purposes of subsection (1)—

(a) to have been born in that territory after commencement; and

(b) to have been born to a parent who at the time of the birth was a British Dependent Territories citizen or settled in a dependent territory.

(3) A person born in a dependent territory after commencement who is not a British Dependent Territories citizen by virtue of subsection (1) or (2) shall be entitled to be registered as such a citizen if, while he is a minor—

(a) his father or mother becomes such a citizen or becomes settled in a dependent territory; and

(b) an application is made for his registration as such a citizen.

(4) A person born in a dependent territory after commencement who is not a British Dependent Territories citizen by virtue of subsection (1) or (2) shall be entitled, on an application for registration as a British Dependent Territories citizen made at any time after he has attained the age of ten years, to be registered as such a citizen if, as regards each of the first ten years of that person's life, the number of days on which he was absent from the territory in that year does not exceed 90.

(5), (6) * * * * *

(7) If in the special circumstances of any particular case the Secretary of State thinks fit, he may for the purposes of subsection (4) treat the person to whom the application relates as fulfilling the requirements specified in that subsection although, as regards any one or more of the first ten years of that person's life, the number of days on which he was absent from the dependent territory there mentioned in that year or each of the years in question exceeds 90.

16 Acquisition by descent

(1) A person born outside the dependent territories after commencment shall be a British Dependent Territories citizen if at the time of the birth his father or mother—

(a) is such a citizen otherwise than by descent; or

(b) is such a citizen and is serving outside the dependent territories in service to which this paragraph applies, his or her recruitment for that service having taken place in a dependent territory.

(2) Paragraph (b) of subsection (1) applies to—

(a) Crown service under the government of a dependent territory; and

(b) service of any description for the time being designated under subsection (3).

(3) For the purposes of this section the Secretary of State may by order made by statutory instrument designate any description of service which he considers to be closely associated with the activities outside the dependent territories of the government of any dependent territory.

(4) Any order made under subsection (3) shall be subject to annulment in pursuance of a resolution of either House of Parliament.

17-25 * * * * *

PART III
BRITISH OVERSEAS CITIZENSHIP

26 Citizens of UK and Colonies who are to become British Overseas citizens at commencement

Any person who was a citizen of the United Kingdom and Colonies immediately before commencement and who does not at commencement become either a British citizen or a British Dependent Territories citizen shall at commencement become a British Overseas citizen.

27-35 * * * * *

PART V
MISCELLANEOUS AND SUPPLEMENTARY

36 * * * * *

37 Commonwealth citizenship

(1) Every person who—

(a) under [the British Nationality Acts 1981 and 1983] is a British citizen, a British Dependent Territories citizen, [a British National (Overseas),] a British Overseas citizen or a British subject; or

(b) under any enctment for the time being in force in any country mentioned in Schedule 3 is a citizen of that country,

shall have the status of a Commonwealth citizen.

(2) Her Majesty may by Order in Council amend Schedule 3 by the alteration of any entry, the removal of any entry, or the insertion of any additional entry.

(3) Any Order in Council made under this section shall be subject to annulment in pursuance of a resolution of either House of Parliament.

(4) After commencement no person shall have the status of a Commonwealth citizen or the status of a British subject otherwise than under this Act.

Note Schedule 3 (not printed) lists those countries currently members of the Commonwealth.

38-39 * * * * *

40 Deprivation of citizenship

(1) Subject to the provisions of this section, the Secretary of State may by order deprive any British citizen to whom the subsection applies of his British citizenship if the Secretary of State is satisfied that the registration or certificate of naturalisation by virtue of which he is such a citizen was obtained by means of fraud, false representation or the concealment of any material fact.

(2) Subsection (1) applies to any British citizen who—

(a) became a British citizen after commencement by virtue of—

(i) his registration as a British citizen under any provision of [the British Nationality Acts 1981 and 1983]; or

(ii) a certificate of naturalisation granted to him under section 6; or

(b) being immediately before commencement a citizen of the United Kingdom and Colonies by virtue of registration as such a citizen under any provision of the British Nationality Acts 1948 to 1964, became at commencement a British citizen; or

(c) at any time before commencement became a British subject (within the meaning of that expression at that time), or a citizen of Eire or of the Republic of Ireland, by virtue of a certificate of naturalisation granted to him or in which his name was included.

(3) Subject to the provisions of this section, the Secretary of State may by order deprive any British citizen to whom this subsection applies of his British citizenship if the Secretary of State is satisfied that that citizen—

(a) has shown himself by act or speech to be disloyal or disaffected towards Her Majesty; or

(b) has, during any war in which Her Majesty was engaged, unlawfully traded or communicated with an enemy or been engaged in or associated with any business that was to his knowledge carried on in such a manner as to assist an enemy in that war; or

(c) has, within the period of five years from the relevant date, been sentenced in any country to imprisonment for a term of not less than twelve months.

(4) Subsection (3) applies to any British citizen who falls within paragraph (a) or (c) of subsection (2); and in subsection (3) "the relevant date", in relation to a British citizen to whom subsection (3) applies, means the date of the registration by virtue of which he is such a citizen or, as the case may be, the date of the grant of the certificate of naturalisation by virtue of which he is such a citizen.

(5) The Secretary of State—

(a) shall not deprive a person of British citizenship under this section unless he is satisfied that it is not conducive to the public good that that person should continue to be a British citizen; and

(b) shall not deprive a person of British citizenship under subsection (3) on the ground mentioned in paragraph (c) of that subsection if it appears to him that that person would thereupon become stateless.

(6) Before making an order under this section the Secretary of State shall give the person against whom the order is proposed to be made notice in writing informing him of the ground or grounds on which it is proposed to be made and of his right to an inquiry under this section.

(7) If the person against whom the order is proposed to be made applies in the prescribed manner for an inquiry, the Secretary of State shall, and in any other case the Secretary of State may, refer the case to a committee of inquiry consisting of a chairman, being a person possessing judicial experience, appointed by the Secretary of State and of such other members appointed by the Secrtetary of State as he thinks proper.

(8)-(10) * * * * *

41 * * * * *

42 Registration and naturalisation: general provisions

(1) Subject to subsection (2)—

(a) a person shall not be registered under any provision of this Act as a citizen of any description or as a British subject; and

(b) a certificate of naturalisation shall not be granted to a person under any provision of this Act,

unless—

(i) any fee payable by virtue of this Act in connection with the registration or as the case may be, the grant of the certificate has been paid; and

(ii) the person concerned has within the prescribed time taken an oath of allegiance in the form indicated in Schedule 5.

(2) So much of subsection (1) as requires the taking of an oath of allegiance shall not apply to a person who—

(a) is not of full age; or

(b) is already a British citizen, a British Dependent Territories citizen, [a British National (Overseas),] a British Overseas citizen, a British subject, or a citizen of any country of which Her Majesty is Queen.

(3) Any provision of this Act which provides for a person to be entitled to registration as a citizen of any description or as a British subject shall have effect subject to the preceding provisions of this section.

(4) A person registered under any provision of this Act as a British citizen, or as a British Dependent Territories citizen [, or as a British National (Overseas),] or as a British Overseas citizen, or as a British subject, shall be a citizen of that description or, as the case may be, [a British National (Overseas) or] a British subject as from the date on which he is so registered.

(5) A person to whom a certificate of naturalisation as a British citizen or as a British Dependent Territories citizen is granted under any provision of this Act shall be a citizen of that description as from the date on which the certificate is granted.

43 * * * * *

44 Decisions involving exercise of discretion

(1) Any discretion vested by or under this Act in the Secretary of State, a Governor or a Lieutenant-Governor shall be exercised without regard to the race, colour or religion of any person who may be affected by its exercise.

(2) The Secretary of State, a Governor or a Lieutenant-Governor, as the case may be, shall not be required to assign any reason for the grant or refusal of any application under this Act the decision on which is at his discretion; and the decision of the Secretary of State or a Governor or Lieutenant-Governor on any such application shall not be subject to appeal to, or review in, any court.

(3) Nothing in this section affects the jurisdiction of any court to entertain proceedings of any derscription concerning the rights of any person under any provision of this Act.

45-46 * * * * *

47 Legitimated children

(1) A person born out of wedlock and legitimated by the subsequent marriage of his parents shall, as from the date of the marriage, be treated for the purposes of this Act as if he had been born legitimate.

(2) A person shall be deemed for the purposes of this section to have been legitimated by the subsequent marriage of his parents if by the law of the place in which his father was domiciled at the time of the marriage the marriage operated immediately or subsequently to legitimate him, and not otherwise.

48 Posthumous children

Any reference in this Act to the status or descriptions of the father or mother of a person at the time of that person's birth shall, in relation to a person born after the death of his father or mother, be construed as a reference to the status or description of the parent in question at the time of that parent's death; and where that death occurred before, and the birth occurs after, commencement, the status or description which would have been applicable to the father or mother had he or she died after commencement shall be deemed to be the status or description applicable to him or her at the time of his or her death.

49 . . .

50 Interpretation

(1) In this Act, unless the context otherwise requires—

"the 1948 Act" means the British Nationality Act 1948:

"alien" means a person who is neither a Commonwealth citizen nor a British protected person nor a citizen of the Republic of Ireland;

"association" means an unincorporated body of persons;

["British National (Overseas)" means a person who is a British National (Overseas) under the Hong Kong (British Nationality) Order 1986, and "status of a British National (Overseas)" shall be construed accordingly;

"British Overseas citizen" includes a person who is a British Overseas citizen under the Hong Kong (British Nationality) Order 1986;]

"British protected person" means a person who is a member of any class of person declared to be British protected persons by an Order in Council for the time being in force under section 38 or is a British protected person by virtue of the Solomon Islands Act 1978;

* * * * *

"Crown service" means the service of the Crown, whether within Her Majesty's dominions or elsewhere;

"Crown service under the government of the United Kingdom" means Crown service under Her Majesty's government in the United Kingdom or under Her Majesty's government in Northern Ireland;

"dependent territory" means a territory mentioned in Schedule 6;

"enactment" includes an enactment comprised in Northern Ireland legislation;

"foreign country" means a country other than the United Kingdom, a dependent territory, a country mentioned in Schedule 3 and the Republic of Ireland;

* * * * *

"immigration laws"—

(a) in relation to the United Kingdom, means the Immigration Act 1971 and any law for purposes similar to that Act which is for the time being or has at any time been in force in any part of the United Kingdom;

(b) in relation to a dependent territory, means any law for purposes similar to the Immigration Act 1971 which is for the time being or has at any time been in force in that territory;

"the Islands" means the Channel Islands and the Isle of Man;

"minor" means a person who has not attained the age of eighteen years;

"prescribed" means prescribed by regulations made under section 41;

"settled" shall be construed in accordance with subsections (2) to (4);

"ship" includes a hovercraft;

* * * * *

"United Kingdom consulate" means the office of a consular officer of Her Majesty's government in the United Kingdom where a register of births is kept or, where there is no such office, such office as may be prescribed.

(2) Subject to subsection (3), references in this Act to a person being settled in the United Kingdom or in a dependent territory are references to his being ordinarily resident in the United Kingdom or, as the case may be, in that territory without being subject under the immigration laws to any restriction on the period for which he may remain.

(3), (4) * * * * *

(5) It is hereby declared that a person is not to be treated for the purpose of any provision of this Act as ordinarily resident in the United Kingdom or in a dependent territory at a time when he is in the United Kingdom or, as the case may be, in that territory in breach of the immigration laws.

(6)-(8) * * * * *

(9) For the purposes of this Act—

(a) the relationship of mother and child shall be taken to exist between a woman and any child (legitimate or illegitimate) born to her; but

(b) subject to section 47, the relationship of father and child shall be taken to exist only between a man and any legitimate child born to him;
and the expressions "mother", "father", "parent", "child" and "descended" shall be construed accordingly.

(10)-(13) * * * * *

51-53 * * * * *

Sections 6, 18

SCHEDULE 1

REQUIREMENTS FOR NATURALISATION

Naturalisation as a British citizen under section 6(1)

1.—(1) Subject to paragraph 2, the requirements for naturalisation as a British citizen under section 6(1) are, in the case of any person who applies for it—

(a) the requirements specified in sub-paragraph (2) of this paragraph, or the alternative requirement specified in sub-paragraph (3) of this paragraph; and

(b) that he is of good character; and

(c) that he has a sufficient knowledge of the English, Welsh or Scottish Gaelic language; and

(d) that either—

(i) his intentions are such that, in the event of a certificate of naturalisation as a British citizen being granted to him, his home or (if he has more than one) his principal home will be in the United Kingdom; or

(ii) he intends, in the event of such a certificate being granted to him, to enter into, or continue in, Crown service under the government of the United Kingdom, or service under an international organisation of which the United Kingdom or Her Majesty's government therein is a member, or service in the employment of a company or association established in the United Kingdom.

(2) The requirements referred to in sub-paragraph (1)(a) of this paragraph are—

(a) that the applicant was in the United Kingdom at the beginning of the period of five years ending with the date of the application, and that the number of days on which he was absent from the United Kingdom in that period does not exceed 450; and

(b) that the number of days on which he was absent from the United Kingdom in the period of twelve months so ending does not exceed 90; and

(c) that he was not at any time in the period of twelve months so ending subject under the immigration laws to any restriction on the period for which he might remain in the United Kingdom; and

(d) that he was not at any time in the period of five years so ending in the United Kingdom in breach of the immigration laws.

(3) The alternative requirement referred to in sub-paragraph (1)(a) of this paragraph is that on the date of the application he is serving outside the United Kingdom in Crown service under the government of the United Kingdom.

2. * * * * *

Naturalisation as a British citizen under section 6(2)

3. Subject to paragraph 4, the requirements for naturalisation as a British citizen under section 6(2) are, in the case of any person who applies for it—

(a) that he was in the United Kingdom at the beginning of the period of three years ending with the date of the application, and that the number of days on which he was absent from the United Kingdom in that period does not exceed 270; and

(b) that the number of days on which he was absent from the United Kingdom in the period of twelve months so ending does not exceed 90; and

(c) that on the date of the application he was not subject under the immigration laws to any restriction on the period for which he might remain in the United Kingdom; and

(d) that he was not at any time in the period of three years ending with the date of the application in the United Kingdom in breach of the immigration laws; and

(e) the requirement specified in paragraph 1(1)(b).

*****

BROADCASTING ACT 1981
(1981, c. 68)

An Act to consolidate the Independent Broadcasting Authority Acts 1973, 1974 and 1978 and the Broadcasting Act 1980 [30 October 1981]

Territorial extent United Kingdom

PART I
THE INDEPENDENT BROADCASTING AUTHORITY

The Authority

1 The Independent Broadcasting Authority

(1) The authority called the Independent Broadcasting Authority shall continue in existence as a body corporate.

(2) The Authority shall consist of—

(a) a Chairman and a Deputy Chairman, and

(b) such number of other members, not being less than five, as the Secretary of State may from time to time determine.

(3) Unless and until the Secretary of State otherwise determines by notice in writing to the Authority, a copy of which shall be laid before each House of Parliament, the number of those other members shall be ten.

2 Function and duties of Authority

(1) The functions of the Authority shall be to provide, in accordance with this Act and until 31st December [2005], television and local sound broadcasting services, additional in each case to those of the BBC and of high quality (both as to the transmission and as to the matter transmitted), for so much of the United Kingdom, the Isle of Man and the Channel Islands as may from time to time be reasonably practicable.

(2) It shall be the duty of the Authority—

(a) to provide the television and local sound broadcasting services as a public service for disseminating information, education and entertainment;

(b) to ensure that the programmes broadcast by the Authority in each area maintain a high general standard in all respects (and in particular in respect of their content and quality), and a proper balance and wide range in their subject matter, having regard both to the programmes as a whole and also to the days of the week on which, and the times of the day at which, the programmes are broadcast; and

(c) to secure a wide showing or (as the case may be) hearing for programmes of merit.

(3)-(6) *****

3 Powers of Authority

(1) The Authority shall (subject to the provisions of this Act) have power to do all such things as are in their opinion necessary for or conducive to the proper discharge of their function under section 2(1) and, in particular, they shall for the purpose of discharging that function have power—

(a) to establish, install and use stations for wireless telegraphy;

(b) to arrange for the provision and equipment of, or (if need be) themselves to provide and equip, studios and other premises for television and sound broadcasting purposes;

(c) by arrangements made for the purpose with [persons providing cable programme services, to provide for the inclusion in the services of programmes broadcast by the Authority].

(2) Notwithstanding section 2(3) the Authority may—

(a) arrange for the provision of parts of programmes otherwise than by programme contractors for the purpose of securing the inclusion in the programmes broadcast by the Authority of items of particular classes which in their opinion are necessary for securing a proper balance in the subject-matter of the programmes and cannot, or cannot as suitably, be provided by programme contractors; * * * * *

(3)-(7) * * * * *

General provisions as to programmes

4 General provisions as to programmes

(1) It shall be the duty of the Authority to satisfy themselves that, so far as possible, the programmes broadcast by the Authority comply with the following requirements, that is to say—

(a) that nothing is included in the programmes which offends against good taste or decency or is likely to encourage or incite to crime or to lead to disorder or to be offensive to public feeling;

(b) that a sufficient amount of time in the programmes is given to news and news features and that all news given in the programmes (in whatever form) is presented with due accuracy and impartiality;

(c) that proper proportions of the recorded and other matter included in the programmes are of British origin and of British performance;

(d) that the programmes broadcast from any station or stations contain a suitable proportion of matter calculated to appeal specially to the tastes and outlook of persons served by the station or stations and, where another language as well as English is in common use among those so served, a suitable proportion of matter in that language;

(e) in the case of local sound broadcasting services, that the programmes broadcast from different stations for reception in different localities do not consist of identical or similar material to an extent inconsistent with the character of the services as local sound broadcasting services; and

(f) that due impartiality is preserved on the part of the persons providing the programmes as respects matters of political or industrial controversy or relating to current public policy.

In applying paragraph (f), a series of programmes may be considered as a whole.

(2) Without prejudice to the generality of subsection (1), it shall be the duty of the Authority to secure the exclusion from the programmes broadcast by them of all expressions of opinion by the Authority or their subsidiary mentioned in section 12(2), or by any programme contractor, on matters other than broadcasting which are of political or industrial controversy or relate to current public policy.

(3) If shall be the duty of the Authority to satisfy themselves that the programmes broadcast by the Authority do not include, whether in an advertisement or otherwise, any technical device which, by using images of very brief duration or by any other means, exploits the posibility of conveying a message to, or otherwise influencing the minds of, members of an audience without their being aware, or fully aware, of what has been done.

(4) Nothing shall be included in any programme broadcast by the Authority, whether in an advertisement or not, which offers any prize of significant value (whether competed for or not) or any gift of significant value, being a prize or gift which is available only to persons receiving that programme, or in relation to which any advantage is given to such persons.

(5) Except with the previous approval of the Authority, there shall not be included in any programme broadcast by the Authority—

(a) any religious service or any propaganda relating to matters of a religious nature;

(b) any item, whether an advertisement or not, which gives or is designed to give publicity to the needs or objects of any association or organisation conducted for charitable or benevolent purposes.

(6) Nothing in subsection (2) or (5) shall apply to a programme broadcast by the Authority so far as the programme consists of proceedings in either House of Parliament or proceedings of a local authority, a committee of a local authority or a joint committee of two or more local authorities.

In this subsection "local authority" means any of the following bodies, namely, a local authority within the meaning of the Local Government Act 1972, a local authority within the meaning of the Local Government (Scotland) Act 1973, a district council in Northern Ireland, the Common Council of the City of London and (without prejudice to the effect of that Act of 1972) the Inner London Education Authority.

(7) *****

Programmes other than advertisements

5 Code for programmes other than advertisements

(1) The Authority shall draw up, and from time to time review, a code giving guidance—

(a) as to the rules to be observed in regard to the showing of violence, and in regard to the inclusion in local sound broadcasts of sounds suggestive of violence, particularly when large numbers of children and young persons may be expected to be watching or listening to the programmes, and

(b) as to such other matters concerning standards and practice for programmes (other than advertisements) broadcast by the Authority as the Authority may consider suitable for inclusion in the code;

and, in considering what other matters ought to be included in the code in pursuance of paragraph (b), the Authority shall have special regard to programmes broadcast when large numbers of children and young persons may be expected to be watching or listening.

(2) The authority shall secure that the provisions of the code under this section are observed in relation to all programmes (other than advertisements) broadcast by them.

(3) The Authority may, in the discharge of their general responsibility for programmes other than advertisements, impose requirements as to standards and practice for such programmes which go beyond, or relate to matters not covered by, the provisions of the code under this section.

(4) *****

6 Submission of programme schedules for Authority's approval

(1) In the case of programmes other than advertisements, the method by which the Authority discharge their duties under sections 2(2) and 5 in relation to television broadcasts shall, and in relation to local sound broadcasts (to such extent as the Authority consider appropriate) may, include consideration of programme schedules submitted by programme contractors to the Authority for approval in accordance with this section.

(2) Subject to subsection (6), no programme (other than an advertisement) provided by a programme contractor—

(a) if it is a television programme, or

(b) if it is a local sound broadcast which the Authority have required to be made in accordance with a programme schedule so approved,

shall be broadcast by the Authority unless it forms part of a programme schedule approved by them in accordance with this section.

(3) A programme schedule—

(a) shall be drawn up in consultation with the Authority, and

(b) shall for a period determined by them;

and the Authority may give to programme contractors such directions as appear to the Authority expedient for the purpose of ensuring that the Authority have sufficient time to discharge their responsibilities in the consideration of programme schedules.

(4)-(7) *****

7 *****

8 Advertisements

(1) The programmes broadcast by the Authority may, so long as the provisions of this Act are complied with in relation thereto, include advertisements inserted therein in consideration of payments to the relevant programme contractor or (in the case of an advertisement included in a programme or part of a programme provided under section 3(2)(b)) to the Authority.

(2) Orders for the insertion of the said advertisements may be received either through advertising or other agents or direct from the advertiser, but neither the Authority nor any programme contractor shall act as an advertising agent.

(3) It shall be the duty of the Authority to secure that the provisions of Schedule 2 are complied with in relation to the advertisements included in the programmes broadcast by the Authority.

(4) After consultation with the Authority the Secretary of State may make regulations amending, repealing, or adding to the provisions of Schedule 2.

(5)-(9) *****

9 Code for advertisements

(1) It shall be the duty of the Authority—

(a) [after consultation with the Cable Authority] to draw up, and from time to time review, a code governing standards and practice in advertising and prescribing the advertisements and methods of advertising to be prohibited, or prohibited in particular circumstances; and

(b) to secure that the provisions of the code are complied with as regards the advertisements included in the programmes broadcast by the Authority.

(2) The Authority may, in the discharge of their general responsibility for advertisements and methods of advertising, impose requirements as to advertisements and method of advertising which go beyond the requirements imposed by the code under this section.

(3)-(5) *****

*****

Provisions applying to all contracts for programmes

22 Provision for news broadcasts

The contracts between the Authority and the various programme contractors shall contain all such provisions as the Authority think necessary or expedient to ensure—

(a) that there is at all times at least one body or organisation effectively equipped and adequately financed to provide news for broadcasting in the programmes supplied to the Authority by the respective programme contractors, and that in so far as any such body or organisation supplies to programme contractors other programmes which it can suitably provide, it is effectively equipped and adequately financed for the purpose;

(b) that each of the programme contractors with whom the Authority enter into contracts for the provision of television programmes is afforded opportunities of obtaining a financial interest in that body or organisation or, if there are two or more such bodies or organisations providing news for broadcasting in the television programmes supplied to the Authority by those contractors, is afforded opportunities of obtaining a financial interest in such of those bodies or organisations as the Authority may in his case direct; and

(c) that the appointment of the manager, editor or other chief executive of any such body or organisation is approved by the Authority.

23 Newspaper shareholdings in programme contractors

(1) Every contract concluded between the Authority and a programme contractor shall, where the programme contractor is a body corporate, contain all such provisions as the Authority think necessary or expedient to ensure that if at any time—

(a) there are newspaper shareholdings in the programme contractor, and

(b) it appears to the Authority that the existence of those shareholdings has led or is leading to results which are contrary to the public interest,

the Authority, with the consent of the Secretary of State, may by notice in writing to the programme contractor, taking effect forthwith or on a date specified in the notice, determine or suspend for such period as may be so specified or until a further notice is given, the Authority's obligation to transmit the programmes supplied by the programme contractor.

(2) Without prejudice to any such provisions contained in a contract between the Authority and a programme contractor, if at any time there are newspaper shareholdings in the programme contractor, and it appears to the Secretary of State that the existence of those shareholdings has led or is leading to results which are contrary to the public interest, he may, after consultation with the Authority, by order—

(a) determine on a date specified in the order the Authority's obligation to transmit the programmes supplied by the programme contractor; or

(b) suspend that obligation for such period as may be so specified, or during a period beginning with a date so specified and continuing so long as the order remains in force; and

(c) whether or not the order provides for the determination or suspension of the said obligation, direct that, while the order remains in force, the Authority shall not enter into any further contract with the programme contractor for the supply of programmes.

(3) Any order under subsection (2) shall be made by statutory instrument; but no such order, other than an order the sole purpose of which is to rescind, postpone commencement of or terminate a period of suspension or to cancel a direction, shall be made unless a draft of the order has been laid before Parliament and approved by a resolution of each House.

(4) The determination or suspension in accordance with this section of the Authority's obligation to transmit the programmes supplied by the programme contractor, whether effected by a notice or by an order, shall not affect the programme contractor's obligation as to the supply of programmes up to the date when the determination or suspension takes effect.

(5) Where such a determination or suspension takes effect, the programme contractor shall not be entitled to any compensation from the Authority or to any refund of any sum previously paid by the programme contractor or to any relief from any liability which has accrued at the date when the determination or suspension takes effect for any sums payable by the programme contractor to the Authority.

(6) For the purposes of this section there are newspaper shareholdings in a body corporate if shares in that body corporate are held by any individual or body corporate being either—

(a) the proprietor of any newspaper, whether national or local, or

(b) a person who has control over any body corporate which is a proprietor of such a newspaper.

* * * * *

Powers of Government in relation to Authority

28 Government control over Authority as to hours of broadcasting

(1) The Secretary of State may from time to time by notice in writing give directions to the Authority—

(a) as to the maximum or minimum time, or both the maximum and the minimum time, which is to be given in any day, week or other period to broadcasts from any of the broadcasting stations used by them, and

(b) as to the hours of the day in which such broadcasts are or are not to be given; and it shall be the duty of the Authority to comply with the notice.

(2)-(4) * * * * *

(5) The powers conferred by this section are in addition to any powers specifically conferred on the Secretary of State by any other provisions of this Act.

29 Government control over Authority as to certain other matters

(1) The Secretary of State or any other Minister of the Crown may, if it appears to him to be necessary or expedient to do so in connection with his functions as such, at any time by notice in writing require the Authority to broadcast, at such times and from such of the stations used by them as may be specified in the notice, any announcement specified in the notice, with or without visual images of any picture, scene or object mentioned in the announcement; and it shall be the duty of the Authority to comply with the notice.

(2) Where the Authority broadcast any announcement in pursuance of a notice under subsection (1) they may, if they think fit, announce that they are doing so in pursuance of such a notice.

(3) Subject to subsection (4), the Secretary of State may at any time by notice in writing require the Authority to refrain from broadcasting any matter or classes of matter specified in the notice; and it shall be the duty of the Authority to comply with the notice.

(4) If the Secretary of State by notice in writing requires the Authority under subsection (3) to refrain from broadcasting anything, the Authority may, if they think fit, broadcast an announcement of the notice or of the revocation or expiration of the notice.

(5)-(8) * * * * *

* * * * *

PART III
THE BROADCASTING COMPLAINTS COMMISSION

Note This part of the Act is printed as amended by the Cable and Broadcasting Act 1984, Sch. 2.

53 The Broadcasting Complaints Commission

(1) The commission named the Broadcasting Complaints Commission shall continue in existence as a body corporate.

(2) The Commission shall consist of not less than three members appointed by the Secretary of State.

(3)-(5) * * * * *

54 Function of Commission

(1) Subject to the provisions of this Part, the function of the Commission shall be to consider and adjudicate upon complaints of—

(a) unjust or unfair treatment in sound or television programmes actually broadcast by a broadcasting body on or after 1st June 1981; or

[(b) unjust or unfair treatment in programmes actually included in a licensed cable programme service after the commencement of section 29 of the Cable and Broadcasting Act 1984 otherwise than by the reception and immediate re-transmission of broadcasts made by a broadcasting body; or

(c) unwarranted infringement of privacy in, or in connection with the obtaining of material included in, sound or television programmes actually so broadcast or programmes actually so included.]

(2) The Commission shall not entertain complaints not falling within subsection (1).

(3) In this Part—

"broadcasting body" means the BBC or the IBA;

["broadcasting complaint" means a complaint in the case of which the relevant programme was broadcast by a broadcasting body;

"cable programme complaint" means a complaint in the case of which the relevant programme was included in a licensed cable programme service otherwise than by the reception and immediate re-transmission of broadcasts made by a broadcasting body;

"complaint" means a complaint to the Commission of any such unjust or unfair treatment or unwarranted infringement of privacy as is mentioned in subsection (1);

"participant", in relation to a programme, means a person who appeared, or whose voice was heard, in the programme;]

"the person affected"—

(a) in relation to any such unjust or unfair treatment as is mentioned in subsection (1), means a participant in the programme in question who was the subject of that treatment or a person who, whether such a participant or not, had a direct interest in the subject-matter of that treatment;

(b) in relation to any such unwarranted infringement of privacy as is so mentioned, means a person whose privacy was infringed;

"the relevant programme", in relation to a complaint, means the programme in which the alleged unjust or unfair treatment occurred or in which, or in connection with the obtaining of material included in which, the alleged unwarranted infringement of privacy occurred;

"unjust or unfair treatment" includes treatment which is unjust or unfair because of the way in which material included in a programme has been selected or arranged;

and references in this Part to television programmes and programme contractors include references to teletext transmission and teletext contractors respectively.

55 Making and entertaining of complaints

(1) Complaints must be made in writing.

(2) A complaint may be made by an individual or by a body of persons, whether incorporated or not, but, subject to subsection (3), shall not be entertained by the Commission unless made by the person affected or by a person authorised by him to make the complaint for him.

(3) Where the person affected is an individual who has died or is for any other reason both unable to make a complaint himself and unable to authorise another person to do so for him, a complaint may be made by the personal representative of the person affected, or by a member of his family, or by some other person or body closely connected with him (whether as his employer, or as a body of which he is or was at his death a member, or in any other way).

(4) The Commission shall not entertain, or proceed with the consideration of, a complaint if it appears to them—

(a) that the complaint relates to the broadcasting of the relevant programme [or its inclusion in a licensed cable programme service] on an occasion more than five years after the death of the person affected; or

(b) that the unjust or unfair treatment or unwarranted infringement of privacy complained of is the subject of proceedings in a court of law in the United Kingdom; or

(c) that the unjust or unfair treatment or unwarranted infringement of privacy complained of is a matter in respect of which the person affected has a remedy by way of proceedings in a court of law in the United Kingdom, and that in the particular circumstances it is not appropriate for the Commission to consider a complaint about it; or

(d) that the complaint is frivolous;

or if it appears to them for any other reason inappropriate for them to entertain, or proceed with the consideration of, the complaint.

(5) The Commission may refuse to entertain a complaint if it appears to them not to have been made within a reasonable time after that occasion on which the relevant programme was broadcast by a broadcasting body [or included in a licensed cable programme service].

(6) Where, in the case of a complaint, the relevant programme was broadcast [or included in a licensed cable programme service] within five years after the death of the person affected, subsection (5) shall apply as if at the end there were added "within five years after the death of the person affected".

(7) The Commission may refuse to entertain—

(a) a complaint of unjust or unfair treatment if the person named as the person affected was not himself the subject of the treatment complained of and it appears to the Commission that he did not have a sufficiently direct interest in the subject-matter thereof to justify the making of a complaint with him as the person affected; or

(b) a complaint made under subsection (3) by a person other than the person affected or a person authorised by him, if it appears to the Commission that the complainant's connection with the person affected is not sufficiently close to justify the making of the complaint by him.

56 Consideration of complaints

(1) Subject to the provisions of section 55, every complaint made to the Commission shall be considered by them either at a hearing or, if they think fit, without a hearing.

(2) Hearings under this section shall be held in private; and where such a hearing is held in respect of a complaint, each of the following persons shall be given an opportunity to attend and be heard, namely—

(a) the complainant;

[(b) in the case of a broadcasting complaint, the broadcasting body by whom the relevant programme was broadcast;

(c) in the case of a cable programme complaint, the Cable Authority and every person providing a licensed cable programme service in which the relevant programme was included; and

(d) in either case, any person not falling within the foregoing paragraphs who appears to the Commission to have been responsible for the making or provision of the relevant programme.]

(3)-(8) * * * * *

57 Publication of Commissions' findings

(1) Where the Commission have considered and adjudicated upon a complaint, they may give [directions requiring the publication, in any manner specified in the directions and within such period as may be specified, of]—

(a) a summary of the complaint approved for the purpose by the Commission; and

(b) the Commission's findings on the complaint or a summary thereof so approved.

[(2) Directions under subsection (1) shall, in the case of a broadcasting complaint, be given to the broadcasting body by whom the relevant programme was broadcast; and it shall be the duty of a broadcasting body to comply with any directions so given.

(2A) Directions under subsection (1) shall, in the case of a cable programme complaint, be given to every person providing a licensed cable programme service in which the relevant programme was included; and it shall be the duty of the Cable Authority to take such steps as they reasonably can to ensure that any directions so given are complied with.]

(3) The Commission shall publish, at such intervals and in such manner as they think fit, reports each containing, as regards every complaint within this subsection dealt with by them in the period covered by the report, a summary of the complaint and of the action taken by them on it and, where they have adjudicated upon it, a summary of their findings.

(4), (5) * * * * *

58 Duty to publicise Commission

(1) It shall be the duty of each broadcasting body to publish (by means of broadcasts or otherwise) regular announcements publicising the Commission and their function of considering and adjudicating upon [broadcasting] complaints.

[(2) It shall be the duty of the Cable Authority to take such steps as they reasonably can to secure the publication (by means of licensed cable programme services or otherwise) of regular announcements publicising the Commission and their function of considering and adjudicating upon cable programme complaints.]

* * * * *

Section 8

SCHEDULE 2
RULES AS TO ADVERTISEMENTS

1.—(1) The advertisements must be clearly distinguishable as such and recognisably separate from the rest of the programme.

(2) Successive advertisements must be recognisably separate.

(3) Advertisements must not be arranged or presented in such a way that any separate advertisement appears to be part of a continuous feature.

(4) Audible matter in advertisements must not be excessively noisy or strident.

2. The standards and practice to be observed in carrying out the requirements of the preceding paragraph shall be such as the Authority may determine either generally or in particular cases.

3. The amount of time given to advertising in the programmes shall not be so great as to detract from the value of the programmes as a medium of information, education and entertainment.

4. Advertisements shall not be inserted otherwise than at the beginning or the end of the programme or in natural breaks therein.

5.—(1) Rules (to be agreed upon from time to time between the Authority and the Secretary of State, or settled by the Secretary of State in default of such agreement) shall be observed as to the classes of broadcasts (which shall in particular include the broadcast of any religious service), in which advertisements may not be inserted, and the interval which must elapse between any such broadcast and any previous or subsequent period given over to advertisements.

(2) The Secretary of State may, after consultation with the Authority, impose rules as to the minimum interval which must elapse between any two periods given over to advertisements, and the rules may make different provision for different circumstances.

6. In the acceptance of advertisements there must be no unreasonable discrimination either against or in favour of any particular advertiser.

7.—(1) The charges made by any programme contractor for advertisements shall be in accordance with tariffs fixed by him from time to time, being tariffs drawn up in such detail and published in such form and manner as the Authority may determine.

(2) Any such tariffs may make provision for different circumstances, and, in particular, may provide, in such detail as the authority may determine, for the making, in special circumstances, of additional special charges.

8. No advertisement shall be permitted which is inserted by or on behalf of any body whose objects are wholly or mainly of a religious or political nature, and no advertisement shall be permitted which is directed towards any religious or political end or has any relation to any industrial dispute.

9. If, in the case of any of the broadcasting stations used by the Authority, there appears to the Authority to be a sufficient local demand to justify that course, provision shall be made for a reasonable allocation of time for local advertisements, of which a suitable proportion shall be short local advertisements.

* * * * *

CONTEMPT OF COURT ACT 1981
(1981, c. 49)

An Act to amend the law relating to contempt of court and related matters [27 July 1981]

Territorial extent United Kingdom (ss. 1-6, 8-11, Sch. 1); England and Wales (ss. 12-14); Scotland (s. 15); England, Wales and Northern Ireland (s. 7). For additional provisions applying to Northern Ireland see Sch. 4.

Strict liability

1 The strict liability rule

In this Act "the strict liability rule" means the rule of law whereby conduct may be treated as a contempt of court as tending to interfere with the course of justice in particular legal proceedings regardless of intent to do so.

2 Limitation of scope of strict liability

(1) The strict liability rule applies only in relation to publications, and for this purpose "publication" includes any speech, writing, broadcast [cable programme] or other communication in whatever form, which is addressed to the public at large or any section of the public.

(2) The strict liability rule applies only to a publication which creates a substantial risk that the course of justice in the proceedings in question will be seriously impeded or prejudiced.

(3) The strict liability rule applies to a publication only if the proceedings in question are active within the meaning of this section at the time of the publication.

(4) Schedule 1 applies for determining the times at which proceedings are to be treated as active within the meaning of this section.

3 Defence of innocent publication or distribution

(1) A person is not guilty of contempt of court under the strict liability rule as the publisher of any matter to which that rule applies if at the time of publication (having taken all reasonable care) he does not know and has no reason to suspect that relevant proceedings are active.

(2) A person is not guilty of contempt of court under the strict liability rule as the distributor of a publication containing any such matter if at the time of distribution (having taken all reasonable care) he does not know that it contains such matter and has no reason to suspect that it is likely to do so.

(3) The burden of proof of any fact tending to establish a defence afforded by this section to any person lies upon that person.

(4) . . .

4 Contemporary reports of proceedings

(1) Subject to this section a person is not guilty of contempt of court under the strict liability rule in respect of a fair and accurate report of legal proceedings held in public, published contemporaneously and in good faith.

(2) In any such proceedings the court may, where it appears to be necessary for avoiding a substantial risk of prejudice to the administration of justice in those proceedings, or in any other proceedings pending or imminent, order that the publication

of any report of the proceedings, or any part of the proceedings, be postponed for such period as the court thinks necessary for that purpose.

(3) *****

(4) . . .

5 Discussion of public affairs

A publication made as or as part of a discussion in good faith of public affairs or other matters of general public interest is not to be treated as a contempt of court under the strict liability rule if the risk of impediment or prejudice to particular legal proceedings is merely incidental to the discussion.

6 Savings

Nothing in the foregoing provisions of this Act—

(a) prejudices any defence available at common law to a charge of contempt of court under the strict liability rule;

(b) implies that any publication is punishable as contempt of court under that rule which would not be so punishable apart from those provisions;

(c) restricts liability for contempt of court in respect of conduct intended to impede or prejudice the administration of justice.

7 Consent required for institution of proceedings

Proceedings for a contempt of court under the strict liability rule (other than Scottish proceedings) shall not be instituted except by or with the consent of the Attorney General or on the motion of a court having jurisdiction to deal with it.

Other aspects of law and procedure

8 Confidentiality of jury's deliberations

(1) Subject to subsection (2) below, it is a contempt of court to obtain, disclose or solicit any particulars of statements made, opinions expressed, arguments advanced or votes cast by members of a jury in the course of their deliberations in any legal proceedings.

(2) This section does not apply to any disclosure of any particulars—

(a) in the proceedings in question for the purpose of enabling the jury to arrive at their verdict, or in connection with the delivery of that verdict, or

(b) in evidence in any subsequent proceedings for an offence alleged to have been committed in relation to the jury in the first mentioned proceedings,

or to the publication of any particulars so disclosed.

(3) Proceedings for a contempt of court under this section (other than Scottish proceedings) shall not be instituted except by or with the consent of the attorney general or on the motion of a court having jurisdiction to deal with it.

9 Use of tape recorders

(1) Subject to subsection (4) below, it is a contempt of court—

(a) to use in court, or bring into court for use, any tape recorder or other instrument for recording sound, except with the leave of the court;

(b) to publish a recording of legal proceedings made by means of any such instrument, or any recording derived directly or indirectly from it, by playing it in the hearing of the public or any section of the public, or to dispose of it or any recording so derived, with a view to such publication;

(c) to use any such recording in contravention of any conditions of leave granted under paragraph (a).

(2) Leave under paragraph (a) of subsection (1) may be granted or refused at the discretion of the court, and if granted may be granted subject to such conditions as the court thinks proper with respect to the use of any recording made pursuant to the leave; and where leave has been granted the court may at the like discretion withdraw or amend it either generally or in relation to any particular part of the proceedings.

(3) Without prejudice to any other power to deal with an act of contempt under paragraph (a) of subsection (1), the court may order the instrument, or any recording made with it, or both, to be forfeited; and any object so forfeited shall (unless the court otherwise determines on application by a person appearing to be the owner) be sold or otherwise disposed of in such manner as the court may direct.

(4) This section does not apply to the making or use of sound recordings for purposes of official transcripts of proceedings.

10 Sources of information

No court may require a person to disclose, nor is any person guilty of contempt of court for refusing to disclose, the source of information contained in a publication for which he is responsible, unless it be established to the satisfaction of the court that disclosure is necessary in the interests of justice or national security or for the prevention of disorder or crime.

11 Publication of matters exempted from disclosure in court

In any case where a court (having power to do so) allows a name or other matter to be withheld from the public in proceedings before the court, the court may give such directions prohibiting the publication of that name or matter in connection with the proceedings as appear to the court to be necessary for the purpose of which it was so withheld.

12 Offences of contempt of magistrates' courts

(1) A magistrates' court has jurisdiction under this section to deal with any person who—

(a) wilfully insults the justice or justices, any witness before or officer of the court or any solicitor or counsel having business in the court, during his or their sitting or attendance in court or in going to or returning from the court; or

(b) wilfully interrupts the proceedings of the court or otherwise misbehaves in court.

(2) In any such case the court may order any officer of the court, or any constable, to take the offender into custody and detain him until the rising of the court; and the court may, if it thinks fit, commit the offender to custody for a specified period not exceeding one month or impose on him a fine not exceeding [£1,000], or both.

(3) . . .

(4), (5) * * * * *

13 * * * * *

Penalties for contempt and kindred offences

14 Proceedings in England and Wales

(1) In any case where a court has power to commit a person to prison for contempt of court and (apart from this provision) no limitation applies to the period of committal, the committal shall (without prejudice to the power of the court to order his earlier discharge) be for a fixed term, and that term shall not on any occasion exceed two years in the case of committal by a superior court, or one month in the case of committal by an inferior court.

(2) In any case where an inferior court has power to fine a person for contempt of court and (apart from the provision) no limit applies to the amount of the fine, the fine shall not on any occasion exceed [£1,000].

(3), (4) * * * * *

[(4A) For the purposes of the preceding provisions of this section a county court shall be treated as a superior court and not as an inferior court.]

(5) * * * * *

15 Penalties for contempt of court in Scottish proceedings

(1) In Scottish proceedings, when a person is committed to prison for contempt of court the committal shall (without prejudice to the power of the court to order his earlier discharge) be for a fixed term.

(2) The maximum penalty which may be imposed by way of imprisonment or fine for contempt of court in Scottish proceedings shall be two years' imprisonment or a fine or both, except that—

(a) where the contempt is dealt with by the sheriff in the course of or in connection with proceedings other than criminal proceedings on indictment, such penalty shall not exceed three months' imprisonment or a fine [not exceeding level 5 on the standard scale] or both; and

(b) where the contempt is dealt with by the district court, such penalty shall not exceed sixty days' imprisonment or a fine of £200 or both.

(3)-(5) * * * * *

16-21 * * * * *

Section 2

SCHEDULE 1

TIMES WHEN PROCEEDINGS ARE ACTIVE FOR PURPOSES OF SECTION 2

Preliminary

1. In this Schedule "criminal proceedings" means proceedings against a person in respect of an offence, not being appellate proceedings or proceedings commenced by motion for committal or attachment in England and Wales or Northern Ireland; and "appellate proceedings" means proceedings on appeal from or for the review of the decision of a court in any proceedings.

2. Criminal, appellate and other proceedings are active within the meaning of section 2 at the times respectively prescribed by the following paragraphs of this Schedule; and in relation to proceedings in which more than one of the steps described in any of those paragraphs is taken, the reference in that paragraph is a reference to the first of those steps.

Criminal proceedings

3. Subject to the following provisions of this Schedule, criminal proceedings are active from the relevant initial step specified in paragraph 4 until concluded as described in paragraph 5.

4. The initial steps of criminal proceedings are:—

(a) arrest without warrant;

(b) the issue, or in Scotland the grant, of a warrant for arrest;

(c) the issue of a summons to appear, or in Scotland the grant of a warrant to cite;

(d) the service of an indictment or other document specifying the charge;

(e) except in Scotland, oral charge.

5. Criminal proceedings are concluded—

(a) by acquittal or, as the case may be, by sentence;

(b) by any other verdict, finding, order or decision which puts an end to the proceedings;

(c) by discontinuance or by operation of law.

6. The reference in paragraph 5(a) to sentence includes any order or decision consequent on conviction or finding of guilt which disposes of the case, either absolutely or subject to future events, and a deferment of sentence under section 1 of the Power of Criminal Courts Act 1973, section 219 or 432 of the Criminal Procedure (Scotland) Act 1975 or Article 14 of the Treatment of Offenders (Northern Ireland) Order 1976.

7. Proceedings are discontinued within the meaning of paragraph 5(c)—

(a) in England and Wales or Northern Ireland, if the charge or summons is withdrawn or a *nolle prosequi* entered;

(b) in Scotland, if the proceedings are expressly abandoned by the prosecutor or are deserted *simpliciter*;

(c) in the case of proceedings in England and Wales or Northern Ireland commenced by arrest without warrant, if the person arrested is released, otherwise than on bail, without having been charged.

8.-10. * * * * *

11. Criminal proceedings against a person which become active on the issue or the grant of a warrant for his arrest cease to be active at the end of the period of twelve months beginning with the date of the warrant unless he has been arrested within that period, but become active again if he is subsequently arrested.

Other proceedings at first instance

12. Proceedings other than criminal proceedings and appellate proceedings are active from the time when arrangements for the hearing are made or, if no such arrangements are previously made, from the time the hearing begins, until the proceedings are disposed of or discontinued or withdrawn; and for the purposes of this paragraph any motion or application made in or for the purposes of any proceedings, and any pre-trial review in the county court, is to be treated as a distinct proceeding.

13. In England and Wales or Northern Ireland arrangements for the hearing of proceedings to which paragraph 12 applies are made within the meaning of that paragraph—

(a) in the case of proceedings in the High Court for which provision is made by rules of court for setting down for trial, when the case is set down;

(b) in the case of any proceedings, when a date for the trial or hearing is fixed.

14. In Scotland arrangements for the hearing of proceedings to which paragraph 12 applies are made within the meaning of that paragraph—

(a) in the case of an ordinary action in the Court of Session or in the sheriff court, when the record is closed;

(b) in the case of a motion or application, when it is enrolled or made;

(c) in any other case, when the date for a hearing is fixed or a hearing is allowed.

Appellate proceedings

15. Appellate proceedings are active from the time when they are commenced—

(a) by application for leave to appeal or apply for review, or by notice of such an application;

(b) by notice of appeal or of application for review;

(c) by other originating process,

until disposed of or abandoned, discontinued or withdrawn.

16. Where, in appellate proceedings relating to criminal proceedings, the court—

(a) remits the case to the court below; or

(b) orders a new trial or a *venire de novo*, or in Scotland grants authority to bring a new prosecution,

any further or new proceedings which result shall be treated as active from the conclusion of the appellate proceedings.

* * * * *

INDECENT DISPLAYS (CONTROL) ACT 1981
(1981, c. 42)

An Act to make fresh provision with respect to the public display of indecent matter; and for purposes connected therewith. [27 July 1981]

Territorial extent England and Wales, Scotland

1 Indecent displays

(1) If any indecent matter is publicly displayed the person making the display and any person causing or permitting the display to be made shall be guilty of an offence.

(2) Any matter which is displayed in or so as to be visible from any public place shall, for the purposes of this section, be deemed to be publicly displayed.

(3) In subsection (2) above, "public place", in relation to the display of any matter, means any place to which the public have or are permitted to have access (whether on payment or otherwise) while that matter is displayed except—

(a) a place to which the public are permitted to have access only on payment which is or includes payment for that display; or

(b) a shop or any part of a shop to which the public can only gain access by passing beyond an adequate warning notice;

but the exclusions contained in paragraphs (a) and (b) above shall only apply where persons under the age of 18 years are not permitted to enter while the display in question is continuing.

(4) Nothing in this section applies in relation to any matter—

(a) included in a television broadcast by the British Broadcasting Corporation or the Independent Broadcasting Authority or a programme [included in a cable programme service which is or does not require to be licensed]; or

(b) included in the display of an art gallery or museum and visible only from within the gallery or museum; or

(c) displayed by or with the authority of, and visible only from within a building occupied by, the Crown or any local authority; or

(d) included in a performance of a play (within the meaning of the Theatres Act 1968); or

[(e) included in a film exhibition as defined in the Cinemas Act 1985—

(i) given in a place which as regards that exhibition is required to be licensed under section 1 of the Act or by virtue only of section 5, 7 or 8 of that Act is not required to be so licensed; or

(ii) which is an exhibition to which section 6 of that Act applies given by an exempted organisation as defined by subsection (6) of that section.]

(5) In this section "matter" includes anything capable of being displayed, except that it does not include an actual human body or any part thereof; and in determining for the purpose of this section whether any displayed matter is indecent—

(a) there shall be disregarded any part of that matter which is not exposed to view; and

(b) account may be taken of the effect of juxtaposing one thing with another.

(6) A warning notice shall not be adequate for the purposes of this section unless it complies with the following requirements—

(a) The warning notice must contain the following words, and no others—

"WARNING

Persons passing beyond this notice will find material on display which they may consider indecent. No admittance to persons under 18 years of age."

(b) The word "WARNING" must appear as a heading.

(c) No pictures or other matter shall appear on the notice.

(d) The notice must be so situated that no one could reasonably gain access to the shop or part of the shop in question without being aware of the notice and it must be easily legible by any person gaining such access.

2 Power of arrest, seizure and entry

(1) . . .

(2) A constable may seize any article which he has reasonable grounds for believing to be or to contain indecent matter and to have been used in the commission of an offence under this Act.

(3) In England and Wales, a justice of the peace if satisfied on information on oath that there are reasonable grounds for suspecting that an offence under this Act has been or is being committed on any premises and, in Scotland, a sheriff or justice of the peace on being so satisfied on evidence on oath, may issue a warrant authorising any constable to enter the premises specified in the information or, as the case may be, evidence (if need be by force) . . . to seize any article which the constable has reaonable grounds for believing to be or to contain indecent matter and to have been used in the commission of an offence under this Act.

3 *****

4 Penalties

(1) In England and Wales, any person guilty of an offence under this Act shall be liable—

(a) on summary conviction, to a fine not exceeding the statutory maximum; or

(b) on conviction on indictment, to imprisonment for a term not exceeding two years or a fine or both.

(2) In Scotland, any person guilty of an offence under this Act shall be liable—

(a) on summary conviction—

(i) in the District Court, to a fine not exceeding [level 4 on the standard scale];

(ii) in the sheriff court, to a fine not exceeding the statutory maximum; or

(b) on conviction on indictment, to imprisonment for a term not exceeding two years or a fine or both.

(3) *****

SUPREME COURT ACT 1981
(1981, c. 54)

An Act to consolidate with amendments the Supreme Court of Judicature (Consolidation) Act 1925 and other enactments relating to the Supreme Court in England and Wales and the administration of justice therein; to repeal certain obsolete or unnecessary enactments so relating; to amend Part VIII of the Mental Health Act 1959, the Courts-Martial (Appeals) Act 1968, the Arbitration Act 1979 and the law relating to county courts; and for connected purposes

[28 July 1981]

Territorial extent England and Wales

PART I
CONSTITUTION OF SUPREME COURT

The Supreme Court

1 The Supreme Court

(1) The Supreme Court of England and Wales shall consist of the Court of Appeal, the High Court of Justice and the Crown Court, each having such jurisdiction as is conferred on it by or under this or any other Act.

(2) The Lord Chancellor shall be president of the Supreme Court.

2, 3 *****

The High Court

4 The High Court

(1) The High Court shall consist of—

(a) the Lord Chancellor;
(b) the Lord Chief Justice;
(c) the President of the Family Division;
(d) the Vice-Chancellor; and
(e) not more than eighty puisne judges of that court.

(2) The puisne judges of the High Court shall be styled "Justices of the High Court".

(3) All the judges of the High Court shall, except where this Act expressly provides otherwise, have in all respects equal power, authority and jurisdiction.

(4)-(6) * * * * *

5-9 * * * * *

10 Appointment of judges of Supreme Court

(1) Whenever the office of Lord Chief Justice, Master of the Rolls, President of the Family Division or Vice-Chancellor is vacant, Her Majesty may by letters patent appoint a qualified person to that office.

(2) Subject to the limits on numbers for the time being imposed by sections 2(1) and 4(1), Her Majesty may from time to time by letters patent appoint qualified persons as Lords Justices of Appeal or as puisne judges of the High Court.

(3) No person shall be qualified for appointment—

(a) as Lord Chief Justice, Master of the Rolls, President of the Family Division or Vice-Chancellor, unless he is qualified for appointment as a Lord Justice of Appeal or is a judge of the Court of Appeal;

(b) as a Lord Justice of Appeal, unless he is a barrister of at least fifteen years' standing or a judge of the High Court; or

(c) as a puisne judge of the High Court, unless he is a barrister of at least ten years' standing.

(4) Every person appointed to an office mentioned in subsection (1) or as a Lord Justice of Appeal or puisne judge of the High Court shall, as soon as may be after his acceptance of office, take the oath of allegiance and the judicial oath, as set out in the Promissory Oaths Act 1868, in the presence of the Lord Chancellor.

11 Tenure of office of judges of Supreme Court

(1) This section applies to the office of any judge of the Supreme Court except the Lord Chancellor.

(2) A person appointed to an office to which this section applies shall vacate it on the day on which he attains the age of seventy-five years unless by virtue of this section he has ceased to hold it before then.

(3) A person appointed to an office to which this section applies shall hold that office during good behaviour, subject to a power of removal by Her Majesty on an address presented to Her by both Houses of Parliament.

(4)-(6) * * * * *

(7) A person who holds an office to which this section applies may at any time resign it by giving the Lord Chancellor notice in writing to that effect.

(8) The Lord Chancellor, if satisfied by means of a medical certificate that a person holding an office to which this section applies—

(a) is disabled by permanent infirmity from the performance of the duties of his office; and

(b) is for the time being incapacitated from resigning his office,

may, subject to subsection (9), by instrument under his hand declare that person's office to have been vacated; and the instrument shall have the like effect for all purposes as if that person had on the date of the instrument resigned his office.

(9) A declaration under subsection (8) with respect to a person shall be of no effect unless it is made—

(a) in the case of any of the Lord Chief Justice, the Master of the Rolls, the President of the Family Division and the Vice-Chancellor, with the concurrence of two others of them;

(b) in the case of a Lord Justice of Appeal, with the concurrence of the Master of the Rolls;

(c) in the case of a puisne judge of any Division of the High Court, with the concurrence of the senior judge of that Division.

(10) *****

12 Salaries etc of judges of Supreme Court

(1) Subject to subsections (2) and (3), there shall be paid to judges of the Supreme Court, other than the Lord Chancellor, such salaries as may be determined by the Lord Chancellor with the concurrence of the Minister for the Civil Service.

(2) Until otherwise determined under this section, there shall be paid to the judges mentioned in subsection (1) the same salaries as at the commencement of this Act.

(3) Any salary payable under this section may be increased, but not reduced, by a determination or further determination under this section.

(4)-(7) *****

13-18 *****

PART II
JURISDICTION
THE HIGH COURT

General jurisdiction

19 General jurisdiction

(1) The High Court shall be a superior court of record.

(2) Subject to the provisions of this Act, there shall be exercisable by the High Court—

(a) all such jurisdiction (whether civil or criminal) as is conferred on it by this or any other Act; and

(b) all such other jurisdiction (whether civil or criminal) as was exercisable by it immediately before the commencment of this Act (including jurisdiction conferred on a judge of the High Court by any statutory provision).

(3), (4) *****

*****

Other particular fields of jurisdiction

29 Orders of mandamus, prohibition and certiorari

(1) The High Court shall have jurisdiction to make orders of mandamus, prohibition and certiorari in those classes of cases in which it had power to do so immediately before the commencement of this Act.

(2) Every such order shall be final, subject to any right of appeal therefrom.

(3) In relation to the jurisdiction of the Crown Court, other than its jurisdiction in matters relating to trial on indictment, the High Court shall have all such jurisdiction to make orders of mandamus, prohibition or certiorari as the High Court possesses in relation to the jurisdiction of an inferior court.

(4) The power of the High Court under any enactment to require justices of the peace or a judge or officer of a county court to do any act relating to the duties of their respective offices, or to require a magistrates' court to state a case for the opinion of the High Court, in any case where the High Court formerly had by virtue of any enactment jurisdiction to make a rule absolute, or an order, for any of those purposes, shall be exercisable by order of mandamus.

(5) In any enactment—

(a) references to a writ of mandamus, of prohibition or of certiorari shall be read as references to the corresponding order; and

(b) references to the issue or award of any such writ shall be read as references to the making of the corresponding order.

30 * * * * *

31 Application for judicial review

(1) An application to the High Court for one or more of the following forms of relief, namely—

(a) an order of mandamus, prohibition or certiorari;

(b) a declaration or injunction under subsection (2); or

(c) an injunction under section 30 restraining a person not entitled to do so from acting in an office to which that section applies,

shall be made in accordance with rules of court by a procedure to be known as an application for judicial review.

(2) A declaration may be made or an injunction granted under this subsection in any case where an application for judicial review, seeking that relief, has been made and the High Court considers that, having regard to—

(a) the nature of the matters in respect of which relief may be granted by orders of mandamus, prohibition or certiorari;

(b) the nature of the persons and bodies against whom relief may be granted by such orders; and

(c) all the circumstances of the case,

it would be just and convenient for the declaration to be made or for the injunction to be granted, as the case may be.

(3) No application for judicial review shall be made unless the leave of the High Court has been obtained in accordance with rules of court; and the court shall not grant leave to make such an application unless it considers that the applicant has a sufficient interest in the matter to which the application relates.

(4) On an application for judicial review the High Court may award damages to the applicant if—

(a) he has joined with his application a claim for damages arising from any matter to which the application relates; and

(b) the court is satisfied that, if the claim had been made in an action begun by the applicant at the time of making his application, he would have been awarded damages.

(5) If, on an application for judicial review seeking an order of certiorari, the High Court quashes the decision to which the application relates, the High Court may remit the matter to the court, tribunal or authority concerned, with a direction to reconsider it and reach a decision in accordance with the findings of the High Court.

(6) Where the High Court considers that there has been undue delay in making an application for judicial review, the court may refuse to grant—

(a) leave for the making of the application; or

(b) any relief sought on the application,

if it considers that the granting of the relief sought would be likely to cause substantial hardship to, or substantially prejudice the rights of, any person or would be detrimental to good administration.

(7) Subsection (6) is without prejudice to any enactment or rule of court which has the effect of limiting the time within which an application for judicial review may be made.

Note The provisions of s. 31 are implemented by Order 53 of the Rules of the Supreme Court, q.v.

* * * * *

CANADA ACT 1982
(1982, c. 11)

An Act to give effect to a request by the Senate and House of Commons of Canada.

[29 March 1982]

Territorial extent Canada

Whereas Canada has requested and consented to the enactment of an Act of the Parliament of the United Kingdom to give effect to the provisions hereinafter set forth and the Senate and the House of Commons of Canada in Parliament assembled have submitted an address to Her Majesty requesting that Her Majesty may graciously be pleased to cause a Bill to be laid before the Parliament of the United Kingdom for that purpose:

Be it therefore enacted by the Queen's Most Excellent Majesty, by and with the advice and consent of the Lords Spiritual and Temporal, and Commons, in this present Parliament assembled, and by the authority of the same, as follows:

1 Constitution Act, 1982 enacted
The Constitution Act, 1982 set out in Schedule B to this Act is hereby enacted for and shall have the force of law in Canada and shall come into force as provided in that Act.

2 Termination of power to legislate for Canada
No Act of the Parliament of the United Kingdom passed after the Constitution Act, 1982 comes into force shall extend to Canada as part of its law.

3 French version
So far as it is not contained in Schedule B, the French version of this Act is set out in Schedule A to this Act and has the same authority in Canada as the English version thereof.

4 Short title
This Act may be cited as the Canada Act 1982.

* * * * *

SCHEDULE B
CONSTITUTION ACT, 1982
PART I
CANADIAN CHARTER OF RIGHTS AND FREEDOMS

Whereas Canada is founded upon principles that recognize the supremacy of God and the rule of law:

Guarantee of Rights and Freedoms

1 Rights and freedoms in Canada
The *Canadian Charter of Rights and Freedoms* guarantees the rights and freedoms set out in it subject only to such reasonable limits prescribed by law as can be demonstrably justified in a free and democratic society.

Fundamental Freedoms

2 Fundamental freedoms
Everyone has the following fundamental freedoms:

(a) freedom of conscience and religion;

(b) freedom of thought, belief, opinion and expression, including freedom of the press and other media of communication;

(c) freedom of peaceful assembly; and

(d) freedom of association.

Democratic Rights

3 Democratic rights of citizens
Every citizen of Canada has the right to vote in an election of members of the House of Commons or of a legislative assembly and to be qualified for membership therein.

4 Maximum duration of legislative bodies
(1) No House of Commons and no legislative assembly shall continue for longer than five years from the date fixed for the return of the writs at a general election of its members.

Continuation in special circumstances
(2) In time of real or apprehended war, invasion or insurrection, a House of Commons may be continued by Parliament and a legislative assembly may be continued by the legislature beyond five years if such continuation is not opposed by the votes of more than one-third of the members of the House of Commons or the legislative assembly, as the case may be.

5 Annual sitting of legislative bodies
There shall be a sitting of Parliament and of each legislature at least once every twelve months.

Mobility Rights

6 Mobility of citizens
(1) Every citizen of Canada has the right to enter, remain in and leave Canada.

Rights to move and gain livelihood
(2) Every citizen of Canada and every person who has the status of a permanent resident of Canada has the right
(a) to move to and take up residence in any province; and
(b) to pursue the gaining of a livelihood in any province.

Limitation
(3) The rights specified in subsection (2) are subject to
(a) any laws or practices of general application in force in a province other than those that discriminate among persons primarily on the basis of province of present or previous residence; and
(b) any laws providing for reasonable residency requirements as a qualification for the receipt of publicly provided social services.

Affirmative action programs
(4) Subsections (2) and (3) do not preclude any law, program or activity that has as its object the amelioration in a province of conditions of individuals in that province who are socially or economically disadvantaged if the rate of employment in that province is below the rate of employment in Canada.

Legal Rights

7 Life, liberty and security of person
Everyone has the right to life, liberty and security of the person and the right not to be deprived thereof except in accordance with the principles of fundamental justice.

8 Search or seizure
Everyone has the right to be secure against unreasonable search or seizure.

9 Detention or imprisonment
Everyone has the right not to be arbitrarily detained or imprisoned.

10 Arrest or detention
Everyone has the right on arrest or detention

(a) to be informed promptly of the reasons therefor;
(b) to retain and instruct counsel without delay and to be informed of that right; and
(c) to have the validity of the detention determined by way of *habeas corpus* and to be released if the detention is not lawful.

11 Proceedings in criminal and penal matters
Any person charged with an offence has the right
(a) to be informed without unreasonable delay of the specific offence;
(b) to be tried within a reasonable time;
(c) not to be compelled to be a witness in proceedings against that person in respect of the offence;
(d) to be presumed innocent until proven guilty according to law in a fair and public hearing by an independent and impartial tribunal;
(e) not to be denied reasonable bail without just cause;
(f) except in the case of an offence under military law tried before a military tribunal, to the benefit of trial by jury where the maximum punishment for the offence is imprisonment for five years or a more severe punishment;
(g) not to be found guilty on account of any act or omission unless, at the time of the act or omission, it constituted an offence under Canadian or international law or was criminal according to the general principles of law recognized by the community of nations;
(h) if finally acquitted of the offence, not to be tried for it again and, if finally found guilty and punished for the offence, not to be tried or punished for it again; and
(i) if found guilty of the offence and if the punishment for the offence has been varied between the time of commission and the time of sentencing, to the benefit of the lesser punishment.

12 Treatment or punishment
Everyone has the right not to be subjected to any cruel and unusual treatment or punishment.

13 Self-crimination
A witness who testifies in any proceedings has the right not to have any incriminating evidence so given used to incriminate that witness in any other proceedings, except in a prosecution for perjury or for the giving of contradictory evidence.

14 Interpreter
A party or witness in any proceedings who does not understand or speak the language in which the proceedings are conducted or who is deaf has the right to the assistance of an interpreter.

Equality Rights

15 Equality before and under law and equal protection and benefit of law
(1) Every individual is equal before and under the law and has the right to the equal protection and equal benefit of the law without discrimination and, in particular, without discrimination based on race, national or ethnic origin, colour, religion, sex, age or mental or physical disability.

Affirmative action programs
(2) Subsection (1) does not preclude any law, program or activity that has as its object the amelioration of conditions of disadvantaged individuals or groups including those that are disadvantaged because of race, national or ethnic origin, colour, religion, sex, age or mental or physical disability.

Official Languages of Canada

16 Official languages of Canada

(1) English and French are the official languages of Canada and have equality of status and equal rights and privileges as to their use in all institutions of the Parliament and government of Canada.

(2), (3) *****

17-23 *****

Enforcement

24 Enforcement of guaranteed rights and freedoms

(1) Anyone whose rights or freedoms, as guaranteed by this Charter, have been infringed or denied may apply to a court of competent jurisdiction to obtain such remedy as the court considers appropriate and just in the circumstances.

Exclusion of evidence bringing administration of justice into disrepute

(2) Where, in proceedings under subsection (1), a court concludes that evidence was obtained in a manner that infringed or denied any rights or freedoms guaranteed by this Charter, the evidence shall be excluded if it is established that, having regard to all the circumstances, the admission of it in the proceedings would bring the administration of justice into disrepute.

General

25 Aboriginal rights and freedoms not affected by Charter

The guarantee in this Charter of certain rights and freedoms shall not be construed so as to abrogate or derogate from any aboriginal, treaty or other rights or freedoms that pertain to the aboriginal peoples of Canada including

(a) any rights or freedoms that have been recognised by the Royal Proclamation of October 7, 1763; and

(b) any rights or freedoms that may be acquired by the aboriginal peoples of Canada by way of land claims settlement.

26 Other rights and freedoms not affected by Charter

The guarantee in this Charter of certain rights and freedoms shall not be construed as denying the existence of any other rights or freedoms that exist in Canada.

27 Multicultural heritage

This Charter shall be interpreted in a manner consistent with the preservation and enhancement of the multicultural heritage of Canadians.

28 Rights guaranteed equally to both sexes

Notwithstanding anything in this Charter, the rights and freedoms referred to in it are guaranteed equally to male and female persons.

29 Rights respecting certain schools preserved

Nothing in this Charter abrogates or derogates from any rights or privileges guaranteed by or under the Constitution of Canada in respect of denominational, separate or dissentient schools.

30 *****

31 Legislative powers not extended

Nothing in this Charter extends the legislative powers of any body or authority.

Application of Charter

32 Application of Charter

(1) This Charter applies

(a) to the Parliament and government of Canada in respect of all matters within the authority of Parliament including all matters relating to the Yukon Territory and Northwest Territories; and

(b) to the legislature and government of each province in respect of all matters within the authority of the legislature of each province.

Exception

(2) Notwithstanding subsection (1), section 15 shall not have effect until three years after this section comes into force.

33 Exceptions where express declaration

(1) Parliament or the legislature of a province may expressly declare in an Act of Parliament or of the legislature, as the case may be, that the Act or a provision thereof shall operate notwithstanding a provision included in section 2 or sections 7 to 15 of this Charter.

Operation of exception

(2) An Act or a provision of an Act in respect of which a declaration made under this section is in effect shall have such operation as it would have but for the provision of this Charter referred to in the declaration.

Five year limitation

(3) A declaration made under subsection (1) shall cease to have effect five years after it comes into force or on such earlier date as may be specified in the declaration.

Re-enactment

(4) Parliament or the legislature of a province may re-enact a declaration made under subsection (1).

Five year limitation

(5) Subsection (3) applies in respect of a re-enactment made under subsection (4).

Citation

34 Citation

This Part may be cited as the *Canadian Charter of Rights and Freedoms*.

* * * * *

Note Schedule A to this Act is a French language version of the Act, and Schedule B is also printed in English and French. Both texts have equal status.

CIVIC GOVERNMENT (SCOTLAND) ACT 1982
(1982, c. 45)

An Act to make provision as regards Scotland for the licensing and regulation of certain activities; for the preservation of public order and safety and the prevention of crime; for prohibiting the taking of and dealing with indecent photographs of children; as to certain powers of constables and others; * * * * * [28 October 1982]

Territorial extent Scotland

51 Obscene material

(1) Subject to subsection (4) below, any person who displays any obscene material in any public place or in any other place where it can be seen by the public shall be guilty of an offence under this section.

(2) Subject to subsection (4) below, any person who publishes, sells or distributes or, with a view to its eventual sale or distribution, makes, prints, has or keeps any obscene material shall be guilty of an offence under this section.

(3) A person guilty of an offence under this section shall be liable, on summary conviction, to a fine not exceeding the prescribed sum or to imprisonment for a period not exceeding two years or to both.

(4) A person shall not be convicted of an offence under this section if he proves that he had used all due diligence to avoid committing the offence.

(5) Under an indictment for or on a complaint of a breach of subsection (1) above, the court may, if satisfied that the person accused is guilty of an offence under section 1(1) of the Indecent Displays (Control) Act 1981 (offence of public display of indecent matter), convict him of a breach of the said section 1(1).

(6) Nothing in this section applies in relation to any matter—

(a) included in a television or sound broadcast by the British Broadcasting Corporation or the Independent Broadcasting Authority [or any such broadcast which is received and immediately re-transmitted by a cable programme service]; or

(b) included in a performance of a play (within the meaning of the Theatres Act 1968).

(7) For section 5(4)(b) of the Indecent Displays (Control) Act 1981 (saving) there shall be substituted the following—

"(b) section 51 of the Civic Government (Scotland) Act 1982".

(8) In this section—

"material" includes any book, magazine, bill, paper, print, film, tape, disk or other kind of recording (whether of sound or visual images or both), photograph, drawing, painting, representation, model or figure [and any matter included in a programme transmitted as part of a cable programme service];

"photograph" includes the negative as well as the positive version;

"public place" has the same meaning as in section 133 of this Act except that it includes any place to which at the material time the public are permitted to have access, whether on payment or otherwise;

"prescribed sum" has the same meaning as in section 289B of the Criminal Procedure (Scotland) Act 1975;

and the reference to publishing includes a reference to [showing] playing, projecting or otherwise reproducing.

52-59 * * * * *

Powers of constables, etc.

60 Powers of search and seizure

Subject to subsections (2) and (3) below, if a constable has reasonable grounds to suspect that a person is in possession of any stolen property, the constable may without warrant—

(a) search that person or anything in his possession, and detain him for as long as is necessary for the purpose of that search;

(b) enter and search any vehicle or vessel in which the constable suspects that that thing may be found, and for that purpose require the person in control of the vehicle or vessel to stop it and keep it stopped;

(c) enter and search any premises occupied by a second-hand dealer or a metal dealer for the purposes of his business;

(d) seize and detain anything found in the course of any such search which appears to the constable to have been stolen or to be evidence of the commission of the crime of theft,

and may, in doing so, use reasonable force.

In this subsection "second-hand dealer" and "metal dealer" have the meanings respectively assigned to them by sections 24(2) and 37(1) of this Act.

(2) The power under subsection (1)(b) above to require the person in charge of a vehicle or vessel to stop it shall be exercisable only by a constable in uniform.

(3) A constable who is not in uniform shall not be entitled to exercise the powers which he may exercise under subsections (1)(a) to (c) above until he has produced his identification—

(a) in relation to the exercise of powers under subsection (1)(a) above, to the person in respect of whom the powers are exercised;

(b) in relation to the exercise of powers under subsections (1)(b) or (c) above, to the person for the time being in charge of the vehicle, vessel or premises and to any other person in or on the vehicle, vessel or premises who, having reasonable cause to do so, requests to see it.

(4) In subsection (1) above "theft" includes any aggravation of theft including robbery.

(5) Nothing in this section prejudices any power of entry or search or any power to seize or detain property or any power to require any vehicle or vessel to be stopped which is exercisable by a constable apart from this section.

(6) Any person who, without reasonable excuse—

(a) fails to allow a constable in pursuance of subsection (1) above to enter and search any premises, vehicle or vessel, or seize and detain anything found in the course of such search;

(b) when required by a constable in pursuance of subsection (1) above to stop a vehicle or vessel and keep it stopped, fails to do so; or

(c) obstructs a constable in the exercise of his powers under subsection (1) above, shall be guilty of an offence and liable, on summary conviction, to a fine not exceeding £200.

61 * * * * *

PART V
PUBLIC PROCESSIONS

62 Notification of processions

(1) A person proposing to hold a procession in public shall give written notice of that proposal in accordance with subsections (2) and (3) below

(a) to the regional or islands council in whose area the procession is to be held, or if it is to be held in the areas of more than one such council, to each such council [and

(b) to the chief constable].

(2) Notice shall be given for the purposes of subsection (1) above by—

(a) its being posted to the main office of the regional or islands council [and to the chief constable] so that in the normal course of post it might be expected to arrive not later than 7 days before the date when the procession is to be held; or

(b) its being delivered by hand to [those offices] not later than 7 days before that date.

(3) The notice to be given under subsection (1) above shall specify—

(a) the date and time when the procession is to be held;

(b) its route;

(c) the number of persons likely to take part in it;

(d) the arrangements for its control being made by the person proposing to hold it; and

(e) the name and address of that person.

(4) A regional or islands council may, on application in accordance with subsection (5) below by a person proposing to hold a procession in public in their area

(a) made to them [and

(b) intimated to the chief constable,]

within the period of 7 days before the date when the procession is to be held, make an order dispensing with the requirements of subsection (2) above in relation to the time limits for the giving of notice of that proposal.

(5) An application under subsection (4) above shall specify the matters mentioned in subsection (3) above and, where an order has been made under the said subsection (4), the application for it shall be treated as notice duly given for the purposes of subsection (1) above.

(6)-(11) * * * * *

(12) In this section and in sections 63 to 65 of this Act—

"procession in public" means a procession in a public place;

"chief constable" means, in relation to a regional or islands council, the chief constable of the police force for the area which comprises or includes the area of the council; and

"public place" has the same meaning as in [Part II of the Public Order Act 1986].

63 Functions of regional and islands councils in relation to processions

(1) The regional or islands council may, after consulting the chief constable in respect of a procession notice of which has been given or falls to be treated as having been given in accordance with section 62(1) of this Act, make an order—

(i) prohibiting the holding of the procession; or

(ii) imposing conditions on the holding of it.

(1A) * * * * *

(2) The conditions which may be imposed under subsection (1) [or (1A)] above on the holding of a procession may include conditions—

(a) as to the date, time and duration of the procession;

(b) as to the route to be taken by it;

(c) prohibiting its entry into any public place specified in the order.

(3) A regional or islands council shall—

(a) where notice of a proposal to hold a procession has been given or falls to be treated as having been given in accordance with section 62(1) of this Act, deliver at least 2 days before the date when, in terms of the notice, the procession is to be held, to the person who gave the notice—

(i) where they have made an order under subsection (1) [or (1A)] above, a copy of it and a written statement of the reasons for it; . . .

(ii) where they decide not to make [an order under subsection (1) above or to revoke an order already made under subsection (1) or (1A) above], notification of that fact;

[(iii) where they have under subsection (1A) above varied such an order, a copy of the order as varied and a written statement of the reasons for the variation; and]

(b) where they have made an order under subsection (1) [or (1A)] above in relation to a proposal to hold a procession, make such arrangements as will ensure that persons who might take or are taking part in that procession are made aware of the fact that the order has been made [and, if the order has been varied under subsection (1A) above, that it has been so varied] and of its effect; [and

(c) where they have revoked an order made under subsection (1) or (1A) above in relation to a proposal to hold a procession, make such arrangements as will ensure that persons who might take or are taking part in that procession are made aware of the fact that the order has been revoked.]

(4) The regional or islands council shall comply with subsection (3) above—

(a) as early as possible;

(b) only in so far as it is reasonably practicable for them to do so.

64 Appeals against orders under section 63

(1) An appeal to the sheriff shall lie at the instance of a person who, in accordance with section 62 of this Act, has or falls to be treated as having given notice of a proposal to hold a procession in public [against—

(a) an order made under section 63(1) or (1A) of this Act; or

(b) a variation under section 63(1A) of this Act of an order made under section 63(1) or (1A), in relation to the procession.

(2) An appeal under this section shall be made by way of summary application and shall be lodged with the sheriff clerk within 14 days from the date on which the copy of the order and statement of reasons were received by the appellant.

(3) On good cause being shown, the sheriff may hear an appeal under this section notwithstanding that it was not lodged within the time mentioned in subsection (2) above.

(4) The sheriff may uphold an appeal under this section only if he considers that the regional or islands council in arriving at their decision to make [or, as the case may be, to vary] the order—

(a) erred in law;

(b) based their decision on any incorrect material fact;

(c) exercised their discretion in an unreasonable manner; or

(d) otherwise acted beyond their powers.

(5)-(9) * * * * *

65 Offences and enforcement

(1) Subject to subsection (3) below, a person who holds a procession in public—

(a) without—

(i) having given or being a person who is treated as having given notice in accordance with section 62 of this Act of his proposal to do so; and

(ii) there being in force in relation to the procession an exempting order under section 62(6) of this Act;

(b) in contravention of an order under section 63(1) [or (1A)] or 64(6)(a)(ii) of this Act prohibiting the holding of it;

(c) otherwise than in accordance with a condition imposed by an order under section 63(1) [or (1A)] or 64(6)(a)(ii) of this Act in relation to the procession; or

(d) otherwise than in accordance with the particulars of its date, time and route specified—

(i) in the notice given under section 62(1) to (3) of this Act; or

(ii) where an order has been made under subsection (4) of that section, in the application for the order,

except to the extent that a condition referred to in paragraph (c) above relates to its date, time or route, shall be guilty of an offence and liable, on summary conviction, to a fine not exceeding £500 or to imprisonment for a period not exceeding 3 months or to both.

(2) Subject to subsection (3) below, a person who takes part in a procession in public—

(a) in respect of which—

(i) notice has not been or is not treated as having been given in accordance with section 62 of this Act; and

(ii) there is not in force an exempting order under section 62(6) of this Act in relation to the procession;

(b) in relation to which an order has been made under section 63(1) [or (1A)] or 64(6)(a)(ii) of this Act prohibiting the holding of it;

(c) which is held otherwise than in accordance with a condition imposed by an order under section 63(1) [or (1A)] or 64(6)(a)(ii) of this Act in relation to the procession; or

(d) which is held otherwise than in accordance with the particulars of its date, time and route specified—

(i) in the notice given under section 62(1) to (3) of this Act; or

(ii) where an order has been made under subsection (4) of that section, in the application for the order

except to the extent that a condition referred to in paragraph (c) above relates to its date, time or route, and refuses to desist when required to do so by a constable in uniform shall be guilty of an offence and liable, on summary conviction, to a fine not exceeding £200.

* * * * *

(4) Subject to subsection (5) below, a constable may arrest without warrant a person whom he reasonably suspects of committing or having committed an offence under this section.

(5) A constable who is not in uniform shall produce his identification if required to do so by any person whom he is arresting under subsection (4) above.

66 Relationship of sections 62 to 65 with Public Order Act 1936

Sections 62 to 65 of this Act are subject to [Part II of the Public Order Act 1986]; and, without prejudice to that generality—

(a) an order under those sections, so far as relating to the same matters as those to which any directions given under section 12 of that Act relate, shall be subject to those directions . . .; and

(b) anything done in conformity with any such directions . . . or omitted, in conformity therewith, to be done shall not be an offence under section 65 of this Act.

* * * * *

LOCAL GOVERNMENT (MISCELLANEOUS PROVISIONS) ACT 1982
(1982, c. 30)

An Act to make amendments for England and Wales of provisions of that part of the law relating to local authorities or highways which is commonly amended by local Acts; to make provision for the control of sex establishments * * * * * [13 July 1982]

Territorial extent England and Wales

1 * * * * *

PART II
CONTROL OF SEX ESTABLISHMENTS

2 Control of sex establishments

(1) A local authority may resolve that Schedule 3 to this Act is to apply to their area; and if a local authority do so resolve, that Schedule shall come into force in their area on the day specified in that behalf in the resolution (which must not be before the expiration of the period of one month beginning with the day on which the resolution is passed).

(2) A local authority shall publish notice that they have passed a resolution under this section in two consecutive weeks in a local newspaper circulating in their area.

(3) The first publication shall not be later than 28 days before the day specified in the resolution for the coming into force of Schedule 3 to this Act in the local authority's area.

(4) The notice shall state the general effect of that Schedule.

(5) In this Part of this Act "local authority" means—

(a) the council of a district;

(b) the council of a London borough; and

(c) the Common Council of the City of London.

* * * * *

Section 2

SCHEDULE 3
CONTROL OF SEX ESTABLISHMENTS

Saving for existing law

1. Nothing in this Schedule—

(a) shall afford a defence to a charge in respect of any offence at common law or under an enactment other than this Schedule; or

(b) shall be taken into account in any way—

(i) at a trial for such an offence; or

(ii) in proceedings for forfeiture under section 3 of the Obscene Publications Act 1959 or section 5 of the Protection of Children Act 1978; or

(iii) in proceedings for condemnation under Schedule 3 to the Customs and Excise Management Act 1979 of goods which section 42 of the Customs Consolidation Act 1876 prohibits to be imported or brought into the United Kingdom as being indecent or obscene; or

(c) shall in any way limit the other powers exercisable under any of those Acts.

Meaning of "sex establishment"

2. In this Schedule "sex establishment" means a sex cinema or a sex shop.

Meaning of "sex cinema"

3.—(1) In this Schedule "sex cinema" means any premises, vehicle, vessel or stall used to a significant degree for the exhibition of moving pictures, by whatever means produced, which—

(a) are concerned primarily with the portrayal of, or primarily deal with or relate to, or are intended to stimulate or encourage—

(i) sexual activity; or

(ii) acts of force or restraint which are associated with sexual activity; or

(b) are concerned primarily with the portrayal of, or primarily deal with or relate to, genital organs or urinary or excretory functions.

but does not include a dwelling-house to which the public is not admitted.

(2) No premises shall be treated as a sex cinema by reason only—

(a) if they are licensed under [section 1 of the Cinemas Act 1985], of their use for a purpose for which a licence under that section is required; or

(b) of their use for an exhibition to which section 6 of that Act (certain non-commercial exhibitions) applies given by an exempted organisation within the meaning of section 6(6) of that Act.]

Meaning of "sex shop" and "sex article"

4.—(1) In this Schedule "sex shop" means any premises, vehicle, vessel or stall used for a business which consists to a significant degree of selling, hiring, exhanging, lending, displaying or demonstrating—

(a) sex articles; or

(b) other things intended for use in connection with, or for the purpose of stimulating or encouraging—

(i) sexual activity; or

(ii) acts of force or restraint which are associated with sexual activity.

(2) No premises shall be treated as a sex shop by reason only of their use for the exhibition of moving pictures by whatever means produced.

(3) In this Schedule "sex article" means—

(a) anything made for use in connection with, or for the purpose of stimulating or encouraging—

(i) sexual activity; or

(ii) acts or force or restraint which are associated with sexual activity; and

(b) anything to which sub-paragraph (4) below applies.

(4) This sub-paragraph applies—

(a) to any article containing or embodying matter to be read or looked at or anything intended to be used, either alone or as one of a set, for the reproduction or manufacture of any such article; and

(b) to any recording of vision or sound,

which—

(i) is concerned primarily with the portrayal of, or primarily deals with or relates to, or is intended to stimulate or encourage, sexual activity or acts of force or restraint which are associated with sexual activity; or

(ii) is concerned primarily with the portrayal of, or primarily deals with or relates to, genital organs, or urinary or excretory functions.

5. * * * * *

Requirement for licences for sex establishments

6.—(1) Subject to the provisions of this Schedule, no person shall in any area in which this Schedule is in force use any premises, vehicle, vessel or stall as a sex establishment except under and in accordance with the terms of a licence granted under this Schedule by the appropriate authority.

(2) Sub-paragraph (1) above does not apply to the sale, supply or demonstration of articles which—

(a) are manufactured for use primarily for the purposes of birth control; or

(b) primarily relate to birth control.

7.—(1) Any person who—

(a) uses any premises, vehicle, vessel or stall as a sex establishment; or

(b) proposes to do so,

may apply to the appropriate authority for them to waive the requirement of a licence.

(3)-(7) * * * * *

Grant, renewal and transfer of licences for sex establishments

8. Subject to paragraph 12(1) below, the appropriate authority may grant to any applicant, and from time to time renew, a licence under this Schedule for the use of any premises, vehicle, vessel or stall specified in it for a sex establishment on such terms and conditions and subject to such restrictions as may be so specified.

9.—(1) Subject to paragraphs 11 and 27 below, any licence under this Schedule shall, unless previously cancelled under paragraph 16 or revoked under paragraph 17(1) below, remain in force for one year or for such shorter period specified in the licence as the appropriate authority may think fit.

(2) Where a licence under this Schedule has been granted to any person, the appropriate authority may, if they think fit, transfer that licence to any other person on the application of that other person.

10., 11. * * * * *

Refusal of licences

12.—(1) A licence under this Schedule shall not be granted—

(a) to a person under the age of 18; or

(b) to a person who is for the time being disqualified under paragraph 17(3) below; or

(c) to a person, other than a body corporate, who is not resident in the United Kingdom or was not so resident throughout the period of six months immediately preceding the date when the application was made; or

(d) to a body corporate which is not incorporated in the United Kingdom; or

(e) to a person who has, within a period of 12 months imediately preceding the date when the application was made, been refused the grant or renewal of a licence for the premises, vehicle, vessel or stall in respect of which the application is made, unless the refusal has been reversed on appeal.

(2) Subject to paragraph 27 below, the appropriate authority may refuse—

(a) an application for the grant or renewal of a licence on one or more of the grounds specified in sub-paragraph (3) below;

(b) an application for the transfer of a licence on either or both of the grounds specified in paragraphs (a) and (b) of that sub-paragraph.

(3) The grounds mentioned in sub-paragraph (2) above are—

(a) that the applicant is unsuitable to hold the licence by reason of having been convicted of an offence or for any other reason;

(b) that if the licence were to be granted, renewed or transferred the business to which it relates would be managed by or carried on for the benefit of a person, other than the applicant, who would be refused the grant, renewal or transfer of such a licence if he made the application himself;

(c) that the number of sex establishments in the relevant locality at the time the application is made is equal to or exceeds the number which the authority consider is appropriate for that locality;

(d) that the grant or renewal of the licence would be inappropriate, having regard—

(i) to the character of the relevant locality; or

(ii) to the use to which any premises in the vicinity are put; or

(iii) to the layout, character or condition of the premises, vehicle, vessel or stall in respect of which the application is made.

(4) Nil may be an appropriate number of the purposes of sub-paragraph (3)(c) above.

(5) In this paragraph "the relevant locality" means—

(a) in relation to premises, the locality where they are situated; and

(b) in relation to a vehicle, vessel or stall, any locality where it is desired to use it as a sex establishment.

13.-16. * * * * *

Revocation of licences

17.—(1) The appropriate authority may, after giving the holder of a licence under this Schedule an opportunity of appearing before and being heard by them, at any time revoke the licence—

(a) on any ground specified in sub-paragraph (1) of paragraph 12 above; or

(b) on either of the grounds specified in sub-paragraph (3)(a) and (b) of that paragraph.

(2) Where a licence is revoked, the appropriate authority shall, if required to do so by the person who held it, give him a statement in writing of the reasons for their decision within 7 days of his requiring them to do so.

(3) Where a licence is revoked, its holder shall be disqualified from holding or obtaining a licence in the area of the appropriate authority for a period of 12 months beginning with the date of revocation.

18. * * * * *

Fees

19. An applicant for the grant, renewal or transfer of a licence under this Schedule shall pay a reasonable fee determined by the appropriate authority.

Enforcement

20.—(1) A person who—

(a) knowingly uses, or knowingly causes or permits the use of, any premises, vehicle, vessel or stall contrary to paragraph 6 above; or

(b) being the holder of a licence for a sex establishment, employs in the business of the establishment any person known to him to be disqualified from holding such a licence; or

(c) being the holder of a licence under this Schedule, without reasonable excuse knowingly contravenes, or without reasonable excuse knowingly permits the contravention of, a term, condition or restriction specified in the licence; or

(d) being the servant or agent of the holder of a licence under this Schedule, without reasonable excuse knowingly contravenes, or without reasonable excuse knowingly permits the contravention of, a term, condition or restriction specified in the licence,

shall be guilty of an offence.

21. Any person who, in connection with an application for the grant, renewal or transfer of a licence under this Schedule, makes a false statement which he knows to be false in any material respect or which he does not believe to be true, shall be guilty of an offence.

22.—(1) A person guilty of an offence under paragraph 20 or 21 above shall be liable on summary conviction to a fine not exceeding £10,000.

(2) A person who, being the holder of a licence under this Schedule, fails without reasonable excuse to comply with paragraph 14(1) above shall be guilty of an offence and liable on summary conviction to a fine not exceeding £200.

Offences relating to persons under 18

23.—(1) A person who, being the holder of a licence for a sex establishment—

(a) without reasonable excuse knowingly permits a person under 18 years of age to enter the establishment; or

(b) employs a person known to him to be under 18 years of age in the business of the establishment,

shall be guilty of an offence.

(2) A person guilty of an offence under this paragraph shall be liable on summary conviction to a fine not exceeding £10,000.

Powers of constables and local authority officers

24. If a constable has reasonable cause to suspect that a person has committed an offence under paragraph 20 or 23 above, he may require him to give his name and address, and if that person refuses or fails to do so, or gives a name or address which the constable reasonably suspects to be false, the constable may arrest him without warrant.

25., 26. * * * * *

Appeals

27.—(1) Subject to sub-paragraphs (2) and (3) below, any of the following persons, that is to say—

(a) an applicant for the grant, renewal or transfer of a licence under this Schedule whose application is refused;

(b) an applicant for the variation of the terms, conditions or restrictions on or subject to which any such licence is held whose application is refused;

(c) a holder of any such licence who is aggrieved by any term, condition or restrictions on or subject to which the licence is held; or

(d) a holder of any such licence whose licence is revoked,

may at any time before the expiration of the period of 21 days beginning with the relevant date appeal to the magistrates' court acting for the relevant area.

(2) An applicant whose application for the grant or renewal of a licence is refused, or whose licence is revoked, on any ground specified in paragraph 12(1) above shall not have a right to appeal under this paragraph unless the applicant seeks to show that the ground did not apply to him.

(3) An applicant whose application for the grant or renewal of a licence is refused on either ground specified in paragraph 12(3)(c) or (d) above shall not have the right to appeal under this paragraph.

(4)-(12) * * * * *

28.-30. * * * * *

BRITISH NATIONALITY (FALKLAND ISLANDS) ACT 1983
(1983, c. 6)

An Act to provide for the acquisition of British citizenship by persons having connections with the Falkland Islands [28 March 1983]

Territorial extent United Kingdom

1 Acquisition of British citizenship at commencement of 1981 Act or by birth or adoption

(1) A person shall at commencement become a British citizen if—

(a) that person becomes a British Dependent Territories citizen at commencement under section 23 of the 1981 Act (persons becoming British Dependent Territories citizens at commencement); and

(b) immediately before commencement either—

(i) that person was a citizen of the United Kingdom and Colonies who had that citizenship by his birth, naturalisation or registration in the Falkland Islands; or

(ii) one of that person's parents, or a parent of one of that person's parents, was, or but for his death would have been, a citizen of the United Kingdom and Colonies who so had that citizenship; or

(iii) that person, being a woman, was, or had at any time been, the wife of a man who by virtue of sub-paragraph (i) or (ii) becomes a British citizen at commencement or would have done so but for his death.

(2) A person born in the Falkland Islands after commencement shall be a British citizen if at the time of the birth his father or mother is—

(a) a British citizen; or

(b) settled in the Falkland Islands.

(3)-(5) * * * * *

2, 3 * * * * *

4 Supplementary provisions

(1) In this Act—

"the 1981 Act" means the British Nationality Act 1981;

"commencement" has the same meaning as in the 1981 Act, that is to say the beginning of 1st January 1983 (that being the day appointed under section 53(2) of that Act for the commencment of all except sections 49 and 53 of that Act);

"the Falkland Islands" means the Colony of the Falkland Islands.

(2), (3) * * * * *

5 Citation, provision for retrospective effect, and extent

(1) This Act may be cited as the British Nationality (Falkland Islands) Act 1983; and this Act and the British Nationality Act 1981 may be cited together as the British Nationality Acts 1981 and 1983.

(2) This Act shall be deemed to have come into force on 1st January 1983 (that is to say at commencement as defined in section 4(1)); and accordingly, subject to subsection (3), where the requirements of any provision of section 1 for the acquisition of British citizenship were satisfied in relation to any person at commencement or at any time between commencement and the passing of this Act, that person shall be treated as having acquired that citizenship at that time.

(3)-(5) * * * * *

NATIONAL AUDIT ACT 1983
(1983, c. 44)

An Act to strengthen Parliamentary control and supervision of expenditure of public money by making new provision for the appointment and status of the Comptroller and Auditor General, establishing a Public Accounts Commission and a National Audit Office and making new provision for promoting economy, efficiency and effectiveness in the use of such money by government departments and other authorities and bodies; to amend or repeal certain provisions of the Exchequer and Audit Departments Acts 1866 and 1921; and for connected purposes.

[13 May 1983]

Territorial extent United Kingdom

* * * * *

PART II
ECONOMY, EFFICIENCY AND EFFECTIVENESS EXAMINATIONS

6 Public departments etc.

(1) The Comptroller and Auditor General may carry out examinations into the economy, efficiency and effectiveness with which any department, authority or other body to which this section applies has used its resources in discharging its functions.

(2) Subsection (1) above shall not be construed as entitling the Comptroller and Auditor General to question the merits of the policy objectives of any department, authority or body in respect of which an examination is carried out.

(3) Subject to subsections (4) and (5) below, this section applies to—

(a) any department in respect of which appropriation accounts are required to be prepared under the Exchequer and Audit Departments Act 1866;

(b) any body required to keep accounts under section 98 of the National Health Service Act 1977 or section 86 of the National Health Service (Scotland) Act 1978;

(c) any other authority or body whose accounts are required to be examined and certified by, or are open to the inspection of, the Comptroller and Auditor General by virtue of any enactment, including an enactment passed after this Act; and

(d) any authority or body which does not fall within section 7 below and whose accounts are required to be examined and certified by, or are open to the inspection of, the Comptroller and Auditor General by virtue of any agreement made, whether before or after the passing of this Act, between that authority or body and a Minister of the Crown.

(4)-(6) * * * * *

(7) In this section—

"authority" includes any person holding a public office;

"Minister" or "Minister of the Crown" includes any department falling within subsection (3)(a) above;

"policy", in relation to any such department, includes any policy of the government so far as relating to the functions of that department;

and references to an agreement made by a Minister include references to conditions imposed by him in pursuance of any statutory power in that behalf, whether in connection with the provision of financial assistance or otherwise.

7 Other bodies mainly supported by public funds

(1) If the Comptroller and Auditor General has reasonable cause to believe that any authority or body to which this section applies has in any of its financial years received more than half its income from public funds he may carry out an examination into the economy, efficiency and effctiveness with which it has in that year used its resources in discharging its functions.

(2) Subsection (1) above shall not be construed as entitling the Comptroller and Auditor General to question the merits of the policy objectives or any authority or body in respect of which an examination is carried out.

(3) In determining for the purposes of subsection (1) above whether the income of an authority or body is such as to bring it within that subsection the Comptroller and Auditor General shall consult that authority or body and the Treasury.

(4) This section applies to any authority or body appointed, or whose members are required to be appointed, by or on behalf of the Crown except a body specified in Schedule 4 to this Act.

(5), (6) * * * * *

8 Right to obtain documents and information

(1) Subject to subsection (2) below, the Comptroller and Auditor General shall have a right of access at all reasonable times to all such documents as he may reasonably require for carrying out any examination under section 6 or 7 above and shall be entitled to require from any person holding or accountable for any such document such information and explanation as are reasonably necessary for that purpose.

(2) Subsection (1) above applies only to documents in the custody or under the control of the department, authority or body to which the examination relates.

9 Reports to House of Commons

The Comptroller and Auditor General may report to the House of Commons the results of any examination carried out by him under section 6 or 7 above.

* * * * *

REPRESENTATION OF THE PEOPLE ACT 1983
(1983, c. 2)

An Act to consolidate the Representation of the People Acts of 1949, 1969, 1977, 1978 and 1980, The Electoral Registers Acts of 1949 and 1953, the Elections (Welsh Forms) Act 1964, Part III of the Local Government Act 1972, sections 6 to 10 of the Local Government (Scotland) Act 1973, the Representation of the People (Armed Forces) Act 1976, the Returning Officers (Scotland) Act 1977, section 3 of the Representation of the People Act 1981, section 62 of and Schedule 2 to the Mental Health (Amendment) Act 1982, and connected provisions; and to repeal as obsolete the Representation of the People Act 1979 and other enactments related to the Representation of the People Acts [8 February 1983]

PART I
PARLIAMENTARY AND LOCAL GOVERNMENT FRANCHISE AND ITS EXERCISE

Parliamentary and local government franchise

1 Parliamentary electors

(1) A person entitled to vote as an elector at a parliamentary election in any constituency is one who—

(a) is resident there on the qualifying date (subject to subsection (2) below in relation to Northern Ireland); and

(b) on that date and on the date of the poll—

(i) is not subject to any legal incapacity to vote (age apart); and

(ii) is either a Commonwealth citizen or a citizen of the Republic of Ireland;

and

(c) is of voting age (that is, 18 years or over) on the date of the poll.

(2) A person is not entitled to vote as an elector at a parliamentary election in any constituency in Northern Ireland unless he was resident in Northern Ireland during the whole of the period of three months ending on the qualifying date for that election.

(3) A person is not entitled to vote as an elector in any constituency unless registered there in the register of parliamentary electors to be used at the election.

(4) A person is not entitled to vote as an elector—

(a) more than once in the same constituency at any parliamentary election;

(b) in more than one constituency at a general election.

* * * * *

75 Prohibition of expenses not authorised by election agent

(1) No expenses shall, with a view to promoting or procuring the election of a candidate at an election, be incurred by any person other than the candidate, his election agent and persons authorised in writing by the election agent on account—

(a) of holding public meetings or organising any public display; or

(b) of issuing advertisements, circulars or publications; or

(c) of otherwise presenting to the electors the candidate or his views or the extent or nature of his backing or disparaging another candidate,

but paragraph (c) of this subsection shall not—

(i) restrict the publication of any matter relating to the election in a newspaper or other periodical or in a broadcast made by the British Broadcasting Corporation or the Independent Broadcasting Authority [or in a programme included in a cable programme service which is or does not require to be licensed]; or

(ii) apply to any expenses not exceeding in the aggregate the sum of [£5] which may be incurred by an individual and are not incurred in pursuance of a plan suggested by or concerted with others, or to expenses incurred by any person in travelling or in living away from home or similar personal expenses.

(2) Where a person incurs any expenses required by this section to be authorised by the election agent—

(a) that person shall [within 21 days after the day on which the result of the election is declared deliver] to the appropriate officer a return of the amount of those expenses, stating the election at which and the candidate in whose support they were incurred, and

(b) the return shall be accompanied by a declaration made by that person (or in the case of an association or body of persons, by a director, general manager, secretary or other similar officer of the association or body) verifying the return and giving particulars of the matters for which the expenses were incurred,

but this subsection does not apply to any person engaged or employed for payment or promise of payment by the candidate or his election agent.

(3) * * * * *

(4) A copy of every return and declaration made under subsection (2) above in relation to a parliamentary election in England, Wales or Northern Ireland shall be sent to the Clerk of the Crown within [21 days after the day on which the result of the election is declared] by the person making the return or declaration, and rule 57 of the parliamentary elections rules applies to any documents sent to the Clerk of the Crown under this subsection.

In this subsection references to the Clerk of the Crown in relation to an election in Northern Ireland are references to the Clerk of the Crown for Northern Ireland.

(5) If a person—

(a) incurs, or aids, abets, counsels or procures any other person to incur, any expenses in contravention of this section, or

(b) knowingly makes the declaration required by subsection (2) falsely,

he shall be guilty of a corrupt practice; and if a person fails to [deliver] or send any declaration or return or a copy of it as required by this section he shall be guilty of an illegal practice, but—

(i) the court before whom a person is convicted under this subsection may, if they think it just in the special circumstances of the case, mitigate or entirely remit any incapacity imposed by virtue of section 173 below; and

(ii) a candidate shall not be liable, nor shall his election be avoided, for a corrupt or illegal practice under this subsection committed by an agent without his consent or connivance.

(6) * * * * *

* * * * *

92 Broadcasting from outside United Kingdom

(1) No person shall, with intent to influence persons to give or refrain from giving their votes at a parliamentary or local government election, use, or aid, abet, counsel or procure the use of, any television or other wireless transmitting station outside the United Kingdom for the transmission of any matter having reference to the election otherwise than in pursuance of—

(a) arrangements made with the British Broadcasting Corporation for it to be received and re-transmitted by that Corporation; or

(b) arrangements made with the Independent Broadcasting Authority or a programme contractor (within the meaning of the Broadcasting Act 1981) for it to be received by the Authority or contractor and re-transmitted by the Authority.

(2) An offence under this section shall be an illegal practice, but the court before whom a person is convicted of an offence under this section may, if they think it just in the special circumstances of the case, mitigate or entirely remit any incapacity imposed by virtue of section 173 below.

(3) * * * * *

93 Broadcasting during elections

(1) In relation to a parliamentary or local government election—

(a) pending such an election it shall not be lawful for any item about the constituency or electoral area to be broadcast from a television or other wireless transmitting station in the United Kingdom if any of the persons who are for the time being candidates at the election takes part in the item and the broadcast is not made with his consent; and

(b) where an item about a constituency or electoral area is so broadcast pending such an election there, then if the broadcast either is made before the latest time for delivery of nomination papers, or is made after that time but without the consent of any candidate remaining validly nominated, any person taking part in the item for the purpose of promoting or procuring his election shall be guilty of an illegal practice, unless the broadcast is so made without his consent.

(2) For the purposes of subsection (1) above—

(a) a parliamentary election shall be deemed to be pending during the period ending with the close of the poll and beginning—

(i) at a general election, with the date of the dissolution of Parliament or any earlier time at which Her Majesty's intention to dissolve Parliament is announced; or

(ii) at a by-election, with the date of the issue of the writ for the election or any earlier date on which a certificate of the vacancy is notified in the London Gazette in accordance with the Recess Elections Act 1975; and

(b) a local government election shall be deemed to be pending during the period ending with the close of the poll and beginning [with the last date on which notice of the election may be published in accordance with rules made under section 36 or, in Scotland, section 42 above].

[(3) References in this section to items being broadcast from a television or other wireless telegraphy transmitting station in the United Kingdom include references to items being included in a cable programme service; and references in this section to the making of broadcasts shall be construed accordingly.]

94 * * * * *

Election meetings

95 Schools and rooms for parliamentary election meetings

(1) Subject to the provisions of this section, a candidate at a parliamentary election is entitled for the purpose of holding public meetings in furtherance of his candidature to the use [free of charge] at reasonable times between the receipt of the writ and [the day preceding] the date of the poll of—

(a) a suitable room in the premises of a school to which this section applies;

(b) any meeting room to which this section applies.

(2) This section applies—

(a) in England and Wales, to county schools and voluntary schools of which the premises are situated in the constituency or an adjoining constituency, and

(b) in Scotland, to any school of which the premises are so situated, not being an independent school within the meaning of the Education (Scotland) Act 1980,

but a candidate is not entitled under this section to the use of a room in school premises outside the constituency if there is a suitable room in other premises in the constituency which are reasonably accessible from the same parts of the constituency as those outside and are premises of a school to which this section applies.

(3) This section applies to meeting rooms situated in the constituency, the expense of maintaining which is payable wholly or mainly out of public funds or out of any rate, or by a body whose expenses are so payable.

(4)-(8) * * * * *

[96 Schools and rooms for local election meetings

(1) Subject to the provisions of this section, a candidate at a local government election is entitled for the purpose of holding public meetings in furtherance of his candidature to the use free of charge at reasonable times between the last day on which notice of the election may be published in accordance with rules made under section 36 or, in Scotland, section 42 above and the day preceding the day of election of—

(a) a suitable room in the premises of a school to which this section applies; or

(b) a meeting room to which this section applies.

(2) This section applies—

(a) in England and Wales, to a county or voluntary school situated in the electoral area for which the candidate is standing (or, if there is no such school in the area, in any such school in an adjacent electoral area) or in a parish or community, as the case may be, in part comprised in that electoral area) and

(b) in Scotland, to any school (not being an independent school within the meaning of the Education (Scotland) Act 1980) situated in the electoral area for which the candidate is standing (or, if there is no such school in the area, any such school in an adjacent electoral area).

(3) This section applies—

(a) in England and Wales, to any meeting room situated in the electoral area for which the candidate is standing or in a parish or community, as the case may be, in part comprised in that electoral area, the expense of maintaining which is payable wholly or mainly out of public funds or out of any rate, or by a body whose expenses are so payable;

(b) in Scotland, to any meeting room the expense of maintaining which is payable by the council of a region, islands area or district.

(4) * * * * *]

97 Disturbances at election meetings

(1) A person who at a lawful public meeting to which this section applies acts, or incites others to act, in a disorderly manner for the purpose of preventing the transaction of the business for which the meeting was called together shall be guilty of an illegal practice.

(2) This section applies to—

(a) a political meeting held in any constituency between the date of the issue of a writ for the return of a member of Parliament for the constituency and the date at which a return to the writ is made;

(b) a meeting held with reference to a local government election in the electoral area for that election [in the period beginning with the last date on which notice of the election may be published in accordance with rules made under section 36 or, in Scotland, section 42 above and ending with] the day of election.

(3) If a constable reasonably suspects any person of committing an offence under subsection (1) above, he may if requested so to do by the chairman of the meeting require that person to declare to him immediately his name and address and, if that person refuses or fails so to declare his name and address or gives a false name and address, he shall be liable on summary conviction to a fine not exceeding [level 1 on the standard scale,] . . .

This subsection does not apply in Northern Ireland.

98, 99 * * * * *

100 Illegal canvassing by police officers

(1) No member of a police force shall by word, message, writing or in any other manner, endeavour to persuade any person to give, or dissuade any person from giving, his vote, whether as an elector or as proxy—

(a) at any parliamentary election for a constituency, or

(b) at any local government election for any electoral area,

wholly or partly within the police area.

(2) A person acting in contravention of subsection (1) above shall be liable [on summary conviction to a fine not exceeding level 3 on the standard scale, but] nothing in that subsection shall subject a member of a police force to any penalty for anything done in the discharge of his duty as a member of the force.

(3) In this section references to a member of a police force and to a police area are to be taken in relation to Northern Ireland as references to a member of the Royal Ulster Constabulary and to Northern Ireland.

* * * * *

CABLE AND BROADCASTING ACT 1984
(1984, c. 46)

An Act to provide for the establishment and functions of a Cable Authority and to make other provision with respect to cable programme services; to amend the Broadcasting Act 1981, to provide for the establishment and functions of a Satellite Broadcasting Board and to make other provision with respect to broadcasting services; and for connected purposes. [26 July 1984]

Territorial extent United Kingdom (all provisions except s. 25 (does not apply to Scotland)).

PART I
CABLE PROGRAMME SERVICES

Introductory

1 The Cable Authority

(1) There shall be an authority to be called the Cable Authority (in this Part referred to as "the Authority") for the purpose of performing the functions assigned to the Authority by this Part.

(2) The Authority shall consist of—

(a) a chairman and deputy chairman; and

(b) such number of other members, not being less than three nor more than ten, as the Secretary of State may from time to time determine.

(3) Schedule 1 to this Act shall have effect with respect to the Authority.

2 Meaning of "cable programme service" etc.

(1) In this Act "cable programme service" means a service which consists wholly or mainly in the sending by any person, by means of a telecommunication system (whether run by him or by any other person), of sounds or visual images or both either—

(a) for reception, otherwise than by wireless telegraphy, at two or more places in the United Kingdom, whether they are so sent for simultaneous reception or at different times in response to requests made by different users of the service; or

(b) for reception, by whatever means, at a place in the United Kingdom for the purpose of their being presented there either to members of the public or to any group of persons.

(2) In this Part "licensable service" means a cable programme service which consists wholly or mainly in the sending by any person, by means of a telecommunication system (whether run by him or by any other person), of sounds or visual images or both either—

(a) for simultaneous reception, otherwise than by wireless telegraphy, in two or more dwelling-houses in the United Kingdom; or

(b) for reception, by whatever means, at a place in the United Kingdom for the purpose of their being presented there either to members of the public or to a group of persons some or all of whom do not have a business interest in hearing or seeing them.

(3)-(8) * * * * *

(9) In this section "dwelling-house" includes a hotel, inn, boarding house or other similar establishment.

Licensing of services by Authority

3 Prohibition on unlicensed services

(1) Subject to any exceptions for which the Secretary of State after consultation with the Authority may by order provide, a person who provides a licensable service shall be guilty of an offence unless he is authorised to provide the service by a licence granted under section 4 below (in this Part referred to as a licence).

(2) A person guilty of an offence under this section shall be liable—

(a) on summary conviction, to a fine not exceeding the statutory maximum;

(b) on conviction on indictment, to a fine.

(3) No proceedings in respect of an offence under this section shall be instituted—

(a) in England and Wales, except by or with the consent of the Director of Public Prosecutions;

(b) in Northern Ireland, except by or with the consent of the Director of Public Prosecutions for Northern Ireland.

(4) Without prejudice to subsection (2) above, compliance with this section shall be enforceable by civil proceedings by the Crown for an injunction or interdict or for any other appropriate relief.

(5) An order under this section shall be made by statutory instrument which shall be subject to annulment in pursuance of a resolution of either House of Parliament.

4 Power to license services

(1) A licence may be granted by the Authority for the provision of such a licensable service as is specified in the licence or is of a description so specified.

(2) A licence shall be in writing and, subject to subsections (3) and (8) and section 17 below, shall continue in force for such period as may be specified in the licence.

(3) A licence for the provision of a prescribed diffusion service (whether as originally granted or as varied under subsection (8) below) shall not continue in force for a period exceeding the relevant maximum period.

(4) For the purposes of subsection (3) above the relevant maximum period is—

(a) fifteen years in the case of a licence for the provision of a prescribed diffusion service in an area—

(i) in which such a service has not previously been provided; or

(ii) in which such a service has previously been so provided, but only in so much of it as in the opinion of the Authority does not amount to a substantial part of it; and

(b) eight years in every other case.

(5) A licence may include—

(a) such conditions as appear to the Authority to be requisite or expedient having regard to the duties imposed on them by this Part and, in the case of a licence for the provision of a prescribed diffusion service, to the information included in the application in pursuance of section 6(1) below;

(b) conditions requiring the rendering to the authority of a payment on the grant of the licence or payments during the currency of the licence or both of such amount or amounts as may be determined by or under the licence; and

(c) conditions requiring the holder of the licence to furnish to the Authority, in such manner and at such times as they may reasonably require, such information as they may require for the purpose of exercising the functions assigned to them by or under this Part.

(6) Without prejudice to the generality of paragraph (a) of subsection (5) above, conditions included in a licence by virtue of that paragraph may require the holder of the licence—

(a) to comply with any direction given by the Authority as to such matters as are specified in the licence or are of a description so specified; and

(b) except in so far as the Authority consent to his doing or not doing them, not to do or to do such things as are specified in the licence or are of a description so specified.

(7)-(9) *****

5, 6 *****

7 Matters to be taken into account

(1) In deciding whether or to whom to grant a licence, the Authority shall take into account all matters appearing to them to be relevant.

(2) Without prejudice to the generality of subsection (1) above, in deciding whether or to whom to grant a licence for the provision of a prescribed diffusion service in any area, the Authority shall take into account the extent to which the applicant or each applicant proposes to do the following things, namely—

(a) to include a range and diversity of programmes;

(b) to include in the programmes matter which originates within the European Economic Community and is performed by nationals of member States;

(c) to include in the programmes an increasing proportion of such matter;

(d) to include programmes of an educational nature, programmes calculated to appeal specially to the taste and outlook of persons living in the area and programmes in which such persons are given an opportunity to participate;

(e) to include programmes provided otherwise than by himself or by associates of his;

(f) to include programmes provided by local voluntary associations and to assist such organisations in the preparation and production of programmes;

(g) to include in the programmes matter which is calculated to promote the understanding or enjoyment of programmes by persons who are deaf;

(h) to provide, or secure the provision of, related services.

(3) In this section "local voluntary organisation" includes a local branch of a national voluntary organisation.

8 Restrictions on the holding of licences

(1) The Authority shall do all that they can to secure that none of the following becomes or remains the holder of a licence for the provision of a diffusion service to which this section applies, that is to say—

(a) an individual who is neither—

(i) a national of a member State who is ordinarily resident within the European Economic Community; nor

(ii) ordinarily resident in the United Kingdom, the Isle of Man or the Channel Islands;

(b) a body corporate which is neither—

(i) a body formed under the law of a member State which has its registered or head office or principal place of business within the European Economic Community; nor

(ii) a body incorporated under the law of the Isle of Man or the Channel Islands;

(c) a local authority;

(d) a body whose objects are wholly or mainly of a religious or political nature;

(e) an individual who is an officer of a body falling within paragraph (d) above; and

(f) a body corporate which is under the control of a person falling within any of the foregoing paragraphs, or any two or more such persons together.

(2) The Authority shall do all that they can to secure that a person who is, or is an associate of,—

(a) a programme contractor for the provision of television programmes for any area;

(b) a programme contractor for the provision of local sound broadcasts for reception in any locality; or

(c) the proprietor of a local newspaper circulating wholly or mainly in any area,

does not become or remain the holder of a licence for the provision in any part of that area or locality of a diffusion service to which this section applies.

(3) The Authority shall do all that they can to secure that a body corporate in which—

(a) any of the persons mentioned in subsection (4) below is a participant; or

(b) any of the persons mentioned in subsection (5) below is a principal participant,

does not become or remain the holder of a licence for the provision of a diffusion service to which this section applies if, in the opinion of the Authority, that person's participation in that body corporate has led, is leading or is likely to lead to results which are adverse to the public interest.

(4) The persons referred to in subsection (3)(a) above are—

(a) a local authority;

(b) a body whose objects are wholly or mainly of a religious or political nature;

(c) the BBC, the IBA and the Welsh Authority; and

(d) a body corporate which is under the control of a person falling within paragraph (a), (b) or (c) above.

(5) The persons referred to in subsection (3)(b) above are—

(a) a person who is a principal participant in another body corporate which is the holder of a licence for the provision of a diffusion service to which this section applies;

(a) a programme contractor, the proprietor of a newspaper and an advertising agent;

(c) a person carrying on a business which consists (wholly or partly) of—

(i) the production, distribution or exhibition of cinematograph films;
(ii) the manufacture of records or the publication of musical works; or
(iii) promoting the broadcasting of sound recordings or the broadcasting or performance of musical works;

(d) an associate of a person falling within paragraph (a), (b) or (c) above;

(e) a person who has control over a body corporate falling within paragraph (a), (b), (c) or (d) above; and

(f) a body corporate which is under the control of a person falling within paragraph (a), (b), (c) or (d) above.

(6) This section applies to any diffusion service in the case of which programmes are included otherwise than by the reception and immediate re-transmission of broadcasts made by a broadcasting authority.

(7) In this section—

"participant", in relation to a body corporate, means a person who (whether alone or jointly with one or more other persons, and whether directly or through one or more nominees) holds or is beneficially entitled to shares, or possesses voting power, in that body corporate;

"principal participant", in relation to a body corporate, means a person who (whether alone or jointly with one or more other persons, and whether directly or through one or more nominees) holds or is beneficially entitled to not less than one-twentieth of the shares, or possesses not less than one-twentieth of the voting power, in that body corporate.

(8) * * * * *

9 * * * * *

Duties of Authority

10 General provisions as to programmes

(1) The Authority shall do all that they can to secure that every licensed service complies with the following requirements, that is to say—

(a) that nothing is included in the programmes which offends against good taste or decency or is likely to encourage or incite to crime or to lead to disorder or to be offensive to public feeling;

(b) that the programmes do not include any technical device which, by using images of very brief duration or by any other means, exploits the possibility of conveying a message to, or otherwise influencing the minds of, members of an audience without their being aware, or fully aware, of what has been done;

(c) that all news given (in whatever form) in programmes which originate in the United Kingdom is presented with due accuracy and impartiality; and

(d) that there are included in the programmes proper proportions of recorded and other matter which originates within the European Economic Community and is performed by nationals of member States.

(2) * * * * *

11-24 * * * * *

Obscenity

25 Obscene programmes

(1) Subject to the following provisions of this section, if—

(a) the inclusion of a programme in a cable programme service involves the publication of an obscene article; or

(b) a programme included in such a service is such that, if any matter included in it were recorded matter, the inclusion of the programme would involve the publication of such an article,

the person providing that service shall be guilty of an offence.

(2) A person guilty of an offence under this section shall be liable—

(a) on summary conviction, to a fine not exceeding the statutory maximum or to imprisonment for a term not exceeding six months;

(b) on conviction on indictment, to a fine or to imprisonment for a term not exceeding three years or both.

(3) Subsection (1) above shall not apply in relation to a programme which is included in a cable programme service by the reception and immediate re-transmission of a broadcast made by a broadcasting authority.

(4) Proceedings for an offence under this section shall not be commenced more than two years after the commission of the offence.

(5) Proceedings for an offence under this section shall not be instituted—

(a) in England and Wales, except by or with the consent of the Director of Public Prosecutions;

(b) In Northern Ireland, except by or with the consent of the Director of Public Prosecutions for Northern Ireland.

(6) A person shall not be proceeded against for an offence at common law—

(a) in respect of a programme included in a cable programme service or anything said or done in the course of such a programme, where it is of the essence of the common law offence that the programme or, as the case may be, what was said or done was obscene, indecent, offensive, disgusting or injurious to morality; or

(b) in respect of an agreement to cause a programme to be included in a cable programme service or to cause anything to be said or done in course of such a programme so included, where the common law offence consists of conspiring to corrupt public morals or to do any act contrary to public morals or decency.

(7) A person shall not be convicted of an offence under this section if he proves that he did not know and had no reason to suspect that the programme in question would be such that it is inclusion in a cable programme service would make him liable to be convicted of an offence under this section.

(8) A person shall not be convicted of an offence under this section if he proves that the inclusion in a cable programme service of the programme in question was justified as being for the public good on the ground that it was in the interests of drama, opera, ballet or any other art, or of literature or learning.

(9) It is hereby declared that the opinion of experts as to the artistic, literary or other merits of a programme may be admitted in any proceedings under this section either to establish or negative the said ground.

(10) In this section expressions used in the Obscene Publications Act 1959 have the same meanings as in that Act.

(11) This section does not extent to Scotland.

26 Obscene programmes in Scotland

[*Amends s. 51 Civic Government (Scotland) Act 1982, printed above as amended.*]

27 Incitement to racial hatred [*Repealed by Sch. 3 Public Order Act 1986; see now ibid. s. 22*] . . .

28 * * * * *

29 Complaints of unjust or unfair treatment etc.

The Broadcasting Complaints Commission shall also have the function of considering and adjudicating upon complaints of—

(a) unjust or unfair treatment in programmes actually included in a licensed service after the commencement of this section otherwise than by the reception and immediate re-transmission of broadcasts made by a broadcasting authority; or

(b) unwarranted infringement of privacy in, or in connection with the obtaining of material included in, programmes actually so included;

and Part III of the 1981 Act (which relates to that Commission) shall accordingly have effect with the amendments made by Schedule 2 to this Act.

* * * * *

POLICE AND CRIMINAL EVIDENCE ACT 1984
(1984, c. 60)

An Act to make further provision in relation to the powers and duties of the police, persons in police detention, criminal evidence, police discipline and complaints against the police; to provide for arrangements for obtaining the views of the community on policing and for a rank of deputy chief constable; to amend the law relating to the Police Federations and Police Forces and Police Cadets in Scotland; and for connected purposes [31 October 1984]

Territorial extent England and Wales.

Note For the application of this Act to investigating officers of the Customs and Excise see the Police and Criminal Evidence Act 1984 (Application to Customs and Excise) Order 1985 (SI 1985 No 1800).

PART I
POWERS TO STOP AND SEARCH

1 Power of constable to stop and search persons, vehicles etc

(1) A constable may exercise any power conferred by this section—

(a) in any place to which at the time when he proposes to exercise the power the public or any section of the public has access, on payment or otherwise, as of right or by virtue of express or implied permission; or

(b) in any other place to which people have ready access at the time when he proposes to exercise the power but which is not a dwelling.

(2) Subject to subsection (3) to (5) below, a constable—

(a) may search—

(i) any person or vehicle;

(ii) anything which is in or on a vehicle,

for stolen or prohibited articles; and

(b) may detain a person or vehicle for the purpose of such a search.

(3) This section does not give a constable power to search a person or vehicle or anything in or on a vehicle unless he has reasonable grounds for suspecting that he will find stolen or prohibited articles.

(4) If a person is in a garden or yard occupied with and used for the purposes of a dwelling or on other land so occupied and used, a constable may not search him in the exercise of the power conferred by this section unless the constable has reasonable grounds for believing—

(a) that he does not reside in the dwelling; and

(b) that he is not in the place in question with the express or implied permission of a person who resides in the dwelling.

(5) If a vehicle is in a garden or yard occupied with and used for the purposes of a dwelling or on other land so occupied and used, a constable may not search the vehicle or anything in or on it in the exercise of the power conferred by this section unless he has reasonable grounds for believing—

(a) that the person in charge of the vehicle does not reside in the dwelling; and

(b) that the vehicle is not in the place in question with the express or implied permission of a person who resides in the dwelling.

(6) If in the course of such a search a constable discovers an article which he has reasonable grounds for suspecting to be a stolen or prohibited article, he may seize it.

(7) An article is prohibited for the purposes of this Part of this Act if it is—
(a) an offensive weapon; or
(b) an article—
(i) made or adapted for use in the course of or in connection with an offence to which this sub-paragraph applies; or
(ii) intended by the person having it with him for such use by him or by some other person.
(8) The offences to which subsection (7)(b)(i) above applies are—
(a) burglary;
(b) theft;
(c) offences under section 12 of the Theft Act 1968 (taking motor vehicle or other conveyance without authority); and
(d) offences under section 15 of that Act (obtaining property by deception).
(9) In this Part of this Act "offensive weapon" means any article—
(a) made or adapted for use for causing injury to persons; or
(b) intended by the person having it with him for such use by him or by some other person.

2 Provisions relating to search under section 1 and other powers
(1) A constable who detains a person or vehicle in the exercise—
(a) of the power conferred by section 1 above; or
(b) of any other power—
(i) to search a person without first arresting him; or
(ii) to search a vehicle without making an arrest,
need not conduct a search if it appears to him subsequently—
(i) that no search is required; or
(ii) that a search is impracticable.
(2) If a constable contemplates a search, other than a search of an unattended vehicle, in the exercise—
(a) of the power conferred by section 1 above; or
(b) of any other power, except the power conferred by section 6 below and the power conferred by section 27(2) of the Aviation Security Act 1982—
(i) to search a person without first arresting him; or
(ii) to search a vehicle without making an arrest,
it shall be his duty, subject to subsection (4) below, to take reasonable steps before he commences the search to bring to the attention of the appropriate person—
(i) if the constable is not in uniform, documentary evidence that he is a constable; and
(ii) whether he is in uniform or not, the matters specified in subsection (3) below;
and the constable shall not commence the search until he has performed that duty.
(3) The matters referred to in subsection (2)(ii) above are—
(a) the constable's name and the name of the police station to which he is attached;
(b) the object of the proposed search;
(c) the constable's grounds for proposing to make it; and
(d) the effect of section 3(7) or (8) below, as may be appropriate.
(4) A constable need not bring the effect of section 3(7) or (8) below to the attention of the appropriate person if it appears to the constable that it will not be practicable to make the record in section 3(1) below.
(5) In this section "the appropriate person" means—
(a) if the constable proposes to search a person, that person; and
(b) if he proposes to search a vehicle, or anything in or on a vehicle, the person in charge of the vehicle.

(6) On completing a search of an unattended vehicle or anything in or on such a vehicle in the exercise of any such power as is mentioned in subsection (2) above a constable shall leave a notice—

(a) stating that he has searched it;

(b) giving the name of the police station to which he is attached;

(c) stating that an application for compensation for any damage caused by the search may be made to that police station; and

(d) stating the effect of section 3(8) below.

(7) * * * * *

(8) The time for which a person or vehicle may be detained for the purposes of such a search is such time as is reasonably required to permit a search to be carried out either at the place where the person or vehicle was first detained or nearby.

(9) Neither the power conferred by section 1 above nor any other power to detain and search a person without first arresting him or to detain and search a vehicle without making an arrest is to be construed—

(a) as authorising a constable to require a person to remove any of his clothing in public other than an outer coat, jacket or gloves; or

(b) as authorising a constable not in uniform to stop a vehicle.

(10) * * * * *

3 Duty to make records concerning searches

(1) Where a constable has carried out a search in the exercise of any such power as is mentioned in section 2(1) above, other than a search—

(a) under section 6 below; or

(b) under section 27(2) of the Aviation Security Act 1982,

he shall make a record of it in writing unless it is not practicable to do so.

(2) If—

(a) a constable is required by subsection (1) above to make a record of a search; but

(b) it is not practicable to make the record on the spot,

he shall make it as soon as practicable after the completion of the search.

(3) The record of a search of a person shall include a note of his name, if the constable knows it, but a constable may not detain a person to find out his name.

(4) If a constable does not know the name of the person whom he has searched, the record of the search shall include a note otherwise describing that person.

(5) The record of a search of a vehicle shall include a note describing the vehicle.

(6) The record of a search of a person or a vehicle—

(a) shall state—

(i) the object of the search;

(ii) the grounds for making it;

(iii) the date and time when it was made;

(iv) the place where it was made;

(v) whether anything, and if so what, was found;

(vi) whether any, and if so what, injury to a person or damage to property appears to the constable to have resulted from the search; and

(b) shall identify the constable making it.

(7) If a constable who conducted a search of a person made a record of it, the person who was searched shall be entitled to a copy of the record if he asks for one before the end of the period specified in subsection (9) below.

(8) If—

(a) the owner of a vehicle which has been searched or the person who was in charge of the vehicle at the time when it was searched asks for a copy of the record of the search before the end of the period specified in subsection (9) below; and

(b) the constable who conducted the search made a record of it,
the person who made the request shall be entitled to a copy.

(9) The period mentioned in subsections (7) and (8) above is the period of 12 months beginning with the date on which the search was made.

(10) * * * * *

4 Road checks

(1) This section shall have effect in relation to the conduct of road checks by police officers for the purpose of ascertaining whether a vehicle is carrying—

(a) a person who has committed an offence other than a road traffic offence or a vehicles excise offence;

(b) a person who is a witness to such an offence;

(c) a person intending to commit such an offence; or

(d) a person who is unlawfully at large.

(2) For the purposes of this section a road check consists of the exercise in a locality of the power conferred by section 159 of the Road Traffic Act 1972 in such a way as to stop during the period for which its exercise in that way in that locality continues all vehicles or vehicles selected by any criterion.

(3) Subject to subsection (5) below, there may only be such a road check if a police officer of the rank of superintendent or above authorises it in writing.

(4) An officer may only authorise a road check under subsection (3) above—

(a) for the purpose specified in subsection (1)(a) above, if he has reasonable grounds—

(i) for believing that the offence is a serious arrestable offence; and

(ii) for suspecting that the person is, or is about to be, in the locality in which vehicles would be stopped if the road check were authorised;

(b) for the purpose specified in subsection (1)(b) above, if he has reasonable grounds for believing that the offence is a serious arrestable offence;

(c) for the purpose specified in subsection (1)(c) above, if he has reasonable grounds—

(i) for believing that the offence would be a serious arrestable offence; and

(ii) for suspecting that the person is, or is about to be, in the locality in which vehicles would be stopped if the road check were authorised;

(d) for the purpose specified in subsection (1)(d) above, if he has reasonable grounds for suspecting that the person is, or is about to be, in that locality.

(5) An officer below the rank of superintendent may authorise such a road check if it appears to him that it is required as a matter of urgency for one of the purposes specified in subsection (1) above.

(6) If an authorisation is given under subsection (5) above, it shall be the duty of the officer who gives it—

(a) to make a written record of the time at which he gives it; and

(b) to cause an officer of the rank of superintendent or above to be informed that it has been given.

(7)-(14) * * * * *

(15) Where a vehicle is stopped in a road check, the person in charge of the vehicle at the time when it is stopped shall be entitled to obtain a written statement of the purpose of the road check if he applies for such a statement not later than the end of the period of twelve months from the day on which the vehicle was stopped.

(16) Nothing in this section affects the exercise by police officers of any power to stop vehicles for purposes other than those specified in subsection (1) above.

5-7 * * * * *

PART II
POWERS OF ENTRY, SEARCH AND SEIZURE

Search warrants

8 Power of justice of the peace to authorise entry and search of premises

(1) If on an application made by a constable a justice of the peace is satisfied that there are reasonable grounds for believing—

(a) that a serious arrestable offence has been committed; and

(b) that there is material on premises specified in the application which is likely to be of substantial value (whether by itself or together with other material) to the investigation of the offence; and

(c) that the material is likely to be relevant evidence; and

(d) that it does not consist of or include items subject to legal privilege, excluded material or special procedure material; and

(e) that any of the conditions specified in subsection (3) below applies,

he may issue a warrant authorising a constable to enter and search the premises.

(2) A constable may seize and retain anything for which a search has been authorised under subsection (1) above.

(3) The conditions mentioned in subsection (1)(e) above are—

(a) that it is not practicable to communicate with any person entitled to grant entry to the premises;

(b) that it is practicable to communicate with a person entitled to grant entry to the premises but it is not practicable to communicate with any person entitled to grant access to the evidence;

(c) that entry to the premises will not be granted unless a warrant is produced;

(d) that the purpose of a search may be frustrated or seriously prejudiced unless a constable arriving at the premises can secure immediate entry to them.

(4) In this Act "relevant evidence", in relation to an offence, means anything that would be admissible in evidence at a trial for the offence.

(5) The power to issue a warrant conferred by this section is in addition to any such power otherwise conferred.

9 Special provisions as to access

(1) A constable may obtain access to excluded material or special procedure material for the purposes of a criminal investigation by making an application under Schedule 1 below and in accordance with that Schedule.

(2) Any Act (including a local Act) passed before this Act under which a search of premises for the purposes of a criminal investigation could be authorised by the issue of a warrant to a constable shall cease to have effect so far as it relates to the authorisation of searches—

(a) for items subject to legal privilege; or

(b) for excluded material; or

(c) for special procedure material consisting of documents or records other than documents.

10 Meaning of "items subject to legal privilege"

(1) Subject to subsection (2) below, in this Act "items subject to legal privilege" means—

(a) communications between a professional legal adviser and his client or any person representing his client made in connection with the giving of legal advice to the client;

(b) communications between a professional legal adviser and his client or any person representing his client or between such an adviser or his client or any such representative and any other person made in connection with or in contemplation of legal proceedings and for the purposes of such proceedings; and

(c) items enclosed with or referred to in such communications and made—
(i) in connection with the giving of legal advice; or
(ii) in connection with or in contemplation of legal proceedings and for the purposes of such proceedings,

when they are in the possession of a person who is entitled to possesion of them.

(2) Items held with the intention of furthering a criminal purpose are not items subject to legal privilege.

11 Meaning of "excluded material"

(1) Subject to the following provisions of this section, in this Act "excluded material" means—

(a) personal records which a person has acquired or created in the course of any trade, business, profession or other occupation or for the purposes of any paid or unpaid office and which he holds in confidence;

(b) human tissue or tissue fluid which has been taken for the purposes of diagnosis or medical treatment and which a person holds in confidence;

(c) journalistic material which a person holds in confidence and which consists—
(i) of documents; or
(ii) of records other than documents.

(2) A person holds material other than journalistic material in confidence for the purposes of this section if he holds it subject—

(a) to an express or implied undertaking to hold it in confidence; or

(b) to a restriction on disclosure or an obligation of secrecy contained in any enactment, including an enactment contained in an Act passed after this Act.

(3) A person holds journalistic material in confidence for the purposes of this section if—

(a) he holds it subject to such an undertaking, restriction or obligation; and

(b) it has been continuously held (by one or more persons) subject to such an undertaking, restriction or obligation since it was first acquired or created for the purposes of journalism.

12 Meaning of "personal records"

In this Part of this Act "personal records" means documentary and other records concerning an individual (whether living or dead) who can be identified from them and relating—

(a) to his physical or mental health;

(b) to spiritual counselling or assistance given or to be given to him; or

(c) to counselling or assistance given or to be given to him, for the purposes of his personal welfare, by any voluntary organisation or by any individual who—
(i) by reason of his office or occupation has responsibilities for his personal welfare; or
(ii) by reason of an order of a court has responsibilities for his supervision.

13 Meaning of "journalistic material"

(1) Subject to subsection (2) below, in this Act "journalistic material" means material acquired or created for the purposes of journalism.

(2) Material is only journalistic material for the purposes of this Act if it is in the possession of a person who acquired or created it for the purposes of journalism.

(3) A person who receives material from someone who intends that the recipient shall use it for the purposes of journalism is to be taken to have acquired it for those purposes.

14 Meaning of "special procedure material"

(1) In this Act "special procedure material" means—

(a) material to which subsection (2) below applies; and

(b) journalistic material, other than excluded material.

(2) Subject to the following provisions of this section, this subsection applies to material, other than items subject to legal privilege and excluded material, in the possession of a person who—

(a) acquired or created it in the course of any trade, business, profession or other occupation or for the purposes of any paid or unpaid office; and

(b) holds it subject—

(i) to an express or implied undertaking to hold it in confidence; or

(ii) to a restriction or obligation such as is mentioned in section 11(2)(b) above.

(3)-(6) * * * * *

15 Search warrants — safeguards

(1) This section and section 16 below have effect in relation to the issue to constables under any enactment, including an enactment contained in an Act passed after this Act, of warrants to enter and search premises; and an entry on or search of premises under a warrant is unlawful unless it complies with this section and section 16 below.

(2) Where a constable applies for any such warrant, it shall be his duty—

(a) to state—

(i) the ground on which he makes the application; and

(ii) the enactment under which the warrant would be issued;

(b) to specify the premises which it is desired to enter and search; and

(c) to identify, so far as is practicable, the articles or persons to be sought.

(3) An application for such a warrant shall be made ex parte and supported by an information in writing.

(4) The constable shall answer on oath any question that the justice of the peace or judge hearing the application asks him.

(5) A warrant shall authorise an entry on one occasion only.

(6) A warrant—

(a) shall specify—

(i) the name of the person who applies for it;

(ii) the date on which it is issued;

(iii) the enactment under which it is issued; and

(iv) the premises to be searched; and

(b) shall identify, so far as is practicable, the articles or persons to be sought.

(7), (8) * * * * *

16 Execution of warrants

(1) A warrant to enter and search premises may be executed by any constable.

(2) Such a warrant may authorise persons to accompany any constable who is executing it.

(3) Entry and search under a warrant must be within one month from the date of its issue.

(4) Entry and search under a warrant must be at a reasonable hour unless it appears to the constable executing it that the purpose of a search may be frustrated on an entry at a reasonable hour.

(5) Where the occupier of premises which are to be entered and searched is present at the time when a constable seeks to execute a warrant to enter and search them, the constable—

(a) shall identify himself to the occupier and, if not in uniform, shall produce to him documentary evidence that he is a constable;

(b) shall produce the warrant to him; and

(c) shall supply him with a copy of it.

(6) Where—

(a) the occupier of such premises is not present at the time when a constable seeks to execute such a warrant; but

(b) some other person who appears to the constable to be in charge of the premises is present,

subsection (5) above shall have effect as if any reference to the occupier were a reference to that other person.

(7) If there is no person present who appears to the constable to be in charge of the premises, he shall leave a copy of the warrant in a prominent place on the premises.

(8) A search under a warrant may only be a search to the extent required for the purpose for which the warrant was issued.

(9) A constable executing a warrant shall make an endorsement on it stating—

(a) whether the articles or persons sought were found; and

(b) whether any articles were seized, other than articles which were sought.

(10)-(12) * * * * *

Entry and search without search warrant

17 Entry for purpose of arrest etc

(1) Subject to the following provisions of this section, and without prejudice to any other enactment, a constable may enter and search any premises for the purpose—

(a) of executing—

(i) a warrant of arrest issued in connection with or arising out of criminal proceedings; or

(ii) a warrant of commitment issued under section 76 of the Magistrates' Courts Act 1980;

(b) of arresting a person for an arrestable offence;

(c) of arresting a person for an offence under—

(i) section 1 (prohibition of uniforms in connection with political objects) . . . of the Public Order Act 1936;

(ii) any enactment contained in sections 6 to 8 or 10 of the Criminal Law Act 1977 (offences relating to entering and remaining on property);

[(iii) section 4 of the Public Order Act 1986 (fear or provocation of violence)].

(d) of recapturing a person who is unlawfully at large and whom he is pursuing; or

(e) of saving life or limb or preventing serious damage to property.

(2) Except for the purpose specified in paragraph (e) of subsection (1) above, the powers of entry and search conferred by this section—

(a) are only exercisable if the constable has reasonable grounds for believing that the person whom he is seeking is on the premises; and

(b) are limited, in relation to premises consisting of two or more separate dwellings, to powers to enter and search—

(i) any parts of the premises which the occupiers of any dwelling comprised in the premises use in common with the occupiers of any other such dwelling; and

(ii) any such dwelling in which the constable has reasonable grounds for believing that the person whom he is seeking may be.

(3) The powers of entry and search conferred by this section are only exercisable for the purposes specified in subsection (1)(c)(ii) above by a constable in uniform.

(4) The power of search conferred by this section is only a power to search to the extent that is reasonably required for the purpose for which the power of entry is exercised.

(5) Subject to subsection (6) below, all the rules of common law under which a constable has power to enter premises without a warrant are hereby abolished.

(6) Nothing in subsection (5) above affects any power of entry to deal with or prevent a breach of the peace.

18 Entry and search after arrest

(1) Subject to the following provisions of this section, a constable may enter and search any premises occupied or controlled by a person who is under arrest for an arrestable offence, if he has reasonable grounds for suspecting that there is on the premises evidence, other than items subject to legal privilege, that relates—

(a) to that offence; or

(b) to some other arrestable offence which is connected with or similar to that offence.

(2) A constable may seize and retain anything for which he may search under subsection (1) above.

(3) The power to search conferred by subsection (1) above is only a power to search to the extent that is reasonably required for the purpose of discovering such evidence.

(4) Subject to subsection (5) below, the powers conferred by this section may not be exercised unless an officer of the rank of inspector or above has authorised them in writing.

(5) A constable may conduct a search under subsection (1) above—

(a) before taking the person to a police station; and

(b) without obtaining an authorisation under subsection (4) above,

if the presence of that person at a place other than a police station is necssary for the effective investigation of the offence.

(6) If a constable conducts a search by virtue of subsection (5) above, he shall inform an officer of the rank of inspector or above that he has made the search as soon as practicable after he has made it.

(7) An officer who—

(a) authorises a search; or

(b) is informed of a search under subsection (6) above, shall make a record in writing—

(i) of the ground for the search; and

(ii) of the nature of the evidence that was sought.

(8) If the person who was in occupation or control of the premises at the time of the search is in police detention at the time the record is to be made, the officer shall make the record as part of his custody record.

Seizure etc.

19 General power of seizure etc

(1) The powers conferred by subsections (2), (3) and (4) below are exercisable by a constable who is lawfully on any premises.

(2) The constable may seize anything which is on the premises if he has reasonable grounds for believing—

(a) that it has been obtained in consequence of the commission of an offence; and

(b) that it is necessary to seize it in order to prevent it being concealed, lost, damaged, altered or destroyed.

(3) The constable may seize anything which is on the premises if he has reasonable grounds for believing—

(a) that it is evidence in relation to an offence which he is investigating or any other offence; and

(b) that it is necessary to seize it in order to prevent the evidence being concealed, lost, altered or destroyed.

(4) The constable may require any information which is contained in a computer and is accessible from the premises to be produced in a form in which it can be taken away and in which it is visible and legible if he has reasonable grounds for believing—

(a) that—

(i) it is evidence in relation to an offence which he is investigating or any other offence; or

(ii) it has been obtained in consequence of the commission of an offence; and

(b) that it is necessary to do so in order to prevent it being concealed, lost, tampered with or destroyed.

(5) The powers conferred by this section are in addition to any power otherwise conferred.

(6) No power of seizure conferred on a constable under any enactment (including an enactment contained in an Act passed after this Act) is to be taken to authorise the seizure of an item which the constable exercising the power has reasonable grounds for believing to be subject to legal privilege.

20 Extension of powers of seizure to computerised information

(1) Every power of seizure which is conferred by an enactment to which this section applies on a constable who has entered premises in the exercise of a power conferred by an enactment shall be construed as including a power to require any information contained in a computer and accessible from the premises to be produced in a form in which it can be taken away and in which it is visible and legible.

(2) This section applies—

(a) to any enactment contained in an Act passed before this Act;

(b) to sections 8 and 18 above;

(c) to paragraph 13 of Schedule 1 to this Act; and

(d) to any enactment contained in an Act passed after this Act.

21 Access and copying

(1) A constable who seizes anything in the exercise of a power conferred by any enactment, including an enactment contained in an Act passed after this Act, shall, if so requested by a person showing himself—

(a) to be the occupier of premises on which it was seized; or

(b) to have had custody or control of it immediately before the seizure,

provide that person with a record of what he seized.

(2) The officer shall provide the record within a reasonable time from the making of the request for it.

(3) Subject to subsection (8) below, if a request for permission to be granted access to anything which—

(a) has been seized by a constable; and

(b) is retained by the police for the purpose of investigating an offence,

is made to the officer in charge of the investigation by a person who had custody or control of the thing immediately before it was so seized or by someone acting on behalf of such a person the officer shall allow the person who made the request access to it under the supervision of a constable.

(4) Subject to subsection (8) below, if a request for a photograph or copy of any such thing is made to the officer in charge of the investigation by a person who had custody or control of the thing immediately before it was so seized, or by someone acting on behalf of such a person, the officer shall—

(a) allow the person who made the rquest access to it under the supervision of a constable for the purpose of photographing or copying it; or

(b) photograph or copy it, or cause it to be photographed or copied.

(5) A constable may also photograph or copy, or have photographed or copied, anything which he has power to seize, without a request being made under subsection (4) above.

(6) Where anything is photographed or copied under subsection (4)(b) above, the photograph or copy shall be supplied to the person who made the request.

(7) The photograph or copy shall be so supplied within a reasonable time from the making of the request.

(8) There is no duty under this section to grant access to, or to supply a photograph or copy of, anything if the officer in charge of the investigation for the purposes of which it was seized has reasonable grounds for believing that to do so would prejudice—

(a) that investigation;

(b) the investigation of an offence other than the offence for the purposes of investigating which the thing was seized; or

(c) any criminal proceedings which may be brought as a result of—

(i) the investigation of which he is in charge; or

(ii) any such investigation as is mentioned in paragraph (b) above.

22 Retention

(1) Subject to subsection (4) below, anything which has been seized by a constable or taken away by a constable following a requirement made by virtue of section 19 or 20 above may be retained so long as is necessary in all the circumstances.

(2) Without prejudice to the generality of subsection (1) above—

(a) anything seized for the purposes of a criminal investigation may be retained, except as provided by subsection (4) below—

(i) for use as evidence at a trial for an offence; or

(ii) for forensic examination or for investigation in connection with an offence; and

(b) anything may be retained in order to establish its lawful owner, where there are reasonable grounds for believing that it has been obtained in consequence of the commission of an offence.

(3) Nothing seized on the ground that it may be used—

(a) to cause physical injury to any person;

(b) to damage property;

(c) to interfere with evidence; or

(d) to assist in escape from police detention or lawful custody,

may be retained when the person from whom it was seized is no longer in police detention or the custody of a court or is in the custody of a court but has been released on bail.

(4) Nothing may be retained for either of the purposes mentioned in subsection (2)(a) above if a photograph or copy would be sufficient for that purpose.

(5) Nothing in this section affects any power of a court to make an order under section 1 of the Police (Property) Act 1897

23 * * * * *

PART III
ARREST

24 Arrest without warrant for arrestable offences

(1) The powers of summary arrest conferred by the following subsections shall apply—

(a) to offences for which the sentence is fixed by law;

(b) to offences for which a person of 21 years of age or over (not previously convicted) may be sentenced to imprisonment for a term of five years (or might be so sentenced but for the restrictions imposed by section 33 of the Magistrates' Courts Act 1980); and

(c) to the offences to which subsection (2) below applies,

and in this Act "arrestable offence" means any such offence.

(2) The offences to which this subsection applies are—

(a) offences for which a person may be arrested under the customs and excise Acts, as defined in section 1(1) of the Customs and Excise Management Act 1979;

(b) offences under the Official Secrets Acts 1911 and 1920 that are not arrestable offences by virtue of the term of imprisonment for which a person may be sentenced in respect of them;

(c) offences under section . . . 22 (causing prostitution of women) or 23 (procuration of girl under 21) of the Sexual Offences Act 1956;

(d) offences under section 12(1) (taking motor vehicle or other conveyance without authority etc) or 25(1) (going equipped for stealing, etc) of the Theft Act 1968; and

(e) offences under section 1 of the Public Bodies Corrupt Practices Act 1889 (corruption in office) or section 1 of the Prevention of Corruption Act 1906 (corrupt transactions with agents).

(3) Without prejudice to section 2 of the Criminal Attempts Act 1981, the powers of summary arrest conferred by the following subsections shall also apply to the offences of—

(a) conspiring to commit any of the offences mentioned in subsection (2) above;

(b) attempting to commit any such offence;

(c) inciting, aiding, abetting, counselling or procuring the commission of any such offence;

and such offences are also arrestable offences for the purposes of this Act.

(4) Any person may arrest without a warrant—

(a) anyone who is in the act of committing an arrestable offence;

(b) anyone whom he has reasonable grounds for suspecting to be committing such an offence.

(5) Where an arrestable offence has been committed, any person may arrest without a warrant—

(a) anyone who is guilty of the offence;

(b) anyone whom he has reasonable grounds for suspecting to be guilty of it.

(6) Where a constable has reasonable grounds for suspecting that an arrestable offence has been committed, he may arrest without a warrant anyone whom he has reasonable grounds for suspecting to be guilty of the offence.

(7) A constable may arrest without a warrant—

(a) anyone who is about to commit an arrestable offence;

(b) anyone whom he has reasonable grounds for suspecting to be about to commit an arrestable offence.

25 General arrest conditions

(1) Where a constable has reasonable grounds for suspecting that any offence which is not an arrestable offence has been committed or attempted, or is being committed or attempted, he may arrest the relevant person if it appears to him that service of a summons is impracticable or inappropriate because any of the general arrest conditions is satisfied.

(2) In this section "the relevant person" means any person whom the constable has reasonable grounds to suspect of having committed or having attempted to commit the offence or of being in the course of committing or attempting to commit it.

(3) The general arrest conditions are—

(a) that the name of the relevant person is unknown to, and cannot be readily ascertained by, the constable;

(b) that the constable has reasonable grounds for doubting whether a name furnished by the relevant person as his name is his real name;

(c) that—

(i) the relevant person has failed to furnish a satisfactory address for service;

or

(ii) the constable has reasonable grounds for doubting whether an address furnished by the relevant person is a satisfactory address for service;

(d) that the constable has reasonable grounds for believing that arrest is necessary to prevent the relevant person—

(i) causing physical injury to himself or any other person;

(ii) suffering physical injury;

(iii) causing loss of or damage to property;

(iv) committing an offence against public decency; or
(v) causing an unlawful obstruction of the highway;

(e) that the constable has reasonable grounds for believing that arrest is necessary to protect a child or other vulnerable person from the relevant person.

(4) For the purposes of subsection (3) above an address is a satisfactory address for service if it appears to the constable—

(a) that the relevant person will be at it for a sufficiently long period for it to be possible to serve him with a summons; or

(b) that some other person specified by the relevant person will accept service of a summons for the relevant person at it.

(5) Nothing in subsection (3)(d) above authorises the arrest of a person under sub-paragraph (iv) of that paragraph except where members of the public going about their normal business cannot reasonably be expected to avoid the person to be arrested.

(6) This section shall not prejudice any power of arrest conferred apart from this section.

26 Repeal of statutory powers of arrest without warrant or order

(1) Subject to subsection (2) below, so much of any Act (including a local Act) passed before this Act as enables a constable—

(a) to arrest a person for an offence without a warrant; or

(b) to arrest a person otherwise than for an offence without a warrant or an order of a court,

shall cease to have effect.

(2) Nothing in subsection (1) above affects the enactments specified in Schedule 2 to this Act.

27 * * * * *

28 Information to be given on arrest

(1) Subject to subsection (5) below, where a person is arrested, otherwise than by being informed that he is under arrest, the arrest is not lawful unless the person arrested is informed that he is under arrest as soon as is practicable after his arrest.

(2) Where a person is arrested by a constable, subsection (1) above applies regardless of whether the fact of the arrest is obvious.

(3) Subject to subsection (5) below, no arrest is lawful unless the person arrested is informed of the ground for the arrest at the time of, or as soon as is practicable after, the arrest.

(4) Where a person is arrested by a constable, subsection (3) above applies regardless of whether the ground for the arrest is obvious.

(5) Nothing in this section is to be taken to require a person to be informed—

(a) that he is under arrest; or

(b) of the ground for the arrest,

if it was not reasonably practicable for him to be so informed by reason of his having escaped from arrest before the information could be given.

29 Voluntary attendance at police station etc

Where for the purpose of assisting with an investigation a person attends voluntarily at a police station or at any other place where a constable is present or accompanies a constable to a police station or any such other place without having been arrested—

(a) he shall be entitled to leave at will unless he is placed under arrest;

(b) he shall be informed at once that he is under arrest if a decision is taken by a constable to prevent him from leaving at will.

30 Arrest elsewhere than at police station

(1) Subject to the following provisions of this section, where a person—

(a) is arrested by a constable for an offence; or

(b) is taken into custody by a constable after being arrested for an offence by a person other than a constable,

at any place other than a police station, he shall be taken to a police station by a constable as soon as practicable after the arrest.

(2) Subject to subsections (3) and (5) below, the police station to which an arrested person is taken under subsection (1) above shall be a designated police station.

(3)-(5) * * * * *

(6) If the first police station to which an arrested person is taken after his arrest is not a designated police station, he shall be taken to a designated police station not more than six hours after his arrival at the first police station unless he is released previously.

(7) A person arrested by a constable at a place other than a police station shall be released if a constable is satisfied, before the person arrested reaches a police station, that there are no grounds for keeping him under arrest.

(8), (9) * * * * *

(10) Nothing in subsection (1) above shall prevent a constable delaying taking a person who has been arrested to a police station if the presence of that person elsewhere is necessary in order to carry out such investigations as it is reasonable to carry out immediately.

(11)-(13) * * * * *

31 Arrest for further offence

Where—

(a) a person—

(i) has been arrested for an offence; and

(ii) is at a police station in consequence of that arrest; and

(b) it appears to a constable that, if he were released from that arrest, he would be liable to arrest for some other offence,

he shall be arrested for that other offence.

32 Search upon arrest

(1) A constable may search an arrested person, in any case where the person to be searched has been arrested at a place other than a police station, if the constable has reasonable grounds for believing that the arrested person may present a danger to himself or others.

(2) Subject to subsections (3) to (5) below, a constable shall also have power in any such case—

(a) to search the arrested person for anything—

(i) which he might use to assist him to escape from lawful custody; or

(ii) which might be evidence relating to an offence; and

(b) to enter and search any premises in which he was when arrested or immediately before he was arrested for evidence relating to the offence for which he has been arrested.

(3) The power to search conferred by subsection (2) above is only a power to search to the extent that is reasonably required for the purpose of discovering any such thing or any such evidence.

(4) The powers conferred by this section to search a person are not to be construed as authorising a constable to require a person to remove any of his clothing in public other than an outer coat, jacket or gloves.

(5) A constable may not search a person in the exercise of the power conferred by subsection (2)(a) above unless he has reasonable grounds for believing that the person to be searched may have concealed on him anything for which a search is permitted under that paragraph.

(6) A constable may not search premises in the exercise of the power conferred by subsection (2)(b) above unless he has reasonable grounds for believing that there is evidence for which a search is permitted under that paragraph on the premises.

(7) In so far as the power of search conferred by subsection (2)(b) above relates to premises consisting of two or more separate dwellings, it is limited to a power to search—

(a) any dwelling in which the arrest took place or in which the person arrested was immediately before his arrest; and

(b) any parts of the premises which the occupier of any such dwelling uses in common with the occupiers of any other dwellings comprised in the premises.

(8) A constable searching a person in the exercise of the power conferred by subsection (1) above may seize and retain anything he finds, if he has reasonable grounds for believing that the person searched might use it to cause physical injury to himself or to any other person.

(9) A constable searching a person in the exercise of the power conferred by subsection (2)(a) above may seize and retain anything he finds, other than an item subject to legal privilege, if he has reasonable grounds for believing—

(a) that he might use it to assist him to escape from lawful custody; or

(b) that it is evidence of an offence or has been obtained in consequence of the commission of an offence.

(10) Nothing in this section shall be taken to affect the power conferred by paragraph 6 of Schedule 3 to the Prevention of Terrorism (Temporary Provisions) Act 1984.

33 *****

PART IV
DETENTION

Detention — conditions and duration

34 Limitations on police detention

(1) A person arrested for an offence shall not be kept in police detention except in accordance with the provisions of this Part of this Act.

(2) Subject to subsection (3) below, if at any time a custody officer—

(a) becomes aware, in relation to any person in police detention, that the grounds for the detention of that person have ceased to apply; and

(b) is not aware of any other grounds on which the continued detention of that person could be justified under the provisions of this Part of this Act,

it shall be the duty of the custody officer, subject to subsection (4) below, to order his immediate release from custody.

(3) No person in police detention shall be released except on the authority of a custody officer at the police station where his detention was authorised or, if it was authorised at more than one station, a custody officer at the station where it was last authorised.

(4) A person who appears to the custody officer to have been unlawfully at large when he was arrested is not to be released under subsection (2) above.

(5), (6) *****

35 Designated police stations

(1) The chief officer of police for each police area shall designate the police stations in his area which, subject to sections 30(3) and (5) above, are to be the stations in that area to be used for the purpose of detention arrested persons.

(2) A chief officer's duty under subsection (1) above is to designate police stations appearing to him to provide enough accommodation for that purpose.

(3), (4) *****

36 Custody officers at police stations

(1) One or more custody officers shall be appointed for each designated police station.

(2) A custody officer for a designated police station shall be appointed—

(a) by the chief officer of police for the area in which the designated police station is situated; or

(b) by such other police officer as the chief officer of police for that area may direct.

(3) No officer may be appointed a custody officer unless he is of at least the rank of sergeant.

(4) An officer of any rank may perform the functions of a custody officer at a designated police station if a custody officer is not readily available to perform them.

(5) Subject to the following provisions of this section and to section 39(2) below, none of the functions of a custody officer in relation to a person shall be performed by an officer who at the time when the function falls to be performed is involved in the investigation of an offence for which that person is in police detention at that time.

(6)-(10) * * * * *

37 Duties of custody officer before charge

(1) Where—

(a) a person is arrested for an offence—

(i) without a warrant; or

(ii) under a warrant not endorsed for bail, or

(b) a person returns to a police station to answer to bail,

the custody officer at each police station where he is detained after his arrest shall determine whether he has before him sufficient evidence to charge that person with the offence for which he was arrested and may detain him at the police station for such period as is necessary to enable him to do so.

(2) If the custody officer determines that he does not have such evidence before him, the person arrested shall be released either on bail or without bail, unless the custody officer has reasonable grounds for believing that his detention without being charged is necessary to secure or preserve evidence relating to an offence for which he is under arrest or to obtain such evidence by questioning him.

(3) If the custody officer has reasonable grounds for so believing, he may authorise the person arrested to be kept in police detention.

(4) Where a custody officer authorises a person who has not been charged to be kept in police detention, he shall, as soon as is practicable, make a written record of the grounds for the detention.

(5) Subject to subsection (6) below, the written record shall be made in the presence of the person arrested who shall at that time be informed by the custody officer of the grounds for his detention.

(6) Subsection (5) above shall not apply where the person arrested is, at the time when the written record is made—

(a) incapable of understanding what is said to him;

(b) violent or likely to become violent; or

(c) in urgent need of medical attention.

(7) Subject to section 41(7) below, if the custody officer determines that he has before him sufficient evidence to charge the person arrested with the offence for which he was arrested, the person arrested—

(a) shall be charged; or

(b) shall be released without charge, either on bail or without bail.

(8) * * * * *

(9) If the person arrested is not in a fit state to be dealt with under subsection (7) above, he may be kept in police detention until he is.

(10) The duty imposed on the custody officer under subsection (1) above shall be carried out by him as soon as practicable after the person arrested arrives at the police station or, in the case of a person arrested at the police station, as soon as practicable after the arrest.

(11) Where—

(a) an arrested juvenile who was arrested without a warrant is not released under subsection (2) above; and

(b) it appears to the custody officer that a decision falls to be taken in pursuance of section 5(2) of the Children and Young Persons Act 1969 whether to lay an information in respect of an offence alleged to have been committed by the arrested juvenile,

it shall be the duty of the custody officer to inform him that such a decision falls to be taken and to specify the offence.

(12) It shall also be the duty of the custody officer—

(a) to take such steps as are practicable to ascertain the identity of a person responsible for the welfare of the arrested juvenile; and

(b) if—

(i) he ascertains the identity of any such person; and

(ii) it is practicable to give that person the information which subsection (11) above requires the custody officer to give to the arrested juvenile,

to give that person the information as soon as it is practicable to do so.

(13) For the purposes of subsection (12) above the persons who may be responsible for the welfare of an arrested juvenile are—

(a) his parent or guardian; and

(b) any other person who has for the time being assumed responsibility for his welfare.

(14)-(15) *****

38 Duties of custody officer after charge

(1) Where a person arrested for an offence otherwise than under a warrant endorsed for bail is charged with an offence, the custody officer shall order his release from police detention, either on bail or without bail, unless—

(a) if the person arrested is not an arrested juvenile—

(i) his name or address cannot be ascertained or the custody officer has reasonable grounds for doubting whether a name or address furnished by him as his name or address is his real name or address;

(ii) the custody officer has reasonable grounds for believing that the detention of the person arrested is necessary for his own protection or to prevent him from causing physical injury to any other person or from causing loss of or damage to property; or

(iii) the custody officer has reasonable grounds for believing that the person arrested will fail to appear in court to answer to bail or that his detention is necessary to prevent him from interfering with the administration of justice or with the investigation of offences or of a particular offence;

(b) if he is an arrested juvenile—

(i) any of the requirements of paragraph (a) above is satisfied; or

(ii) the custody officer has reasonable grounds for believing that he ought to be detained in his own interests.

(2) If the release of a person arrested is not required by subsection (1) above, the custody officer may authorise him to be kept in police detention.

(3) Where a custody officer authorises a person who has been charged to be kept in police detention, he shall, as soon as practicable, make a written record of the grounds for the detention.

(4) Subject to subsection (5) below, the written record shall be made in the presence of the person charged who shall at that time be informed by the custody officer of the grounds for his detention.

(5) Subsection (4) above shall not apply where the person charged is, at the time when the written record is made—

(a) incapable of understanding what is said to him;

(b) violent or likely to become violent; or

(c) in urgent need of medical attention.

(6) Where a custody officer authorises an arrested juvenile to be kept in police detention under subsection (1) above, the custody officer shall, unless he certifies that it is impracticable to do so, make arrangements for the arrested juvenile to be taken into the care of a local authority and detained by the authority; and it shall be lawful to detain him in pursuance of the arrangements.

(7)-(8) *****

39 Responsibilities in relation to persons detained

(1) Subject to subsection (2) and (4) below, it shall be the duty of the custody officer at a police station to ensure—

(a) that all persons in police detention at that station are treated in accordance with this Act and any code of practice issued under it and relating to the treatment of persons in police detention; and

(b) that all matters relating to such persons which are required by this Act or by such codes of practice to be recorded are recorded in the custody records relating to such persons.

(2)-(5) *****

(6) Where—

(a) an officer of higher rank than the custody officer gives directions relating to a person in police detention; and

(b) the directions are at variance—

(i) with any decision made or action taken by the custody officer in the performance of a duty imposed on him under this Part of this Act; or

(ii) with any decision or action which would be for the directions have been made or taken by him in the performance of such a duty,

the custody officer shall refer the matter at once to an officer of the rank of superintendent or above who is responsible for the police station for which the custody officer is acting as custody officer.

40 Review of police detention

(1) Reviews of the detention of each person in police detention in connection with the investigation of an offence shall be carried out periodically in accordance with the following provisions of this section—

(a) in the case of a person who has been arrested and charged, by the custody officer; and

(b) in the case of a person who has been arrested but not charged, by an officer of at least the rank of inspector who has not been directly involved in the investigation.

(2) The officer to whom it falls to carry out a review is referred to in this section as a "review officer".

(3) Subject to subsection (4) below—

(a) the first review shall be not later than six hours after the detention was first authorised;

(b) the second review shall be not later than nine hours after the first;

(c) subsequent reviews shall be at intervals of not more than nine hours.

(4) A review may be postponed—

(a) if, having regard to all the circumstances prevailing at the latest time for it specified in subsection (3) above, it is not practicable to carry out the review at that time;

(b) without prejudice to the generality of paragraph (a) above—

(i) if at that time the person in detention is being questioned by a police officer and the review officer is satisfied that an interruption of the questioning for the purpose of carrying out the review would prejudice the investigation in connection with which he is being questioned; or

(ii) if at that time no review officer is readily available.

(5) If a review is postponed under subsection (4) above it shall be carried out as soon as practicable after the latest time specified for it in subsection (3) above.

(6) If a review is carried out after postponement under subsection (4) above, the fact that it was so carried out shall not affect any requirement of this section as to the time at which any subsequent review is to be carried out.

(7) The review officer shall record the reasons for any postponement of a review in the custody record.

(8) Subject to subsection (9) below, where the person whose detention is under review has not been charged before the time of the review, section 37(1) to (6) above shall have effect in relation to him, but with the substitution—

(a) of references to the person whose detention is under review for references to the person arrested; and

(b) of references to the review officer for references to the custody officer.

(9) Where a person has been kept in police detention by virtue of section 37(9) above, section 37(1) to (6) shall not have effect in relation to him but it shall be the duty of the review officer to determine whether he is yet in a fit state.

(10) Where the person whose detention is under review has been charged before the time of the review, section 38(1) to (6) above shall have effect in relation to him, with the sutstitution of references to the person whose detention is under review for references to the person arrested.

(11) Where—

(a) an officer of higher rank than the review officer gives directions relating to a person in police detention; and

(b) the directions are at variance—

(i) with any decision made or action taken by the review officer in the performance of a duty imposed on him under this Part of this Act; or

(ii) with any decision or action which would but for the directions have been made or taken by him in the performance of such a duty,

the review officer shall refer the matter at once to an officer of the rank of superintendent or above who is responsible for the police station for which the review officer is acting as review officer in connection with the detention.

(12) Before determining whether to authorise a person's continued detention the review officer shall give—

(a) that person (unless he is asleep); or

(b) any solicitor representing him who is available at the time of the review,

an opportunity to make representations to him abut the detention.

(13), (14) * * * * *

41 Limits on period of detention without charge

(1) Subject to the following provisions of this section and to sections 42 and 43 below, a person shall not be kept in police detention for more than 24 hours without being charged.

(2) The time from which the period of detention of a person is to be calculated (in this Act referred to as "the relevant time")—

(a) in the case of a person to whom this paragraph applies, shall be—

(i) the time at which that person arrives at the relevant police station; or
(ii) the time 24 hours after the time of that person's arrest,
whichever is the earlier;
(b) in the case of a person arrested outside England and Wales, shall be—
(i) the time at which that person arrives at the first police station to which he is taken in the police area in England or Wales in which the offence for which he was arrested is being investigated; or
(ii) the time 24 hours after the time of that person's entry into England and Wales,
whichever is the earlier;
(c) in the case of a person who—
(i) attends voluntarily at a police station; or
(ii) accompanies a constable to a police station without having been arrested,
and is arrested at the police station, the time of his arrest;
(d) in any other case, except where subsection (5) below applies, shall be the time at which the person arrested arrives at the first police station to which he is taken after his arrest.
(3)-(6) * * * * *
(7) Subject to subsection (8) below, a person who at the expiry of 24 hours after the relevant time is in police detention and has not been charged shall be released at that time either on bail or without bail.
(8) Subsection (7) above does not apply to a person whose detention for more than 24 hours after the relevant time has been authorised or is otherwise permitted in accordance with section 42 or 43 below.
(9) * * * * *

42 Authorisation of continued detention

(1) Where a police officer of the rank of superintendent or above who is responsible for the police station at which a person is detained has reasonable grounds for believing that—
(a) the detention of that person without charge is necessary to secure or preserve evidence relating to an offence for which he is under arrest or to obtain such evidence by questioning him;
(b) an offence for which he is under arrest is a serious arrestable offence; and
(c) the investigation is being conducted diligently and expeditiously,
he may authorise the keeping of that person in police detention for a period expiring at or before 36 hours after the relevant time.
(2) Where an officer such as is mentioned in subsection (1) above has authorised the keeping of a person in police detention for a period expiring less than 36 hours after the relevant time, such an officer may authorise the keeping of that person in police detention for a further period expiring not more than 36 hours after that time if the conditions specified in subsection (1) above are still satisfied when he gives the authorisation.
(3) If it is proposed to transfer a person in police detention to another police area, the officer determining whether or not to authorise keeping him in detention under subsection (1) above shall have regard to the distance and the time the journey would take.
(4) No authorisation under subsection (1) above shall be given in respect of any person—
(a) more than 24 hours after the relevant time; or
(b) before the second review of his detention under section 40 above has been carried out.
(5) Where an officer authorises the keeping of a person in police detention under subsection (1) above, it shall be his duty—

(a) to inform that person of the grounds for his continued detention; and

(b) to record the grounds in that person's custody record.

(6) Before determining whether to authorise the keeping of a person in detention under subsection (1) or (2) above, an officer shall give—

(a) that person; or

(b) any solicitor representing him who is available at the time when it falls to the officer to determine whether to give the authorisation,

an opportunity to make representations to him about the detention.

(7), (8) * * * * *

(9) Where—

(a) an officer authorises the keeping of a person in detention under subsection (1) above; and

(b) at the time of the authorisation he has not yet exercised a right conferred on him by section 56 or 58 below,

the officer—

(i) shall inform him of that right;

(ii) shall decide whether he should be permitted to exercise it;

(iii) shall record the decision in his custody record; and

(iv) if the decision is to refuse to permit the exercise of the right, shall also record the grounds for the decision in that record.

(10) Where an officer has authorised the keeping of a person who has not been charged in detention under subsection (1) or (2) above, he shall be released from detention, either on bail or without bail, not later than 36 hours after the relevant time, unless—

(a) he has been charged with an offence; or

(b) his continued detention is authorised or otherwise permitted in accordance with section 43 below.

(11) A person released under subsection (10) above shall not be re-arrested without a warrant for the offence for which he was previously arrested unless new evidence justifying a further arrest has come to light since his release.

43 Warrants of further detention

(1) Where, on an application on oath made by a constable and supported by an information, a magistrate's court is satisfied that there are reasonable grounds for believing that the further detention of the person to whom the application relates is justified, it may issue a warrant of further detention authorising the keeping of that person in police detention.

(2) A court may not hear an application for a warrant of further detention unless the person to whom the application relates—

(a) has been furnished with a copy of the information; and

(b) has been brought before the court for the hearing.

(3) The person to whom the application relates shall be entitled to be legally represented at the hearing and, if he is not so represented but wishes to be so represented—

(a) the court shall adjourn the hearing to enable him to obtain representation; and

(b) he may be kept in police detention during the adjournment.

(4) A person's further detention is only justified for the purposes of this section or section 44 below if—

(a) his detention without charge is necessary to secure or preserve evidence relating to an offence for which he is under arrest or to obtain such evidence by questioning him;

(b) an offence for which he is under arrest is a serious arrestable offence; and

(c) the investigation is being conducted diligently and expeditiously.

(5) Subject to subsection (7) below, an application for a warrant of further detention may be made—

(a) at any time before the expiry of 36 hours after the relevant time; or
(b) in a case where—
(i) it is not practicable for the magistrates' court to which the application will be made to sit at the expiry of 36 hours after the relevant time; but
(ii) the court will sit during the 6 hours following the end of that period, at any time before the expiry of the said 6 hours.

(6) In a case to which subsection (5)(b) above applies—
(a) the person to whom the application relates may be kept in police detention until the application is heard; and
(b) the custody officer shall make a note in that person's custody record—
(i) of the fact that he was kept in police detention for more than 36 hours after the relevant time; and
(ii) of the reason why he was so kept.

(7) If—
(a) an application for a warrant of further detention is made after the expiry of 36 hours after the relevant time; and
(b) it appears to the magistrates' court that it would have been reasonable for the police to make it before the expiry of that period,
the court shall dismiss the application.

(8) Where on an application such as is mentioned in subsection (1) above a magistrates' court is not satisfied that there are reasonable grounds for believing that the further detention of the person to whom the application relates is justified, it shall be its duty—
(a) to refuse the application; or
(b) to adjourn the hearing of it until a time not later than 36 hours after the relevant time.

(9) The person to whom the application relates may be kept in police detention during the adjournment.

(10) A warrant of further detention shall—
(a) state the time at which it is issued;
(b) authorise the keeping in police detention of the person to whom it relates for the period stated in it.

(11) Subject to subsection (12) below, the period stated in a warrant of further detention shall be such period as the magistrates' court thinks fit, having regard to the evidence before it.

(12) The period shall not be longer than 36 hours.

(13) * * * * *

(14) Any information submitted in support of an application under this section shall state—
(a) the nature of the offence for which the person to whom the application relates has been arrested;
(b) the general nature of the evidence on which that person was arrested;
(c) what inquiries relating to the offence have been made by the police and what further inquiries are proposed by them;
(d) the reasons for believing the continued detention of that person to be necessary for the purposes of such further inquiries.

(15) Where an application under this section is refused, the person to whom the application relates shall forthwith be charged or, subject to subsection (16) below, released, either on bail or without bail.

(16) A person need not be released under subsection (15) above—
(a) before the expiry of 24 hours after the relevant time; or
(b) before the expiry of any longer period for which his continued detention is or has been authorised under section 42 above.

(17) Where an application under this section is refused, no further application shall be made under this section in repect of the person to whom the refusal relates, unless supported by evidence which has come to light since the refusal.

(18) Where a warrant of further detention is issued, the person to whom it relates shall be released from police detention, either on bail or without bail, upon or before the expiry of the warrant unless he is charged.

(19) A person released under subsection (18) above shall not be re-arrested without a warrant for the offence for which he was previously arrested unless new evidence justifying a further arrest has come to light since his release.

44 Extension of warrants of further detention

(1) On an application on oath made by a constable and supported by an information a magistrates' court may extend a warrant of further detention issued under section 43 above if it is satisfied that there are reasonable grounds for believing that the further detention of the person to whom the application relates is justified.

(2) Subject to subsection (3) below, the period for which a warrant of further detention may be extended shall be such period as the court thinks fit, having regard to the evidence before it.

(3) The period shall not—

(a) be longer than 36 hours; or

(b) end later than 96 hours after the relevant time.

(4) Where a warrant of further detention has been extended under subsection (1) above, or further extended under this subsection, for a period ending before 96 hours after the relevant time, on an application such as is mentioned in that subsection a magistrates' court may further extend the warrant if it is satisfied as there mentioned; and subsections (2) and (3) above apply to such further extensions as they apply to extensions under subsection (1) above.

(5) A warrant of further detention shall, if extended or further extended under this section, be endorsed with a note of the period of the extension.

(6) Subsections (2), (3), and (14) of section 43 above shall apply to an application made under this section as they apply to an application made under that section.

(7), (8) * * * * *

45 Detention before charge — supplementary

(1) In sections 43 and 44 of this Act "magistrates' court" means a court consisting of two or more justices of the peace sitting otherwise than in open court.

(2) Any reference in this Part of this Act to a period of time or a time of day is to be treated as approximate only.

Detention — miscellaneous

46 Detention after charge

(1) Where a person—

(a) is charged with an offence; and

(b) after being charged—

(i) is kept in police detention; or

(ii) is detained by a local authority in pursuance of arrangements made under section 38(6) above,

he shall be brought before a magistrates' court in accordance with the provisions of this section.

(2) If he is to be brought before a magistrates' court for the petty sessions area in which the police station at which he was charged is situated, he shall be brought before such a court as soon as is practicable and in any event not later than the first sitting after he is charged with the offence.

(3) If no magistrates' court for that area is due to sit either on the day on which he is charged or on the next day, the custody officer for the police station at which he was charged shall inform the clerk to the justices for the area that there is a person in the area to whom subsection (2) above applies.

(4) If the person charged is to be brought before a magistrates' court for a petty sessions area other than that in which the police station at which he was charged is situated, he shall be removed to that area as soon as is practicable and brought before such a court as soon as is practicable after this arrival in the area and in any event not later than the first sitting of a magistrates' court for that area after this arrival in the area.

(5) If no magistrates' court for that area is due to sit either on the day on which he arrives in the area or on the next day—

(a) he shall be taken to a police station in the area; and

(b) the custody officer at that station shall inform the clerk to the justices for the for the area that there is a person in the area to whom subsection (4) applies.

(6) Subject to subsection (8) below, where a clerk to the justices for a petty sessions area has been informed—

(a) under subsection (3) above that there is a person in the area to whom subsection (2) above applies; or

(b) under subsection (5) above that there is a person in the area to whom subsection (4) above applies,

the clerk shall arrange for a magistrates' court to sit not later than the day next following the relevant day.

(7) In this section "the relevant day"—

(a) in relation to a person who is to be brought before a magistrates' court for the petty sessions area in which the police station at which he was charged is situated, means the day on which he was charged; and

(b) in relation to a person who is to be brought before a magistrates' court for any other petty sessions area, means the day on which he arrives in the area.

(8) Where the day next following the relevant day is Christmas Day, Good Friday or a Sunday, the duty of the clerk under subsection (6) above is a duty to arrange for a magistrates' court to sit not later than the first day after the relevant day which is not one of those days.

(9) * * * * *

47 Bail after arrest

Subject to subsection (2) below, a release on bail of a person under this Part of this Act shall be a release on bail granted in accordance with the Bail Act 1976.

(2) Nothing in the Bail Act 1976 shall prevent the re-arrest without warrant of a person released on bail subject to a duty to attend at a police station if new evidence justifying a further arrest has come to light since his release.

(3)-(8) * * * * *

48-52 * * * * *

PART V
QUESTIONING AND TREATMENT OF PERSONS BY POLICE

53 Abolition of certain powers of constables to search persons

(1) Subject to subsection (2) below, there shall cease to have effect any Act (including a local Act) passed before this Act in so far as it authorises—

(a) any search by a constable of a person in police detention at a police station; or

(b) an intimate search of a person by a constable;

and any rule of common law which authorises a search such as is mentioned in paragraph (a) or (b) above is abolished.

(2) Nothing in subsection (1)(a) above shall affect paragraph 6(2) of Schedule 3 to the Prevention of Terrorism (Temporary Provisions) Act 1984.

54 Search of detained persons

(1) The custody officer at a police station shall ascertain and record or cause to be recorded everything which a person has with him when he is—

(a) brought to the station after being arrested elsewhere or after being committed to custody by an order or sentence of a court; or

(b) arrested at the station after—

(i) having attended voluntarily there; or

(ii) having accompanied a constable there without having been arrested.

(2) In the case of an arrested person the record shall be made as part of his custody record.

(3) Subject to subsection (4) below, a custody officer may seize and retain any such thing or cause any such thing to be seized and retained.

(4) Clothes and personal effects may only be seized if the custody officer—

(a) believes that the person from whom they are seized may use them—

(i) to cause physical injury to himself or any other person;

(ii) to damage property;

(iii) to interfere with evidence; or

(iv) to assist him to escape; or

(b) has reasonable grounds for believing that they may be evidence relating to an offence.

(5) Where anything is seized, the person from whom it is seized shall be told the reason for the seizure unless he is—

(a) violent or likely to become violent; or

(b) incapable of understanding what is said to him.

(6) Subject to subsection (7) below, a person may be searched if the custody officer considers it necessary to enable him to carry out his duty under subsection (1) above and to the extent that the custody officer considers necessary for that purpose.

(7) An intimate search may not be conducted under this section.

(8) A search under this section shall be carried out by a constable.

(9) The constable carrying out a search shall be of the same sex as the person searched.

55 Intimate searches

(1) Subject to the following provisions of this section, if an officer of at least the rank of superintendent has reasonable grounds for believing—

(a) that a person who has been arrested and is in police detention may have concealed on him anything which—

(i) he could use to cause physical injury to himself or others; and

(ii) he might so use while he is in police detention or in the custody of a court; or

(b) that such a person—

(i) may have a Class A drug concealed on him; and

(ii) was in possession of it with the appropriate criminal intention before his arrest,

he may authorise such a search of that person.

(3) *****

(4) An intimate search which is only a drug offence search shall be by way of examination by a suitably qualified person.

(5) Except as provided by subsection (4) above, an intimate search shall be by way of examination by a suitably qualified person unless an officer of at least the rank of superintendent considers that this is not practicable.

(6) An intimate search which is not carried out as mentioned in subsection (5) above shall be carried out by a constable.

(7) A constable may not carry out an intimate search of a person of the opposite sex.

(8) No intimate search may be carried out except—

(a) at a police station;

(b) at a hospital;

(c) at a registered medical practitioner's surgery; or

(d) at some other place used for medical purposes.

(9) An intimate search which is only a drug offence search may not be carried out at a police station.

(10) If an intimate search of a person is carried out, the custody record relating to him shall state—

(a) which parts of his body were searched; and

(b) why they were searched.

(11) *****

(12) This custody officer at a police station may seize and retain anything which is found on an intimate search of a person, or cause any such thing to be seized and retained—

(a) if he believes that the person from whom it is seized may use it—

(i) to cause physical injury to himself or any other person;

(ii) to damage property;

(iii) to interfere with evidence; or

(iv) to assist him to escape; or

(b) if he has reasonable grounds for believing that it may be evidence relating to an offence.

(13) Where anything is seized under this section, the person from whom it is seized shall be told the reason for the seizure unless he is—

(a) violent or likely to become violent; or

(b) incapable of understanding what is said to him.

(14)-(16) *****

(17) In this section—

*****

"Class A drug" has the meaning assigned to it by section 2(1)(b) of the Misuse of Drugs Act 1971;

"drug offence search" means an intimate search for a Class A drug which an officer has authorised by virtue of subsection (1)(b) above; and

"suitably qualified person" means—

(a) a registered medical practitioner; or

(b) a registered nurse.

56 Right to have someone informed when arrested

(1) Where a person has been arrested and is being held in custody in a police station or other premises, he shall be entitled, if he so requests, to have one friend or relative or other person who is known to him or who is likely to take an interest in his welfare told, as soon as is practicable except to the extent that delay is permitted by this section, that he has been arrested and is being detained there.

(2) Delay is only permitted—

(a) in the case of a person who is in police detention for a serious arrestable offence; and

(b) if an officer of at least the rank of superintendent authorises it.

(3) In any case the person in custody must be permitted to exercise the right conferred by subsection (1) above within 36 hours from the relevant time as defined in section 41(2) above.

(4) *****

(5) [Subject to subsection (5A) below] an officer may only authorise delay where he has reasonable grounds for believing that telling the named person of the arrest—

(a) will lead to interference with or harm to evidence connected with a serious arrestable offence or interference with or physical injury to other persons; or

(b) will lead to the alerting of other persons suspected of having committed such an offence but not yet arrested for it; or

(c) will hinder the recovery of any property obtained as a result of such an offence.

[(5A) An officer may also authorise delay where the serious arrestable offence is a drug trafficking offence and the officer has reasonable grounds for believing—

(a) that the detained person has benefited from drug trafficking, and

(b) that the recovery of the value of that person's proceeds of drug trafficking will be hindered by telling the named person of the arrest.]

(6) If a delay is authorised—

(a) the detained person shall be told the reason for it; and

(b) the reason shall be noted on his custody record.

(7) The duties imposed by subsection (6) above shall be performed as soon as is practicable.

(8) The rights conferred by this section on a person detained at a police station or other premises are exercisable whenever he is transferred from one place to another; and this section applies to each subsequent occasion on which they are exercisable as it applies to the first such occasion.

(9) There may be no further delay in permitting the exercise of the right conferred by subsection (1) above once the reason for authorising delay ceases to subsist.

(10) In the foregoing provisions of this section references to a person who has been arrested include references to a person who has been detained under the terrorism provisions and "arrest" includes detention under those provisions.

(11) In its application to a person who has been arrested or detained under the terrorism provisions—

(a) subsection (2)(a) above shall have effect as if for the words "for a serious arrestable offence" there were substituted the words "under the terrorism provisions";

(b) subsection (3) above shall have effect as if for the words from "within" onwards there were substituted the words "before the end of the period beyond which he may no longer be detained without the authority of the Secretary of State"; and

(c) subsection (5) above shall have effect as if at the end there were added "or

(d) will lead to interference with the gathering of information about the commission, preparation or instigation of an act of terrorism; or

(e) by alerting any person, will make it more difficult—

(i) to prevent an act of terrorism; or

(ii) to secure the apprehension, prosecution or conviction of any person in connection with the commission, preparation or instigation of an act of terrorism.".

57 * * * * *

58 Access to legal advice

(1) A person arrested and held in custody in a police station or other premises shall be entitled, if he so requests, to consult a solicitor privately at any time.

(2) Subject to subsection (3) below, a request under subsection (1) above and the time at which it was made shall be recorded in the custody record.

(3) Such a request need not be recorded in the custody record of a person who makes it at a time while he is at a court after being charged with an offence.

(4) If a person makes such a request, he must be permitted to consult a solicitor as soon as is practicable except to the extent that delay is permitted by this section.

(5) In any case he must be permitted to consult a solicitor within 36 hours from the relevant time, as defined in section 41(2) above.

(6) Delay in compliance with a request is only permitted—

(a) in the case of a person who is in police detention for a serious arrestable offence; and

(b) if an officer of at least the rank of superintendent authorises it.

(7) An officer may give an authorisation under subsection (6) above orally or in writing but, if he gives it orally, he shall confirm it in writing as soon as is practicable.

(8) [Subject to subsection (8A) below] an officer may only authorise delay where he has reasonable grounds for believing that the exercise of the right conferred by subsection (1) above at the time when the person detained desires to exercise it—

(a) will lead to interference with or harm to evidence connected with a serious arrestable offence or interference with or physical injury to other persons; or

(b) will lead to the alerting of other persons suspected of having committed such an offence but not yet arrested for it; or

(c) will hinder the recovery of any property obtained as a result of such an offence.

[(8A) An officer may also authorise delay where the serious arrestable offence is a drug trafficking offence and the officer has reasonable grounds for believing—

(a) that the detained person has benefited from drug trafficking, and

(b) that the recovery of the value of that person's proceeds of drug trafficking will be hindered by the exercise of the right conferred by subsection (1) above.]

(9) If delay is authorised—

(a) the detained person shall be told the reason for it; and

(b) the reason shall be noted on his custody record.

(10) The duties imposed by subsection (9) above shall be performed as soon as is practicable.

(11) There may be no further delay in permitting the exercise of the right conferred by subsection (1) above once the reason for authorising delay ceases to subsist.

(12) The reference in subsection (1) above to a person arrested includes a reference to a person who has been detained under the terrorism provisions.

(13) In the application of this section to a person who has been arrested or detained under the terrorism provisions—

(a) subsection (5) above shall have effect as if for the words from "within" onwards there were substituted the words "before the end of the period beyond which he may no longer be detained without the authority of the Secretary of State";

(b) subsection (6)(a) above shall have effect as if for the words "for a serious arrestable offence" there were substituted the words "under the terrorism provisions"; and

(c) subsection (8) above shall have effect as if at the end there were added "or

(d) will lead to interference with the gathering of information about the commission, preparation or instigation of acts of terrorism; or

(e) by alerting any person, will make it more difficult—

(i) to prevent an act of terrorism; or

(ii) to secure the apprehension, prosecution or conviction of any person in connection with the commission, preparation or instigation of an act of terrorism.".

(14) If an officer of appropriate rank has reasonable grounds for believing that, unless he gives a direction under subsection (15) below, the exercise by a person arrested or detained under the terrorism provisions of the right conferred by subsection (1) above will have any of the consequences specified in subsection (8) above (as it has effect by virtue of subsection (13) above), he may give a direction under that subsection.

(15) A direction under this subsection is a direction that a person desiring to exercise the right conferred by subsection (1) above may only consult a solicitor in the sight and hearing of a qualified officer of the uniformed branch of the force of which the officer giving the direction is a member.

(16) An officer is qualified for the purpose of subsection (15) above if—

(a) he is of at least the rank of inspector; and

(b) in the opinion of the officer giving the direction he has no connection with the case.

(17) An officer is of appropriate rank to give a direction under subsection (15) above if he is of at least the rank of Commander or Assistant Chief Constable.

(18) A direction under subsection (15) above shall cease to have effect once the reason for giving it ceases to subsist.

59 *****

60 Tape-recording of interviews

(1) It shall be the duty of the Secretary of State—

(a) to issue a code of practice in connection with the tape-recording of interviews of persons suspected of the commission of criminal offences which are held by police officers at police stations; and

(b) to make an order requiring the tape-recording of interviews of persons suspected of the commission of criminal offences, or of such descriptions of criminal offences as may be specified in the order, which are so held, in accordance with the code as it has effect for the time being.

(2) An order under subsection (1) above shall be made by statutory instrument and shall be subject to annulment in pursuance of a resolution of either House of Parliament.

61 Fingerprinting

(1) Except as provided by this section no person's fingerprints may be taken without the appropriate consent.

(2) Consent to the taking of a person's fingerprints must be in writing if it is given at a time when he is at a police station.

(3) The fingerprints of a person detained at a police station may be taken without the appropriate consent—

(a) if an officer of at least the rank of superintendent authorises then to be taken; or

(b) if—

(i) he has been charged with a recordable offence or informed that he will be reported for such an offence; and

(ii) he has not had his fingerprints taken in the course of the investigation of the offence by the police.

(4) An officer may only give an authorisation under subsection (3)(a) above if he has reasonable grounds—

(a) for suspecting the involvement of the person whose fingerprints are to be taken in a criminal offence; and

(b) for believing that his fingerprints will tend to confirm or disprove his involvement.

(5) An officer may give an authorisation under subsection (3)(a) above orally or in writing but, if he gives it orally, he will confirm it in writing as soon as is practicable.

(6) Any person's fingerprints may be taken without the appropriate consent if he has been convicted of a recordable offence.

(7) In a case where by virtue of subsection (3) or (6) above a person's fingerprints are taken without the appropriate consent—

(a) he shall be told the reason before his fingerprints are taken; and

(b) the reason shall be recorded as soon as is practicable after the fingerprints are taken.

(8) If he is detained at a police station when the fingerprints are taken, the reason for taking them shall be recorded on his custody record.

(9) Nothing in this section—

(a) affects any power conferred by paragraph 18(2) of Schedule 2 to the Immigration Act 1971; or

(b) applies to a person arrested or detained under the terrorism provisions.

62 Intimate samples

(1) An intimate sample may be taken from a person in police detention only—

(a) if a police officer of at least the rank of superintendent authorises it to be taken; and

(b) if the appropriate consent is given.

(2) An officer may only give an authorisation if he has reasonable grounds—

(a) for suspecting the involvement of the person from whom the sample is to be taken in a serious arrestable offence; and

(b) for believing that the sample will tend to confirm or disprove his involvement.

(3) An officer may give an authorisation under subsection (1) above orally or in writing but, if he gives it orally, he shall confirm it in writing as soon as is practicable.

(4) The appropriate consent must be given in writing.

(5) Where—

(a) an authorisation has been given; and

(b) it is proposed that an intimate sample shall be taken in pursuance of the authorisation,

an officer shall inform the person from whom the sample is to be taken—

(i) of the giving of the authorisation; and

(ii) of the grounds for giving it.

(6) The duty imposed by subsection (5)(ii) above includes a duty to state the nature of the offence in which it is suspected that the person from whom the sample is to be taken has been involved.

(7) If an intimate sample is taken from a person—

(a) the authorisation by virtue of which it was taken;

(b) the grounds for giving the authorisation; and

(c) the fact that the appropriate consent was given,

shall be recorded as soon as is practicable after the sample is taken.

(8) If an intimate sample is taken from a person detained at a police station, the matters required to be recorded by subsection (7) above shall be recorded in his custody record.

(9) An intimate sample, other than a sample of urine or saliva, may only be taken from a person by a registered medical practitioner.

(10) Where the appropriate consent to the taking of an intimate sample from a person was refused without good cause, in any proceedings against that person for an offence—

(a) the court, in determining—

(i) whether to commit that person for trial; or

(ii) whether there is a case to answer; and

(b) the court or jury, in determining whether that person is guilty of the offence charged,

may draw such inferences from the refusal as appear proper; and the refusal may, on the basis of such inferences, be treated as, or as capable of amounting to corroboration of any evidence against the person in relation to which the refusal is material.

(11) Nothing in this section affects sections 5 to 12 of the Road Traffic Act 1972.

63 Other samples

(1) Except as provided by this section, a non-intimate sample may not be taken from a person without the appropriate consent.

(2) Consent to the taking of a non-intimate sample must be given in writing.

(3) A non-intimate sample may be taken from a person without the appropriate consent if—

(a) he is in police detention or is being held in custody by the police on the authority of a court; and

(b) an officer of at least the rank of superintendent authorises it to be taken without the appropriate consent.

(4) An officer may only give an authorisation under subsection (3) above if he has reasonable grounds—

(a) for suspecting the involvement of the person from whom the sample is to be taken in a serious arrestable offence; and

(b) for believing that the sample will tend to confirm or disprove his involvement.

(5) An officer may give an authorisation under subsection (3) above orally or in writing but, if he gives it orally, he shall confirm it in writing as soon as is practicable.

(6) Where—

(a) an authorisation has been given; and

(b) it is proposed that a non-intimate sample shall be taken in pursuance of the authorisation,

an officer shall inform the person from whom the sample is to be taken—

(i) of the giving of the authorisation; and

(ii) of the grounds for giving it.

(7) the duty imposed by subsection (6)(ii) above includes a duty to state the nature of the offence in which it is suspected that the person from whom the sample is to be taken has been involved.

(8) If a non-intimate sample is taken from a person by virtue of subsection (3) above—

(a) the authorisation by virtue of which it was taken; and

(b) the grounds for giving the authorisation,

shall be recorded as soon as is practicable after the sample is taken.

(9) If a non-intimate sample is taken from a person detained at a police station, the matters required to be recorded by subsection (8) above shall be recorded in his custody record.

64 Destruction of fingerprints and samples

(1) If—

(a) fingerprints or samples are taken from a person in connection with the investigation of an offence; and

(b) he is cleared of that offence,

they must be destroyed as soon as is practicable after the conclusion of the proceedings.

(2) If—

(a) fingerprints or samples are taken from a person in connection with such an investigation; and

(b) it is decided that he shall not be prosecuted for the offence and he has not admitted it and been dealt with by way of being cautioned by a constable,

they must be destroyed as soon as is practicable after that decision is taken.

(3) If—

(a) fingerprints or samples are taken from a person in connection with the investigation of an offence; and

(b) that person is not suspected of having committed the offence,

they must be destroyed as soon as they have fulfilled the purpose for which they were taken.

(4)-(7) * * * * *

65 Part V — supplementary

In this Part of this Act—

"appropriate consent" means—

(a) in relation to a person who has attained the age of 17 years, the consent of that person;

(b) in relation to a person who has not attained that age but has attained the age of 14 years, the consent of that person and his parent or guardian; and

(c) in relation to a person who has not attained the age of 14 years, the consent of his parent or guardian;

"fingerprints" includes palm prints;

"intimate sample" means a sample of blood, semen or any other tissue fluid, urine, saliva or pubic hair, or a swab taken from a person's body orifice;

"non-intimate sample" means—

(a) a sample of hair other than pubic hair;

(b) a sample taken from a nail or from under a nail;

(c) a swab taken from any part of a person's body other than a body orifice;

(d) a footprint or a similar impression of any part of a person's body other than a part of his hand;

"the terrorism provisions" means—

(a) section 12(1) of the Prevention of Terrorism (Temporary Provisions) Act 1984; and

(b) any provision conferring a power of arrest or detention and contained in an order under section 13 of that Act; and

"terrorism" has the meaning assigned to it by section 14(1) of that Act.

PART VI
CODES OF PRACTICE — GENERAL

66 Codes of practice

The Secretary of State shall issue codes of practice in connection with—

(a) the exercise by police officers of statutory powers—

(i) to search a person without first arresting him; or

(ii) to search a vehicle without making an arrest;

(b) the detention, treatment, questioning and indication of persons by police officers;

(c) searches of premises by police officers; and

(d) the seizure of property found by police officers on persons or premises.

67 Codes of practice — supplementary

(1) When the Secretary of State proposes to issue a code of practice to which this section applies, he shall prepare and publish a draft of that code, shall consider any representations made to him about the draft and may modify the draft accordingly.

(2) This section applies to a code of practice under section 60 or 66 above.

(3) The Secretary of State shall lay before both Houses of Parliament a draft of any code of practice prepared by him under this section.

(4) When the Secretary of State has laid the draft of a code before Parliament, he may bring the code into operation by order made by statutory instrument.

(5) No order under subsection (4) above shall have effect until approved by a resolution of each House of Parliament.

(6) An order bringing a code of practice into operation may contain such transitional provisions or savings as appear to the Secretary of State to be necessary or expedient in connection with the code of practice thereby brought into operation.

(7) The Secretary of State may from time to time revise the whole or any part of a code of practice to which this section applies and issue that revised code; and the foregoing provisions of this section shall apply (with appropriate modifications) to such a revised code as they apply to the first issue of a code.

(8) A police officer shall be liable to disciplinary proceedings for a failure to comply with any provision of such a code, unless such proceedings are precluded by section 104 below.

(9) Persons other than police officers who are charged with the duty of investigating offences or charging offenders shall in the discharge of that duty have regard to any relevant provision of such a code.

(10) A failure on the part—

(a) of a police officer to comply with any provision of such a code; or

(b) of any person other than a police officer who is charged with the duty of investigating offences or charging offenders to have regard to any relevant provision of such a code in the discharge of the duty,

shall not of itself render him liable to any criminal or civil proceedings.

(11) In all criminal and civil proceedings any such code shall be admissible in evidence; and if any provision of such a code appears to the court or tribunal conducting the proceedings to be relevant to any question arising in the proceedings it shall be taken into account in determining that question.

(12) * * * * *

PART VIII
EVIDENCE IN CRIMINAL PROCEEDINGS — GENERAL

68-75 * * * * *

Confessions

76 Confessions

(1) In any proceedings a confession made by an accused person may be given in evidence against him in so far as it is relevant to any matter in issue in the proceedings and is not excluded by the court in pursuance of this section.

(2) If, in any proceedings where the prosecution proposes to give in evidence a confession made by an accused person, it is represented to the court that the confession was or may have been obtained—

(a) by oppression of the person who made it; or

(b) in consequence of anything said or done which was likely, in the circumstances existing at the time, to render unreliable any confession which might be made by him in consequence thereof,

the court shall not allow the confession to be given in evidence against him except in so far as the prosecution proves to the court beyond reasonable doubt that the confession (notwithstanding that it may be true) was not obtained as aforesaid.

(3) In any proceedings where the prosecution proposes to give in evidence a confession made by an accused person, the court may of its own motion require the prosecution, as a condition of allowing it to do so, to prove that the confession was not obtained as mentioned in subsection (2) above.

(4) The fact that a confession is wholly or partly excluded in pursuance of this section shall not affect the admissibility in evidence—

(a) of any facts discovered as a result of the confession; or

(b) where the confession is relevant as showing that the accused speaks, writes or expresses himself in a particular way, of so much of the confession as is necessary to show that he does so.

(5) Evidence that a fact to which this subsection applies was discovered as a result of a statement made by an accused person shall not be admissible unless evidence of how it was discovered is given by him or on his behalf.

(6) Subsection (5) above applies—

(a) to any fact discovered as a result of a confession which is wholly excluded in pursuance of this section; and

(b) to any fact discovered as a result of a confession which is partly so excluded, if that fact is discovered as a result of the excluded part of the confession.

(7) Nothing in Part VII of this Act shall prejudice the admissibility of a confession made by an accused person.

(8) In this section "oppression" includes torture, inhuman or degrading treatment, and the use or threat of violence (whether or not amounting to torture).

77 Confessions by mentally handicapped persons

(1) Without prejudice to the general duty of the court at a trial on indictment to direct the jury on any matter on which it appears to the court appropriate to do so, where at such a trial—

(a) the case against the accused depends wholly or substantially on a confession by him; and

(b) the court is satisfied—

(i) that he is mentally handicapped; and

(ii) that the confession was not made in the presence of an independent person,

the court shall warn the jury that there is special need for caution before convicting the accused in reliance on the confession, and shall explain that the need arises because of the circumstances mentioned in paragraphs (a) and (b) above, but in doing so shall not be required to use any particular form of words.

(2) In any case where at the summary trial of a person for an offence it appears to the court that a warning under subsection (1) above would be required if the trial were on indictment, the court shall treat the case as one in which there is a special need for caution before convicting the accused on his confession.

(3) In this section—

"independent person" does not include a police officer or a person employed for, or engaged on police purposes;

"mentally handicapped", in relation to a person, means that he is in a state of arrested or incomplete development of mind which includes significant impairment of intelligence and social functioning; and

"police purposes" has the meaning assigned to it by section 64 of the Police Act 1964.

Note The Police and Criminal Evidence Act 1984 (Application to Customs and Excise) Order 1985 (SI 1985 No. 1800), Art. 10, provides that subsection (3) above "shall be modified to the extent that the definition of 'independent person' shall, in addition to the persons mentioned therein, also include an officer or any other person acting under the authority of the Commissioners of Customs and Excise".

Miscellaneous

78 Exclusion of unfair evidence

(1) In any proceedings the court may refuse to allow evidence on which the prosecution proposes to rely to be given if it appears to the court that, having regard to all the circumstances, including the circumstances in which the evidence was obtained, the admission of the evidence would have such an adverse effect on the fairness of the proceedings that the court ought not to admit it.

(2) Nothing in this section shall prejudice any rule of law requiring a court to exclude evidence.

79-81 * * * * *

Part VIII — supplementary

82 Part VIII — interpretation

(1) In this Part of this Act—

"confession" includes any statement wholly or partly adverse to the person who made it, whether made to a person in authority or not and whether made in words or otherwise;

*****

(2) *****

(3) Nothing in this Part of this Act shall prejudice any power of a court to exclude evidence (whether by preventing questions from being put or otherwise) at its discretion.

PART IX
POLICE COMPLAINTS AND DISCIPLINE

The Police Complaints Authority

83 Establishment of the Police Complaints Authority

(1) There shall be an authority to be known as "the Police Complaints Authority" and in this Part of this Act referred to as "the Authority."

(2) Schedule 4 to this Act shall have effect in relation to the Authority.

(3) The Police Complaints Board is hereby abolished.

Handling of complaints etc

84 Preliminary

(1) Where a complaint is submitted to the chief officer of police for a police area, it shall be his duty to take any steps that appear to him to be desirable for the purpose of obtaining or preserving evidence relating to the conduct complained of.

(2) After performing the duties imposed on him by subsection (1) above, the chief officer shall determine whether he is the appropriate authority in relation to the officer against whom the complaint was made.

(3) If he determines that he is not the appropriate authority, it shall be his duty—

(a) to send the complaint or, if it was made orally, particulars of it, to the appropriate authority; and

(b) to give notice that he has done so to the person by or on whose behalf the complaint was made.

(4) In this Part of this Act—

"complaint" means any complaint about the conduct of a police officer which is submitted—

(a) by a member of the public; or

(b) on behalf of a member of the public and with his written consent;

"the appropriate authority" means—

(a) in relation to an officer of the metropolitan police, the Commissioner of Police of the Metropolis; and

(b) in relation to an officer of any other police force—

(i) if he is a senior officer, the police authority for the force's area; and

(ii) if he is not a senior officer, the chief officer of the force;

"senior officer" means an officer holding a rank above the rank of chief superintendent.

(5) Nothing in this Part of this Act has effect in relation to a complaint in so far as it relates to the direction or control of a police force by the chief officer or the person performing the functions of the chief officer.

(6) If any conduct to which a complaint wholly or partly relates is or has been the subject of criminal or disciplinary proceedings, none of the provisions of this Part of this Act which relate to the recording and investigation of complaints have effect in relation to the complaint in so far as it relates to that conduct.

85 Investigation of complaints: standard procedure

(1) If a chief officer determines that he is the appropriate authority in relation to an officer about whose conduct a complaint has been made and who is not a senior officer, he shall record it.

(2) After doing so he shall consider whether the complaint is suitable for informal resolution and may appoint an officer from his force to assist him.

(3) If it appears to the chief officer that the complaint is not suitable for informal resolution, he shall appoint an officer from his force or some other force to investigate it formally.

(4) If it appears to him that it is suitable for informal resolution, he shall seek to resolve it informally and may appoint an officer from his force to do so on his behalf.

(5) If it appears to the chief officer, after attempts have been made to resolve a complaint informally—

(a) that informal resolution of the complaint is impossible; or

(b) that the complaint is for any other reason not suitable for informal resolution,

he shall appoint an officer from his force or some other force to investigate it formally.

(6) An officer may not be appointed to investigate a complaint formally if he has previously been appointed to act in relation to it under subsection (4) above.

(7) If a chief officer requests the chief officer of some other force to provide an officer of his force for appointment under subsection (3) or (5) above, that chief officer shall provide an officer to be so appointed.

(8) No officer may be appointed under this section unless he is—

(a) of at least the rank of chief inspector; and

(b) of at least the rank of the officer against whom the complaint is made.

(9) Unless the investigation is supervised by the Authority under section 89 below, the investigating officer shall submit his report on the investigation to the chief officer.

(10) A complaint is not suitable for informal resolution unless—

(a) the member of the public concerned gives his consent; and

(b) the chief officer is satisfied that the conduct complained of, even if proved, would not justify a criminal or disciplinary charge.

86 Investigation of complaints against senior officers

(1) Where a complaint about the conduct of a senior officer—

(a) is submitted to the appropriate authority; or

(b) is sent to the appropriate authority under section 84(3) above,

it shall be the appropriate authority's duty to record it and, subject to subsection (2) below, to investigate it.

(2) The appropriate authority may deal with the complaint according to the appropriate authority's discretion, if satisfied that the conduct complained of, even if proved, would not justify a criminal or disciplinary charge.

(3) In any other case the appropriate authority shall appoint an officer from the appropriate authority's force or from some other force to investigate the complaint.

(4) A chief officer shall provide an officer to be appointed, if a request is made to him for one to be appointed under subsection (3) above.

(5) No officer may be appointed unless he is of at least the rank of the officer against whom the complaint is made.

(6) Unless an investigation under this section is supervised by the Authority under section 89 below, the investigating officer shall submit his report on it to the appropriate authority.

87 References of complaints to Authority

(1) The appropriate authority—

(a) shall refer to the Authority—

(i) any complaint alleging that the conduct complained of resulted in the death of or serious injury to some other person; and

(ii) any complaint of a description specified for the purposes of this section in regulations made by the Secretary of State; and

(b) may refer to the Authority any complaint which is not required to be referred to them.

(2), (3) *****

(4) In this Part of this Act "serious injury" means a fracture, damage to an internal organ, impairment of bodily function, a deep cut or a deep laceration.

88 References of other matters to Authority

The appropriate authority may refer to the Authority any matter which—

(a) appears to the appropriate authority to indicate that an officer may have committed a criminal offence or an offence against discipline; and

(b) is not the subject of a complaint,

if it appears to the appropriate authority that it ought to be referred by reason—

(i) of its gravity; or

(ii) of exceptional circumstances.

89 Supervision of investigations by Authority

(1) The Authority shall supervise the investigation—

(a) of any complaint alleging that the conduct of a police officer resulted in the death of or serious injury to some other person; and

(b) of any other description of complaint specified for the purposes of this section in regulations made by the Secretary of State.

(2) The Authority shall supervise the investigation—

(a) of any complaint the investigation of which they are not required to supervise under subsection (1) above; and

(b) of any matter referred to them under section 88 above,

if they consider that it is desirable in the public interest that they should supervise that investigation.

(3) Where the Authority have made a determination under this section, it shall be their duty to notify it to the appropriate authority.

(4), (5) *****

(6) At the end of an investigation which the Authority have supervised the investigating officer—

(a) shall submit a report on the investigation to the Authority; and

(b) shall send a copy to the appropriate authority.

(7)-(14) *****

90 Steps to be taken after investigation — general

(1) It shall be the duty of the appropriate authority, on receiving—

(a) a report concerning the conduct of a senior officer which is submitted to them under section 86(6) above; or

(b) a copy of a report concerning the conduct of a senior officer which is sent to them under section 89(6) above,

to send a copy of the report to the Director of Public Prosecutions unless the report satisfies them that no criminal offence has been committed.

(2) Nothing in the following provisions of this section or in sections 91 to 94 below has effect in relation to senior officers.

(3) On receiving—

(a) a report concerning the conduct of an officer who is not a senior officer which is submitted to him under section 85(9) above; or

(b) a copy of a report concerning the conduct of such an officer which is sent to him under section 89(6) above it shall be the duty of a chief officer of police—

(i) to determine whether the report indicates that a criminal offence may have been committed by a member of the police force for his area; and

(ii) if he determines that it does, to consider whether the offence indicated is such that the officer ought to be charged with it.

(4) If the chief officer—

(a) determines that the report does indicate that a criminal offence may have been committed by a member of the police force for his area; and

(b) considers that the offence indicated is such that the officer ought to be charged with it,

he shall send a copy of the report to the Director of Public Prosecutions.

(5) Subject to section 91(1) below, after the Director has dealt with the question of criminal proceedings, the chief officer shall send the Authority a memorandum, signed by him and stating whether he has preferred disciplinary charges in respect of the conduct which was the subject of the investigation and, if not, his reasons for not doing so.

(6) If the chief officer—

(a) determines that the report does indicate that a criminal offence may have been committed by a member of the police force for his area; and

(b) considers that the offence indicated is not such that the officer ought to be charged with it,

he shall send the Authority a memorandum to that effect, signed by him and stating whether he proposes to prefer disciplinary charges in respect of the conduct which was the subject of the investigation and, if not, his reasons for not proposing to do so.

(7) Subject to section 91(1) below, if the chief officer considers that the report does not indicate that a criminal offence may have been committed by a member of the police force for his area, he shall send the Authority a memorandum to that effect, signed by him and stating whether he has preferred disciplinary charges in respect of the conduct which was the subject of the investigation and, if not, his reasons for not doing so.

(8)-(10) * * * * *

91 Steps to be taken where accused has admitted charges

(1) No memorandum need be sent to the Authority under section 90 above if disciplinary charges have been preferred in respect of the conduct which was the subject of the investigation and the accused has admitted the charges and has not withdrawn his admission.

(2) In any such case the chief officer shall send to the Authority, after the conclusion of the disciplinary proceedings (including any appeal to the Secretary of State), particulars of the disciplinary charges preferred and of any punishment imposed.

(3) If—

(a) the charges related to conduct which was the subject of a complaint; and

(b) the investigation of the complaint was not supervised by the Authority,

the chief officer shall also send the Authority—

(i) a copy of the complaint or of the record of the complaint; and

(ii) a copy of the report of the investigation.

92 Powers of Authority to direct reference of reports etc to Director of Public Prosecutions

(1) When a chief officer of police has performed all duties imposed on him by sections 90 and 91 above in relation to the report of an investigation concerning the conduct of an officer who is not a senior officer, it shall be the duty of the Authority—

(a) to determine whether the report indicates that a criminal offence may have been committed by that officer; and

(b) if so, to consider whether the offence is such that the officer ought to be charged with it.

(2) If the Authority consider that the officer ought to be charged, it shall be their duty to direct the chief officer to send the Director of Public Prosecutions a copy of the report.

(3) When the Authority give a direction under subsection (2) above, they may also direct the chief officer to send the Director the information contained in the memorandum under section 90 above.

(4) If the investigation was an investigation of a complaint, the Authority shall direct the chief officer to send the Director a copy of the complaint or of the record of the complaint.

(5) It shall be the duty of a chief officer to comply with any direction under this section.

(6) Sections 90 and 91 above shall apply where a copy of a report is sent to the Director under this section as they apply where a copy is sent to him under section 90(4) above.

93 Powers of Authority as to disciplinary charges

(1) Where a memorandum under section 90 above states that a chief officer of police has not preferred disciplinary charges or does not propose to do so, the Authority may recommend him to prefer such disciplinary charges as they may specify.

(2) Subject to subsection (6) below, a chief officer may not withdraw charges which he has preferred in accordance with a recommendation under subsection (1) above.

(3) If after the Authority have made a recommendation under this section and consulted the chief officer he is still unwilling to prefer such charges as the Authority consider appropriate, they may direct him to prefer such charges as they may specify.

(4) Where the Authority give a chief officer a direction under this section, they shall furnish him with a written statement of their reasons for doing so.

(5) Subject to subsection (6) below, it shall be the duty of a chief officer to prefer and proceed with charges specified in such a direction.

(6) The Authority may give a chief officer leave—

(a) not to prefer charges which section 90(10) above or subsection (5) above would otherwise oblige him to prefer; or

(b) not to proceed with charges with which section 90(10) above or subsection (2) or (5) above would otherwise oblige him to proceed.

(7) The Authority may request a chief officer of police to furnish them with such information as they may reasonably require for the purpose of discharging their functions under this section.

(8) It shall be the duty of a chief officer to comply with any such request.

94 Disciplinary tribunals

(1) Where a chief officer of police prefers a disciplinary charge in respect of a matter to which a memorandum under section 90 above relates, this section applies—

(a) to the hearing of any charge in pursuance of a direction under section 93 above; and

(b) to the hearing of any other charge to which the Authority direct that it shall apply.

(2) The Authority may direct that this section shall apply to the hearing of a charge if they consider that to be desirable by reason of any exceptional circumstances affecting the case.

(3) Where this section applies to the hearing of a disciplinary charge—

(a) the function of determining whether the accused is guilty of the charge shall be discharged by a tribunal consisting of—

(i) a chairman who shall, subject to subsection (4) below, be the chief officer of police by whom that function would fall to be discharged apart from this section; and

(ii) two members of the Authority nominated by the Authority, being members who have not been concerned with the case; and

(b) the function of determining any punishment to be imposed shall, subject to subsection (7) below, be discharged by the chairman after consulting the other members of the tribunal.

(4) Where—

(a) the accused is a member of the metropolitan police force; and

(b) the function of determining whether he is guilty of the charge would, apart from this section, fall to be discharged by a person or persons other than a chief officer of police (whether the Commissioner of Police of the Metropolis or the chief officer of another police force),

the chairman of the tribunal shall be—

(i) a person nominated by the Commissioner, being either an Assistant Commissioner of Police of the Metropolis or an officer of the metropolitan police force of such rank as may be prescribed by regulations made by the Secretary of State; or

(ii) in default of any such nomination, the Commissioner.

(5)-(9) * * * * *

95 Information as to the manner of dealing with complaints etc

Every police authority in carrying out their duty with respect to the maintenance of an adequate and efficient police force, and inspectors of constabulary in carrying out their duties with respect to the efficiency of any police force, shall keep themselves informed as to the working of sections 84 to 93 above in relation to the force.

96 * * * * *

97 Reports

(1) The Authority shall, at the request of the Secretary of State, report to him on such matters relating generally to their functions as the Secretary of State may specify, and the Authority may for that purpose carry out research into any such matters.

(2) The Authority may make a report to the Secretary of State on any matters coming to their notice under this Part of this Act to which they consider that his attention should be drawn by reason of their gravity or of other exceptional circumstances; and the Authority shall send a copy of any such report to the police authority and to the chief officer of police of any police force which appears to the Authority to be concerned or, if the report concerns any such body of constables as is mentioned in section 96 above, to the authority maintaining it and the officer having the direction and the control of it.

(3) As soon as practicable after the end of each calendar year the Authority shall make to the Secretary of State a report on the discharge of their functions during that year.

(4) The Authority shall keep under review the working of sections 84 to 96 above and shall make to the Secretary of State a report on it at least once in every three years after the coming into force of this section.

(5) The Secretary of State shall lay before Parliament a copy of every report received by him under this section and shall cause every such report to be published.

(6) The Authority shall send to every police authority—

(a) a copy of every report made by the Authority under subsection (3) above; and

(b) any statistical or other general information which relates to the year dealt with by the report and to the area of that authority and which the Authority consider should be brought to the police authority's attention in connection with their functions under section 95 above.

98-100 * * * * *

Amendments of discipline provisions

101 Discipline regulations

(1) Regulations under section 33(2)(e) of the Police Act 1964 (discipline regulations) shall provide—

(a) for the determination of questions whether offences against discipline have been committed;

(b) for racially discriminatory behaviour to be made a specific disciplinary offence; and

(c) for members of police forces who are found to have committed such offences to be punished by way of dismissal, requirement to resign, reduction in rank, reduction in rate of pay, fine, reprimand or caution.

(2)-(9) * * * * *

102 Representation at disciplinary proceedings

(1) On the hearing of a disciplinary charge against a police officer of the rank of chief superintendent or below the punishment of dismissal, requirement to resign or reduction in rank may not be awarded unless he has been given an opportunity to elect to be legally represented at the hearing.

(2) Where such an officer so elects, he may be represented at the hearing, at his option, either by counsel or by a solicitor.

(3) Except in a case where such an officer has been given an opportunity to elect to be legally represented and has so elected, he may only be represented at the hearing of a disciplinary charge by another member of a police force.

(4)-(6) * * * * *

103 * * * * *

General

104 Restrictions on subsequent proceedings

(1) Where a member of a police force has been convicted or acquitted of a criminal offence he shall not be liable to be charged with any offence against discipline which is in substance the same as the offence of which he has been convicted or acquitted.

(2) Subsection (1) above shall not be construed as applying to a charge in respect of an offence against discipline which consists in having been found guilty of a criminal offence.

(3) Subject to subsection (4) below, no statement made by any person for the purpose of the informal resolution of a complaint shall be admissible in any subsequent criminal, civil or disciplinary proceedings.

(4) A statement is not rendered inadmissible by subsection (3) above if it consists of or includes an admission relating to a matter which does not fall to be resolved informally.

105 * * * * *

PART X
POLICE — GENERAL

106 Arrangements for obtaining the views of the community on policing

(1) Arrangements shall be made in each police area for obtaining the views of people in that area about matters concerning the policing of the area and for obtaining their co-operation with the police in preventing crime in the area.

(2) Except as provided by subsections (3) to (7) below, arrangements for each police area shall be made by the police authority after consulting the chief constable as to the arrangements that would be appropriate.

(3) The Secretary of State shall issue guidance to the Commissioner of Police of the Metropolis concerning arrangements for the Metropolitan Police District; and the Commissioner shall make such arrangements after taking account of that guidance.

(4) The Commissioner shall make separate arrangements—
(a) for each London borough;
(b) for each district which falls wholly within the Metropolitan Police District; and
(c) for each part of a district which falls partly within that District.
(5) The Commissioner shall consult the council of each London borough as to the arrangements that would be appropriate for the borough.
(6)-(12) *****

107-115 *****

PART XI
MISCELLANEOUS AND SUPPLEMENTARY

116 Meaning of "serious arrestable offence"

(1) This section has effect for determining whether an offence is a serious arrestable offence for the purposes of this Act.
(2) The following arrestable offences are always serious—
(a) an offence (whether at common law or under any enactment) specified in Part I of Schedule 5 to this Act; and
[(aa) any of the offences mentioned in paragraphs (a) to (d) of the definition of "drug trafficking offence" in section 38(1) of the Drug Trafficking Offences Act 1986]; and
(b) an offence under an enactment specified in Part II of that Schedule.
(3) Subject to subsections (4) and (5) below, any other arrestable offence is serious only if its commission—
(a) has led to any of the consequences specified in subsection (6) below; or
(b) is intended or is likely to lead to any of those consequences.
(4) An arrestable offence which consists of making a threat is serious if carrying out the threat would be likely to lead to any of the consequences specified in subsection (6) below.
(5) An offence under section 1, 9 or 10 of the Prevention of Terrorism (Temporary Provisions) Act 1984 is always a serious arrestable offence for the purposes of section 56 or 58 above, and an attempt or conspiracy to commit any such offence is also always a serious arrestable offence for those purposes.
(6) The consequences mentioned in subsections (3) and (4) above are
(a) serious harm to the security of the State or to public order;
(b) serious interference with the administration of justice or with the investigation of offences or of a particular offence;
(c) the death of any person;
(d) serious injury to any person;
(e) substantial financial gain to any person; and
(f) serious financial loss to any person.
(7) Loss is serious for the purposes of this section if, having regard to all the circumstances, it is serious for the person who suffers it.
(8) In this section "injury" includes any disease and any impairment of a person's physical or mental condition.

117 Power of constable to use reasonable force

Where any provision of this Act—
(a) confers a power on a constable; and
(b) does not provide that the power may only be exercised with the consent of some person, other than a police officer,
the officer may use reasonable force, if necessary, in the exercise of the power.

118 General interpretation

(1) In this Act—

*****

"intimate search" means a search which consists of the physical examination of a person's body orifices;

*****

(2) A person is in police detention for the purposes of this Act if—

(a) he has been taken to a police station after being arrested for an offence; or

(b) he is arrested at a police station after attending voluntarily at the station or accompanying a constable to it,

and is detained there or is detained elsewhere in the charge of a constable, except that a person who is at a court after being charged is not in police detention for those purposes.

*****

Section 9

SCHEDULE 1
SPECIAL PROCEDURE

Making of orders by circuit judge

1. If on an application made by a constable a circuit judge is satisfied that one or other of the sets of access conditions is fulfilled, he may make an order under paragraph 4 below.

2. The first set of access conditions is fulfilled if—

(a) there are reasonable grounds for believing—

(i) that a serious arrestable offence has been committed;

(ii) that there is material which consists of special procedure material or includes special procedure material and does not also include excluded material on premises specified in the application;

(iii) that the material is likely to be of substantial value (whether by itself or together with other material) to the investigation in connection with which the application is made; and

(iv) that the material is likely to be relevant evidence;

(b) other methods of obtaining the material—

(i) have been tried without success; or

(ii) have not been tried because it appeared that they were bound to fail; and

(c) it is in the public interest, having regard—

(i) to the benefit likely to accrue to the investigation if the material is obtained; and

(ii) to the circumstances under which the person in possession of the material holds it,

that the material should be produced or that access to it should be given.

3. The second set of access conditions is fulfilled if—

(a) there are reasonable grounds for believing that there is material which consists of or includes excluded material or special procedure material on premises specified in the application;

(b) but for section 9(2) above a search of the premises for that material could have been authorised by the issue of a warrant to a constable under an enactment other than this Schedule; and

(c) the issue of such a warrant would have been appropriate.

4. An order under this paragraph is an order that the person who appears to the circuit judge to be in possession of the material to which the application relates shall—

(a) produce it to a constable for him to take away; or

(b) give a constable access to it,

not later than the end of the period of seven days from the date of the order or the end of such longer period as the order may specify.

5. Where the material consists of information contained in a computer—

(a) an order under paragraph 4(a) above shall have effect as an order to produce the material in a form in which it can be taken away and in which it is visible and legible; and

(b) an order under paragraph 4(b) above shall have effect as an order to give a constable access to the material in a form in which it is visible and legible.

6. For the purposes of sections 21 and 22 above material produced in pursuance of an order under paragraph 4(a) above shall be treated as if it were material seized by a constable.

Notices of applications for orders

7. An application for an order under paragraph 4 above shall be made inter partes.

8. Notice of an application for such an order may be served on a person either by delivering it to him or by leaving it at his proper address or by sending it by post to him in a registered letter or by the recorded delivery service.

9. Such a notice may be served—

(a) on a body corporate, by serving it on the body's secretary or clerk or other similar officer; and

(b) on a partnership, by serving it on one of the partners.

10. For the purposes of this Schedule, and of section 7 of the Interpretation Act 1978 in its application to this Schedule, the proper address of a person, in the case of secretary or clerk or other similar officer of a body corporate, shall be that of the registered or principal office of that body, in the case of a partner of a firm shall be that of the principal office of the firm, and in any other case shall be the last known address of the person to be served.

11. Where notice of an application for an order under paragraph 4 above has been served on a person, he shall not conceal, destroy, alter or dispose of the material to which the application relates except—

(a) with the leave of a judge; or

(b) with the written permission of a constable,

until—

(i) the application is dismissed or abandoned; or

(ii) he has complied with an order under paragraph 4 above made on the application.

Issue of warrants by circuit judge

12. If on an application made by a constable a circuit judge—

(a) is satisfied—

(i) that either set of access conditions is fulfilled; and

(ii) that any of the further conditions set out in paragraph 14 below is also fulfilled; or

(b) is satisfied—

(i) that the second set of access conditions is fufilled; and

(ii) that an order under paragraph 4 above relating to the material has not been complied with,

he may issue a warrant authorising a constable to enter and search the premises.

13. A constable may seize and retain anything for which a search has been authorised under paragraph 12 above.

14. The further conditions mentioned in paragraph 12(a)(ii) above are—

(a) that it is not practicable to communicate with any person entitled to grant entry to the premises to which the application relates;

(b) that it is practicable to communicate with a person entitled to grant entry to the premises but it is not practicable to communicate with any person entitled to grant access to the material;

(c) that the material contains information which—
(i) is subject to a restriction or obligation such as is mentioned in section 11(2)(b) above; and
(ii) is likely to be disclosed in breach of it if a warrant is not issued;
(d) that service of notice of an application for an order under paragraph 4 above may seriously prejudice the investigation.

15.—(1) If a person fails to comply with an order under paragraph 4 above, a circuit judge may deal with him as if he had committed a contempt of the Crown Court.

(2) Any enactment relating to contempt of the Crown Court shall have effect in relation to such a failure as if it were such a contempt.

16. * * * * *

* * * * *

Section 116

SCHEDULE 5
SERIOUS ARRESTABLE OFFENCES

PART I
OFFENCES MENTIONED IN SECTION 116(2)(a)

1. Treason.
2. Murder.
3. Manslaughter.
4. Rape.
5. Kidnapping.
6. Incest with a girl under the age of 13.
7. Buggery with—
   (a) a boy under the age of 16; or
   (b) a person who has not consented.
8. Indecent assault which constitutes an act of gross indecency.

PART II
OFFENCES MENTIONED IN SECTION 116(2)(b)

Explosive Substances Act 1883 (c. 3)

1. Section 2 (causing explosion likely to endanger life or property).

Sexual Offences Act 1956 (c. 69)

2. Section 5 (intercourse with a girl under the age of 13).

Firearms Act 1968 (c. 27)

3. Section 16 (possession of firearms with intent to injure).
4. Section 17(1) (use of firearms and imitation firearms to resist arrest).
5. Section 18 (carrying firearms with criminal intent).

Road Traffic Act 1972 (c. 20)

6. Section 1 (causing death by reckless driving).

Taking of Hostages Act 1982 (c. 28)

7. Section 1 (hostage-taking).

Aviation Security Act 1982 (c. 36)

8. Section 1 (hi-jacking).

* * * * *

PREVENTION OF TERRORISM (TEMPORARY PROVISIONS) ACT 1984
(1984, c.8)

An Act to repeal and re-enact with amendments the provisions of the Prevention of Terrorism (Temporary Provisions) Act 1976 [22 March 1984]

Territorial extent United Kingdom, except that Part I does not extend to Northern Ireland.

PART I
PROSCRIBED ORGANISATIONS

1 Proscribed organisations

(1) Subject to subsection (7) below, if any person—

(a) belongs or professes to belong to a proscribed organisation;

(b) solicits or invites financial or other support for a proscribed organisation, or knowingly makes or receives any contribution in money or otherwise to the resources of a proscribed organisation; or

(c) arranges or assists in the arrangement or management of, or addresses, any meeting of three or more persons (whether or not it is a meeting to which the public are admitted) knowing that the meeting—

(i) is to support a proscribed organisation;

(ii) is to further the activities of such an organisation; or

(iii) is to be addressed by a person belonging or professing to belong to such an organisation,

he shall be guilty of an offence.

(2) A person guilty of an offence under subsection (1) above shall be liable—

(a) on summary conviction to imprisonment for a term not exceeding six months, or to a fine not exceeding the statutory maximum, or both; or

(b) on conviction on indictment to imprisonment for a term not exceeding five years, or to a fine, or both.

(3) Any organisation for the time being specified in Schedule 1 to this Act is a proscribed organisation for the purposes of this Act; and any organisation which passes under a name mentioned in that Schedule shall be treated as proscribed, whatever relationship (if any) it has to any other organisation of the same name.

(4) The Secretary of State may by order made by statutory instrument add to Schedule 1 to this Act any organisation that appears to him to be concerned in terrorism occurring in the United Kingdom and connected with Northern Irish affairs, or in promoting or encouraging it.

(5) The Secretary of State may also by order so made remove an organisation from Schedule 1 to this Act.

(6) In this section and section 2 below "organisation" includes any association or combination of persons.

(7) A person belonging to a proscribed organisation shall not be guilty of an offence under this section by reason of belonging to the organisation if he shows—

(a) that he became a member when it was not a proscribed organisation under the current legislation; and

(b) that he has not since he became a member taken part in any of its activities at any time while it was a proscribed organisation under that legislation.

(8), (9) * * * * *

(10) The court by or before which a person is convicted of an offence under this section may order the forfeiture of any money or other property which, at the time of the offence, he had in his possession or under his control for the use or benefit of the proscribed organisation.

2 Display of support in public for a proscribed organisation

(1) Any person who in a public place—

(a) wears any item of dress; or

(b) wears, carries or displays any article,

in such a way or in such circumstances as to arouse reasonable apprehension that he is a member or supporter of a proscribed organisation, shall be guilty of an offence, and shall be liable on summary conviction—

(i) to imprisonment for a term not exceeding six months; or

(ii) to a fine of an amount not exceeding level 5 on the standard scale,

or to both.

(2) . . .

(3) In this section "public place" includes any highway [, or in Scotland any road within the meaning of the Roads (Scotland) Act 1984,] and any other premises or place to which at the material time the public have, or are permitted to have, access, whether on payment or otherwise.

PART II
EXCLUSION ORDERS

3 Exclusion orders: general

(1) The Secretary of State may exercise the powers conferred on him by this Part of this Act in such way as appears to him expedient to prevent acts of terrorism to which this Part of this Act applies.

(2) An order under section 4, 5 or 6 below is referred to in this Act as an "exclusion order."

(3) An exclusion order may be revoked at any time by a further order made by the Secretary of State.

(4) An exclusion order shall, unless revoked earlier, expire at the end of the period of three years beginning with the day on which it is made.

(5) The fact that an exclusion order against a person has been revoked or has expired shall not prevent the making of a further exclusion order against him.

(6) The acts of terrorism to which this Part of this Act applies are acts of terrorism designed to influence public opinion or Government policy with respect to affairs in Northern Ireland.

4 Orders excluding persons from Great Britain

(1) If the Secretary of State is satisfied that any person—

(a) is or has been concerned in the commission, preparation or instigation of acts of terrorism to which this Part of this Act applies; or

(b) is attempting or may attempt to enter Great Britain with a view to being concerned in the commission, preparation or instigation of such acts of terrorism,

the Secretary of State may make an exclusion order against him.

(2) An exclusion order under this section is an order prohibiting a person from being in, or entering, Great Britain.

(3) In deciding whether to make an exclusion order under this section against a person who is ordinarily resident in Great Britain, the Secretary of State shall have regard to the question whether that person's connection with any country or territory outside Great Britain is such as to make it appropriate that such an order should be made.

(4) An exclusion order shall not be made under this section against a person who is a British citizen and who—

(a) is at the time ordinarily resident in Great Britain, and has then been ordinarily resident in Great Britain throughout the last three years; or

(b) is at the time subject to an order under section 5 below.

(5) Subsection (4)(a) above shall be construed in accordance with Schedule 2 to this Act.

5 Orders excluding persons from Northern Ireland

(1) If the Secretary of State is satisfied that any person—

(a) is or has been concerned in the commission, preparation or instigation of acts of terrorism to which this Part of this Act applies; or

(b) is attempting or may attempt to enter Northern Ireland with a view to being concerned in the commission, preparation or instigation of such acts of terrorism,

the Secretary of State may make an exclusion order against him.

(2) In deciding whether to make an exclusion order under this section against a person who is ordinarily resident in Northern Ireland, the Secretary of State shall have regard to the question whether that person's connection with any country or territory outside Northern Ireland is such as to make it appropriate that such an order should be made.

(4) An exclusion order shall not be made under this section against a person who is a British citizen and who—

(a) is at the time ordinarily resident in Northern Ireland, and has been ordinarily resident in Northern Ireland throughout the last three years; or

(b) is at the time subject to an order under section 4 above.

(5) Subsection (4)(a) above shall be construed in accordance with Schedule 2 to this Act.

6 Orders excluding persons from the United Kingdom

(1) If the Secretary of State is satisfied that any person—

(a) is or has been concerned in the commission, preparation or instigation of acts of terrorism to which this Part of this Act applies; or

(b) is attempting or may attempt to enter Great Britain or Northern Ireland with a view to being concerned in the commission, preparation or instigation of such acts of terrorism,

the Secretary of State may make an exclusion order against him.

(2) An exclusion order under this section is an order prohibiting a person from being in, or entering, the United Kingdom.

(3), (4) * * * * *

7 Right to make representations to Secretary of State etc

(1) As soon as may be after the making of an exclusion order, notice of the making of the order shall be served on the person against whom it has been made; and the notice—

(a) shall set out the rights afforded to him by this section; and

(b) shall specify the manner in which those rights are to be exercised.

(2) Subsection (1) above shall not impose an obligation to take any steps to serve a notice on a person at a time when he is outside the United Kingdom.

(3) After service of the notice, if the person against whom the exclusion order has been made objects to the order—

(a) he may make representations in writing to the Secretary of State setting out the grounds of his objections; and

(b) he may include in those representations a request for a personal interview with the person or persons nominated by the Secretary of State under subsection (6) below.

(4) Subject to subsection (5) below, a person against whom an exclusion order has been made must exercise the rights conferred by subsection (3) above within seven days of the service of the notice.

(5) Where before the expiry of that period—

(a) he has consented to his removal under section 8 below from Great Britain, Northern Ireland or the United Kingdom, as the case may be; and

(b) he has been removed accordingly,

he may exercise the rights conferred by subsection (3) above within fourteen days of his removal.

(6)-(13) * * * * *

8, 9 * * * * *

PART III
MISCELLANEOUS OFFENCES

10 Contributions towards acts of terrorism

(1) If any person—

(a) solicits or invites any other person to give, lend or otherwise make available, whether for consideration or not, any money or other property; or

(b) receives or accepts from any other person, whether for consideration or not, any money or other property,

intending that it shall be applied or used for or in connection with the commission, preparation or instigation of acts of terrorism to which this Part of this Act applies, he shall be guilty of an offence.

(2) If any person gives, lends or otherwise makes available to any other person, whether for consideration or not, any money or other property, knowing or suspecting that it will or may be applied or used for or in connection with the commission, preparation or instigation of acts of terrorism to which this Part of this Act applies, he shall be guilty of an offence.

(3) A person guilty of an offence under subsection (1) or (2) above shall liable—

(a) on summary conviction to imprisonment for a term not exceeding six months, or to a fine not exceeding the statutory maximum, or both; or

(b) on conviction on indictment to imprisonment for a term not exceeding five years, or to a fine, or both.

(4) The court by or before which a person is convicted of an offence under subsection (1) above may order the forfeiture of any money or other property—

(a) which, at the time of the offence, he had in his possession or under his control; and

(b) which, at that time, he intended should be applied or used for or in connection with the commission, preparation or instigation of acts of terrorism to which this Part of this Act applies.

(5) The acts of terrorism to which this Part of this Act applies are acts of terrorism connected with Northern Irish affairs.

(6) In this section "property" includes—

(a) in England and Wales and Northern Ireland, both real and personal property; and

(b) in Scotland, both heritable and moveable property.

11 Information about acts of terrorism

(1) If a person who has information which he knows or believes might be of material assistance—

(a) in preventing the commission by any other person of an act of terrorism to which this Part of this Act applies; or

(b) in securing the apprehension, prosecution or conviction of any other person for an offence involving the commission, preparation or instigation of an act of terrorism to which this Part of this Act applies,

fails without reasonable excuse to disclose that information as soon as reasonably practicable—

(i) in England and Wales, to a constable;

(ii) in Scotland, to a constable or the procurator fiscal; or

(iii) in Northern Ireland, to a constable or a member of Her Majesty's forces,

he shall be guilty of an offence.

(2) A person guilty of an offence under subsection (1) above shall be liable—

(a) on summary conviction to imprisonment for a term not exceeding six months, or to a fine not exceeding the statutory maximum, or both;

(b) on conviction on indictment to imprisonment for a term not exceeding five years, or to a fine, or both.

(3) Proceedings for an offence under this section may be taken, and the offence may for the purpose of those proceedings be treated as having been committed, in a place where the person to be charged is or has at any time been since he first knew or believed that the information might be of material assistance as mentioned in subsection (1) above.

PART IV
ARREST, DETENTION AND PORT POWERS

12 Powers of arrest and detention

(1) Subject to subsection (2) below, a constable may arrest without warrant a person whom he has reasonable grounds for suspecting to be—

(a) a person guilty of an offence under section 1, 9 or 10 above;

(b) a person who is or has been concerned in the commission, preparation or instigation of acts of terrorism to which this Part of this Act applies;

(c) a person subject to an exclusion order.

(2) The power of arrest conferred by subsection (1)(c) above is exercisable only—

(a) in Great Britain, if the exclusion order was made under section 4 above; and

(b) in Northern Ireland, if it was made under section 5 above.

(3) The acts of terrorism to which this Part of this Act applies are—

(a) acts of terrorism connected with the affairs of Northern Ireland; and

(b) acts of terrorism of any other description except acts connected solely with the affairs of the United Kingdom or any part of the United Kingdom other than Northern Ireland.

(4) A person arrested under this section shall not be detained in right of the arrest for more than forty-eight hours after his arrest; but the Secretary of State may, in any particular case, extend the period of forty-eight hours by a period or periods specified by him.

(5) Any such further period or periods shall not exceed five days in all.

(6)-(8) * * * * *

13 * * * * *

PART V
GENERAL

14 Supplementary

(1)-(3) * * * * *

(4) The powers conferred by Part II of this Act and section 13 above shall be exercisable notwithstanding the rights conferred by section 1 of the Immigration Act 1971 (general principles regulating entry into and staying in the United Kingdom).

(5) Any reference in a provision of this Act to a person's having been concerned in the commission, preparation or instigation of acts of terrorism shall be taken to be a reference to his having been so concerned at any time, whether before or after the passing of this Act.

(6) When any question arises under this Act whether or not a person is exempted from the provisions of section 4, 5 or 6 above, it shall lie on the person asserting it to prove that he is.

15, 16 * * * * *

17 Duration, expiry and revival of certain provisions

(1) The following provisions of this Act—

sections 1 to 13;

section 14 except in so far as it relates to orders under subsection (2)(a) or (b) below;
subsection (2)(c) below; and
the Schedules,

shall remain in force until the end of the period of twelve months beginning with the passing of this Act and shall then expire unless continued in force by an order under subsection (2)(a) below.

(2) The Secretary of State may by order made by statutory instrument provide—

(a) that all or any of the said provisions which are for the time being in force (including any in force by virtue of an order under this paragraph or paragraph (c) below) shall continue in force for a period not exceeding twelve months from the coming into operation of the order;

(b) that all or any of the said provisions which are for the time being in force shall cease to be in force; or

(c) that all or any of the said provisions which are not for the time being in force shall come into force again and remain in force for a period not exceeding twelve months from the coming into operation of the order.

(3) This Act shall cease to have effect at the end of the period of five years beginning with the date on which it is passed.

18, 19 *****

Section 1

SCHEDULE 1

PROSCRIBED ORGANISATIONS

Irish Republican Army

Irish National Liberation Army

Sections 4 and 5

SCHEDULE 2

EXCLUSION ORDERS: CALCULATION OF PERIOD OF RESIDENCE

1.—(1) It is hereby declared that a person is not to be treated—

(a) as ordinarily resident in Great Britain for the purpose of the exemption in section 4(4)(a) of this Act; or

(b) as ordinarily resident in Northern Ireland for the purpose of the exemption in section 5(4)(a) of this Act,

at a time when he is there in breach of—

(i) an exclusion order;

(ii) the Immigration Act 1971; or

(iii) any law for purposes similar to that Act in force in the United Kingdom after the passing of this Act.

(2) In each of those exemptions "the last three years" is to be taken as a period amounting in total to three years exclusive of any time during which the person claiming exemption was undergoing imprisonment or detention for a period of six months or more by virtue of a sentence passed for an offence on a conviction in the United Kingdom and Islands.

2., 3. *****

Section 14

SCHEDULE 3

SUPPLEMENTAL PROVISIONS FOR SECTIONS 1 TO 13

*****

PART II

OFFENCES, DETENTION ETC

Prosecution of offences

3. Proceedings shall not be instituted—

(a) in England and Wales for an offence under section 1, 2, 9, 10 or 11 of this Act, except by, or with the consent of, the Attorney General; or

(b) in Northern Ireland for an offence under section 9, 10 or 11 of this Act, except by, or with the consent of, the Attorney General for Northern Ireland.

Search warrants

4.—(1) If a justice of the peace is satisfied that there is reasonable ground for suspecting that—

(a) evidence of the commission of an offence under section 1, 9 or 10 of this Act; or

(b) evidence sufficient to justify the making of an order under section 1 of this Act or an exclusion order,

is to be found at any premises or place, he may grant a search warrant authorising entry to the premises or place.

(2) An application for a warrant under sub-paragraph (1) above shall be made by a member of a police force of a rank not lower than inspector, and he shall give his information to the justice on oath.

(3) The warrant shall authorise the applicant, and any other member of any police force, to enter the premises or place, if necessary by force, and to search the premises or place and every person found therein and to seize anything found on the premises or place, or on any such person, which any member of a police force acting under the warrant has reasonable grounds for suspecting to be evidence falling within sub-paragraph (1) above.

(4) If a member of a police force of a rank not lower than superintendent has reasonable grounds for believing that the case is one of great emergency and that in the interests of the State immediate action is necessary, he may by a written order signed by him give to any member of a police force the authority which may be given by a search warrant under this paragraph.

(5) Where an authority is given under sub-paragraph (4) above, particulars of the case shall be notified as soon as may be to the Secretary of State.

(6) A search of a person under this paragraph may only be carried out—

(a) by a person of the same sex as the person searched; or

(b) by a medical practitioner.

(7), (8) * * * * *

5. * * * * *

Powers of search without warrant

6.—(1) In any circumstances in which a constable has power under section 12 of this Act to arrest a person, he may also, for the purpose of ascertaining whether he has in his possession any document or other article which may constitute evidence that he is a person liable to arrest, stop that person, and search him.

(2) Where a constable has arrested a person under that section, for any reason other than for the commission of a criminal offence, he or any other constable, may search him for the purpose of ascertaining whether he has in his possession any document or other article which may constitute evidence that he is a person liable to arrest.

(3) A search under this paragraph may only be carried out—

(a) by a person of the same sex as the person searched; or

(b) by a medical practitioner.

7., 8. * * * * *

VIDEO RECORDINGS ACT 1984
(1984, c. 39)

An Act to make provision for regulating the distribution of video recordings and for connected purposes. [12 July 1984]

Territorial extent United Kingdom

Preliminary

1 Interpretation of terms

(1) The provisions of this section shall have effect for the interpretation of terms used in this Act.

(2) "Video work" means any series of visual images (with or without sound)—

(a) produced electronically by the use of information contained on any disc or magnetic tape, and

(b) shown as a moving picture.

(3) "Video recording" means any disc or magnetic tape containing information by the use of which the whole or a part of a video work may be produced.

(4) "Supply" means supply in any manner, whether or not for reward, and, therefore, includes supply by way of sale, letting on hire, exchange or loan; and references to a supply are to be interpreted accordingly.

2 Exempted works

(1) Subject to subsection (2) below, a video work is for the purposes of this Act an exempted work if, taken as a whole—

(a) it is designed to inform, educate or instruct;

(b) it is concerned with sport, religion or music; or

(c) it is a video game.

(2) A video work is not an exempted work for those purposes if, to any significant extent, it depicts—

(a) human sexual activity of acts of force or restraint associated with such activity;

(b) mutilation or torture of, or other acts of gross violence towards, humans or animals;

(c) human genital organs or human urinary or excretory functions;

or is designed to any significant extent to stimulate or encourage anything falling within paragraph (a) or, in the case of anything falling within paragraph (b), is designed to any extent to do so.

3 Exempted supplies

(1) The provisions of this section apply to determine whether or not a supply of a video recording is an exempted supply for the purposes of this Act.

(2) The supply of a video recording by any person is an exempted supply if it is neither—

(a) a supply for reward, nor

(b) a supply in the course or furtherance of a business.

(3) Where on any premises facilities are provided in the course or furtherance of a business for supplying video recordings, the supply by any person of a video recording on those premises is to be treated for the purposes of subsection (2) above as a supply in the course or furtherance of a business.

(4) Where a person (in this subsection referred to as the "original supplier") supplies a video recording to a person who, in the course of a business, makes video works or supplies video recordings, the supply is an exempted supply—

(a) if it is not made with a view to any further supply of that recording, or

(b) if it is so made, but is not made with a view to the eventual supply of that recording to the original supplier.

(5)-(12) * * * * *

Designated authority

4 Authority to determine suitability of video works for classification

(1) The Secretary of State may by notice under this section designate any person as the authority responsible for making arrangements—

(a) for determining for the purposes of this Act whether or not video works are suitable for classification certificates to be issued in respect of them, having special regard to the likelihood of video works in respect of which such certificates have been issued being viewed in the home,

(b) in the case of works which are determined in accordance with the arrangements to be so suitable—

(i) for making such other determinations as are required for the issue of classification certificates, and

(ii) for issuing such certificates, and

(c) for maintaining a record of such determinations (whether determinations made in pursuance of arrangements made by that person or by any person previously designated under this section), including video recordings of the video works to which the determinations relate.

(2) The power to designate any person by notice under this section includes power—

(a) to designate two or more persons jointly as the authority responsible for making those arrangements, and

(b) to provide that any person holding an office or employment specified in the notice is to be treated as designated while holding that office or employment.

(3) The Secretary of State shall not make any designation under this section unless he is satisfied that adequate arrangements will be made for an appeal by any person against a determination that a video work submitted by him for the issue of a classification certificate—

(a) is not suitable for a classification certificate to be issued in respect of it, or

(b) is not suitable for viewing by persons who have not attained a particular age, or against a determination that no video recording containing the work is to be supplied other than in a licensed sex shop.

(4) The Secretary of State may at any time designate another person in place of any person designated under this section and, if he does so, may give directions as to the transfer of any record kept in pursuance of the arrangements referred to in subsection (1) above; and it shall be the duty of any person having control of any such record or any part of it to comply with the directions.

(5)-(8) *****

5 Parliamentary procedure for designation

(1) Where the Secretary of State proposes to make a designation under section 4 of this Act, he shall lay particulars of his proposal before both Houses of Parliament and shall not make the proposed designation until after the end of the period of forty days beginning with the day on which the particulars of his proposal were so laid.

(2), (3) *****

6 Annual report

(1) The designated authority shall, as soon as it is reasonably practicable to do so after 31st December, make a report to the Secretary of State on the carrying out in the year ending with that date of the arrangements referred to in section 4(1) and (3) of this Act (together with a statement of accounts) and on such other matters (if any) as the designated authority consider appropriate or the Secretary of State may require.

(2) The Secretary of State shall lay a copy of any report made to him under this section before each House of Parliament.

Classification and labelling

7 Classification certificates

(1) In this Act "classification certificate" means a certificate—

(a) issued in respect of a video work in pursuance of arrangements made by the designated authority; and

(b) satisfying the requirements of subsection (2) below.

(2) Those requirements are that the certificate must contain—

(a) a statement that the video work concerned is suitable for general viewing and unrestricted supply (with or without any advice as to the desirability of parental guidance with regard to the viewing of the work by young children or as to the particular suitability of the work for viewing by children); or

(b) a statement that the video work concerned is suitable for viewing only by persons who have attained the age (not being more than eighteen years) specified in the certificate and that no video recording containing that work is to be supplied to any person who has not attained the age so specified; or

(c) the statement mentioned in paragraph (b) above together with a statement that no video recording containing that work is to be supplied other than in a licensed sex shop.

8 Requirements as to labelling, etc.

(1) The Secretary of State may, in relation to video works in respect of which classification certificates have been issued, by regulations require such indication as may be specified by the regulations of any of the contents of any classification certificate to be shown in such a manner as may be so specified on any video recording containing the video work in respect of which the certificate was issued or any spool, case or other thing on or in which such a video recording is kept.

(2), (3) *****

Offences and penalties

9 Supplying video recording of unclassified work

(1) A person who supplies or offers to supply a video recording containing a video work in respect of which no classification certificate has been issued is guilty of an offence unless—

(a) the supply is, or would if it took place be, an exempted supply, or

(b) the video work is an exempted work.

(2) It is a defence to a charge of committing an offence under this section to prove that the accused believed on reasonable grounds—

(a) that the video work concerned or, if the video recording contained more than one work to which the charge relates, each of those works was either an exempted work or a work in respect of which a classification certificate had been issued, or

(b) that the supply was, or would if it took place be, an exempted supply by vitrue of section 3(4) or (5) of this Act.

10 Possession of video recording or unclassified work for the purposes of supply

(1) Where a video recording contains a video work in respect of which no classification certificate has been issued, a person who has the recording in his possession for the purpose of supplying it is guilty of an offence unless—

(a) he has it in his possession for the purpose only of a supply which, if it took place, would be an exempted supply, or

(b) the video work is an exempted work.

(2) It is a defence to a charge of committing an offence under this section to prove—

(a) that the accused believed on reasonable grounds that the video work concerned or, if the video recording contained more than one work to which the charge relates, each of those works was either an exempted work or a work in respect of which a classification certificate had been issued,

(b) that the accused had the video recording in his possession for the purpose only of a supply which he believed on reasonable grounds would, if it took place, be an exempted supply by virtue of section 3(4) or (5) of the Act, or

(c) that the accused did not intend to supply the video recording until a classification certificate had been issued in respect of the video work concerned.

11 Supplying video recording of classified work in breach of classification

(1) Where a classification certificate issued in respect of a video work states that no video recording containing that work is to be supplied to any person who has not attained the age specified in the certificate, a person who supplies or offers to supply a video recording containing that work to a person who has not attained the age so specified is guilty of an offence unless the supply is, or would if it took place be, an exempted supply.

(2) It is a defence to a charge of committing an offence under this section to prove—

(a) that the accused neither knew nor had reasonable grounds to believe that the classification certificate contained the statement concerned,

(b) that the accused neither knew nor had reasonable grounds to believe that the person concerned had not attained that age, or

(c) that the accused believed on reasonable grounds that the supply was, or would if it took place be, an exempted supply by virtue of section 3(4) or (5) of this Act.

12 Certain video recordings only to be supplied in licensed sex shops

(1) Where a classification certificate issued in respect of a video work states that no video recording containing that work is to be supplied other than in a licensed sex shop, a person who at any place other than in a sex shop for which a licence is in force under the relevant enactment—

(a) supplies a video recording containing the work, or

(b) offers to do so,

is guilty of an offence unless the supply is, or would if it took place be, an exempted supply.

(2)-(6) * * * * *

13, 14 * * * * *

15 Penalties

(1) A person guilty of an offence under section 9 or 10 of this Act shall be liable, on summary conviction, to a fine not exceeding £20,000.

(2) In relation to England and Wales, Scotland or Northern Ireland, the Secretary of State may by order amend subsection (1) above so as to substitute for the sum specified in that subsection (whether at the passing of this Act or by a previous order made under this subsection) such other sum as appears to him to be justified by a change in the value of money appearing to him to have taken place since the passing of this Act or the date of the previous order made under this subsection, as the case may be.

(3) A person guilty of an offence under any other provision of this Act shall be liable, on summary conviction, to a fine not exceeding level 5 on the standard scale.

(4), (5) * * * * *

16 * * * * *

17 Entry, search and seizure

(1) If a justice of the peace is satisfied by information on oath that there are reasonable grounds for suspecting—

(a) that an offence under this Act has been or is being committed on any premises, and

(b) that evidence that the offence has been or is being committed is on those premises,

he may issue a warrant under his hand authorising any constable to enter and search the premises within one month from the date of issue of the warrant.

(2) A constable entering or searching any premises in pursuance of a warrant under subsection (1) above may use reasonable force if necessary and may seize anything found there which he has reasonable grounds to believe may be required to be used in evidence in any proceedings for an offence under this Act.

(3) In subsection (1) above—

(a) the reference to a justice of the peace is, in Scotland, a reference to the sheriff or a justice of the peace and, in Northern Ireland, a reference to a resident magistrate, and

(b) the reference to information is, in Scotland, a reference to evidence and, in Northern Ireland, a reference to a complaint.

18 Arrest

(1) If a constable has reasonable grounds for suspecting that a person has committed an offence under this Act, he may require him to give his name and address and, if that person refuses or fails to do so or gives a name and address which the constable reasonably suspects to be false, the constable may arrest him without warrant.

(2) This section does not extend to Scotland.

19, 20 * * * * *

21 Forfeiture

(1) Where a person is convicted of any offence under this Act, the court may order any video recording—

(a) produced to the court, and

(b) shown to the satisfaction of the court to relate to the offence,

to be forfeited.

(2) The court shall not order any video recording to be forfeited under subsection (1) above if a person claiming to be the owner of it or otherwise interested in it applies to be heard by the court, unless an opportunity has been given to him to show cause why the order should not be made.

(3) References in this section to a video recording include a reference to any spool, case or other thing on or in which the recording is kept.

(4), (5) * * * * *

* * * * *

CINEMAS ACT 1985
(1985, c. 13)

An Act to consolidate the Cinematograph Acts 1909 to 1982 and certain related enactments, with an amendment to give effect to a recommendation of the Law Commission. [27 March 1985]

Territorial extent England and Wales, Scotland.

Control of exhibitions

1 Licence required for exhibitions

(1) Subject to sections 5 to 8 below, no premises shall be used for a film exhibition unless they are licensed for the purpose under this section.

(2) A licensing authority may grant a licence under this section to such a person as they think fit to use any premises specified in the licence for the purpose of film exhibitions on such terms and conditions and subject to such restrictions as, subject to regulations under section 4 below, they may determine.

(3) Without prejudice to the generality of subsection (2) above, it shall be the duty of a licensing authority, in granting a licence under this section as respects any premises,—

(a) to impose conditions or restrictions prohibiting the admission of children to film exhibitions involving the showing of works designated, by the authority or by such other body as may be specified in the licence, as works unsuitable for children; and

(b) to consider what (if any) conditions or restrictions should be imposed as to the admission of children to other film exhibitions involving the showing of works designated, by the authority or by such other body as may be specified in the licence, as works of such other description as may be so specified.

2 Consent required for exhibitions for children

(1) Subject to sections 5 and 6 below, no premises shall be used, except with the consent of the licensing authority, for a film exhibition organised wholly or mainly as an exhibition for children.

(2) * * * * *

3-4 * * * * *

Exempted exhibitions

5 Exhibitions in private dwelling-houses

(1) This section applies to any film exhibition which—

(a) is given in a private dwelling-house,

(b) is one to which the public are not admitted, and

(c) satisfies the condition mentioned in subsection (2) below.

(2) The condition referred to in subsection (1)(c) above is that either—

(a) the exhibition is not promoted for private gain, or

(b) the sole or main purpose of the exhibition is to demonstrate any product, to advertise any goods or services or to provide information, education or instruction.

(3) The following exemptions have effect in relation to any film exhibition to which this section applies, that is to say—

(a) a licence shall not be required by reason only of the giving of the exhibition;

(b) where the exhibition is given in premises in respect of which a licence is in force, no condition or restriction on or subject to which the licence was granted shall apply to the exhibition;

(c) regulations under section 4 above shall not apply to the exhibition.

6 Other non-commercial exhibitions

(1) Subject to subsections (4) and (5) below, this section applies to any film exhibition (other than one to which section 5 above applies) which—

(a) is one to which the public are not admitted or are admitted without payment, or

(b) does not fall within paragraph (a) above but is given by an exempted organisation,

and (in either case) satisfies the condition mentioned in subsection (2) below.

(2) The condition referred to in subsection (1) above is that either—

(a) the exhibition is not promoted for private gain, or

(b) the sole or main purpose of the exhibition is to demonstrate any product, to advertise any goods or services or to provide information, education or instruction.

(3) The following exemptions have effect in relation to any film exhibition to which this section applies, that is to say—

(a) a licence under section 1 above shall not be required by reason only of the giving of the exhibition unless the pictures are produced by means specified in regulations under section 4 above as means involving such risk that it is inexpedient that this paragraph should have effect;

(b) where the exhibition is given in premises in respect of which a licence under section 1 above is in force, no condition or restriction on or subject to which the licence was granted shall apply to the exhibition except so far as it relates to the matters specified in section 4(2)(a) above;

(c) a consent under section 2 above shall not be required by reason only of the giving of the exhibition;

(d) where the exhibition is given in premises in respect of which a consent under section 2 above is in force, no condition or restriction on or subject to which the consent was granted shall apply to the exhibition;

(e) regulations under section 4 above making such provision as is mentioned in subsection (2)(b) of that section shall not apply to the exhibition and regulations under that section making such provision as is mentioned in subsection (2)(a) of that section shall not apply to the exhibition unless it is given in premises in respect of which a licence under section 1 above is in force.

(4) A film exhibition is excluded from being one to which this section applies if it is organised solely or mainly as an exhibition for children who are members of a club, society or association the principal object of which is attendance at film exhibitions, unless the exhibition is given in a private dwelling-house or as part of the activities of an educational or religious institution.

(5) A film exhibition is excluded from being one to which this section applies by virtue of paragraph (b) of subsection (1) above if on more than three out of the last preceding seven days the premises in question were used for the giving of a film exhibition to which this section applied by virtue of that paragraph.

(6) In this section "exempted organisation" means a society, institution, committee or other organisation with respect to which there is in force at the time of the exhibition in question a certificate given by the Secretary of State certifying that he is satisfied that the organisation is not conducted or established for profit; and there shall be paid to the Secretary of State in respect of the giving of such a certificate such reasonable fee as he may determine.

(7), (8) * * * * *

7 Exhibitions in premises used occasionally

(1) Where the premises in which it is proposed to give a film exhibition are premises used occasionally and exceptionally only, and not on more than six days in any one calendar year, for the purposes of such an exhibition, it shall not be necessary to obtain a licence under section 1 above if—

(a) the occupier of the premises has given to the licensing authority, to the fire authority and to the chief officer of police, not less than seven days' notice in writing of his intention so to use the premises; and

(b) he complies with any regulations under section 4 above and, subject to any such regulations, with any conditions imposed by the licensing authority and notified to him in writing.

(2) For the purposes of subsection (1) above, the giving in any premises of an exhibition to which section 5 or 6 above applies shall be disregarded.

8-20 * * * * *

21 Interpretation

(1) In this Act, except where the contrary intention appears,—

* * * * *

"child" means a person under the age of sixteen;

"film exhibition" means any exhibition of moving pictures which is produced otherwise than by the simultaneous reception and exhibition of—

(a) television programmes broadcast by the British Broadcasting Corporation or the Independent Broadcasting Authority, or

(b) programmes included in a cable programme service which is, or does not require to be, licensed under section 4 of the Cable and Broadcasting Act 1984;

* * * * *

(2) Any reference in this Act to an exhibition which requires a licence under section 1 above is a reference to an exhibition to which that section applies; and any reference in this Act to an exhibition which requires a consent under section 2 above is a reference to an exhibition to which that section applies.

* * * * *

INTERCEPTION OF COMMUNICATIONS ACT 1985
(1985, c. 56)

An Act to make new provision for and in connection with the interception of communications sent by post or by means of public telecommunication systems and to amend section 45 of the Telecommunications Act 1984. [25 July 1985]

Territorial extent United Kingdom

1 Prohibition on interception

(1) Subject to the following provisions of this section, a person who intentionally intercepts a communication in the course of its transmission by post or by means of a public telecommunication system shall be guilty of an offence and liable—

(a) on summary conviction, to a fine not exceeding the statutory maximum;

(b) on conviction on indictment, to imprisonment for a term not exceeding two years or to a fine or to both.

(2) A person shall not be guilty of an offence under this section if—

(a) the communication is intercepted in obedience to a warrant issued by the Secretary of State under section 2 below; or

(b) that person has reasonable grounds for believing that the person to whom, or the person by whom, the communication is sent has consented to the interception.

(3) A person shall not be guilty of an offence under this section if—

(a) the communication is intercepted for purposes connected with the provision of postal or public telecommunication services or with the enforcement of any enactment relating to the user of those services; or

(b) the communication is being transmitted by wireless telegraphy and is intercepted, with the authority of the Secretary of State, for purposes connected with the issue of licences under the Wireless Telegraphy Act 1949 or the prevention or detection of interference with wireless telegraphy.

(4) No proceedings in respect of an offence under this section shall be instituted—

(a) in England and Wales, except by or with the consent of the Director of Public Prosecutions;

(b) In Northern Ireland, except by or with the consent of the Director of Public Prosecutions for Northern Ireland.

2 Warrants for interception

(1) Subject to the provisions of this section and section 3 below, the Secretary of State may issue a warrant requiring the person to whom it is addressed to intercept, in the course of their transmission by post or by means of public telecommunication system, such communications as are described in the warrant; and such a warrant may also require the person to whom it is addressed to disclose the intercepted material to such persons and in such manner as are described in the warrant.

(2) The Secretary of State shall not issue a warrant under this section unless he considers that the warrant is necessary—

(a) in the interests of national security;

(b) for the purpose of preventing or detecting serious crime or;

(c) for the purpose of safeguarding the economic well-being of the United Kingdom.

(3) The matters to be taken into account in considering whether a warrant is necessary as mentioned in subsection (2) above shall include whether the information which it is considered necessary to acquire could reasonably be acquired by other means.

(4) A warrant shall not be considered necessary as mentioned in subsection (2)(c) above unless the information which it is considered necessary to acquire is information relating to the acts or intentions of persons outside the British Islands.

(5) References in the following provisions of this Act to a warrant are references to a warrant under this section.

3 Scope of warrants

(1) Subject to subsection (2) below, the interception required by a warrant shall be the interception of—

(a) such communications as are sent to or from one or more addresses specified in the warrant, being an address or addresses likely to be used for the transmission of communications to or from—

(i) one particular person specified or described in the warrant; or

(ii) one particular set of premises so specified or described; and

(b) such other communications (if any) as it is necessary to intercept in order to intercept communications falling within paragraph (a) above.

(2) Subsection (1) above shall not apply to a warrant if—

(a) the interception required by the warrant is the interception, in the course of their transmission by means of a public telecommunication system, of—

(i) such external communications as are described in the warrant; and

(ii) such other communications (if any) as it is necessary to intercept in order to intercept such external communications as are so described; and

(b) at the time when the warrant is issued, the Secretary of State issues a certificate certifying the descriptions of intercepted material the examination of which he considers necessary as mentioned in section 2(2) above.

(3) A certificate such as is mentioned in subsection (2) above shall not specify an address in the British Islands for the purpose of including communications sent to or from that address in the certified material unless—

(a) the Secretary of State considers that the examination of communications sent to or from that address is necessary for the purpose of preventing or detecting acts of terrorism; and

(b) communications sent to or from that address are included in the certified material only in so far as they are sent within such a period, not exceeding three months, as is specified in the certificate.

(4) A certificate such as is mentioned in subsection (2) above shall not be issued except under the hand of the Secretary of State.

(5) References in the following provisions of this Act to a certificate are references to a certificate such as is mentioned in subsection (2) above.

4 Issue and duration of warrants

(1) A warrant shall not be issued except—

(a) under the hand of the Secretary of State; or

(b) in an urgent case where the Secretary of State has expressly authorised its issue and a statement of that fact is endorsed thereon, under the hand of an official of his department of or above the rank of Assistant Under Secretary of State.

(2) A warrant shall, unless renewed under subsection (3) below, cease to have effect at the end of the relevant period.

(3) The Secretary of State may, at any time before the end of the relevant period, renew a warrant if he considers that the warrant continues to be necessary as mentioned in section 2(2) above.

(4) If, at any time before the end of the relevant period, the Secretary of State considers that a warrant is no longer necessary as mentioned in section 2(2) above, he shall cancel the warrant.

(5) A warrant shall not be renewed except by an instrument under the hand of the Secretary of State.

(6) In this section "the relevant period"—

(a) in relation to a warrant which has not been renewed, means—

(i) if the warrant was issued under subsection (1)(a) above, the period of two months beginning with the day on which it was issued; and

(ii) if the warrant was issued under subsection (1)(b) above, the period ending with the second working day following that day;

(b) in relation to a warrant which was last renewed within the period mentioned in paragraph (a)(ii) above, means the period of two months beginning with the day on which it was so renewed; and

(c) in relation to a warrant which was last renewed at any other time, means—

(i) if the instrument by which it was so renewed is endorsed with a statement that the renewal is considered necessary as mentioned in section 2(2)(a) or (c) above, the period of six months beginning with the day on which it was so renewed; and

(ii) if that instrument is not so endorsed, the period of one month beginning with that day.

5 * * * * *

6 Safeguards

(1) Where the Secretary of State issues a warrant he shall, unless such arrangements have already been made, make such arrangements as he considers necessary for the purpose of securing—

(a) that the requirements of subsections (2) and (3) below are satisfied in relation to the intercepted material; and

(b) where a certificate is issued in relation to the warrant, that so much of the intercepted material as is not certified by the certificate is not read, looked at or listened to by any person.

(2) The requirements of this subsection are satisfied in relation to any intercepted material if each of the following, namely—

(a) the extent to which the material is disclosed;

(b) the number of persons to whom any of the material is disclosed;

(c) the extent to which the material is copied; and

(d) the number of copies made of any of the material,

is limited to the minimum that is necessary as mentioned in section 2(2) above.

(3) The requirements of this subsection are satisfied in relation to any intercepted material if each copy made of any of that material is destroyed as soon as its retention is no longer necessary as mentioned in section 2(2) above.

7 The Tribunal

(1) There shall be a tribunal (in this Act referred to as "the Tribunal") in relation to which the provisions of Schedule 1 to this Act shall apply.

(2) Any person who believes that communications sent to or by him have been intercepted in the course of their transmission by post or by means of a public telecommunication system may apply to the Tribunal for an investigation under this section.

(3) On such an application (other than one appearing to the Tribunal to be frivolous or vexatious), the Tribunal shall investigate—

(a) whether there is or has been a relevant warrant or a relevant certificate; and

(b) where there is or has been such a warrant or certificate, whether there has been any contravention of sections 2 to 5 above in relation to that warrant or certificate.

(4) If, on an investigation, the Tribunal, applying the principles applicable by a court on an application for judicial review, conclude that there has been a contravention of sections 2 to 5 above in relation to a relevant warrant or a relevant certificate, they shall—

(a) give notice to the applicant stating that conclusion;

(b) make a report of their findings to the Prime Minister; and

(c) if they think fit, make an order under subsection (5) below.

(5) An order under this subsection may do one or more of the following, namely—

(a) quash the relevant warrant or the relevant certificate;

(b) direct the destruction of copies of the intercepted material or, as the case may be, so much of it as is certified by the relevant certificate;

(c) direct the Secretary of State to pay to the applicant such sum by way of compensation as may be specified in the order.

(6), (7) * * * * *

(8) The decisions of the Tribunal (including any decisions as to their jurisdiction) shall not be subject to appeal or liable to be questioned in any court.

(9) * * * * *

8 The Commissioner

(1) The Prime Minister shall appoint a person who holds or has held a high judicial office (in this section referred to as "the Commissioner") to carry out the following functions, namely—

(a) to keep under review the carrying out by the Secretary of State of the functions conferred on him by sections 2 to 5 above and the adequacy of any arrangements made for the purposes of section 6 above; and

(b) to give to the Tribunal all such assistance as the Tribunal may require for the purpose of enabling them to carry out their functions under this Act.

(2) The Commissioner shall hold office in accordance with the terms of his appointment and there shall be paid to him out of money provided by Parliament such allowances as the Treasury may determine.

(3) It shall be the duty of every person holding office under the Crown or engaged in the business of the Post Office or in the running of a public telecommunication system to disclose or give to the Commissioner such documents or information as he may require for the purpose of enabling him to carry out his functions under this section.

(4) It shall be the duty of the Tribunal to send to the Commissioner a copy of every report made by them under section 7(4) above.

(5) If at any time it appears to the Commissioner—

(a) that there has been a contravention of sections 2 to 5 above which has not been the subject of a report made by the Tribunal under section 7(4) above; or

(b) that any arrangements made for the purposes of section 6 above have proved inadequate,

he shall make a report to the Prime Minister with respect to that contravention or those arrangements.

(6) As soon as practicable after the end of each calendar year, the Commissioner shall make a report to the Prime Minister with respect to the carrying out of his functions under this section.

(7) The Prime Minister shall lay before each House of Parliament a copy of every annual report made by the Commissioner under subsection (6) above together with a statement as to whether any matter has been excluded from that copy in pursuance of subsection (8) below.

(8) If it appears to the Prime Minister, after consultation with the Commissioner, that the publication of any matter in an annual report would be prejudicial to national security, to the prevention or detection of serious crime or to the economic well-being of the United Kingdom, the Prime Minister may exclude that matter from the copy of the report as laid before each House of Parliament.

9 Exclusion of evidence

(1) In any proceedings before any court or tribunal no evidence shall be adduced and no question in cross-examination shall be asked which (in either case) tends to suggest—

(a) that an offence under section 1 above has been or is to be committed by any of the persons mentioned in subsection (2) below; or

(b) that a warrant has been or is to be issued to any of those persons.

(2) The persons referred to in subsection (1) above are—

(a) any person holding office under the Crown;

(b) the Post Office and any person engaged in the business of the Post Office; and

(c) any public telecommunications operator and any person engaged in the running of a public telecommunication system.

(3) Subsection (1) above does not apply—

(a) in relation to proceedings for a relevant offence or proceedings before the Tribunal; or

(b) where the evidence is adduced or the question in cross-examination is asked for the purpose of establishing the fairness or unfairness of a dismissal on grounds of an offence under section 1 above or of conduct from which such an offence might be inferred; and paragraph (a) of that subsection does not apply where a person has been convicted of the offence under that section.

(4) *****

10 Interpretation

(1), (2) *****

(3) For the purposes of this Act conduct which constitutes or, if it took place in the United Kingdom, would constitute one or more offences shall be regarded as serious crime if, and only if—

(a) it involves the use of violence, results in substantial financial gain or is conduct by a large number of persons in pursuit of a common purpose; or

(b) the offence or one of the offences is an offence for which a person who has attained the age of twenty-one and has no previous convictions could reasonably be expected to be sentenced to imprisonment for a term of three years or more.

*****

PROSECUTION OF OFFENCES ACT 1985
(1985, c. 23)

An Act to provide for the establishment of a Crown Prosecution Service for England and Wales; to make provision as to costs in criminal cases; to provide for the imposition of time limits in relation to preliminary stages of criminal proceedings; to amend section 42 of the Supreme Court Act 1981 and section 3 of the Children and Young Persons Act 1969; to make provision with respect to consents to prosecutions; to repeal section 9 of the Perjury Act 1911; and for connected purposes. [23 May 1985]

Territorial extent England and Wales

PART I
THE CROWN PROSECUTION SERVICE

Constitution and functions of Service

1 The Crown Prosecution Service

(1) There shall be a prosecuting service for England and Wales (to be known as the "Crown Prosecution Service") consisting of—

(a) the Director of Public Prosecutions, who shall be head of the Service;

(b) the Chief Crown Prosecutors, designated under subsection (4) below, each of whom shall be the member of the Service responsible to the Director for supervising the operation of the service in his area; and

(c) the other staff appointed by the Director under this section.

(2) The Director shall appoint such staff for the Service as, with the approval of the Treasury as to numbers, remuneration and other terms and conditions of service, he considers necessary for the discharge of his functions.

(3) The Director may designate any member of the Service who is a barrister or solicitor for the purposes of this subsection, and any person so designated shall be known as a Crown Prosecutor.

(4) The Director shall divide England and Wales into areas and, for each of those areas, designate a Crown Prosecutor for the purposes of this subsection and any person so designated shall be known as a Chief Crown Prosecutor.

(5) The Director may, from time to time, vary the division of England and Wales made for the purpose of subsection (4) above.

(6) Without prejudice to any functions which may have been assigned to him in his capacity as a member of the Service, every Crown Prosecutor shall have all the powers of the Director as to the institution and conduct of proceedings but shall exercise those powers under the direction of the Director.

(7) Where any enactment (whenever passed)—

(a) prevents any step from being taken without the consent of the Director or without his consent or the consent of another; or

(b) requires any step to be taken by or in relation to the Director;

any consent given by or, as the case may be, step taken by or in relation to, a Crown Prosecutor shall be treated, for the purposes of that enactment, as given by or, as the case may be, taken by or in relation to the Director.

2 The Director of Public Prosecutions

(1) The Director of Public Prosecutions shall be appointed by the Attorney General.

(2) The Director must be a barrister or solicitor of not less than ten years' standing.

(3) *****

3 Functions of the Director

(1) The Director shall discharge his functions under this or any other enactment under the superintendence of the Attorney General.

(2) It shall be the duty of the Director—

(a) to take over the conduct of all criminal proceedings, other than specified proceedings, instituted on behalf of a police force (whether by a member of that force or by any other person);

(b) to institute and have the conduct of criminal proceedings in any case where it appears to him that—

(i) the importance or difficulty of the case makes it appropriate that proceedings should be instituted by him; or

(ii) it is otherwise appropriate for proceedings to be instituted by him;

(c) to take over the conduct of all binding over proceedings instituted on behalf of a police force (whether by a member of that force or by any other person);

***** and

(g) to discharge such other functions as may from time to time be assigned to him by the Attorney General in pursuance of this paragraph.

(3), (4) *****

4 Crown Prosecutors

(1) Crown Prosecutors shall have, in any court, the rights of audience enjoyed by solicitors holding practising certificates and shall have such additional rights of audience in the Crown Court as may be given by virtue of subsection (3) below.

(2) The reference in subsection (1) above to rights of audience enjoyed in any court by solicitors includes a reference to rights enjoyed in the Crown Court by virtue of any direction given by the Lord Chancellor under section 83 of the Supreme Court Act 1981.

(3) For the purpose of giving Crown Prosecutors additional rights of audience in the Crown Court, the Lord Chancellor may give any such direction as respects Crown Prosecutors as he could give under section 83 of the Act of 1981 in respect of solicitors.

(4)-(6) *****

5 *****

6 Prosecutions instituted and conducted otherwise than by the Service

(1) Subject to subsection (2) below, nothing in this Part shall preclude any person from instituting any criminal proceedings or conducting any criminal proceedings to which the Director's duty to take over the conduct of proceedings does not apply.

(2) Where criminal proceedings are instituted in circumstances in which the Director is not under a duty to take over their conduct, he may nevertheless do so at any stage.

7-9 * * * * *

Guidelines

10 Guidelines for Crown Prosecutors

(1) The Director shall issue a Code for Crown Prosecutors giving guidance on general principles to be applied by them—

(a) in determining, in any case—

(i) whether proceedings for an offence should be instituted or, where proceedings have been instituted, whether they should be discontinued; or

(ii) what charges should be preferred; and

(b) in considering, in any case, representations to be made by them to any magistrates' court about the mode of trial suitable for that case.

(2) The Director may from time to time make alterations in the Code.

(3) The provisions of the Code shall be set out in the Director's report under section 9 of this Act for the year in which the Code is issued; and any alteration in the Code shall be set out in his report under that section for the year in which the alteration is made.

11-21 * * * * *

PART III
MISCELLANEOUS

22 Power of Secretary of State to set time limits in relation to preliminary stages of criminal proceedings

(1) The Secretary of State may by regulations make provision, with respect to any specified preliminary stage of proceedings for an offence, as to the maximum period—

(a) to be allowed to the prosecution to complete that stage;

(b) during which the accused may, while awaiting completion of that stage, be—

(i) in the custody of a magistrates' court; or

(ii) in the custody of the Crown Court;

in relation to that offence.

(2) The regulations may, in particular—

(a) be made so as to apply only in relation to proceedings instituted in specified areas;

(b) make different provision with respect to proceedings instituted in different areas;

(c) make such provision with respect to the procedure to be followed in criminal proceedings as the Secretary of State considers appropriate in consequence of any other provision of the regulations;

(d) provide for the Magistrates' Courts Act 1980 and the Bail Act 1976 to apply in relation to cases to which custody or overall time limits apply subject to such modifications as may be specified (being modifications which the Secretary of State considers necessary in consequence of any provision made by the regulations); and

(e) make such transitional provision in relation to proceedings instituted before the commencement of any provision of the regulations as the Secretary of State considers appropriate.

(3) The appropriate court may, at any time before the expiry of a time limit imposed by the regulations, extend, or further extend, that limit if it is satisfied—

(a) that there is good and sufficient cause for doing so; and

(b) that the prosecution has acted with all due expedition.

(4) Where, in relation to any proceedings for an offence, an overall time limit has expired before the completion of the stage of the proceedings to which the limit applies, the accused shall be treated, for all purposes, as having been acquitted of that offence.

(5)-(13) * * * * *

* * * * *

REPRESENTATION OF THE PEOPLE ACT 1985
(1985, c. 50)

An Act to amend the law relating to parliamentary elections in the United Kingdom and local government elections in Great Britain, to provide for combining polls taken on the same date at such elections and elections to the Assembly of the European Communities, to extend the franchise at elections to that Assembly, to amend the law relating to the effect of the demise of the Crown on the summoning and duration of a new Parliament and to repeal section 21(3) of the Representation of the People Act 1918. [16 July 1985]

Territorial extent United Kingdom (ss. 1, 2)

Extension of franchise to British citizens overseas

1 Extension of parliamentary franchise

(1) Subject to section 1(3) of the principal Act, a person is entitled (notwithstanding anything in section 1(2) of that Act) to vote as an elector at a parliamentary election in any constituency if—

(a) he qualifies as an overseas elector in respect of that constituency on the qualifying date, and

(b) on that date and on the date of the poll he is not subject to any legal incapacity to vote and is a British citizen.

(2) For the purposes of this and the principal Act, a person qualifies as an overseas elector in respect of a constituency on the qualifying date if—

(a) on that date he is not resident in the United Kingdom, and

(b) he satisfies the following conditions.

(3) Those conditions are that—

(a) he was included in a register of parliamentary electors in respect of an address at a place that is situated within the constituency concerned,

(b) on the date by reference to which the register was prepared, he was resident or treated for the purposes of registration as resident at that address,

(c) that date fell within the period of five years ending immediately before the qualifying date, and

(d) if he was included in any register of parliamentary electors prepared by reference to a date later than the date referred to in paragraph (b) above, he was not resident or treated for the purposes of registration as resident at an address in the United Kingdom on that later date.

(4) The reference in subsection (1) above to a person being subject to a legal incapacity to vote on the qualifying date does not include a reference to his being below the age of 18 on that date.

* * * * *

Note The 'principal Act' is the Representation of the People Act 1983.

AUSTRALIA ACT 1986
(1986, c. 2)

An Act to give effect to a request by the Parliament and Government of the Commonwealth of Australia. [17 February 1986]

Territorial extent Australia

1 Termination of power of Parliament of United Kingdom to legislate for Australia
No Act of the Parliament of the United Kingdom passed after the commencement of this Act shall extend, or be deemed to extend, to the Commonwealth, to a State or to a Territory as part of the law of the Commonwealth, of the State or of the Territory.

2-11 * * * * *

12 Amendment of Statute of Westminster
Sections 4, 9(2) and (3) and 10(2) of the Statute of Westminster 1931, in so far as they are part of the law of the Commonwealth, of a State or of a Territory, are hereby repealed.

13, 14 * * * * *

15 Method of repeal or amendment of this Act or Statute of Westminster
(1) This Act or the Statute of Westminster 1931, as amended and in force from time to time, in so far as it is part of the law of the Commonwealth, of a State or of a Territory, may be repealed or amended by an Act of the Parliament of the Commonwealth passed at the request or with the concurrence of the Parliaments of all the States and, subject to subsection (3) below, only in that manner.
(2) For the purposes of subsection (1) above, an Act of the Parliament of the Commonwealth that is repugnant to this Act or the Statute of Westminster 1931, as amended and in force from time to time, or to any provision of this Act or of that Statute as so amended and in force, shall, to the extent of the repugnancy, be deemed an Act to repeal or amend the Act, Statute or provision to which it is repugnant.
(3) Nothing in subsection (1) above limits or prevents the exercise by the Parliament of the Commonwealth of any powers that may be conferred upon that Parliament by any alteration to the Constitution of the Commonwealth made in accordance with section 128 of the Constitution of the Commonwealth after the commencement of this Act.

* * * * *

EDUCATION (NO. 2) ACT 1986
(1986, c. 61)

An Act to amend the law relating to education. [7 November 1986]

* * * * *

PART IV
MISCELLANEOUS

43 Freedom of speech in universities, polytechnics and colleges
(1) Every individual and body of persons concerned in the government of any establishment to which this section applies shall take such steps as are reasonably practicable to ensure that freedom of speech within the law is secured for members, students and employees of the establishment and for visiting speakers.
(2) The duty imposed by subsection (1) above includes (in particular) the duty to ensure, so far as is reasonably practicable, that the use of any premises of the establishment is not denied to any individual or body of persons on any ground connected with—
(a) the beliefs or views of that individual or of any member of that body; or
(b) the policy or objectives of that body.

(3) The governing body of every such establishment shall, with a view to facilitating the discharge of the duty imposed by subsection (1) above in relation to that establishment, issue and keep up to date a code of practice setting out—

(a) the procedures to be followed by members, students and employees of the establishment in connection with the organisation—

(i) of meetings which are to be held on premises of the establishment and which fall within any class of meeting specified in the code; and

(ii) of other activities which are to take place on those premises and which fall within any class of activity so specified; and

(b) the conduct required of such persons in connection with any such meeting or activity;

and dealing with such other matters as the governing body consider appropriate.

(4) Every individual and body of persons concerned in the government of any such establishment shall take such steps as are reasonably practicable (including where appropriate the initiation of disciplinary measures) to secure that the requirements of the code of practice for that establishment, issued under subsection (3) above, are complied with.

(5) The establishments to which this section applies are—

(a) any university;

(b) any establishment which is maintained by a local education authority and for which section 1 of the 1968 (No. 2) Act (government and conduct of colleges of education and other institutions providing further education) requires there to be an instrument of government; and

(c) any establishment of further education designated by or under regulations made under section 27 of the 1980 Act as an establishment substantially dependent for its maintenance on assistance from local education authorities or on grants under section 100(1)(b) of the 1944 Act.

(6) * * * * *

(7) Where any establishment—

(a) falls within subsection (5)(b) above; or

(b) falls within subsection (5)(c) above by virtue of being substantially dependent for its maintenance on assistance from local education authorities;

the local education authority or authorities maintaining or (as the case may be) assisting the establishment shall, for the purposes of this section, be taken to be concerned in its government.

(8) Where a students' union occupies premises which are not premises of the establishment in connection with which the union is constituted, any reference in this section to the premises of the establishment shall be taken to include a reference to the premises occupied by the students' union.

44 Political indoctrination

(1) The local education authority by whom any county, voluntary or special school is maintained, and the governing body and head teacher of the school shall forbid—

(a) the pursuit of partisan political activities by any of those registered pupils at the school who are junior pupils; and

(b) the promotion of partisan political views in the teaching of any subject in the school.

(2) In the case of activities which take place otherwise than on the premises of the school concerned, subsection (1)(a) above applies only where arrangements for junior pupils to take part in the activities are made by any member of the staff of the school (in his capacity as such) or by anyone acting on his, or the school's behalf.

45 Duty to secure balanced treatment of political issues

The local education authority by whom any county, voluntary or special school is maintained, and the governing body and head teacher of the school, shall take such steps as are reasonably practicable to secure that where political issues are brought to the attention of pupils while they are—

(a) at the school; or

(b) taking part in extra-curricular activities which are provided or organised for registered pupils at the school by or on behalf of the school;

they are offered a balanced presentation of opposing views.

* * * * *

PARLIAMENTARY CONSTITUENCIES ACT 1986
(1986, c. 56)

An Act to consolidate the House of Commons (Redistribution of Seats) Acts 1949 to 1979 and certain related enactments. [7 November 1986]

Territorial extent United Kingdom

1 Parliamentary constituencies

(1) There shall for the purpose of parliamentary elections be the county and borough constituencies (or in Scotland the county and burgh constituencies), each returning a single member, which are described in Orders in Council made under this Act.

(2) In this Act and, except where the context otherwise requires, in any Act passed after the Representation of the People Act 1948, "constituency" means an area having separate representation in the House of Commons.

2 The Boundary Commissions

(1) For the purposes of the continuous review of the distribution of seats at parliamentary elections, there shall continue to be four permanent Boundary Commissions, namely a Boundary Commission for England, a Boundary Commission for Scotland, a Boundary Commission for Wales and a Boundary Commission for Northern Ireland.

(2) Schedule 1 to this Act shall have effect with respect to the constitution of, and other matters relating to, the Boundary Commissions.

3 Reports of the Commissions

(1) Each Boundary Commission shall keep under review the representation in the House of Commons of the part of the United Kingdom with which they are concerned and shall, in accordance with subsection (2) below, submit to the Secretary of State reports with respect to the whole of that part of the United Kingdom, either—

(a) showing the constituencies into which they recommend that it should be divided in order to give effect to the rules set out in paragraphs 1 to 6 of Schedule 2 to this Act (read with paragraph 7 of that Schedule), or

(b) stating that, in the opinion of the Commission, no alteration is required to be made in respect of that part of the United Kingdom in order to give effect to the said rules (read with paragraph 7).

(2) Reports under subsection (1) above shall be submitted by a Boundary Commission not less than ten or more than fifteen years from the date of the submission of their last report under that subsection.

(3) Any Boundary Commission may also from time to time submit to the Secretary of State reports with respect to the area comprised in any particular constituency or constituencies in the part of the United Kingdom with which they are concerned, showing the constituencies into which they recommend that that area should be divided in order to give effect to the rules set out in paragraphs 1 to 6 of Schedule 2 to this Act (read with paragraph 7 of that Schedule).

(4) A report of a Boundary Commission under this Act showing the constituencies into which they recommend that any area should be divided shall state, as respects each constituency, the name by which they recommend that it should be known, and whether they recommend that it should be a county constituency or a borough constituency (or in Scotland a county constituency or a burgh constituency).

(5) As soon as may be after a Boundary Commission have submitted a report to the Secretary of State under this Act, he shall lay the report before Parliament together, except in a case where the report states that no alteration is required to be made in respect of the part of the United Kingdom with which the Commission are concerned, with the draft of an Order in Council for giving effect, whether with or without modifications, to the recommendations contained in the report.

(6) Schedule 2 to this Act which contains the rules referred to above and related provisions shall have effect.

4 Orders in Council

(1) The draft of any Order in Council laid before Parliament by the Secretary of State under this Act for giving effect, whether with or without modifications, to the recommendations contained in the report of a Boundary Commission may make provision for any matters which appear to him to be incidental to, or consequential on, the recommendations.

(2) Where any such draft gives effect to any such recommendations with modifications, the Secretary of State shall lay before Parliament together with the draft a statement of the reasons for the modifications.

(3) If any such draft is approved by resolution of each House of Parliament, the Secretary of State shall submit it to Her Majesty in Council.

(4) If a motion for the approval of any such draft is rejected by either House of Parliament or withdrawn by leave of the House, the Secretary of State may amend the draft and lay the amended draft before Parliament, and if the draft as so amended is approved by resolution of each House of Parliament, the Secretary of State shall submit it to Her Majesty in Council.

(5) * * * * *

(6) The coming into force of any such Order shall not affect any parliamentary election until a proclamation is issued by Her Majesty summoning a new Parliament, or affect the constitution of the House of Commons until the dissolution of the Parliament then in being.

(7) The validity of any Order in Council purporting to be made under this Act and reciting that a draft of the Order has been approved by resolution of each House of Parliament shall not be called in question in any legal proceedings whatsoever.

5 Notices

(1) Where a Boundary Commission intend to consider making a report under this Act they shall, by notice in writing, inform the Secretary of State accordingly, and a copy of the notice shall be published—

(a) in a case where it was given by the Boundary Commission for England or the Boundary Commission for Wales, in the London Gazette,

(b) in a case where it was given by the Boundary Commission for Scotland, in the Edinburgh Gazette, and

(c) in a case where it was given by the Boundary Commission for Northern Ireland, in the Belfast Gazette.

(2) Where a Boundary Commission have provisionally determined to make recommendations affecting any constituency, they shall publish in at least one newspaper circulating in the constituency a notice stating—

(a) the effect of the proposed recommendations and (except in a case where they propose to recommend that no alteration be made in respect of the constituency) that a copy of the recommendations is open to inspection at a specified place within the constituency, and

(b) that representations with respect to the proposed recommendations may be made to the Commission within one month after the publication of the notice;

and the Commission shall take into consideration any representations duly made in accordance with any such notice.

(3) Where a Boundary Commission revise any proposed recommendations after publishing a notice of them under subsection (2) above, the Commission shall comply again with that subsection in relation to the revised recommendations, as if no earlier notice had been published.

6 Local inquiries

(1) A Boundary Commission may, if they think fit, cause a local inquiry to be held in respect of any constituency or constituencies.

(2) Where, on the publication of the notice under section 5(2) above of a recommendation of a Boundary Commission for the alteration of any constituencies, the Commission receive any representation objecting to the proposed recommendation from an interested authority or from a body of electors numbering one hundred or more, the Commission shall not make the recommendation unless, since the publication of the notice, a local inquiry has been held in respect of the constituencies.

(3) Where a local inquiry was held in respect of the constituencies before the publication of the notice mentioned in subsection (2) above, that subsection shall not apply if the Commission, after considering the matters discussed at the local inquiry, the nature of the representations received on the publication of the notice and any other relevant circumstances, are of opinion that a further local inquiry would not be justified.

(4)-(7) * * * * *

* * * * *

Section 2

SCHEDULE 1
THE BOUNDARY COMMISSIONS

Constitution

1. The Speaker of the House of Commons shall be the chairman of each of the four Commissions.

2. Each of the four Commissions shall consist of the chairman, a deputy chairman and two other members appointed by the Secretary of State.

3. The deputy chairman—

(a) in the case of the Commission for England shall be a judge of the High Court appointed by the Lord Chancellor,

(b) in the case of the Commission for Scotland shall be a judge of the Court of Session appointed by the Lord President of the Court of Session,

(c) in the case of the Commission for Wales shall be a judge of the High Court appointed by the Lord Chancellor,

(d) in the case of the Commission for Northern Ireland shall be a judge of the High Court in Northern Ireland appointed by the Lord Chief Justice of Northern Ireland.

4. A member of any Commission (other than the chairman) shall hold his appointment for such term and on such conditions as may be determined before his appointment by the person appointing him.

5.-12. * * * * *

Section 3

SCHEDULE 2
RULES FOR REDISTRIBUTION OF SEATS

The rules

1.—(1) The number of constituencies in Great Britain shall not be substantially greater or less than 613.

(2) The number of constituencies in Scotland shall not be less than 71.

(3) The number of constituencies in Wales shall not be less than 35.

(4) The number of constituencies in Northern Ireland shall not be greater than 18 or less than 16, and shall be 17 unless it appears to the Boundary Commission for Northern Ireland that Northern Ireland should for the time being be divided into 16 or (as the case may be) into 18 constituencies.

2. Every constituency shall return a single member.

3. There shall continue to be a constituency which shall include the whole of the City of London and the name of which shall refer to the City of London.

4.—(1) So far as is practicable having regard to rules 1 to 3—

(a) in England and Wales,—

(i) no county or part of a county shall be included in a constituency which includes the whole or part of any other county or the whole or part of a London borough,

(ii) no London borough or any part of a London borough shall be included in a constituency which includes the whole or part of any other London borough,

(b) in Scotland, regard shall be had to the boundaries of local authority areas,

(c) in Northern Ireland, no ward shall be included partly in one constituency and partly in another.

(2) In sub-paragraph (1)(b) above "area" and "local authority" have the same meanings as in the Local Government (Scotland) Act 1973.

5. The electorate of any constituency shall be as near the electoral quota as is practicable having regard to rules 1 to 4; and a Boundary Commission may depart from the strict application of rule 4 if it appears to them that a departure is desirable to avoid an excessive disparity between the electorate of any constituency and the electoral quota, or between the electorate of any constituency and that of neighbouring constituencies in the part of the United Kingdom with which they are concerned.

6. A Boundary Commission may depart from the strict application of rules 4 and 5 if special geographical considerations, including in particular the size, shape and accessibility of a constituency, appear to them to render a departure desirable.

General and supplementary

7. It shall not be the duty of a Boundary Commission to aim at giving full effect in all circumstances to the above rules, but they shall take account, so far as they reasonably can—

(a) of the inconveniences attendant on alterations of constituencies other than alterations made for the purposes of rule 4, and

(b) of any local ties which would be broken by such alterations.

8., 9. * * * * *

PUBLIC ORDER ACT 1986
(1986, c. 64)

An Act to abolish the common law offences of riot, rout, unlawful assembly and affray and certain statutory offences relating to public order; to create new offences relating to public order; to control public processions and assemblies; to control the stirring up of racial hatred; to provide for the exclusion of certain offenders from sporting events; to create a new offence relating to the contamination of or interference with goods; to confer power to direct certain trespassers to leave land; to amend section 7 of the Conspiracy and Protection of Property Act 1875, section 1 of the Prevention of Crime Act 1953, Part V of the Criminal Justice (Scotland) Act 1980 and the Sporting Events (Control of Alcohol etc.) Act 1985; to repeal certain obsolete or unnecessary enactments; and for connected purposes. [7 November 1986]

Territorial extent England and Wales (ss. 1-9, 13, 39, 40(4)); England and Wales, Scotland (remainder).

PART I
NEW OFFENCES

1 Riot

(1) Where 12 or more persons who are present together use or threaten unlawful violence for a common purpose and the conduct of them (taken together) is such as would cause a person of reasonable firmness present at the scene to fear for his personal safety, each of the persons using unlawful violence for the common purpose is guilty of riot.

(2) It is immaterial whether or not the 12 or more use or threaten unlawful violence simultaneously.

(3) The common purpose may be inferred from conduct.

(4) No person of reasonable firmness need actually be, or be likely to be, present at the scene.

(5) Riot may be committed in private as well as in public places.

(6) A person guilty of riot is liable on conviction on indictment to imprisonment for a term not exceeding ten years or a fine or both.

2 Violent disorder

(1) Where 3 or more persons who are present together use or threaten unlawful violence and the conduct of them (taken together) is such as would cause a person of reasonable firmness present at the scene to fear for his personal safety, each of the persons using or threatening unlawful violence is guilty of violent disorder.

(2) It is immaterial whether or not the 3 or more use or threaten unlawful violence simultaneously.

(3) No person of reasonable firmness need actually be, or be likely to be, present at the scene.

(4) Violent disorder may be committed in private as well as in public places.

(5) A person guilty of violent disorder is liable on conviction on indictment to imprisonment for a term not exceeding 5 years or a fine or both, or on summary conviction to imprisonment for a term not exceeding 6 months or a fine not exceeding the statutory maximum or both.

3 Affray

(1) A person is guilty of affray if he uses or threatens unlawful violence towards another and his conduct is such as would cause a person of reasonable firmness present at the scene to fear for his personal safety.

(2) Where 2 or more persons use or threaten the unlawful violence, it is the conduct of them taken together that must be considered for the purposes of subsection (1).

(3) For the purposes of this section a threat cannot be made by the use of words alone.

(4) No person of reasonable firmness need actually be, or be likely to be, present at the scene.

(5) Affray may be committed in private as well as in public places.

(6) A constable may arrest without warrant anyone he reasonably suspects is committing affray.

(7) A person guilty of affray is liable on conviction on indictment to imprisonment for a term not exceeding 3 years or a fine or both, or on summary conviction to imprisonment for a term not exceeding 6 months or a fine not exceeding the statutory maximum or both.

4 Fear or provocation of violence

(1) A person is guilty of an offence if he—

(a) uses towards another person threatening, abusive or insulting words or behaviour, or

(b) distributes or displays to another person any writing, sign or other visible representation which is threatening, abusive or insulting,

with intent to cause that person to believe that immediate unlawful violence will be used against him or another by any person, or to provoke the immediate use of unlawful violence by that person or another, or whereby that person is likely to believe that such violence will be used or it is likely that such violence will be provoked.

(2) An offence under this section may be committed in a public or a private place, except that no offence is committed where the words or behaviour are used, or the writing, sign or other visible representation is distributed or displayed, by a person inside a dwelling and the other person is also inside that or another dwelling.

(3) A constable may arrest without warrant anyone he reasonably suspects is committing an offence under this section.

(4) A person guilty of an offence under this section is liable on summary conviction to imprisonment for a term not exceeding 6 months or a fine not exceeding level 5 on the standard scale or both.

5 Harassment, alarm or distress

(1) A person is guilty of an offence if he—

(a) uses threatening, abusive or insulting words or behaviour, or disorderly behaviour, or

(b) displays any writing, sign or other visible representation which is threatening, abusive or insulting,

within the hearing or sight of a person likely to be caused harassment, alarm or distress thereby.

(2) An offence under this section may be committed in a public or a private place, except that no offence is committed where the words or behaviour are used, or the writing, sign or other visible representation is displayed, by a person inside a dwelling and the other person is also inside that or another dwelling.

(3) It is a defence for the accused to prove—

(a) that he had no reason to believe that there was any person within hearing or sight who was likely to be caused harassment, alarm or distress, or

(b) that he was inside a dwelling and had no reason to believe that the words or behaviour used, or the writing, sign or other visible representation displayed, would be heard or seen by a person outside that or any other dwelling, or

(c) that his conduct was reasonable.

(4) A constable may arrest a person without warrant if—

(a) he engages in offensive conduct which the constable warns him to stop, and

(b) he engages in further offensive conduct immediately or shortly after the warning.

(5) In subsection (4) "offensive conduct" means conduct the constable reasonably suspects to constitute an offence under this section, and the conduct mentioned in paragraph (a) and the further conduct need not be of the same nature.

(6) A person guilty of an offence under this section is liable on summary conviction to a fine not exceeding level 3 on the standard scale.

6 Mental element: miscellaneous

(1) A person is guilty of riot only if he intends to use violence or is aware that his conduct may be violent.

(2) A person is guilty of violent disorder or affray only if he intends to use or threaten violence or is aware that his conduct may be violent or threaten violence.

(3) A person is guilty of an offence under section 4 only if he intends his words or behaviour, or the writing, sign or other visible representation, to be threatening, abusive or insulting, or is aware that it may be threatening, abusive or insulting.

(4) A person is guilty of an offence under section 5 only if he intends his words or behaviour, or the writing, sign or other visible representation, to be threatening, abusive or insulting, or is aware that it may be threatening, abusive or insulting or (as the case may be) he intends his behaviour to be or is aware that it may be disorderly.

(5) For the purposes of this section a person whose awareness is impaired by intoxication shall be taken to be aware of that of which he would be aware if not intoxicated, unless he shows either that his intoxication was not self-induced or that it was caused solely by the taking or administration of a substance in the course of medical treatment.

(6) In subsection (5) "intoxication" means any intoxication, whether caused by drink, drugs or other means, or by a combination of means.

(7) Subsections (1) and (2) do not affect the determination for the purposes of riot or violent disorder of the number of persons who use or threaten violence.

7 Procedure: miscellaneous

(1) No prosecution for an offence of riot or incitement to riot may be instituted except by or with the consent of the Director of Public Prosecutions.

(2)-(4) * * * * *

8 Interpretation

In this Part—

"dwelling" means any structure or part of a structure occupied as a person's home or as other living accommodation (whether the occupation is separate or shared with others) but does not include any part not so occupied, and for this purpose "structure" includes a tent, caravan, vehicle, vessel or other temporary or movable structure;

"violence" means any violent conduct, so that—

(a) except in the context of affray, it includes violent conduct towards property as well as violent conduct towards persons, and

(b) it is not restricted to conduct causing or intended to cause injury or damage but includes any other violent conduct (for example, throwing at or towards a person a missile of a kind capable of causing injury which does not hit or falls short).

9 Offences abolished

(1) The Common Law offences of riot, rout, unlawful assembly and affray are abolished.

(2) * * * * *

10 * * * * *

PART II
PROCESSIONS AND ASSEMBLIES

11 Advance notice of public processions

(1) Written notice shall be given in accordance with this section of any proposal to hold a public procession intended—

(a) to demonstrate support for or opposition to the views or actions of any person or body of persons,

(b) to publicise a cause or campaign, or

(c) to mark or commemorate an event,

unless it is not reasonably practicable to give any advance notice of the procession.

(2) Subsection (1) does not apply where the procession is one commonly or customarily held in the police area (or areas) in which it is proposed to be held or is a funeral procession organised by a funeral director acting in the normal course of his business.

(3) The notice must specify the date when it is intended to hold the procession, the time when it is intended to start it, its proposed route, and the name and address of the person (or of one of the persons) proposing to organise it.

(4) Notice must be delivered to a police station—

(a) in the police area in which it is proposed the procession will start, or

(b) where it is proposed the procession will start in Scotland and cross into England, in the first police area in England on the proposed route.

(5) If delivered not less than 6 clear days before the date when the procession is intended to be held, the notice may be deliverd by post by the recorded delivery service; but section 7 of the Interpretation Act 1978 (under which a document sent by post is deemed to have been served when posted and to have been delivered in the ordinary course of post) does not apply.

(6) If not delivered in accordance with subsection (5), the notice must be delivered by hand not less than 6 clear days before the date when the procession is intended to be held or, if that is not reasonably practicable, as soon as delivery is reasonably practicable.

(7) Where a public procession is held, each of the persons organising it is guilty of an offence if—

(a) the requirements of this section as to notice have not been satisfied, or

(b) the date when it is held, the time when it starts, or its route, differs from the date, time or route specified in the notice.

(8) It is a defence for the accused to prove that he did not know of, and neither suspected nor had reason to suspect, the failure to satisfy the requirements or (as the case may be) the difference of date, time or route.

(9) To the extent that an alleged offence turns on a difference of date, time or route, it is a defence for the accused to prove that the difference arose from circumstances beyond his control or from something done with the agreement of a police officer or by his direction.

(10) A person guilty of an offence under subsection (7) is liable on summary conviction to a fine not exceeding level 3 on the standard scale.

12 Imposing conditions on public processions

(1) If the senior police officer, having regard to the time or place at which and the circumstances in which any public procession is being held or is intended to be held and to its route or proposed route, reasonably believes that—

(a) it may result in serious public disorder, serious damage to property or serious disruption to the life of the community, or

(b) the purpose of the persons organising it is the intimidation of others with a view to compelling them not to do an act they have a right to do, or to do an act they have a right not to do,

he may give directions imposing on the persons organising or taking part in the procession such conditions as appear to him necessary to prevent such disorder, damage, disruption or intimidation, including conditions as to the route of the procession or prohibiting it from entering any public place specified in the directions.

(2) In subsection (1) "the senior police officer" means—

(a) in relation to a procession being held, or to a procession intended to be held in a case where persons are assembling with a view to taking part in it, the most senior in rank of the police officers present at the scene, and

(b) in relation to a procession intended to be held in a case where paragraph (a) does not apply, the chief officer of police.

(3) A direction given by a chief officer of police by virtue of subsection (2)(b) shall be given in writing.

(4) A person who organises a public procession and knowingly fails to comply with a condition imposed under this section is guilty of an offence, but it is a defence for him to prove that the failure arose from circumstances beyond his control.

(5) A person who takes part in a public procession and knowingly fails to comply with a condition imposed under this section is guilty of an offence, but it is a defence for him to prove that the failure arose from circumstances beyond his control.

(6) a person who incites another to commit an offence under subsection (5) is guilty of an offence.

(7) A constable in uniform may arrest without warrant anyone he reasonably suspects is committing an offence under subsection (4), (5) or (6).

(8) A person guilty of an offence under subsection (4) is liable on summary conviction to imprisonment for a term not exceeding 3 months or a fine not exceeding level 4 on the standard scale or both.

(9) A person guilty of an offence under subsection (5) is liable on summary conviction to a fine not exceeding level 3 on the standard scale.

(10) A person guilty of an offence under subsection (6) is liable on summary conviction to imprisonment for a term not exceeding 3 months or a fine not exceeding level 4 on the standard scale or both, notwithstanding section 45(3) of the Magistrates' Courts Act 1980 (inciter liable to same penalty as incited).

(11) In Scotland this section applies only in relation to a procession being held, and to a procession intended to be held in a case where persons are assembling with a view to taking part in it.

13 Prohibiting public processions

(1) If at any time the chief officer of police reasonably believes that, because of particular circumstances existing in any district or part of a district, the powers under section 12 will not be sufficient to prevent the holding of public processions in that district or part from resulting in serious public disorder, he shall apply to the council of the district for an order prohibiting for such period not exceeding 3 months as may be specified in the application the holding of all public processions (or of any class of public procession so specified) in the district or part concerned.

(2) On receiving such an application, a council may with the consent of the Secretary of State make an order either in the terms of the application or with such modifications as may be approved by the Secretary of State.

(3) Subsection (1) does not apply in the City of London or the metropolitan police district.

(4) If at any time the Commissioner of Police for the City of London or the Commissioner of Police of the Metropolis reasonably believes that, because of particular circumstances existing in his police area or part of it, the powers under section 12 will not be sufficient to prevent the holding of public processions in that area or part from resulting in serious public disorder, he may with the consent of the Secretary of State make an order prohibiting for such period not exceeding 3 months as may be specified in the order the holding of all public processions (or of any class of public procession so specified) in the area or part concerned.

(5) An order made under this section may be revoked or varied by a subsequent order made in the same way, that is, in accordance with subsections (1) and (2) or subsection (4), as the case may be.

(6) An order under this section shall, if not made in writing, be recorded in writing as soon as practicable after being made.

(7) A person who organises a public procession the holding of which he knows is prohibited by virtue of an order under this section is guilty of an offence.

(8) A person who takes part in a public procession the holding of which he knows is prohibited by virtue of an order under this section is guilty of an offence.

(9) A person who incites another to commit an offence under subsection (8) is guilty of an offence.

(10) A constable in uniform may arrest without warrant anyone he reasonably suspects is committing an offence under subsection (7), (8) or (9).

(11) A person guilty of an offence under subsection (7) is liable on summary conviction to imprisonment for a term not exceeding 3 months or a fine not exceeding level 4 on the standard scale or both.

(12) A person guilty of an offence under subsection (8) is liable on summary conviction to a fine not exceeding level 3 on the standard scale.

(13) A person guilty of an offence under subsection (9) is liable on summary conviction to imprisonment for a term not exceeding 3 months or a fine not exceeding level 4 on the standard scale or both, notwithstanding section 45(3) of the Magistrates' Courts Act 1980.

14 Imposing conditions on public assemblies

(1) If the senior police officer, having regard to the time or place at which and the circumstances in which any public assembly is being held or is intended to be held, reasonably believes that—

(a) it may result in serious public disorder, serious damage to property or serious disruption to the life of the community, or

(b) the purpose of the persons organising it is the intimidation of others with a view to compelling them not to do an act they have a right to do, or to do an act they have a right not to do,

he may give directions imposing on the persons organising or taking part in the assembly such conditions as to the place at which the assembly may be (or continue to be) held, its maximum duration, or the maximum number of persons who may constitute it, as appear to him necessary to prevent such disorder, damage, disruption or intimidation.

(2) In subsection (1) "the senior police officer" means—

(a) in relation to an assembly being held, the most senior in rank of the police officers present at the scene, and

(b) in relation to an assembly intended to be held, the chief officer of police.

(3) A direction given by a chief officer of police by virtue of subsection (2)(b) shall be given in writing.

(4) A person who organises a public assembly and knowingly fails to comply with a condition imposed under this section is guilty of an offence, but it is a defence for him to prove that the failure arose from circumstances beyond his control.

(5) A person who takes part in a public assembly and knowingly fails to comply with a condition imposed under this section is guilty of an offence, but it is a defence for him to prove that the failure arose from circumstances beyond his control.

(6) A person who incites another to commit an offence under subsection (5) is guilty of an offence.

(7) A constable in uniform may arrest without warrant anyone he reasonably suspects is committing an offence under subsection (4), (5) or (6).

(8) A person guilty of an offence under subsection (4) is liable on summary conviction to imprisonment for a term not exceeding 3 months or a fine not exceeding level 4 on the standard scale or both.

(9) A person guilty of an offence under subsection (5) is liable on summary conviction to a fine not exceeding level 3 on the standard scale.

(10) A person guilty of an offence under subsection (6) is liable on summary conviction to imprisonment for a term not exceeding 3 months or a fine not exceeding level 4 on the standard scale or both, notwithstanding section 45(3) of the Magistrates' Courts Act 1980.

15 Delegation

(1) The chief officer of police may delegate, to such extent and subject to such conditions as he may specify, any of his functions under sections 12 to 14 to a deputy or assistant chief constable; and references in those subsections to the person delegating shall be construed accordingly.

(2) Subsection (1) shall have effect in the City of London and the metropolitan police district as if "a deputy or assistant chief constable" read "an assistant commissioner of police".

16 Interpretation

In this Part—

*****

"public assembly" means an assembly of 20 or more persons in a public place which is wholly or partly open to the air;

"public place" means—

(a) any highway, or in Scotland any road within the meaning of the Roads (Scotland) Act 1984, and

(b) any place to which at the material time the public or any section of the public has access, on payment or otherwise, as of right or by virtue of express or implied permission;

"public procession" means a procession in a public place.

PART III
RACIAL HATRED

Meaning of "racial hatred"

17 Meaning of "racial hatred"

In this Part "racial hatred" means hatred against a group of persons in Great Britain defined by reference to colour, race, nationality (including citizenship) or ethnic or national origins.

Acts intended or likely to stir up racial hatred

18 Use of words or behaviour or display of written material

(1) A person who uses threatening, abusive or insulting words or behaviour, or displays any written material which is threatening, abusive or insulting, is guilty of an offence if—

(a) he intends thereby to stir up racial hatred, or

(b) having regard to all the circumstances racial hatred is likely to be stirred up thereby.

(2) An offence under this section may be committed in a public or a private place, except that no offence is committed where the words or behaviour are used, or the written material is displayed, by a person inside a dwelling and are not heard or seen except by other persons in that or another dwelling.

(3) A constable may arrest without warrant anyone he reasonably suspects is committing an offence under this section.

(4) In proceedings for an offence under this section it is a defence for the accused to prove that he was inside a dwelling and had no reason to believe that the words or behaviour used, or the written material displayed, would be heard or seen by a person outside that or any other dwelling.

(5) A person who is not shown to have intended to stir up racial hatred is not guilty of an offence under this section if he did not intend his words or behaviour, or the written material, to be, and was not aware that it might be, threatening, abusive or insulting.

(6) This section does not apply to words or behaviour used, or written material displayed, solely for the purpose of being included in a programme broadcast or included in a cable programme service.

19 Publishing or distributing written material

(1) A person who publishes or distributes written material which is threatening, abusive or insulting is guilty of an offence if—

(a) he intends thereby to stir up racial hatred, or

(b) having regard to all the circumstances racial hatred is likely to be stirred up thereby.

(2) In proceedings for an offence under this section it is a defence for an accused who is not shown to have intended to stir up racial hatred to prove that he was not aware of the content of the material and did not suspect, and had no reason to suspect, that it was threatening, abusive or insulting.

(3) References in this Part to the publication or distribution of written material are to its publication or distribution to the public or a section of the public.

20 Public performance of play

(1) If a public performance of a play is given which involves the use of threatening, abusive or insulting words or behaviour, any person who presents or directs the performance is guilty of an offence if—

(a) he intends thereby to stir up racial hatred, or

(b) having regard to all the circumstances (and, in particular, taking the performance as a whole) racial hatred is likely to be stirred up thereby.

(2)-(6) * * * * *

21 Distributing, showing or playing a recording

(1) A person who distributes, or shows or plays, a recording of visual images or sounds which are threatening, abusive or insulting is guilty of an offence if—

(a) he intends thereby to stir up racial hatred, or

(b) having regard to all the circumstances racial hatred is likely to be stirred up thereby.

(2) In this Part "recording" means any record from which visual images or sounds may, by any means, be reproduced; and references to the distribution, showing or playing of a recording are to its distribution, showing or playing to the public or a section of the public.

(3) In proceedings for an offence under this section it is a defence for an accused who is not shown to have intended to stir up racial hatred to prove that he was not aware of the content of the recording and did not suspect, and had no reason to suspect, that it was threatening, abusive or insulting.

(4) This section does not apply to the showing or playing of a recording solely for the purpose of enabling the recording to be broadcast or included in a cable programme service.

22 Broadcasting or including programme in cable programme service

(1) If a programme involving threatening, abusive or insulting visual images or sounds is broadcast, or included in a cable programme service, each of the persons mentioned in subsection (2) is guilty of an offence if—

(a) he intends thereby to stir up racial hatred, or

(b) having regard to all the circumstances racial hatred is likely to be stirred up thereby.

(2) The persons are—

(a) the person providing the broadcasting or cable programme service,

(a) any person by whom the programme is produced or directed, and

(c) any person by whom offending words or behaviour are used.

(3)-(6) * * * * *

(7) This section does not apply—

(a) to the broadcasting of a programme by the British Broadcasting Corporation or the Independent Broadcasting Authority, or

(b) to the inclusion of a programme in a cable programme service by the reception and immediate re-transmission of a broadcast by either of those authorities.

(8) * * * * *

Racially inflammatory material

23 Possession of racially inflammatory material

(1) A person who has in his possession written material which is threatening, abusive or insulting, or a recording of visual images or sounds which are threatening, abusive or insulting, with a view to—

(a) in the case of written material, its being displayed, published, distributed, broadcast or included in a cable programme service, whether by himself or another, or

(b) in the case of a recording, its being distributed, shown, played, broadcast or included in a cable programme service, whether by himself or another,

is guilty of an offence if he intends racial hatred to be stirred up thereby or, having regard to all the circumstances, racial hatred is likely to be stirred up thereby.

(2) For this purpose regard shall be had to such display, publication, distribution, showing, playing, broadcasting or inclusion in a cable programme service as he has, or it may reasonably be inferred that he has, in view.

(3) In proceedings for an offence under this section it is a defence for an accused who is not shown to have intended to stir up racial hatred to prove that he was not aware of the content of the written material or recording and did not suspect, and had no reason to suspect, that it was threatening, abusive or insulting.

(4) This section does not apply to the possession of written material or a recording by or on behalf of the British Broadcasting Corporation or the Independent Broadcasting Authority or with a view to its being broadcast by either of those authorities.

24 Powers of entry and search

(1) If in England and Wales a justice of the peace is satisfied by information on oath laid by a constable that there are reasonable grounds for suspecting that a person has possession of written material or a recording in contravention of section 23, the justice may issue a warrant under his hand authorising any constable to enter and search the premises where it is suspected the material or recording is situated.

(2) If in Scotland a sheriff or justice of the peace is satisfied by evidence on oath that there are reasonable grounds for suspecting that a person has possession of written material or a recording in contravention of section 23, the sheriff or justice may issue a warrant authorising any constable to enter and search the premises where it is suspected the material or recording is situated.

(3) A constable entering or searching premises in pursuance of a warrant issued under this section may use reasonable force if necessary.

(4) * * * * *

25 * * * * *

Supplementary provisions

26 Savings for reports of parliamentary or judicial proceedings

(1) Nothing in this Part applies to a fair and accurate report of proceedings in Parliament.

(2) Nothing in this Part applies to a fair and accurate report of proceedings publicly heard before a court or tribunal exercising judicial authority where the report is published contemporaneously with the proceedings or, if it is not reasonably practicable or would be unlawful to publish a report of them contemporaneously, as soon as publication is reasonably practicable and lawful.

27 Procedure and punishment

(1) No proceedings for an offence under this Part may be instituted in England and Wales except by or with the consent of the Attorney General.

(2) For the purposes of the rules in England and Wales against charging more than one offence in the same count or information, each of sections 18 to 23 creates one offence.

(3) A person guilty of an offence under this Part is liable—

(a) on conviction on indictment to imprisonment for a term not exceeding two years or a fine or both;

(b) on summary conviction to imprisonment for a term not exceeding six months or a fine not exceeding the statutory maximum or both.

28-38 * * * * *

PART V
MISCELLANEOUS AND GENERAL

39 Power to direct trespassers to leave land

(1) If the senior police officer reasonably believes that two or more persons have entered land as trespassers and are present there with the common purpose of residing there for any period, that reasonable steps have been taken by or on behalf of the occupier to ask them to leave and—

(a) that any of those persons has caused damage to property on the land or used threatening, abusive or insulting words or behaviour towards the occupier, a member of his family or an employee or agent of his, or

(b) that those persons have between them brought twelve or more vehicles on to the land,

he may direct those persons, or any of them, to leave the land.

(2) If a person knowing that such a direction has been given which applies to him—

(a) fails to leave the land as soon as reasonably practicable, or

(b) having left again enters the land as a trespasser within the period of three months beginning with the day on which the direction was given,

he commits an offence and is liable on summary conviction to imprisonment for a term not exceeding three months or a fine not exceeding level 4 on the standard scale, or both.

(3) A constable in uniform who reasonably suspects that a person is committing an offence under this section may arrest him without warrant.

(4) In proceedings for an offence under this section it is a defence for the accused to show—

(a) that his original entry on the land was not as a trespasser, or

(b) that he had a reasonable excuse for failing to leave the land as soon as reasonably practicable or, as the case may be, for again entering the land as a trespasser.

(5) In this section—

* * * * *

"senior police officer" means the most senior in rank of the police officers present at the scene;

* * * * *

40 Amendments repeals and savings

(1)-(3) * * * * *

(4) Nothing in this Act affects the common law powers in England and Wales to deal with or prevent a breach of the peace.

(5) As respects Scotland, nothing in this Act affects any power of a constable under any rule of law.

* * * * *

CROWN PROCEEDINGS (ARMED FORCES) ACT 1987
(1987, c. 25)

An Act to repeal section 10 of the Crown Proceedings Act 1947 and to provide for the revival of that section in certain circumstances. [15 May 1987]

Territorial extent United Kingdom

1 Repeal of s. 10 of the Crown Proceedings Act 1947

Subject to section 2 below, section 10 of the Crown Proceedings Act 1947 (exclusions from liability in tort in cases involving the armed forces) shall cease to have effect except in relation to anything suffered by a person in consequence of an act or omission committed before the date on which this Act is passed.

2 Revival of s. 10

(1) Subject to the following provisions of this section, the Secretary of State may, at any time after the coming into force of section 1 above, by order—

(a) revive the effect of section 10 of the Crown Proceedings Act 1947 either for all purposes or for such purposes as may be described in the order; or

(b) where that section has effect for the time being in pursuance of an order made by virtue of paragraph (a) above, provide for that section to cease to have effect either for all of the purposes for which it so has effect or for such of them as may be so described.

(2) The Secretary of State shall not make an order reviving the effect of the said section 10 for any purposes unless it appears to him necessary or expedient to do so—

(a) by reason of any imminent national danger or of any great emergency that has arisen; or

(b) for the purposes of any warlike operations in any part of the world outside the United Kingdom or of any other operations which are or are to be carried out in connection with the warlike activity of any persons in any such part of the world.

(3) Subject to subsection (4) below, an order under this section describing purposes for which the effect of the said section 10 is to be revived, or for which that section is to cease to have effect, may describe those purposes by reference to any matter whatever and may make different provision for different cases, circumstances or persons.

(4) Nothing in any order under this section shall revive the effect of the said section 10, or provide for that section to cease to have effect, in relation to anything suffered by a person in consequence of an act or omission committed before the date on which the order comes into force.

(5) The power to make an order under this section shall be exercisable by statutory instrument subject to annulment in pursuance of a resolution of either House of Parliament.

* * * * *

IMMIGRATION (CARRIERS' LIABILITY) ACT 1987
(1987, c. 24)

An Act to require carriers to make payments to the Secretary of State in respect of passengers brought by them to the United Kingdom without proper documents. [15 May 1987]

1 Liability of carriers for passengers without proper documents

(1) Where a person requiring leave to enter the United Kingdom arrives in the United Kingdom by ship or aircraft and, on being required to do so by an immigration officer, fails to produce—

(a) either a valid passport with photograph or some other document satisfactorily establishing his identity and nationality or citizenship; and

(b) if he is a person who under the immigration rules requires a visa for entry into the United Kingdom, a visa valid for that purpose,

the owners or agents of the ship or aircraft shall, in respect of that person, be liable to pay the Secretary of State on demand the sum of £1,000 or such other sum as may be prescribed.

(2) No liability shall be incurred under subsection (1) above in respect of any person who is shown by the owners or agents to have produced to them or an employee of theirs the document or documents specified in that subsection when embarking on the ship or aircraft for the voyage or flight to the United Kingdom.

(3) In subsection (1) above "prescribed" means prescribed by an order made by the Secretary of State by statutory instrument subject to annulment in pursuance of a resolution of either House of Parliament.

(4), (5) * * * * *

MINISTRY OF DEFENCE POLICE ACT 1987
(1987, c. 4)

An Act to make fresh provision for the Ministry of Defence Police. [5 March 1987]

Territorial extent United Kingdom

1 The Ministry of Defence Police

(1) There shall be a police force to be known as the Ministry of Defence Police and consisting—

(a) of persons nominated by the Secretary of State; and

(b) of persons who at the coming into force of this Act are special constables by virtue of appointment under section 3 of the Special Constables Act 1923 on the Nomination of the Defence Council.

(2) A person nominated under subsection (1) above shall—

(a) in England and Wales be attested as a constable by making the declaration required of a member of a police force maintained under the Police Act 1964 before a justice of the peace;

(b) in Scotland make the declaration required of a person on appointment to the office of constable of a police force maintained under the Police (Scotland) Act 1967 before a person before whom such a declaration may be made by a person appointed to that office; and

(c) in Northern Ireland be attested as a constable by taking and subscribing the oath required of a member of the Royal Ulster Constabulary before a justice of the peace.

(3) The Secretary of State shall appoint a chief constable for the Ministry of Defence Police, and they shall operate under the chief constable's direction and control.

(4) The Secretary of State shall have power—

(a) to suspend a member of the Ministry of Defence Police from duty; and

(b) to terminate a person's membership.

(5), (6) * * * * *

2 Jurisdiction

(1) In any place in the United Kingdom to which subsection (2) below for the time being applies, members of the Ministry of Defence Police shall have the powers and privileges of constables.

(2) The places to which this subsection applies are—

(a) land, vehicles, vessels, aircraft and hovercraft in the possession, under the control or used for the purposes of—

(i) the Secretary of State for Defence;

(ii) the Defence Council;

(iii) a headquarters or defence organisation; or

(iv) the service authorities of a visiting force;

(b) land, vehicles, vessels, aircraft and hovercraft which are—

(i) in the possession, under the control or used for the purposes of an ordnance company; and

(ii) used for the purpose of, or for purposes which include, the making or development of ordnance or otherwise for naval, military or air force purposes;

(c) land, vehicles, vessels, aircraft and hovercraft which are—

(i) in the possession, under the control or used for the purposes of a dockyard contractor; and

(ii) used for the purpose of, or for purposes which include, providing designated services or otherwise for naval, military or air force purposes;

(d) land which is in the vicinity of land mentioned in any of paragraphs (a) to (c) above and on which a constable of the police force for the police area in which the first-mentioned land is situated, or, in Northern Ireland, of the Royal Ulster Constabulary, has asked the Ministry of Defence Police to assist him in the execution of his duties; and

(e) land where the Secretary of State has agreed to provide the services of the Ministry of Defence Police under an agreement notice of which has been published in the appropriate Gazette.

(3) Members of the Ministry of Defence Police shall also have the powers and privileges of constables in any place in the United Kingdom to which subsection (2) above does not for the time being apply, but only—

(a) in relation to Crown property, international defence property, ordnance property and dockyard property;

(b) in relation to persons—

(i) subject to the control of the Defence Council;

(ii) employed under or for the purposes of the Ministry of Defence or the Defence Council; or

(iii) in respect of whom the service courts and service authorities of any country may exercise powers by virtue of section 2 of the Visiting Forces Act 1952;

(c) in relation to matters connected with anything done under a contract entered into by the Secretary of State for Defence for the purposes of his Department or the Defence Council; and

(d) for the purpose of securing the unimpeded passage of any such property as is mentioned in paragraph (a) above.

(4), (5) * * * * *

3-5 * * * * *

6 Causing disaffection

Any person who causes, or attempts to cause, or does any act calculated to cause, disaffection amongst the members of the Ministry of Defence Police, or induces or attempts to induce, or does any act calculated to induce, any member of the Ministry of Defence Police to withhold his services or to commit breaches of discipline, shall be guilty of an offence and liable—

(a) on summary conviction, to imprisonment for a term not exceeding six months or to a fine not exceeding the statutory maximum, or to both;

(b) on conviction on indictment, to imprisonment for a term not exceeding two years or to a fine or to both.

* * * * *

NORTHERN IRELAND (EMERGENCY PROVISIONS) ACT 1987
(1987, c. 30)

An Act to amend the Northern Ireland (Emergency Provisions) Act 1978; to confer certain rights on persons detained in police custody in Northern Ireland under or by virtue of Part IV of the Prevention of Terrorism (Temporary Provisions) Act 1984; to regulate the provision of security services there; and for connected purposes. [15 May 1987]

Territorial extent Northern Ireland

* * * * *

PART II
RIGHTS OF PERSONS DETAINED UNDER TERRORISM PROVISIONS IN POLICE CUSTODY

Note Sections 14 and 15 contain provisions broadly similar to ss. 56 and 58 of the Police and Criminal Evidence Act 1984, q.v.

PART II
OTHER CONSTITUTIONAL MATERIALS

THE CONSTITUTION OF THE UNITED STATES

We the People of the United States, in order to form a more perfect Union, establish Justice, ensure Domestic Tranquillity, provide for the common Defence, promote the general Welfare, and secure the Blessings of Liberty to ourselves and our Posterity, do ordain and establish this CONSTITUTION for the United States of America.

Articles I-VII
* * * * *

AMENDMENTS TO THE CONSTITUTION

Article I
Congress shall make no law respecting an establishment of religion, or prohibiting the free exercise thereof; or abridging the freedom of speech or of the press; or the right of the people peaceably to assemble, and to petition the government for a redress of grievances.

Article II
A well-regulated militia being necessary to the security of a free state, the right of the people to keep and bear arms shall not be infringed.

Article III
No soldier shall, in time of peace, be quartered in any house without the consent of the owner, nor in time of war but in a manner to be prescribed by law.

Article IV
The right of the people to be secure in their persons, houses, papers, and effects, against unreasonable searches and seizures, shall not be violated, and no warrants shall issue but upon probable cause, supported by oath or affirmation, and particularly describing the place to be searched, and the persons or things to be seized.

Article V
No person shall be held to answer for a capital or other infamous crime unless on a presentment or indictment of a grand jury, except in cases arising in the land or naval forces, or in the militia, when in actual service, in time of war or public danger; nor shall any person be subject for the same offence to be twice put in jeopardy of life or limb; nor shall be compelled in any criminal case to be a witness against himself, nor be deprived of life, liberty, or property, without due process of law; nor shall private property be taken for public use without just compensation.

Article VI
In all criminal prosecutions, the accused shall enjoy the right to a speedy and public trial, by an impartial jury of the state and district wherein the crime shall have been committed, which district shall have been previously ascertained by law, and to be informed of the nature and cause of the accusation; to be confronted with the witnesses against him; to have compulsory process for obtaining witnesses in his favor, and to have the assistance of counsel for his defence.

Article VII
In suits at common law, where the value in controversy shall exceed twenty dollars, the right of trial by jury shall be preserved, and no fact tried by a jury shall be otherwise re-examined in any court of the United States than according to the rules of the common law.

Article VIII
Excessive bail shall not be required, nor excessive fines imposed, nor cruel and unusual punishments inflicted.

Article IX
The enumeration in the constitution of certain rights shall not be construed to deny or disparage others retained by the people.

Article X
The powers not delegated to the United States by the constitution, nor prohibited by it to the states, are reserved to the states respectively, or to the people.

[*The foregoing ten amendments were adopted at the first session of Congress, and were declared to be in force, December 15, 1791.*]

Articles XI-XIII
* * * * *

Article XIV
1. All persons born or naturalized in the United States, and subject to the jurisdiction thereof, are citizens of the United States and of the state wherein they reside. No state shall make or enforce any law which shall abridge the privileges or immunities of citizens of the United States; nor shall any state deprive any person of life, liberty, or property without due process of law; nor deny to any person within its jurisdiction the equal protection of the law.

2.-4. * * * * *

5. The Congress shall have power to enforce, by appropriate legislation, the provisions of this article.

[*Declared in force, July 28, 1868.*]

* * * * *

EUROPEAN CONVENTION FOR THE PROTECTION OF HUMAN RIGHTS AND FUNDAMENTAL FREEDOMS (1950)

[*The European Convention on Human Rights*]

The Governments signatory hereto, being Members of the Council of Europe,

Considering the Universal Declaration of Human Rights proclaimed by the General Assembly of the United Nations on 10 December 1948;

Considering that this Declaration aims at securing the universal and effective recognition and observance of the Rights therein declared;

Considering that the aim of the Council of Europe is the achievement of greater unity between its Members and that one of the methods by which the aim is to be pursued is the maintenance and further realization of Human Rights and Fundamental Freedoms;

Reaffirming their profound belief in those Fundamental Freedoms which are the foundation of justice and peace in the world and are best maintained on the one hand by an effective political democracy and on the other by a common understanding and observance of the Human Rights upon which they depend;

Being resolved, as the Governments of European countries which are like-minded and have a common heritage of political traditions, ideals, freedom and the rule of law to take the first steps for the collective enforcement of certain of the Rights stated in the Universal Declaration;

Have agreed as follows:

Article 1
The High Contracting Parties shall secure to everyone within their jurisdiction the rights and freedoms defined in Section I of this Convention.

SECTION I

Article 2

1. Everyone's right to life shall be protected by law. No one shall be deprived of his life intentionally save in the execution of a sentence of a court following his conviction of a crime for which this penalty is provided by law.

2. Deprivation of life shall not regarded as inflicted in contravention of this article when it results from the use of force which is no more than absolutely necessary:

(a) in defence of any person from unlawful violence;

(b) in order to effect a lawful arrest or to prevent the escape of a person lawfully detained;

(c) in action lawfully taken for the purpose of quelling a riot or insurrection.

Article 3

No one shall be subjected to torture or to inhuman or degrading treatment or punishment.

Article 4

1. No one shall be held in slavery or servitude.

2. No one shall be required to perform forced or compulsory labour.

3. For the purpose of this article the term 'forced or compulsory labour' shall not include:

(a) any work required to be done in the ordinary course of detention imposed according to the provisions of Article 5 of this Convention or during conditional release from such detention;

(b) any service of a military character or, in case of conscientious objectors in countries where they are recognized, service exacted instead of compulsory military service;

(c) any service exacted in case of an emergency or calamity threatening the life or well-being of the community;

(d) any work or service which forms part of normal civic obligations.

Article 5

1. Everyone has the right to liberty and security of person.

No one shall be deprived of his liberty save in the following cases and in accordance with a procedure prescribed by law:

(a) the lawful detention of a person after conviction by a competent court;

(b) the lawful arrest or detention of a person for non-compliance with the lawful order of a court or in order to secure the fulfilment of any obligation prescribed by law;

(c) the lawful arrest or detention of a person effected for the purpose of bringing him before the competent legal authority on reasonable suspicion of having committed an offence or when it is reasonably considered necessary to prevent his committing an offence or fleeing after having done so;

(d) the detention of a minor by lawful order for the purpose of educational supervision or his lawful detention for the purpose of bringing him before the competent legal authority;

(e) the lawful detention of persons for the prevention of the spreading of infectious diseases, of persons of unsound mind, alcoholics or drug addicts, or vagrants;

(f) the lawful arrest or detention of a person to prevent his effecting an unauthorized entry into the country or of a person against whom action is being taken with a view to deportation or extradition.

2. Everyone who is arrested shall be informed promptly, in a language which he understands, of the reasons for his arrest and of any charge against him.

3. Everyone arrested or detained in accordance with the provisions of paragraph 1(c) of this article shall be brought promptly before a judge or other officer authorized by law to

exercise judicial power and shall be entitled to trial within a reasonable time or to release pending trial. Release may be conditioned by guarantees to appear for trial.

4. Everyone who is deprived of his liberty by arrest or detention shall be entitled to take proceedings by which the lawfulness of his detention shall be decided speedily by a court and his release ordered if the detention is not lawful.

5. Everyone who has been the victim of arrest or detention in contravention of the provisions of this article shall have an enforceable right to compensation.

Article 6

1. In the determination of his civil rights and obligations or of any criminal charge against him, everyone is entitled to a fair and public hearing within a reasonable time by an independent and impartial tribunal established by law. Judgment shall be pronounced publicly but the press and public may be excluded from all or part of the trial in the interest of morals, public order or national security in a democratic society, where the interests of juveniles or the protection of the private life of the parties so require, or to the extent strictly necessary in the opinion of the court in special circumstances where publicity would prejudice the interests of justice.

2. Everyone charged with a criminal offence shall be presumed innocent until proved guilty according to law.

3. Everyone charged with a criminal offence has the following minimum rights:

(a) to be informed promptly, in a language which he understands and in detail, of the nature and cause of the accusation against him;

(b) to have adequate time and facilities for the preparation of his defence;

(c) to defend himself in person or through legal assistance of his own choosing or, if he has not sufficient means to pay for legal assistance, to be given it free when the interests of justice so require;

(d) to examine or have examined witnesses against him and to obtain the attendance and examination of witnesses on his behalf under the same conditions as witnesses against him;

(e) to have the free assistance of an interpreter if he cannot understand or speak the language used in court.

Article 7

1. No one shall be held guilty of any criminal offence on account of any act or omission which did not constitute a criminal offence under national or international law at the time when it was committed. Nor shall a heavier penalty be imposed than the one that was applicable at the time the criminal offence was committed.

2. This article shall not prejudice the trial and punishment of any person for any act or omission which, at the time when it was committed, was criminal according to the general principles of law recognized by civilized nations.

Article 8

1. Everyone has the right to respect for his private and family life, his home and his correspondence.

2. There shall be no interference by a public authority with the exercise of this right except such as is in accordance with the law and is necessary in a democratic society in the interests of national security, public safety or the economic well-being of the country, for the prevention of disorder or crime, for the protection of health or morals, or for the protection of the rights and freedoms of others.

Article 9

1. Everyone has the right to freedom of thought, conscience and religion; this right includes freedom to change his religion or belief, and freedom, either alone or in community with others and in public or private, to manifest his religion or belief, in worship, teaching, practice and observance.

2. Freedom to manifest one's religion or beliefs shall be subject only to such limitations as are prescribed by law and are necessary in a democratic society in the interests of public safety, for the protection of public order, health or morals, or for the protection of the rights and freedoms of others.

Article 10

1. Everyone has the right to freedom of expression. This right shall include freedom to hold opinions and to receive and impart information and ideas without interference by public authority and regardless of frontiers. This article shall not prevent States from requiring the licensing of broadcasting, television or cinema enterprises.

2. The exercise of these freedoms, since it carries with it duties and responsibilities, may be subject to such formalities, conditions, restrictions or penalties as are prescribed by law and are necessary in a democratic society, in the interests of national security, territorial integrity or public safety, for the prevention of disorder or crime, for the protection of health or morals, for the protection of the reputation or rights of others, for preventing the disclosure of information received in confidence, or for maintaining the authority and impartiality of the judiciary.

Article 11

1. Everyone has the right to freedom of peaceful assembly and to freedom of association with others, including the right to form and to join trade unions for the protection of his interests.

2. No restrictions shall be placed on the exercise of these rights other than such as are prescribed by law and are necessary in a democratic society in the interests of national security or public safety, for the prevention of disorder or crime, of the protection of health or morals or for the protection of the rights and freedoms of others. This article shall not prevent the imposition of lawful restrictions on the exercise of these rights by members of the armed forces, of the police or of the administration of the State.

Article 12

Men and women of marriageable age have the right to marry and to found a family, according to the national laws governing the exercise of this right.

Article 13

Everyone whose rights and freedoms as set forth in this Convention are violated shall have an effective remedy before a national authority notwithstanding that the violation has been committed by persons acting in an official capacity.

Article 14

The enjoyment of the rights and freedoms set forth in this Convention shall be secured without discrimination on any ground such as sex, race, colour, language, religion, political or other opinion, national or social origin, association with a national minority, property, birth or other status.

Article 15

1. In time of war or other public emergency threatening the life of the nation any High Contracting Party may take measures derogating from its obligations under this Convention to the extent strictly required by the exigencies of the situation, provided that such measures are not inconsistent with its other obligations under international law.

2. No derogation from Article 2, except in respect of deaths resulting from lawful acts of war, or from Articles 3, 4 (paragraph 1) and 7 shall be made under this provision.

3. Any High Contracting Party availing itself of this right of derogation shall keep the Secretary-General of the Council of Europe fully informed of the measures which it has taken and the reasons therefor. It shall also inform the Secretary-General of the Council of Europe when such measures have ceased to operate and the provisions of the Convention are again being fully executed.

Article 16
Nothing in Articles 10, 11, and 14 shall be regarded as preventing the High Contracting Parties from imposing restrictions on the political activity of aliens.

Article 17
Nothing in this Convention may be interpreted as implying for any State, group or person any right to engage in any activity or perform any act aimed at the destruction of any of the rights and freedoms set forth herein or at their limitation to a greater extent than is provided for in the Convention.

Article 18
The restrictions permitted under this Convention to the said rights and freedoms shall not be applied for any purpose other than those for which they have been prescribed.

SECTION II

Article 19
To ensure the observance of the engagements undertaken by the High Contracting Parties in the present Convention, there shall be set up:

1. A European Commission of Human Rights hereinafter referred to as 'the Commission';
2. A European Court of Human Rights, hereinafter referred to as 'the Court'.

SECTION III

Article 20
The Commission shall consist of a number of members equal to that of the High Contracting Parties. No two members of the Commission may be nationals of the same State.

Article 21

1. The members of the Commission shall be elected by the Committee of Ministers by an absolute majority of votes, from a list of names drawn up by the Bureau of the Consultative Assembly; each group of the Representatives of the High Contracting Parties in the Consultative Assembly shall put forward three candidates, of whom two at least shall be its nationals.
2. As far as applicable, the same procedure shall be followed to complete the Commission in the event of other States subsequently becoming Parties to this Convention, and in filling casual vacancies.

Article 22

1. The members of the Commission shall be elected for a period of six years. They may be re-elected. However, of the members elected at the first election, the terms of seven members shall expire at the end of three years.
2. The members whose terms are to expire at the end of the initial period of three years shall be chosen by lot by the Secretary-General of the Council of Europe immediately after the first election has been completed.

3.-6. *****

Article 23
The members of the Commission shall sit on the Commission in their individual capacity.

Article 24
Any High Contracting Party may refer to the Commission, through the Secretary-General of the Council of Europe, any alleged breach of the provisions of the Convention by another High Contracting Party.

Article 25

1. The Commission may receive petitions addressed to the Secretary-General of the Council of Europe from any person, non-governmental organization or group of individuals claiming to be the victim of a violation by one of the High Contracting Parties of the rights set forth in this Convention, provided that the High Contracting Party against which the complaint has been lodged has declared that it recognizes the competence of the Commission to receive such petitions. Those of the High Contracting Parties who have made such a declaration undertake not to hinder in any way the effective exercise of this right.

2. Such declarations may be made for a specific period.

3. The declarations shall be deposited with the Secretary-General of the Council of Europe who shall transmit copies thereof to the High Contracting Parties and publish them.

4. The Commission shall only exercise the powers provided for in this article when at least six High Contracting Parties are bound by declarations made in accordance with the preceding paragraphs.

Article 26

The Commission may only deal with the matter after all domestic remedies have been exhausted, according to the generally recognized rules of international law, and within a period of six months from the date on which the final decision was taken.

Article 27

1. The Commission shall not deal with any petition submitted under Article 25 which

(a) is anonymous, or

(b) is substantially the same as a matter which has already been examined by the Commission or has already been submitted to another procedure or international investigation or settlement and if it contains no relevant new information.

2. The Commission shall consider inadmissible any petition submitted under Article 25 which it considers incompatible with the provisions of the present Convention, manifestly ill-founded, or an abuse of the right of petition.

3. The Commission shall reject any petition referred to it which it considers inadmissible under Article 26.

Article 28

In the event of the Commission accepting a petition referred to it:

(a) it shall, with a view to ascertaining the facts undertake together with the representatives of the parties an examination of the petition and, if need be, an investigation, for the effective conduct of which the States concerned shall furnish all necessary facilities, after an exchange of views with the Commission:

(b) it shall place itself at the disposal of the parties concerned with a view to securing a friendly settlement of the matter on the basis of respect for Human Rights as defined in this Convention.

Article 29

[After it has accepted a petition submitted under Article 25, the Commission may nevertheless decide unanimously to reject the petition if, in the course of its examination, it finds that the existence of one of the grounds for non-acceptance provided for in Article 27 has been established.

In such a case, the decision shall be communicated to the parties.]

Article 30

If the [Commission] succeeds in effecting a friendly settlement in accordance with Article 28, it shall draw up a Report which shall be sent to the States concerned, to the Committee of Ministers and to the Secretary-General of the Council of Europe for publication. This Report shall be confined to a brief statement of the facts and of the solution reached.

Article 31

1. If a solution is not reached, the Commission shall draw up a Report on the facts and state its opinion as to whether the facts found disclose a breach by the State concerned of its obligations under the Convention. The opinions of all the members of the Commission on this point may be stated in the Report.

2. The Report shall be transmitted to the Committee of Ministers. It shall also be transmitted to the States concerned, who shall not be at liberty to publish it.

3. In transmitting the Report to the Committee of Ministers the Commission may make such proposals as it thinks fit.

Article 32

1. If the question is not referred to the Court in accordance with Article 48 of this Convention within a period of three months from the date of the transmission of the Report to the Committee of Ministers, the Committee of Ministers shall decide by a majority of two-thirds of the members entitled to sit on the Committee whether there has been a violation of the Convention.

2. In the affirmative case the Committee of Ministers shall prescribe a period during which the Contracting Party concerned must take the measures required by the decision of the Committee of Ministers.

3. If the High Contracting Party concerned has not taken satisfactory measures within the prescribed period, the Committee of Ministers shall decide by the majority provided for in paragraph 1 above what effect shall be given to its original decision and shall publish the Report.

4. The High Contracting Parties undertake to regard as binding on them any decision which the Committee of Ministers may take in application of the preceding paragraphs.

Article 33

The Commission shall meet *in camera*.

Article 34

[Subject to the provisions of Article 29, the] Commission shall take its decision by a majority of the Members present and voting; . . .

Article 35

The Commission shall meet as the circumstances require. The meetings shall be convened by the Secretary-General of the Council of Europe.

Article 36

The Commission shall draw up its own rules of procedure.

Article 37

* * * * *

SECTION IV

Article 38

The European Court of Human Rights shall consist of a number of judges equal to that of the Members of the Council of Europe. No two judges may be nationals of the same State.

Article 39

1. The members of the Court shall be elected by the Consultative Assembly by a majority of the votes cast from a list of persons nominated by the Members of the Council of Europe; each Member shall nominate three candidates, of whom two at least shall be its nationals.

2. As far as applicable, the same procedure shall be followed to complete the Court in the event of the admission of new members of the Council of Europe, and in filling casual vacancies.

3. The candidates shall be of high moral character and must either possess the qualifications required for appointment to high judicial office or be jurisconsults of recognized competence.

Article 40

1. The members of the Court shall be elected for a period of nine years. They may be re-elected. However, of the members elected at the first election the terms of four members shall expire at the end of three years, and the terms of four more members shall expire at the end of six years.

2. The members whose terms are to expire at the end of the initial periods of three and six years shall be chosen by lot by the Secretary-General immediately after the first election has been completed.

3.-6. * * * * *

Article 41

The Court shall elect its President and Vice-President for a period of three years. They may be re-elected.

Articles 42, 43

* * * * *

Article 44

Only the High Contracting Parties and the Commission shall have the right to bring a case before the Court.

Article 45

The jurisdiction of the Court shall extend to all cases concerning the interpretation and application of the present Convention which the High Contracting Parties or the Commission shall refer to it in accordance with Article 48.

Article 46

1. Any of the High Contracting Parties may at any time declare that it recognizes as compulsory *ipso facto* and without special agreement the jurisdiction of the Court in all matters concerning the interpretation and application of the present Convention.

2. The declarations referred to above may be made unconditionally or on condition of reciprocity on the part of several or certain other High Contracting Parties or for a specified period.

3. These declarations shall be deposited with the Secretary-General of the Council of Europe who shall transmit copies thereof to the High Contracting Parties.

Article 47

The Court may only deal with a case after the Commission has acknowledged the failure of efforts for a friendly settlement and within the period of three months provided for in Article 32.

Article 48

The following may bring a case before the Court, provided that the High Contracting Party concerned, if there is only one, or the High Contracting Parties concerned, if there is more than one, are subject to the compulsory jurisdiction of the Court or, failing that, with the consent of the High Contracting Party concerned, if there is only one, or of the High Contracting Parties concerned if there is more than one:

(a) the Commission;
(b) a High Contracting Party whose national is alleged to be a victim;
(c) a High Contracting Party which referred the case to the Commission;
(d) a High Contracting Party against which the complaint has been lodged.

Article 49
In the event of dispute as to whether the Court has jurisdiction, the matter shall be settled by the decision of the Court.

Article 50
If the Court finds that a decision or a measure taken by a legal authority or any other authority of a High Contracting Party, is completely or partially in conflict with the obligations arising from the present Convention, and if the internal law of the said Party allows only partial reparation to be made for the consequences of this decision or measure, the decision of the Court shall, if necessary, afford just satisfaction to the injured party.

Article 51
1. Reasons shall be given for the judgment of the Court.
2. If the judgment does not represent in whole or in part the unanimous opinion of the judges, any judge shall be entitled to deliver a separate opinion.

Article 52
The judgment of the Court shall be final.

Article 53
The High Contracting Parties undertake to abide by the decision of the Court in any case to which they are parties.

Articles 54-59
* * * * *

SECTION V

Article 60
Nothing in this Convention shall be construed as limiting or derogating from any of the human rights and fundamental freedoms which may be ensured under the laws of any High Contracting Party or under any other agreement to which it is a Party.

Articles 61-63
* * * * *

Article 64
1. Any State may, when signing this Convention or when depositing its instrument of ratification, make a reservation in respect of any particular provision of the Convention to the extent that any law then in force in its territory is not in conformity with the provision. Reservations of a general character shall not be permitted under this article.
2. Any reservation made under this article shall contain a brief statement of the law concerned.
* * * * *

Protocols

1. Enforcement of certain Rights and Freedoms not included in Section I of the Convention
The Governments signatory hereto, being Members of the Council of Europe,

Being resolved to take steps to ensure the collective enforcement of certain rights and freedoms other than those already included in Section I of the Convention for the Protection of Human Rights and Fundamental Freedoms signed at Rome on 4th November 1950 (hereinafter referred to as 'the Convention'),

Have agreed as follows:

Article 1
Every natural or legal person is entitled to the peaceful enjoyment of his possessions. No one shall be deprived of his possessions except in the public interest and subject to the conditions provided for by law and by the general principles of international law.

The preceding provisions shall not, however, in any way impair the right of a State to enforce such laws as it deems necessary to control the use of property in accordance with the general interest or to secure the payment of taxes or other contributions or penalties.

Article 2

No person shall be denied the right to education. In the exercise of any functions which it assumes in relation to education and to teaching, the State shall respect the right of parents to ensure such education and teaching in conformity with their own religious and philosophical convictions.

Article 3

The High Contracting Parties undertake to hold free elections at reasonable intervals by secret ballot, under conditions which will ensure the free expression of the opinion of the people in the choice of the legislature.

* * * * *

4. *Protecting certain Additional Rights*

The Governments signatory hereto, being Members of the Council of Europe.

Being resolved to take steps to ensure the collective enforcement of certain rights and freedoms other than those already included in Section I of the Convention for the Protection of Human Rights and Fundamental Freedoms signed at Rome on 4 November 1950 (hereinafter referred to as 'the Convention') and in Articles 1 to 3 of the First Protocol to the Convention, signed at Paris on 20 March 1952,

Have agreed as follows:

Article 1

No one shall be deprived of his liberty merely on the ground of inability to fulfil a contractual obligation.

Article 2

1. Everyone lawfully within the territory of a State shall, within that territory, have the right to liberty of movement and freedom to choose his residence.
2. Everyone shall be free to leave any country, including his own.
3. No restrictions shall be placed on the exercise of these rights other than such as are in accordance with law and are necessary in a democratic society in the interests of national security or public safety, for the maintenance of 'ordre public', for the prevention of crime, for the protection of the rights and freedoms of others.
4. The rights set forth in paragraph 1 may also be subject, in particular areas, to restrictions imposed in accordance with law and justified by the public interest in a democratic society.

Article 3

1. No one shall be expelled, by means either of an individual or of a collective measure, from the territory of the State of which he is a national.
2. No one shall be deprived of the right to enter the territory of the State of which he is a national.

Article 4

Collective expulsion of aliens is prohibited.

* * * * *

Note This Protocol has not yet been ratified by the United Kingdom.

6. *Concerning the Abolition of the Death Penalty*

The member States of the Council of Europe, signatory to this Protocol to the Convention for the Protection of Human Rights and Fundamental Freedoms, signed at Rome on 4 November 1950 (hereinafter referred to as "the Convention").

Considering that the evolution that has occurred in several member States of the Council of Europe expresses a general tendency in favour of abolition of the death penalty.

Have agreed as follows:

Article 1
The death penalty shall be abolished. No one shall be condemned to such penalty or executed.

Article 2
A state may make provision in its law for the death penalty in respect of acts committed in time of war or of imminent threat of war; such penalty shall be applied only in the instance laid down in the law and in accordance with its provisions. The State shall communicate to the Secretary General of the Council of Europe the relevant provisions of that law.

Article 3
No derogation from the provision of this Protocol shall be made under Article 15 of the Convention.

Article 4
No reservation may be made under Article 64 of the Convention in respect of the provisions of this Protocol.

Note Not ratified by the United Kingdom. Protocols 7 and 8 are not included as they are not yet in force and have not been ratified by the UK.

TREATY
establishing
THE EUROPEAN ECONOMIC COMMUNITY
(Rome, 25 March 1957)

Article 1
By this Treaty, the High Contracting Parties establish among themselves a EUROPEAN ECONOMIC COMMUNITY.

Article 2
The Community shall have as its task, by establishing a common market and progressively approximating the economic policies of Member States, to promote throughout the Community a harmonious development of economic activities, a continuous and balanced expansion, an increase in stability, an accelerated raising of the standard of living and closer relations between the States belonging to it.

Article 3
For the purposes set out in Article 2, the activities of the Community shall include, as provided in this Treaty and in accordance with the timetable set out therein:

(a) the elimination, as between Member States, of customs duties and of quantitative restrictions on the import and export of goods, and of all other measures having equivalent effect;

(b) the establishment of a common customs tariff and of a common commercial policy towards third countries;

(c) the abolition, as between Member States, of obstacles to freedom of movement for persons, services and capital;

(d) the adoption of a common policy in the sphere of agriculture;

(e) the adoption of a common policy in the sphere of transport;

(f) the institution of a system ensuring that competition in the common market is not distorted;

(g) the application of procedures by which the economic policies of Member States can be coordinated and disequilibria in their balances of payments remedied;

(h) the approximation of the laws of Member States to the extent required for the proper functioning of the common market;

(i) the creation of a European Social Fund in order to improve employment opportunities for workers and to contribute to the raising of their standard of living;

(j) the establishment of a European Investment Bank to facilitate the economic expansion of the Community by opening up fresh resources;

(k) the association of the overseas countries and territories in order to increase trade and to promote jointly economic and social development.

Article 4

1. The tasks entrusted to the Community shall be carried out by the following institutions:

an ASSEMBLY
a COUNCIL,
a COMMISSION,
a COURT OF JUSTICE.

Each institution shall act within the limits of the powers conferred upon it by this Treaty.

2. The Council and the Commission shall be assisted by an Economic and Social Committee acting in an advisory capacity.

[3. The audit shall be carried out by a Court of Auditors acting within the limits of the powers conferred upon it by this Treaty.]

Article 5

Member States shall take all appropriate measures; whether general or particular, to ensure fulfilment of the obligations arising out of this Treaty or resulting from action taken by the institutions of the Community. They shall facilitate the achievement of the Community's tasks.

They shall abstain from any measure which could jeopardise the attainment of the objectives of this Treaty.

Article 6

1. Member States shall, in close cooperation with the institutions of the Community, coordinate their respective economic policies to the extent necessary to attain the objectives of this Treaty.

2. The institutions of the Community shall take care not to prejudice the internal and external financial stability of the Member States.

Article 7

Within the scope of application of this Treaty, and without prejudice to any special provisions contained therein; any discrimination on grounds of nationality shall be prohibited.

The Council may, on a proposal from the Commission and after consulting the Assembly, adopt, by a qualified majority, rules designed to prohibit such discrimination.

★★★★★

Article 30

Quantitative restrictions on imports and all measures having equivalent effect shall, without prejudice to the following provisions, be prohibited between Member States.

★★★★★

Article 36

The provisions of Articles 30 to 34 shall not preclude prohibitions or restrictions on imports, exports or goods in transit justified on grounds of public morality, public policy or public security; the protection of health and life of humans, animals or plants; the protection of national treasures possessing artistic, historic or archaeological value; or the protection of industrial and commercial property. Such prohibitions or restrictions shall not, however, constitute a means of arbitrary discrimination or a disguised restriction on trade between Member States.

* * * * *

Article 48

1. Freedom of movement for workers shall be secured within the Community by the end of the transitional period at the latest.
2. Such freedom of movement shall entail the abolition of any discrimination based on nationality between workers of the Member States as regards employment, remuneration and other conditions of work and employment.
3. It shall entail the right, subject to limitations justified on grounds of public policy, public security or public health:
   (a) to accept offers of employment actually made;
   (b) to move freely within the territory of Member States for this purpose;
   (c) to stay in a Member State for the purpose of employment in accordance with the provisions governing the employment of nationals of that State laid down by law, regulation or administrative action;
   (d) to remain in the territory of a Member State after having been employed in that State, subject to conditions which shall be embodied in implementing regulations to be drawn up by the Commission.
4. The provisions of this Article shall not apply to employment in the public service.

* * * * *

Article 59

Within the framework of the provisions set out below, restrictions on freedom to provide services within the Community shall be progressively abolished during the transitional period in respect of nationals of Member States who are established in a State of the Community other than that of the person for whom the services are intended.

The Council may, acting unanimously on a proposal from the Commission, extend the provisions of this Chapter to nationals of a third country who provide services and who are established within the Community.

Article 60

Services shall be considered to be "services" within the meaning of this Treaty where they are normally provided for remuneration, in so far as they are not governed by the provisions relating to freedom of movement for goods, capital and persons.

"Services" shall in particular include:

(a) activities of an industrial character,
(b) activities of a commercial character;
(c) activities of craftsmen;
(d) activities of the professions.

Without prejudice to the provisions of the Chapter relating to the right of establishment, the person providing a service may, in order to do so, temporarily pursue his activity in the State where the service is provided, under the same conditions as are imposed by that State on its own nationals.

* * * * *

Article 119

Each Member State shall during the first stage ensure and subsequently maintain the application of the principle that men and women should receive equal pay for equal work.

For the purpose of this Article, "pay" means the ordinary basic or minimum wage or salary and any other consideration, whether in cash or in kind, which the worker receives, directly or indirectly, in respect of his employment from his employer.

Equal pay without discrimination based on sex means:

(a) that pay for the same work at piece rates shall be calculated on the basis of the same unit of measurement;

(b) that pay for work at time rates shall be the same for the same job.

* * * * *

Article 169

If the Commission considers that a Member State has failed to fulfil an obligation under this Treaty, it shall deliver a reasoned opinion on the matter after giving the State concerned the opportunity to submit its observations.

If the State concerned does not comply with the opinion within the period laid down by the Commission, the latter may bring the matter before the Court of Justice.

Article 170

A Member State which considers that another Member State has failed to fulfil an obligation under this Treaty may bring the matter before the Court of Justice.

Before a Member State brings an action against another Member State for an alleged infringement of an obligation under this Treaty, it shall bring the matter before the Commission.

The Commission shall deliver a reasoned opinion after each of the States concerned has been given the opportunity to submit its own case and its observations on the other party's case both orally and in writing.

If the Commission has not delivered an opinion within three months of the date on which the matter was brought before it, the absence of such opinion shall not prevent the matter from being brought before the Court of Justice.

Article 171

If the Court of Justice finds that a Member State has failed to fulfil an obligation under this Treaty, the State shall be required to take the necessary measures to comply with the judgment of the Court of Justice.

Article 172

Regulations made by the Council pursuant to the provisions of this Treaty may give the Court of Justice unlimited jurisdiction in regard to the penalties provided for in such regulations.

Article 173

The Court of Justice shall review the legality of acts of the Council and the Commission other than recommendations or opinions. It shall for this purpose have jurisdiction in actions brought by a Member State, the Council or the Commission on grounds of lack of competence, infringement of an essential procedural requirement, infringement of this Treaty or of any rule of law relating to its application, or misuse of powers.

Any natural or legal person may, under the same conditions, institute proceedings against a decision addressed to that person or against a decision which, although in the form of a regulation or a decision addressed to another person, is of direct and individual concern to the former.

The proceedings provided for in this Article shall be instituted within two months of the publication of the measure, or of its notification to the plaintiff, or, in the absence thereof, of the day on which it came to the knowledge of the latter, as the case may be.

Article 174

If the action is well founded, the Court of Justice shall declare the act concerned to be void.

In the case of a regulation, however, the Court of Justice shall, if it considers this necessary, state which of the effects of the regulation which it has declared void shall be considered as definitive.

* * * * *

Article 177

The Court of Justice shall have jurisdiction to give preliminary rulings concerning:

(a) the interpretation of this Treaty;

(b) the validity and interpretation of acts of the institutions of the Community;

(c) the interpretation of the statutes of bodies established by an act of the Council, where those statutes so provide.

Where such a question is raised before any court or tribunal of a Member State, that court or tribunal may, if it considers that a decision on the question is necessary to enable it to give judgment, request the Court of Justice to give a ruling thereon.

Where any such question is raised in a case pending before a court or tribunal of a Member State, against whose decisions there is no judicial remedy under national law, that court or tribunal shall bring the matter before the Court of Justice.

* * * * *

Article 189

In order to carry out their task the Council and the Commission shall, in accordance with the provisions of this Treaty, make regulations, issue directives, take decisions, make recommendations or deliver opinions.

A regulation shall have general application. It shall be binding in its entirety and directly applicable in all Member States.

A directive shall be binding, as to the result to be achieved, upon each Member State to which it is addressed, but shall leave to the national authorities the choice of form and methods.

A decision shall be binding in its entirety upon those to whom it is addressed.

Recommendations and opinions shall have no binding force.

* * * * *

REGULATION (EEC) No 1612/68 OF THE COUNCIL of 15 October 1968

on freedom of movement for workers within the Community

THE COUNCIL OF THE EUROPEAN COMMUNITIES.

Having regard to the Treaty establishing the European Economic Community, and in particular Article 49 thereof;

Having regard to the proposal from the Commission;

Having regard to the Opinion of the European Parliament;

Having regard to the Opinion of the Economic and Social Committee;

Whereas freedom of movement for workers should be secured within the Community by the end of the transitional period at the latest; whereas the attainment of this objective entails the abolition of any discrimination based on nationality between workers of the Member States as regards employment, remuneration and other conditions of work and employment, as well as the right of such workers to move freely within the Community in order to pursue activities as employed persons subject to any limitations justified on grounds of public policy, public security or public health;

Whereas by reason in particular of the early establishment of the customs union and in order to ensure the simultaneous completion of the principal foundations of the Community, provisions should be adopted to enable the objectives laid down in Articles 48 and 49 of the Treaty in the field of freedom of movement to be achieved and to perfect measures adopted successively under Regulation No 15 on the first steps for attainment of freedom of movement and under Council Regulation No 38/64/EEC of 25 March 1964 on freedom of movement for workers within the Community;

Whereas freedom of movement constitutes a fundamental right of workers and their families; whereas mobility of labour within the Community must be one of the means by which the worker is guaranteed the possibility of improving his living and working conditions and promoting his social advancement, while helping to satisfy the requirements of the economies of the Member States; whereas the right of all workers in the Member States to pursue the activity of their choice within the Community should be affirmed;

Whereas such right must be enjoyed without discrimination by permanent, seasonal and frontier workers and by those who pursue their activities for the purpose of providing services;

Whereas the right of freedom of movement, in order that it may be exercised, by objective standards, in freedom and dignity, requires that equality of treatment shall be ensured in fact and in law in respect of all matters relating to the actual pursuit of activities as employed persons and to eligibility for housing, and also that obstacles to the mobility of workers shall be eliminated, in particular as regards the worker's right to be joined by his family and the conditions for the integration of that family into the host country;

Whereas the principle of non-discrimination between Community workers entails that all nationals of Member States have the same priority as regards employment as is enjoyed by national workers;

★ ★ ★ ★ ★

Note Parts of the Preamble relating to those parts of the Regulation not reproduced herein are omitted.

HAS ADOPTED THIS REGULATION:

PART 1: EMPLOYMENT AND WORKERS' FAMILIES

TITLE I—ELIGIBILITY FOR EMPLOYMENT

Article 1

1. Any national of a Member State, shall, irrespective of his place of residence, have the right to take up an activity as an employed person, and to pursue such activity, within the territory of another Member State in accordance with the provisions laid down by law, regulation or administrative action governing the employment of nationals of that State.

2. He shall, in particular, have the right to take up available employment in the territory of another Member State with the same priority as nationals of that State.

Article 2

Any national of a Member State and any employer pursuing an activity in the territory of a Member State may exchange their applications for and offers of employment, and may conclude and perform contracts of employment in accordance with the provisions in force laid down by law, regulation or administrative action, without any discrimination resulting therefrom.

Article 3

1. Under this Regulation, provisions laid down by law, regulation or administrative action or administrative practices of a Member State shall not apply:

—where they limit application for and offers of employment, or the right of foreign nationals to take up and pursue employment or subject these to conditions not applicable in respect of their own nationals; or

—where, though applicable irrespective of nationality, their exclusive or principal aim or effect is to keep nationals of other Member States away from the employment offered.

This provision shall not apply to conditions relating to linguistic knowledge required by reason of the nature of the post to be filled.

2. *****

Article 4

*****

Article 5

A national of a Member State who seeks employment in the territory of another Member State shall receive the same assistance there as that afforded by the employment offices in that State to their own nationals seeking employment.

Article 6

*****

TITLE II—EMPLOYMENT AND EQUALITY OF TREATMENT

Article 7

1. A worker who is a national of a Member State may not, in the territory of another Member State, be treated differently from national workers by reason of his nationality in respect of any conditions of employment and work, in particular as regards remuneration, dismissal, and should he become unemployed, reinstatement or re-employment.

2. He shall enjoy the same social and tax advantages as national workers.

3. He shall also, by virtue of the same right and under the same conditions as national workers, have access to training in vocational schools and retraining centres.

4. Any clause of a collective or individual agreement or of any other collective regulation concerning eligibility for employment, employment, remuneration and other conditions of work or dismissal shall be null and void in so far as it lays down or authorises discriminatory conditions in respect of workers who are nationals of the other Member States.

Article 8

1. A worker who is a national of a Member State and who is employed in the territory of another Member State shall enjoy equality of treatment as regards membership of trade unions and the exercise of rights attaching thereto, including the right to vote; he may be excluded from taking part in the management of bodies governed by public law and from holding an office governed by public law. Furthermore, he shall have the right of eligibility for workers' representative bodies in the undertaking. The provisions of this Article shall not affect laws or regulations in certain Member States which grant more extensive rights to workers coming from the other Member States.

2. . . .

Article 9

*****

TITLE III—WORKERS' FAMILIES

Article 10

1. The following shall, irrespective of their nationality, have the right to install themselves with a worker who is a national of one Member State and who is employed in the territory of another Member State:

(a) his spouse and their descendants who are under the age of 21 years or are dependants;

(b) dependent relatives in the ascending line of the worker and his spouse.

2. Member States shall facilitate the admission of any member of the family not coming within the provisions of paragraph 1 if dependent on the worker referred to above or living under his roof in the country whence he comes.

3. For the purposes of paragraphs 1 and 2, the worker must have available for his family housing considered as normal for national workers in the region where he is employed; this provision, however must not give rise to discrimination between national workers and workers from the other Member States.

EEC COUNCIL DIRECTIVE 64/221 of 25 February 1964

On the Co-ordination of Special Measures concerning the movement and residence of Foreign Nationals which are justified on Grounds of Public Policy, Public Security or Public Health

THE COUNCIL OF THE EUROPEAN ECONOMIC COMMUNITY,

Having regard to the Treaty establishing the European Economic Community, and in particular Article 56(2) thereof;

Having regard to Council Regulation 15 of August 16, 1961 (J.O. 1961, 1073), on initial measures to bring about free movement of workers within the Community, and in particular Article 47 thereof;

Having regard to Council directive of August 16, 1961 (J.O. 1961, 1513), on administrative procedures and practices governing the entry into and employment and residence in a Member State of workers and their families from other Member States of the Community;

Having regard to the General Programmes for the abolition of restrictions on freedom of establishment and on freedom to provide services, and in particular Title II of each such programme;

Having regard to the Council directive of February 25, 1964 (J.O. 1964, 845), on the abolition of restrictions on movement and residence within the Community for nationals of Member States with regard to establishment and the provision of services;

Having regard to the proposal from the Commission;

Having regard to the Opinion of the European Parliament;

Having regard to the Opinion of the Economic and Social Committee;

Whereas co-ordination of provisions laid down by law, regulation or administrative action which provide for special treatment for foreign nationals on grounds of public policy, public security or public health should in the first place deal with the conditions for entry and residence of nationals of Member States moving within the Community either in order to pursue activities as employed or self-employed persons, or as recipients of services;

Whereas such co-ordination presupposes in particular an approximation of the procedures followed in each Member State when invoking grounds of public policy, public security or public health in matters connected with the movement or residence of foreign nationals;

Whereas, in each Member State, nationals of other Member States should have adequate remedies available to them in respect of the decisions of the administration in such matters;

Whereas it would be of little practical use to compile a list of diseases and disabilities which might endanger public health, public policy or public security and it would be difficult to make such a list exhaustive; whereas it is sufficient to classify such diseases and disabilities in groups;

HAS ADOPTED THIS DIRECTIVE:

Article 1

1. The provisions of this directive shall apply to any national of a Member State who resides in or travels to another Member State of the Community, either in order to pursue an activity as an employed or self-employed person, or as a recipient of services.

2. These provisions shall apply also to the spouse and to members of the family who come within the provisions of the regulations and directives adopted in this field in pursuance of the Treaty.

Article 2

1. This directive relates to all measures concerning entry into their territory, issue or renewal of residence permits, or expulsion from their territory, taken by Member States on grounds of public policy, public security or public health.

2. Such grounds shall not be invoked to service economic ends.

Article 3

1. Measures taken on grounds of public policy or of public security shall be based exclusively on the personal conduct of the individual concerned.

2. Previous criminal convictions shall not in themselves constitute grounds for the taking of such measures.

3. Expiry of the identity card or passport used by the person concerned to enter the host country and to obtain a residence permit shall not justify expulsion from the territory.

4. The State which issued the identity card or passport shall allow the holder of such document to re-enter its territory without any formality even if the document is no longer valid or the nationality of the holder is in dispute.

Article 4

1. The only diseases or disabilities justifying refusal of entry into a territory or refusal to issue a first residence permit shall be those listed in the Annex to this directive. [*Not printed.*]

2. Diseases or disabilities occurring after a first residence permit has been issued shall not justify refusal to renew the residence permit or expulsion from the territory.

3. Member States shall not introduce new provisions or practices which are more restrictive than those in force at the date of notification of this directive.

Article 5

1. A decision to grant or to refuse a first residence permit shall be taken as soon as possible and in any event not later than six months from the date of application for the permit.

The person concerned shall be allowed to remain temporarily in the territory pending a decision either to grant or to refuse a residence permit.

2. The host country may, in cases where this is considered essential, request the Member State of origin of the applicant, and if need be other Member States, to provide information concerning any previous police record. Such enquiries shall not be made as a matter of routine. The Member State consulted shall give its reply within two months.

Article 6

The person concerned shall be informed of the grounds of public policy, public security, or public health upon which the decision taken in his case is based, unless this is contrary to the interests of the security of the State involved.

Article 7

The person concerned shall be officially notified of any decision to refuse the issue or renewal of a residence permit or to expel him from the territory. The period allowed for leaving the territory shall be stated in this notification. Save in cases of urgency, this period shall be not less than 15 days if the person concerned has not yet been granted a residence permit and not less than one month in all other cases.

Article 8

The person concerned shall have the same legal remedies in respect of any decision concerning entry, or refusing the issue or renewal of a residence permit, or ordering expulsion from the territory, as are available to nationals of the State concerned in respect of acts of the administration.

Articles 9-11

*****

CODE OF PRACTICE FOR THE EXERCISE BY POLICE OFFICERS OF STATUTORY POWER OF STOP AND SEARCH (CODE A)

Note This code of practice was issued by the Home Secretary as required by sections 66 and 67 of the Police and Criminal Evidence Act 1984, and was drafted following a process of public consultation to give effect to the recommendation of the Royal Commission on Criminal Procedure (1981, Cmnd. 8092) that there be clear guidelines under which the police should operate. Its legal status is set out in s. 67(11) of the 1984 Act. The notes for guidance (which do not have legal force) are not included in these extracts.

*****

2 Action before a search is carried out

2.1 Where an officer has the reasonable grounds for suspicion necessary to exercise a power of stop and search he may detain the person concerned for the purposes of and with a view to searching him. There is no power to stop or detain a person against his will in order to find grounds for a search.

2.2 Before carrying out a search the officer may question the person about his behaviour or his presence in circumstances which gave rise to the suspicion, since he may have a satisfactory explanation which will make a search unnecessary. If, as a result of any questioning preparatory to a search, or other circumstances which come to the attention of the officer, there cease to be reasonable grounds for suspecting that an article is being carried of a kind for which there is a power of stop and search, no search may take place.

2.3 The reasonable grounds for suspicion which are necessary for the exercise of the initial power to detain may be confirmed or eliminated as a result of the questioning of a person detained for the purposes of a search (or such questioning may reveal reasonable grounds to suspect the possession of a different kind of unlawful article from that originally suspected); but the reasonable grounds for suspicion without which any search or detention for the purposes of a search is unlawful cannot be retrospectively provided by such questioning during his detention or by his refusal to answer any question put to him.

2.4 Before any search of a detained person or attended vehicle takes place the officer must give the person to be searched or in charge of the vehicle the following information:

(i) his name and the name of the police station to which he is attached;
(ii) the object of the search; and
(iii) his grounds for undertaking it.

2.5 If the officer is not in uniform he must show his warrant card.

2.6 Unless it appears to the officer that it will not be practicable to make a record of the search, he must also inform the person to be searched (or the owner or person in charge of a vehicle that is to be searched, as the case may be) that he is entitled to a copy of the record of the search if he asks for it within a year. If the person wishes to have a copy and is not given one on the spot, he should be advised to which police station he should apply.

2.7 If the person to be searched, or in charge of a vehicle to be searched, does not understand what is being said, the officer must take reasonable steps to bring the information in paragraphs 2.4 to 2.6 to his attention. If the person has someone with him then the officer must establish whether that person can interpret.

3 Conduct of the search

3.1 Every reasonable effort must be made to reduce to the minimum the embarrassment that a person being searched may experience.

3.2 Although force may only be used as a last resort, reasonable force may be used if necessary to conduct a search or to detain a person or vehicle for the purposes of a search. A compulsory search may be made only if it has been established that the person is unwilling to co-operate (e.g. by opening a bag).

3.3 The length of time for which a person or vehicle may be detained will depend on the circumstances, but must in all circumstances be reasonable and not extend beyond the time taken for the search. The thoroughness and extent of a search must depend on what is suspected of being carried, and by whom. If the suspicion relates to a particular article, for example an offensive weapon, which is seen to be slipped into a person's pocket then, in the absence of other grounds for suspicion or an opportunity for the article to be moved elsewhere, the search must be confined to that pocket. In the case of a small article which can readily be concealed, such as a drug, and which might be concealed anywhere on the person, a more extensive search may be necessary.

3.4 The search must be conducted at the place where the person or vehicle was first detained or nearby.

3.5 Searches in public must be restricted to superficial examination of outer clothing. There is no power to require a person to remove any clothing in public other than an outer coat, jacket or gloves. Where on reasonable grounds it is considered necessary to conduct a more thorough search (e.g. by requiring someone to take off a T-shirt or headgear), this should be done out of public view (e.g. in a police van or a nearby police station if there is one). Any search involving the removal of more than an outer coat, jacket, gloves, headgear or footwear may only be made by an officer of the same sex as the person searched and may not be made in the presence of anyone of the opposite sex.

4 *****

ANNEX A *****

ANNEX B

REASONABLE GROUNDS FOR SUSPICION [1.5]

1 Reasonable suspicion does not require *certainty* that an unlawful article is being carried; nor does the officer concerned have to be satisfied of this beyond reasonable doubt. Reasonable suspicion, in contrast to *mere* suspicion must be founded on fact. There must be some concrete basis for the officer's suspicion, related to the individual person concerned, which can be considered and evaluated by an objective third person. Mere suspicion, in contrast, is a hunch or instinct which cannot be explained or justified to an objective observer. An officer who has such a hunch or instinct may well be justified in continuing to keep the person under observation or speak to him, but additional grounds which bring up mere suspicion to the level of reasonable suspicion are needed before he may exercise the powers dealt with in this code.

2 Reasonable suspicion may arise from the nature of the property observed or being carried or suspected of being carried coupled with other factors including the time, the place or the suspicious behaviour of the person concerned or those with him. The decision to search must be based on all the facts which, to a careful officer, bear on the likelihood that an article of a certain kind will be found, and not only on what can be seen at the time. So an officer with prior knowledge of the behaviour of someone he sees in a certain situation, or acting on information received (such as a description of a suspected offender) may have reasonable grounds for searching him although another officer would not.

3 Reasonable suspicion cannot be supported on the basis simply of a higher than average chance that the person has committed or is committing an offence, for example because he belongs to a group within which offenders of a certain kind are relatively common, or because of a combination of factors such as these. For example, a person's colour of itself can never be a reasonable ground for suspicion. The mere fact alone that a person is carrying a particular kind of property or is dressed in a certain way or has a certain hairstyle is likewise not of itself sufficient. Nor is the fact that a person is known to have a previous conviction for unlawful possession of an article.

4 The degree or level of suspicion required to establish the reasonable grounds justifying the exercise of powers of stop and search is no less than the degree or level of suspicion required to effect an arrest without warrant for any of the suspected offences to which these powers relate. The powers of stop and search provide an opportunity to establish the commission or otherwise of certain kinds of offences without arrest and may therefore render arrest unnecessary.

5 Paragraph 4 above is subject to the principle that where a police officer has reasonable grounds to suspect that a person is in *innocent* possession of a stolen or prohibited article, the power of stop and search exists notwithstanding that there would be no power of arrest. However every effort should be made to secure the voluntary production of the article before the power is resorted to.

CODE OF PRACTICE FOR THE SEARCHING OF PREMISES BY POLICE OFFICERS AND THE SEIZURE OF PROPERTY FOUND BY POLICE OFFICERS ON PERSONS OR PREMISES (CODE B)

Note See note to Code A (*supra*).

1 General

1.1 This code of practice must be readily available at all police stations for consultation by police officers, detained persons and members of the public.

1.2 The notes for guidance included are not provisions of this code, but are guidance to police officers and others about its application and interpretation.

1.3 This code applies to the following searches of premises:

(a) searches of premises undertaken for the purposes of an investigation into an alleged offence, with the occupier's consent, other than routine scenes of crime searches and searches following the activation of burglar or fire alarms or bomb threat calls;

(b) searches of premises under the powers conferred by sections 17, 18 and 32 of the Police and Criminal Evidence Act 1984;

(c) searches of premises undertaken in pursuance of a search warrant issued in accordance with section 15 of, or Schedule 1 to, that Act.

'Premises' is a wide term which may include vessels and, in certain circumstances, vehicles.

2 Search warrants and production orders

(a) Action to be taken before an application is made

2.1 Where information is received which appears to justify an application, the officer concerned must take reasonable steps to check that the information is accurate, recent and has not been provided maliciously or irresponsibly. An application may not be made on the basis of information from an anonymous source where corroboration has not been sought.

2.2 The officer shall ascertain as specifically as is possible in the circumstances the nature of the articles concerned and their location.

2.3 The officer shall also make enquiries to establish what, if anything, is known about the likely occupier of the premises and the nature of the premises themselves; and whether they have been previously searched and if so how recently; and to obtain any other information relevant to the application.

2.4 No application for a search warrant may be made without the authority of an officer of at least the rank of inspector (or, in a case of urgency where no officer of this rank is readily available, the senior officer on duty). No application for a production order or warrant under Schedule 1 to the Police and Criminal Evidence Act 1984 may be made without the authority of an officer of at least the rank of superintendent.

2.5 Except in a case of urgency, if there is reason to believe that a search might have an adverse effect on relations between the police and the community then the local police community liaison officer shall be consulted before it takes place.

(b) Making an application

2.6 An application for a search warrant must be supported by an information in writing, stating:

(i) the enactment under which the application is made;
(ii) as specifically as is reasonably practicable the premises to be searched and the object of the search; and
(iii) the grounds on which the application is made (including, where the purpose of the proposed search is to find evidence of an alleged offence, an indication of how the evidence relates to the investigation).

2.7 An application for a search warrant under paragraph 12(a) of Schedule 1 to the Police and Criminal Evidence Act 1984 shall also, where appropriate, indicate why it is believed that service of notice of an application for a production order may seriously prejudice the investigation.

2.8 If an application is refused, no further application may be made for a warrant to search those premises unless supported by additional grounds.

3 * * * * *

4 Search with consent

4.1 Subject to paragraph 4.3 below, if it is proposed to search premises with the consent of a person entitled to grant entry to the premises the consent must be given in writing.

4.2, 4.3 * * * * *

5 * * * * *

6 Seizure and retention of property

(a) Seizure

6.1 Subject to paragraph 6.2 below, an officer who is searching any premises under any statutory power or with the consent of the occupier may seize:

(a) anything covered by a warrant; and
(b) anything which he has reasonable grounds for believing is evidence of an offence or has been obtained in consequence of the commission of an offence.

Items under (b) may only be seized where this is necessary to prevent their concealment, alteration, loss, damage or destruction.

6.2 No item may be seized which is subject to legal privilege (as defined in section 10 of the Police and Criminal Evidence Act 1984).

6.3 An officer who decides that it is not appropriate to seize property because of an explanation given by the person holding it, but who has reasonable grounds for believing that it has been obtained in consequence of the commission of an offence by some person, shall inform the holder of his suspicions and shall explain that, if he disposes of the property, he may be liable to civil or criminal proceedings.

6.4 An officer may photograph or copy, or have photographed or copied, any document or other article which he has power to seize in accordance with paragraph 6.1 above.

6.5 Where an officer considers that a computer may contain information that could be used in evidence, he may require the information to be produced in a form that can be taken away and in which it is visible and legible.

(b) Retention

6.6 Subject to paragraph 6.7 below anything which has been seized in accordance with the above provisions may be retained only for as long as is necessary in the circumstances. It may be retained, among other purposes:

(i) for use as evidence at a trial for an offence;

(ii) for forensic examination or for other investigation in connection with an offence; or

(iii) where there are reasonable grounds for believing that it has been stolen or obtained by the commission of an offence, in order to establish its lawful owner.

6.7 Property shall not be retained in accordance with sub-paragraphs 6.6(i) and (ii) (i.e. for use as evidence or for the purposes of investigation) if a photograph or copy would suffice for those purposes.

6.8, 6.9 * * * * *

7 Action to be taken after searches

7.1 Where premises have been searched in circumstances to which this code applies, other than in the circumstances covered by paragraph 4.3 above, the officer in charge of the search shall, on arrival at a police station, make or have made a record of the search. The record shall include:

(i) the address of the premises searched;

(ii) the date, time and duration of the search;

(iii) the authority under which the search was made. Where the search was made in the exercise of a statutory power to search premises without warrant, the record shall include the power under which the search was made; and where the search was made under warrant, or with written consent, a copy of the warrant or consent shall be appended to the record or kept in a place identified in the record;

(iv) the names of the officers who conducted the search;

(v) the names of any persons on the premises if they are known;

(vi) either a list of any articles seized or a note of where such a list is kept and, if not covered by a warrant, the reason for their seizure;

(vii) whether force was used and, if so, the reason why it was used;

(viii) details of any damage caused during the search, and the circumstances in which it was caused.

7.2 Where premises have been searched under warrant, the warrant shall be endorsed to show:

(i) whether any articles specified in the warrant were found;

(ii) whether any other articles were seized;

(iii) the date and time at which it was executed;

(iv) the names of the officers who executed it; and

(v) whether a copy was handed to the occupier or left on the premises and if so where on them.

7.3 Any warrant which has been executed or which has not been executed within one month of its issue shall be returned, if it was issued by a justice of the peace, to the clerk to the justices for the petty sessions area concerned or, if issued by a judge, to the appropriate officer of the court from which he issued it.

8 * * * * *

CODE OF PRACTICE FOR THE DETENTION, TREATMENT AND QUESTIONING OF PERSONS BY POLICE OFFICERS (CODE C)

Note See note to Code A (*supra*).

1 General

1.1 All persons in custody must be dealt with expeditiously, and released as soon as the need for detention has ceased to apply.

1.2 This code of practice must be readily available at all police stations for consultation by police officers, detained persons and members of the public.

1.3 The notes for guidance included are not provisions of this code, but are guidance to police officers and others about its application and interpretation. Provisions in the annexes to this code are provisions of this code.

1.4 If an officer has any suspicion, or is told in good faith, that a person of any age may be mentally ill or mentally handicapped, or mentally incapable of understanding the significance of questions put to him or his replies, then that person shall be treated as a mentally ill or mentally handicapped person for the purposes of this code.

1.5 If anyone appears to be under the age of 17 then he shall be treated as a juvenile for the purposes of this code in the absence of clear evidence to show that he is older.

1.6 If a person appears to be blind or seriously visually handicapped, deaf, unable to read or unable to communicate orally with the officer dealing with him at the time, he should be treated as such for the purposes of this code in the absence of clear evidence to the contrary.

1.7 In this code 'the appropriate adult' means:

(a) in the case of a juvenile:

(i) his parent or guardian (or, if he is in care, the care authority or organisation);

(ii) a social worker; or

(iii) failing either of the above, another responsible adult who is not a police officer or employed by the police.

(b) in the case of a person who is mentally ill or mentally handicapped:

(i) a relative, guardian or other person responsible for his care or custody;

(ii) someone who has experience of dealing with mentally ill or mentally handicapped persons but is not a police officer or employed by the police; or

(iii) failing either of the above, some other responsible adult who is not a police officer or employed by the police.

1.8 Whenever this code requires a person to be given certain information he does not have to be given it if he is incapable at the time of understanding what is said to him or is violent or likely to become violent or is in urgent need of medical attention, but he must be given it as soon as practicable.

1.9 Any reference to a custody officer in this code includes an officer who is performing the functions of a custody officer.

1.10 In its application to persons who are in custody at police stations, this code applies whether or not they have been arrested for an offence, except section 16 which applies solely to persons in police detention.

2 Custody records

2.1 A separate custody record must be opened as soon as practicable for each person who is brought to a police station under arrest or is arrested at the police station having attended there voluntarily. All information which has to be recorded under this code must be recorded as soon as practicable, in the custody record unless otherwise specified.

2.2 In the case of any action requiring the authority of an officer of a specified rank, his name and rank must be noted in the custody record.

2.3 The custody officer is responsible for the accuracy and completeness of the custody record and for ensuring that the record or a copy of the record accompanies a detained person if he is transferred to another police station. The record shall show the time of and reason for transfer and the time a person is released from detention.

2.4 When a person leaves police detention he or his legal representative shall be supplied on request with a copy of the custody record as soon as practicable. This entitlement lasts for twelve months after his release.

2.5 All entries in custody and written interview records must be timed and signed by the maker.

2.6 Any refusal by a person to sign either a custody or an interview record when asked to do so in accordance with the provisions of this code must itself be recorded.

3 Initial action

(a) Detained persons: normal procedure

3.1 When a person is brought to a police station under arrest or is arrested at the police station having attended there voluntarily, the custody officer must inform him of the following rights and of the fact that they need not be exercised immediately:

(i) the right to have someone informed of his arrest in accordance with section 5 below;

(ii) the right to consult a solicitor in accordance with section 6 below; and

(iii) the right to consult this and the other codes of practice.

3.2 The custody officer must also give the person a written notice setting out the above three rights, the right to a copy of the custody record in accordance with paragraph 2.4 above and the caution in the terms prescribed in section 10 below. The custody officer shall ask the person to sign the custody record to acknowledge receipt of this notice.

3.3 If the custody officer authorises a person's detention he must inform him of the grounds as soon as practicable and in any case before that person is then questioned about any offence.

3.4 The person shall be asked to sign on the custody record to signify whether or not he wants legal advice at this point.

(b) Detained persons: special groups

3.5 If the person does not understand English or appears to be deaf and the custody officer cannot communicate with him then the custody officer must as soon as practicable call an interpreter, and ask him to provide the information required above.

3.6 If the person is a juvenile, is mentally handicapped or is suffering from mental illness then the custody officer must as soon as practicable inform the appropriate adult of the grounds for his detention and his whereabouts, and ask the adult to come to the police station to see the person. If the appropriate adult is already at the police station when information is given to the person as required in paragraphs 3.1 to 3.3 above then the information must be given to the detained person in his presence. If the appropriate adult is not at the police station when the information is given then the information must be given to the detained person again in the presence of the appropriate adult once that person arrives.

3.7 If the person is blind or seriously visually handicapped or is unable to read, the custody officer should ensure that his solicitor, relative, the appropriate adult or some other person likely to take an interest in him is available to help in checking any documentation. Where this code requires written consent or signification, then the person who is assisting may be asked to sign instead if the detained person so wishes.

3.8 In the case of a juvenile who is known to be subject to a supervision order, reasonable steps must also be taken to notify the person supervising him.

(c) Persons attending a police station voluntarily

3.9 Any person attending a police station voluntarily for the purpose of assisting with an investigation may leave at will unless placed under arrest. If it is decided that he would not be allowed to do so then he must be informed at once that he is under arrest and brought before the custody officer. If he is not placed under arrest but is cautioned in accordance with section 10 below, the officer who gives the caution must at the same time inform him that he is not under arrest, that he is not obliged to remain at the police station but that if he remains at the police station he may obtain legal advice if he wishes.

(d) Documentation

3.10 The grounds for a person's detention shall be recorded, in his presence if practicable.

3.11 Action taken under paragraphs 3.5 to 3.8 shall be recorded.

4 Detained persons' property

(a) Action

4.1 The custody officer is responsible for:

(a) ascertaining:

(i) what property a detained person has with him when he comes to the police station (whether on arrest, re-detention on answering to bail, commitment to prison custody on the order or sentence of a court, on lodgement at the police station with a view to his production in court from such custody, or on arrival at a police station on transfer from detention at another station or from hospital);

(ii) what property he might have acquired for an unlawful or harmful purpose while in custody.

(b) the safekeeping of any property which is taken from him and which remains at the police station.

To these ends the custody officer may search him or authorise his being searched to the extent that he considers necessary (provided that a search of intimate parts of the body or involving the removal of more than outer clothing may only be made in accordance with Annex A to this Code). A search may only be carried out by an officer of the same sex as the person searched.

4.2 A detained person may retain clothing and personal effects at his own risk unless the custody officer considers that he may use them to cause harm to himself or others, interfere with evidence, damage property or effect an escape or they are needed as evidence. In this event the custody officer can withhold such articles as he considers necessary. If he does so he must tell the person why.

4.3 Personal effects are those items which a person may lawfully need to use or refer to while in detention but do not include cash and other items of value.

(b) Documentation

4.4 The custody officer is responsible for recording all property brought to the police station that a detained person had with him, or had taken from him on arrest. The detained person shall be allowed to check and sign the record of property as correct.

4.5 If a detained person is not allowed to keep any article of clothing or personal effects the reason must be recorded.

5 Right not to be held incommunicado

(a) Action

5.1 Any person to whom paragraphs 2.1 and 3.9 apply may on request have one person known to him or who is likely to take an interest in his welfare informed at public expense as soon as practicable of his whereabouts. If the person cannot be contacted the person who has made the request may choose up to two alternatives. If they too cannot be contacted the custody officer has discretion to allow further attempts until the information has been conveyed.

5.2 The exercise of the above right in respect of each of the persons nominated may be delayed only in accordance with Annex B to this code.

5.3 The above right may be exercised on each occasion that a person is taken to another police station.

5.4 The person may receive visits at the custody officer's discretion.

5.5 Where an enquiry as to the whereabouts of the person is made by a friend, relative or person with an interest in his welfare, this information shall be given, if he agrees and if Annex B does not apply.

5.6 The person shall be supplied on request with writing materials. Any letter or other message shall be sent as soon as practicable unless Annex B applies.

5.7 He may also speak on the telephone for a reasonable time to one person unless Annex B applies.

5.8 Before any letter or message is sent, or telephone call made, the person shall be informed that what he says in any letter, call or message (other than in the case of a communication to a solicitor) may be read or listened to as appropriate and may be given in evidence. A telephone call may be terminated if it is being abused. The costs can be at public expense at the discretion of the custody officer.

(b) Documentation

5.9 A record must be kept of:

(a) any request made under this section and the action taken on it;

(b) any letters or messages sent, calls made or visits received; and

(c) any refusal on the part of a person to have information about himself or his whereabouts given to an outside enquirer.

6 Right to legal advice

(a) Action

6.1 Subject to paragraph 6.2, any person may at any time consult and communicate privately, whether in person, in writing or on the telephone with a solicitor.

6.2 The exercise of the above right may be delayed only in accordance with Annex B to this code.

6.3 A person who asks for legal advice may not be interviewed or continue to be interviewed until he has received it unless:

(a) Annex B applies; or

(b) an officer of the rank of superintendent or above has reasonable grounds for believing that:

(i) delay will involve an immediate risk of harm to persons or serious loss of, or damage to, property; or

(ii) where a solicitor, including a duty solicitor, has been contacted and has agreed to attend, awaiting his arrival would cause unreasonable delay to the processes of investigation; or

(c) the solicitor nominated by the person, or selected by him from a list:

(i) cannot be contacted;

(ii) has previously indicated that he does not wish to be contacted; or

(iii) having been contacted, has declined to attend;

and the person has been advised of the Duty Solicitor Scheme (where one is in operation) but has declined to ask for the duty solicitor, or the duty solicitor is unavailable; or

(d) the person has given his agreement in writing or on tape that the interview may be started at once.

6.4 Where sub-paragraph 6.3(b)(i) applies, once sufficient information to avert the risk has been obtained, questioning must cease until the person has received legal advice or sub-paragraphs 6.3(a), (b)(ii), (c) or (d) apply.

6.5 Where a person has been permitted to consult a solicitor and the solicitor is available at the time the interview begins or is in progress, he must be allowed to have his solicitor present while he is interviewed.

6.6 The solicitor may only be required to leave the interview if his conduct is such that the investigating officer is unable properly to put questions to the suspect.

6.7 If the investigating officer considers that a solicitor is acting in such a way, he will stop the interview and consult an officer not below the rank of superintendent, if one is readily available, and otherwise an officer not below the rank of inspector who is not connected with the investigation. After speaking to the solicitor, the officer who has been consulted will decide whether or not the interview should continue in the presence of that solicitor. If he decides that it should not, the suspect will be given the opportunity to consult another solicitor before the interview continues and that solicitor will be given an opportunity to be present at the interview.

6.8 The removal of a solicitor from an interview is a serious step and if it occurs, the officer of superintendent rank or above who took the decision will consider whether the incident should be reported to The Law Society. If the decision to remove the solicitor has been taken by an officer below the rank of superintendent, the facts must be reported to an officer of superintendent rank or above who will similarly consider whether a report to The Law Society would be appropriate.

6.9 In this code 'solicitor' means a solicitor qualified to practise in accordance with the Solicitors Act 1974. If a solicitor wishes to send a clerk or legal executive to provide advice on his behalf, then the clerk or legal executive shall be admitted to the police station for this purpose unless an officer of the rank of inspector or above considers that such a visit will hinder the investigation of crime and directs otherwise. Once admitted to the police station, the provisions of paragraphs 6.3 to 6.7 apply.

6.10 If the inspector refuses access to a clerk or legal executive or a decision is taken that such a person should not be permitted to remain at an interview, he must forthwith notify a solicitor on whose behalf the clerk or legal executive was to have acted or was acting, and give him an opportunity of making alternative arrangements.

(b) Documentation

6.11 Any request for legal advice and the action taken on it shall be recorded.

6.12 If a person has asked for legal advice and an interview is commenced in the absence of a solicitor or his representative (or the solicitor or his representative has been required to leave an interview) a record shall be made in the interview record.

7 *****

8 Conditions of detention

(a) Action

8.1 So far as is practicable, not more than one person shall be detained in each cell.

8.2 Cells in use must be adequately heated, cleaned and ventilated. They must be adequately lit, subject to such dimming as is compatible with safety and security to allow persons detained overnight to sleep. No additional restraints should be used within a locked cell unless absolutely necessary, and then only approved handcuffs.

8.3 Blankets, mattresses, pillows and other bedding supplied should be of a reasonable standard and in a clean and sanitary condition.

8.4 Access to toilet and washing facilities must be provided.

8.5 If it is necessary to remove a person's clothes for the purposes of investigation, for hygiene or health reasons or for cleaning, replacement clothing of a reasonable standard of comfort and cleanliness shall be provided. A person may not be interviewed unless adequate clothing has been offered to him.

8.6 At least two light meals and one main meal shall be offered in any period of 24 hours. Whenever necessary, advice shall be sought from the police surgeon on medical or dietary matters. As far as practicable, meals provided shall offer a varied diet and meet any special dietary needs or religious beliefs that the person may have; he may also have meals supplied by his family or friends at his or their own expense.

8.7 Brief outdoor exercise shall be offered daily if practicable.

8.8 A juvenile shall not be placed in a police cell unless no other secure accommodation is available and the custody officer considers that it is not practicable to supervise him if he is not placed in a cell. He may not be placed in a cell with a detained adult.

8.9. Reasonable force may be used if necessary for the following purposes:

(i) to secure compliance with reasonable instructions, including instructions given in pursuance of the provisions of a code of practice; of

(ii) to prevent escape, injury, damage to property or the destruction of evidence.

8.10 Persons detained should be visited every hour, and those who are drunk, every half hour.

(b) Documentation

8.11 A record must be kept of replacement clothing and meals offered.

8.12 If a juvenile is placed in a cell, the reason must be recorded.

9 Treatment of detained persons

(a) General

9.1 If a complaint is made by or on behalf of a detained person about his treatment since his arrest, or it comes to the notice of any officer that he may have been treated improperly, a report must be made as soon as practicable to an officer of the rank of inspector or above who is not connected with the investigation. If the matter concerns a possible assault or the possibility of the unnecessary or unreasonable use of force then the police surgeon must also be called as soon as practicable.

(b) Medical treatment

9.2 The custody officer must immediately call the police surgeon (or, in urgent cases, send the person to hospital or call the nearest available medical practitioner) if a person brought to a police station or already detained there:

(a) appears to be suffering from physical or mental illness; or

(b) is injured; or

(c) does not show signs of sensibility and awareness or fails to respond normally to questions or conversation (other than through drunkenness alone); or

(d) otherwise appears to need medical attention.

This applies even if the person makes no request for medical attention and whether or not he has recently had medical treatment elsewhere (unless brought to the police station direct from hospital).

9.3 If it appears to the custody officer, or he is told, that a person brought to the police station under arrest may be suffering from an infectious disease of any significance he must take steps to isolate the person and his property until he has obtained medical directions as to where the person should be taken, whether fumigation should take place and what precautions should be taken by officers who have been or will be in contact with him.

9.4 If a detained person requests a medical examination the police surgeon must be called as soon as practicable. He may in addition be examined by a medical practitioner of his own choice at his own expense.

9.5 If a person is required to take or apply any medication in compliance with medical directions, the custody officer is responsible for its safe keeping and for ensuring that he is given the opportunity to take or apply it at the appropriate times. No police officer may administer controlled drugs subject to the Misuse of Drugs Act 1971 for this purpose. A person may administer such drugs to himself only under the personal supervision of the police surgeon.

9.6 If a detained person has in his possession or claims to need medication relating to a heart condition, diabetes, epilepsy or a condition of comparable potential seriousness then, even though paragraph 9.2 may not apply, the advice of the police surgeon must be obtained.

9.7-9.9 * * * * *

10 Cautions

(a) When a caution must be given

10.1 A person whom there are grounds to suspect of an offence must be cautioned before any questions about it (or further questions if it is his answers to previous questions that provide grounds for suspicion) are put to him for the purpose of obtaining evidence which may be given to a court in a prosecution. He therefore need not be cautioned if questions are put for other purposes, for example, to establish his identity, his ownership of, or responsibility for, any vehicle or the need to search him in the exercise of powers of stop and search.

10.2 When a person who is not under arrest is initially cautioned before or during an interview at a police station or other premises he must at the same time be told that he is not under arrest, is not obliged to remain with the officer but that if he does, may obtain legal advice if he wishes.

10.3 A person must be cautioned upon arrest for an offence unless:

(a) it is impracticable to do so by reason of his condition or behaviour at the time; or

(b) he has already been cautioned immediately prior to arrest in accordance with paragraph 10.1 above.

(b) Action: general

10.4 The caution shall be in the following terms:

"You do not have to say anything unless you wish to do so, but what you say may be given in evidence."

Minor deviations do not constitute a breach of this requirement provided that the sense of the caution is preserved.

10.5 When there is a break in questioning under caution the interviewing officer must ensure that the person being questioned is aware that he remains under caution. If there is any doubt the caution should be given again in full when the interview resumes.

(c) Documentation

10.6 A record shall be made when a caution is given under this section, either in the officer's pocket book or in the interview record as appropriate.

11 Interviews: general

(a) Action

11.1 No police officer may try to obtain answers to questions or to elicit a statement by the use of oppression, or shall indicate, except in answer to a direct question, what action will be taken on the part of the police if the person being interviewed answers questions, makes a statement or refuses to do either. If the person asks the officer directly what action will be taken in the event of his answering questions, making a statement or refusing to do either, then the officer may inform the person what action the police propose to take in that event provided that that action is itself proper and warranted.

11.2 As soon as a police officer who is making enquiries of any person about an offence believes that a prosecution should be brought against him and that there is sufficient evidence for it to succeed, he shall without delay cease to question him.

(b) Interview records

11.3 (a) An accurate record must be made of each interview with a person suspected of an offence, whether or not the interview takes place at a police station.

(b) If the interview takes place in the police station or other premises:

(i) the record must state the place of the interview, the time it begins and ends, the time the record is made (if different), any breaks in the interview and the names of all those present; and must be made on the forms provided for this purpose or in the officer's pocket book or in accordance with the code of practice for the tape recording of police interviews with suspects;

(ii) the record must be made during the course of the interview, unless in the investigating officer's view this would not be practicable or would interfere with the conduct of the interview, and must constitute either a verbatim record of what has been said or, failing this, an account of the interview which adequately and accurately summarises it.

11.4 If an interview record is not made during the course of the interview it must be made as soon as practicable after its completion.

11.5 Written interview records must be timed and signed by the maker.

11.6 If an interview record is not completed in the course of the interview the reason must be recorded in the officer's pocket book.

11.7 Any refusal by a person to sign an interview record when asked to do so in accordance with the provisions of this code must itself be recorded.

12 Interviews in police stations

(a) Action

12.1 If a police officer wishes to interview, or conduct enquiries which require the presence of, a detained person the custody officer is responsible for deciding whether to deliver him into his custody.

12.2 In any period of 24 hours a detained person must be allowed a continuous period of at least 8 hours for rest, free from questioning, travel or any interruption arising out of the investigation concerned. This period should normally be at night. The period of rest may not be interrupted or delayed unless there are reasonable grounds for believing that it would:

(i) involve a risk of harm to persons or serious loss of, or damage to, property;

(ii) delay unnecessarily the person's release from custody; or

(iii) otherwise prejudice the outcome of the investigation.

If a person is arrested at a police station after going there voluntarily, the period of 24 hours runs from the time of arrival at the police station and not the time of his arrest.

12.3 A detained person may not be supplied with intoxicating liquor except on medical directions. No person who is unfit through drink or drugs to the extent that he is unable to appreciate the significance of questions put to him and his answers may be questioned about an alleged offence in that condition except in accordance with Annex C.

12.4 As far as practicable interviews shall take place in interview rooms which must be adequately heated, lit and ventilated.

12.5 Persons being questioned or making statements shall not be required to stand.

12.6 Before the commencement of an interview each interviewing officer shall identify himself and any other officers present by name and rank to the person being interviewed.

12.7 Breaks from interviewing shall be made at recognised meal times. Short breaks for refreshment shall also be provided at intervals of approximately two hours, subject to the interviewing officer's discretion to delay a break if there are reasonable grounds for believing that it would:

(i) involve a risk of harm to persons or serious loss of, or damage to, property;

(ii) delay unnecessarily the person's release from custody; or

(iii) otherwise prejudice the outcome of the investigation.

12.8 If in the course of the interview a complaint is made by the person being questioned or on his behalf, concerning the provisions of this code then the interviewing officer shall:

(i) record it in the interview record; and

(ii) inform the custody officer, who is then responsible for dealing with it in accordance with section 9 of this code.

12.9-12.15 *****

13-16 *****

17 Charging of detained persons

(a) Action

17.1 When an officer considers that there is sufficient evidence to prosecute a detained person he should without delay bring him before the custody officer who shall then be responsible for considering whether or not he should be charged. Any resulting action should be taken in the presence of the appropriate adult if the person is a juvenile or mentally ill or mentally handicapped.

17.2 When a detained person is charged with or informed that he may be prosecuted for an offence he shall be cautioned in the terms of paragraph 10.4 above.

17.3 At the time a person is charged he shall be given a written notice showing particulars of the offence with which he is charged and including the name of the officer in the case, his police station and the reference number for the case. So far as possible the particulars of the charge shall be stated in simple terms, but they shall also show the precise offence in law with which he is charged. The notice shall begin with the following words:

> "You are charged with the offence(s) shown below. You do not have to say anything unless you wish to do so, but what you say may be given in evidence."

If the person is a juvenile or is mentally ill or mentally handicapped the notice shall be given to the appropriate adult.

17.4 If at any time after a person has been charged with or informed he may be prosecuted for an offence a police officer wishes to bring to the notice of that person any written statement made by another person or the content of an interview with another person, he shall hand to that person a true copy of any such written statement or bring to his attention the content of the interview record, but shall say or do nothing to invite any reply or comment save to caution him in the terms of paragraph 10.4 above. If the person cannot read then the officer may read it to him. If the person is a juvenile or mentally ill or mentally handicapped the copy shall also be given to, or the interview record brought to the attention of, the appropriate adult.

17.5 Questions relating to an offence may not be put to a person after he has been charged with that offence, or informed that he may be prosecuted for it, unless they are necessary for the purpose of preventing or minimising harm or loss to some other person or to the public or for clearing up an ambiguity in a previous answer or statement, or where it is in the interests of justice that the person should have put to him and have an opportunity to comment on information concerning the offence which has come to light since he was charged or informed that he might be prosecuted. Before any such questions are put he shall be cautioned in the terms of paragraph 10.4 above.

17.6 Where a juvenile is charged with an offence and the custody officer authorises his continuing detention he must try to make arrangements for the juvenile to be taken into the care of a local authority to be detained pending appearance in court unless he certifies that it is impracticable to do so in accordance with section 38(6) of the Police and Criminal Evidence Act 1984.

(b) Documentation

17.7 A record shall be made of anything a detained person says when charged.

17.8 Any questions put after charge and answers given relating to the offence shall be contemporaneously recorded in full on the forms provided and the record signed by that person or, if he refuses, by the interviewing officer and any third parties present. If the questions are tape recorded the arrangements set out in the relevant code of practice apply.

17.9 If it is not practicable to make arrangements for the transfer of a juvenile into local authority care in accordance with paragraph 17.6 above the custody officer must record the reasons and make out a certificate to be produced before the court together with the juvenile.

ANNEX A-E *****

Note Code D (Identification of persons by Police Officers) is not reproduced herein.

INDEX

BLACKSTONE'S STATUTES

TITLES IN THE SERIES

Civil Liability Statutes
Public Law Statutes
Employment Law Statutes
Criminal Law Statutes
Criminal Procedure: Evidence and Sentencing Statutes
Family Law Statutes
Land Law Statutes
Commercial Law Statutes
Company Law Statutes